THE NEW COMPLETE BOOK OF BRIDGE

Albert Dormer

in consultation with

Ron Klinger

VICTOR GOLLANCZ

in association with

PETER CRAWLEY

First published in Great Britain in 1996
in association with Peter Crawley
by Victor Gollancz
An imprint of The Orion Publishing Group Ltd
Wellington House, 125 Strand, London WC2R 0BB
First paperback edition published 1999

A catalogue record for this book
is available from the British Library

ISBN 0 575 06738 1

Printed in Great Britain by
Clays Ltd, St Ives plc

THE NEW COMPLETE BOOK
OF BRIDGE

Also by Albert Dormer

DORMER ON DEDUCTION

CONTENTS

PART TWO – THE PLAY

FOREWORD

This book gives a full account of modern Acol and of the whole range of defensive and competitive bidding. It is suitable for players up to a high standard but will readily be understood by less experienced players as each topic starts with the fundamentals.

The play of the cards is covered in all important aspects, with an emphasis on mental approach and on principles of wide application. Deals are presented in a way that allows the reader to develop his thoughts and arrive at solutions. There are many hints of practical value that will stay in the mind.

The treatment of bidding reflects the best current practice. It is therefore a work of consolidation, which in the Author's view is much needed, rather than innovation, which is in over-supply. It owes much to the views of Ron Klinger, one of the world's leading bridge teachers and authors, whose record as a player includes an Olympiad brilliancy prize when representing Australia. No one of his authority is in closer touch with mainstream Acol and I was delighted when he agreed to collaborate with me in the writing of *The New Complete Book of Bridge*.

I am indebted also to Andrew Kambites, one of Britain's leading authors and teachers, who made many helpful suggestions.

PART ONE

THE BIDDING

Chapter 1

THE OPENING BID

When to open 1NT – Openings of 1♣, 1◇, 1♡ and 1♠ – The choice of suit – Third and fourth hand openings – The finer points of valuation

Logically, any discussion of bidding should start by setting the range of the 1NT opening, as this affects the meaning not just of notrump sequences but of many sequences that begin with one of a suit.

For example, when you open with one of a suit and on the next round bid notrumps at any level, the points shown depend on what 1NT would have shown, had you opened with that call.

Opener	Responder
1♡	1♠
1NT	

In any well-ordered system the points denoted by opener in this sequence must differ from those of a 1NT opening.

It follows that the traditional Acol notrump – weak and strong – meant that one was to an important extent playing two separate systems, making it difficult to draw consistent inferences.

When Acol was more free and easy – some might say, more hit and miss – this did not matter too much, but the system is now much more precise and there are many inferential sequences. Today it is standard to play an unvarying notrump.

The accepted strength for those who set the tone for Acol bidding is 12 to 14. Hands in this range with balanced or semi-balanced pattern can be a headache when opened with one of a suit.

Bidding theorists have always recognised that a 1NT opening is a *good* opening, for fundamental reasons. And by playing 12–14 you are able to open 1NT more often than when playing a higher range.

It is indispensable that any rebid in notrumps now shows a hand too strong for a notrump opening:

(1)	Opener	Responder	(2)	Opener	Responder
	1♣	1♠		1♡	2◇
	1NT			2NT	

In each case the notrump rebid shows a type similar to a notrump opening, but the strength is at least 15 points. The complete scheme of notrump rebids is discussed later.

WHEN TO OPEN 1NT

The favoured style today is to open 1NT on most – fundamentalists would say all – 12–14 point hands that include:

no singleton;
no 5-card major suit;
no 5–4 pattern.

As will shortly be seen, this does not entirely exhaust the patterns that may be opened with 1NT.

It is not necessary to have a guard in every suit, or even in three suits. 1NT remains the preferred opening when the high cards are quite heavily concentrated:

♠ 9 6 2　♡ A K J 7　◇ A 10 9 3　♣ 10 4

With this type it used to be thought best to open 1♡ and rebid 2◇, but this style is *passé*. To bring definition to later sequences, the rule now is: *A player who opens with one of a major and bids two of a new suit on the next round is firmly presumed to have at least five cards in the first suit.*

So, with 4–4 suits, touching or not, you open 1NT. In only one case is there an alternative. When the suits are clubs and spades, 1♣ is an option because the second suit can be shown at the one level:

(1)　　♠ A Q J 5　　♡ J 7　　◇ 10 8 3　　♣ K Q 10 6
(2)　　♠ K 8 6 2　　♡ K 4　　◇ K J 2　　♣ K J 4 2

With (1), considering how strong the two suits are, it makes sense to open 1♣ and bid 1♠ over 1♡ or 1◇. With (2), it is perhaps more canny to open 1NT than to bid two moderate suits. But tactics – position at table and so on – come into it too.

With 5–3–3–2, 1NT is the normal opening when the suit is a minor, however strong. With a 5-card major, the suit opening is much preferred unless it may leave you with a difficult rebid:

(3)　　♠ Q 10 9 7 3　　♡ A K J　　◇ Q 2　　♣ J 10 6
(4)　　♠ J 8 5　　♡ 10 4　　◇ A K Q 9 2　　♣ K 10 4
(5)　　♠ 8 7　　♡ 10 7 4 3 2　　◇ A Q 4　　♣ A K 2

Hand (3) is opened with 1♠ as this spade holding is eminently rebiddable in the modern style.

With (4) the opening is 1NT, not 1◇. Either way you are likely to end up in notrumps, so it is better to open in that strain, with a better chance of shutting out opponents.

With (5) you could open 1NT but – at duplicate, especially – you might prefer to open 1♡ with the intention of rebidding 2◇. You do not wish to stress this weak 5-card suit, but nor do you want to conceal it.

With a 5–4 pattern it is uncommon, but not unknown, to open 1NT when the 5-card suit is a minor or when you might otherwise be faced with an awkward rebid:

♠ K 5   ♡ Q 10 3 2   ◇ A Q   ♣ J 8 7 4 3

If you opened 1♣ and partner responded 1♠ you would not be well placed; so, open 1NT.

An option not to be sneezed at is that it is conceivable to pass with 12 points. You would be within your constitutional rights to do so with this collection:

♠ A K 7   ♡ J 7 4 3   ◇ Q 8 3 2   ♣ Q 5

However, if you prefer to open, 1NT is the only choice: a sequence initiated in any other way would be actively misleading. When a moderate balanced hand is not worth a 1NT opening, it is not worth opening at all.

The 5-card major

A 4♡ or 4♠ contract with five trumps opposite three is so often the right spot that the major-suit opening is usually preferred to 1NT even when the suit is very weak: otherwise the best contract may be lost, not only when partner has 4-card support in a balanced hand and does not activate the Stayman convention but also with this type:

Opener	Responder
♠ 8 7	♠ A 9 5
♡ 10 7 4 3 2	♡ A K 5
◇ A K 3	◇ Q 7 4
♣ A Q 2	♣ J 7 5 4

After a 1NT opening the responder will not consider anything but 3NT, yet this could fail with a spade lead, while 4♡ needs only a 3–2 break.

In general, then, it is preferable to open the major suit with this type. You intend to pass a 1NT response and rebid 2◇, not such a terrible fib, over a 1♠ or 2♣ response. Over a 2◇ response a raise to 3◇ will suggest a 5-card heart suit as well as diamond support.

Opener can very often gauge that the risk of having to rebid a weak suit is within acceptable limits:

♠ A 9 3   ♡ Q 8 5 3 2   ◇ 10 4   ♣ A K 6

With 5–3 in hearts and spades, a 1♡ opening is attractive, as you can raise a response of 1♠. Here, 2♣ from partner can also be raised. It would be too bad if partner chose this moment to respond 2◇: there would then be no choice but to rebid 2♡.

A further consideration is that opponents today are less reluctant to compete against 1NT. Suppose you open 1NT with a 5-card heart suit and next hand overcalls with 2♠, which comes back to you: it is difficult for you to compete further, yet you may have a heart fit with which you could have pushed opponents one range higher. If you open 1♡, a fit or absence of fit comes immediately to light and puts you in a better position if the auction becomes competitive.

When undecided, you might make it a rule to open 1NT with eight losers but open the major suit with seven. (See the Losing Trick Count, Chapter 6.) This is better than spinning a coin.

OPENINGS OF 1♣, 1◇, 1♡ AND 1♠

What is the lower limit of strength for a suit opening, and how is strength to be measured? For notrump bidding the 4–3–2–1 count is simple and effective, but for a suit opening, distribution as well as high cards must be considered.

There are methods of adding points for long suits or short suits, and teachers find this helpful for getting beginners started, but no scheme of that kind can match the judgment of an experienced player. When the grizzled professionals talk about points, they always mean plain high-card points. You never hear them say, 'I had 18 points, including distribution.' Instead they will say, 'I had a good 16 and a 6-card suit.' Or, 'I had a bad eleven, 4–4–4–1.' Or whatever.

In bridge jargon, 'good' and 'bad' sum up the net effect of
the range of distributional features that affect a hand's potential. A good eleven may be opened, a bad 12 may be passed,
and so on. A 13-point hand is always opened unless it has very
negative features, such as bare honour cards or a looming
rebid problem:

♠ K Q   ♡ A K   ♢ 9 7 5 4 2   ♣ J 7 6 3

A 13-point hand has to be as bad as this before you even
think of passing. If you open 1♢ and rebid 2♣ you will be
bidding two very poor suits and may land in the wrong
contract even when your partner has a good hand, as your
points are not where he will expect. To bid weak suits is
sometimes unavoidable, but here you could pass, especially
as the bare honours in spades and hearts should be devalued.
If a pass is too conservative for your taste, the opening should
be 1NT.

An 11-point hand may be opened when it has a positive
feature, such as a good 6-card major or a 5–4 pattern with
most of the points in the suits. If the suits are adjacent,
allowing an easy rebid, so much the better.

(1)   ♠ A Q J 9 8 6   ♡ 10 4   ♢ K J 2   ♣ 8 3
(2)   ♠ 7   ♡ A K 9 8 6 ♢ Q J 10 8 ♣ J 4 3

With (1) you open 1♠, prepared to rebid the suit until the
cows come home.

With (2) it is perfectly sound to open 1♡ and follow with
2♢. Always be willing to open light when the character of the
hand will be well described by the intended sequence.

A hand with only ten points has to have genuine oomph: a
self-supporting 6-card spade suit, perhaps, with top cards, not
queens and jacks, outside. Or a 5–5 or 6–5 pattern with
strong suits:

♠ A J 10 8 6   ♡ 5   ♢ 3   ♣ K Q 10 9 5 2

This hand should be opened with 1♣ at any vulnerability.

THE CHOICE OF SUIT

In the discussion that follows it is to be borne in mind that a rebid in notrumps is always an option with 15+ and a suitable pattern, but never with less.

When more than one suit is held it is mightily important to open with the correct one: that is, the suit that leaves you with a sound, or at any rate not loathsome, rebid over any likely response.

The choice is simplest when only 5-card or longer suits are held. With two 5-card suits, the higher-ranking is opened unless the suits are clubs and spades. In that case, in theory, to start with 1♣ is cheaper, but in practice it often works out that opener is unable to define his 5-card length in spades – the more important feature. It is often better to open 1♠ unless the club suit is strong and the spades weak.

The choice of opening with 5–4

The modern style is to bid always the 5-card suit first. On most hands this works smoothly enough:

(1)	♠ 8 3		♡ A Q 7 5 2		◇ K J 6 5		♣ A 5
(2)	♠ K Q J 9 2		♡ J 4		◇ Q 10 8 2		♣ A 7

With (1) you open 1♡: a rebid of 2◇ on the next round will then suggest 5–4. With (2) you open 1♠, again intending to rebid 2◇ if partner's response is 1NT or 2♣. However, over a response of 2♡ you would have to rebid 2♠, as a bid of 3◇ would show a distinctly stronger hand.

When the 5-card suit is very weak you must decide whether you are willing to face a rebid that may not rejoice the heart:

(3)	♠ 10 8 5 4 2		♡ 8		◇ K Q 6		♣ A K J 2

After 1♠–2♡ you would have no option but to rebid 2♠. If this appals you, the solution is to open 1♣, treating the pattern as 4–4.

When the suits are adjacent and the 5-card suit is lower-ranking, you should still bid the longer suit first – even when this is a weak minor and the 4-card suit is a strong major:

   (4)   ♠ K 5   ♡ A Q J 8   ◇ J 8 6 4 3   ♣ Q 3

With this type, which is not strong enough for a reverse sequence, Acol players used to open 1♡ and rebid 2◇, but such a sequence now shows at least a 5-card heart suit. Players today argue with sound logic that since they would open 1◇ with 4–4 in diamonds and hearts (a pattern discussed later), it can hardly be wrong to do so when holding five diamonds, however weak.

The 6–5 pattern

With non-touching suits, open the longer. With touching suits, open the higher-ranking unless you are willing to reverse – at a high level if necessary. This is because when you have long suits, so will opponents, and they may crowd the auction.

   (1)   ♠ –   ♡ A Q J 7 2   ◇ K J 8 5 3 2   ♣ 8 4
   (2)   ♠ 7   ♡ K Q J 8 3   ◇ A K J 7 6 4   ♣ 8

With (1) a 1♡ opening is more likely to work out. If you were to open 1◇ you might find it difficult to mention hearts in a contested auction. With hand (2), which is strong enough for a reverse in competition, the opening is 1◇.

The 4–4–4–1 pattern

There are now two important objectives. First you must avoid opening in a major suit and rebidding in a minor, as such a sequence requires at least 5–4. Secondly, you must make it as easy as possible for partner to show any 4-card suit. The best scheme is this:

With a spade singleton, open 1◇;
With a heart or diamond singleton, open 1♣;
With a club singleton, open 1♡.

With this protocol there is only one type and one sequence that can be awkward:

(1)	♠ Q	♡ K 9 7 6	◇ K Q J 2	♣ A 10 9 4
(2)	♠ Q 8 7 4	♡ 5	◇ A 9 5 3	♣ A K 7 2
(3)	♠ A J 7 3	♡ K J 4 2	◇ K Q J 3	♣ 10

With (1), no problem: you open 1◇ and rebid 1NT over 1♠. If you were below 15 points you would rebid 2♣. It is primarily the responder's job to see that a 4–4 heart fit is not missed.

With (2), again no problem: you open 1♣, not 1◇. Now it will be possible while still at the one level to locate a fit in any suit.

Hand (3) is potentially the 'awkward' type. By opening 1♡ rather than 1♠ you allow partner to bid the other major economically, and with the hand shown, if the response is 2♣ you can go to 2NT, as you have 15 points.

However, when you are below 15 points you may have to rebid 2◇, with the disadvantage that your partner will presume you to have five hearts. But this is just one more risk in what is essentially a risk-taking game.

The 4–4–3–2 and 4–3–3–3 patterns

The count will always be 15 or more, for otherwise you would open 1NT. With 4–3–3–3 you bid the 4-card suit, regardless:

♠ K Q 8   ♡ 10 8 7 3   ◇ A J 8   ♣ K Q 4

After an opening 1♡, a rebid of 1NT over a 1♠ response will indicate 15–17. Over a response of 2♣ or 2◇ you would bid 2NT with this hand but, as will be seen later, the range could now be 15–19.

With 4–4 in touching suits you open the lower-ranking suit so that responder can readily bid the higher-ranking suit if he has it:

♠ A Q 9 3   ♡ A 10 5 2   ♢ Q 10 4   ♣ K 7

Bid 1♡. Over a 2♣ or 2♢ response, the rebid is 2NT. To open 1♠ and rebid 2♡ would suggest at least a 5–4 pattern and would incur the further disadvantage of not defining the point count. You would also open the lower suit with 4–4 in diamonds and hearts or in clubs and diamonds.

With 4–4 in non-touching suits – hearts and clubs or diamonds and spades – it is always permissible to open the minor suit, and when you are eager to find a fit, that is what you should do. However, when the hand is so suitable for a rebid in notrumps that you prefer not to show both suits, the major suit may be opened;

♠ A 10   ♡ A 9 8 4   ♢ A Q 2   ♣ K J 7 3

Obviously, to open 1♡ and continue with 2NT on the next round is a satisfactory sequence, especially when partner has passed and there is no risk of missing a slam in clubs. You may also elect to open the major when this suit is very strong and the minor suit weak; but only with non-touching suits.

The net effect of this scheme of rebids is that a 1♠ opening will always show a 5-card suit or 15+. The same is true of a 1♡ opening with the sole exception of the sequence 1♡–2♣–2♢, which may be 4–4–4–1 with a club singleton.

Openings and rebids when playing a strong 1NT

Many sequences are similar to those described, but there are two important differences. With a 4–3–3–3 pattern and 12–14 it is usual to open 1♣, no matter where the 4-card suit is located. This is done to allow a rebid of 1NT on the next round, which may be the only sound move:

♠ K 8 3   ♡ Q J 7 2   ♢ A K 5   ♣ 9 8 2

If you were to open 1♡ you would have no good rebid over a 2♣ or 2♢ response, as a rebid of 2NT is normally played as showing extra values. Instead, open 1♣ and rebid 1NT, denoting a minimum.

With a 4–4–3–2 pattern not strong enough for 1NT, the choice is again governed by the need to have a sound rebid. With touching suits, you now open the higher. With non-touching suits, when one is clubs the opening is 1♣. With four spades and four diamonds, you open the suit next in rank above the 3-card holding:

♠ A J 8 7　♡ 9 7 6　♢ A K 8 2　♣ J 5

Open 1♠, intending to raise 2♡ to three and to bid 2♢ over 2♣.

THIRD AND FOURTH HAND OPENINGS

It is now an option to bid one of a suit, intending to pass the response, instead of opening 1NT. This may be done to show a strong feature or to suggest a lead:

♠ K Q J 8　♡ Q 9 3　♢ A 7 2　♣ 10 9 5

In first or second position you would open 1NT, to keep the faith. In third or fourth position, 1♠ clearly makes more sense; but it is not done very often, as 1NT is such a good tactical move.

THE FINER POINTS OF VALUATION

When an expert describes a hand as a good or bad 15 points, or whatever, he is not taking a moral position but reflecting the sum of good and bad features. So, what are these, and how much do they count for?

Aces are worth more than four points, because of their controlling power. Queens are worth less than two. Tens and nines have their value, especially in combination with higher cards. Think of the potential, at notrumps, of K–10–9–x as against K–5–3–2 or even K–10–5–3.

Bare honours are worth distinctly less than face value unless partner bids the suit, and even then the lack of a developing low card is a negative factor. Think of the difference between a singleton king opposite A–J–x–x–x, compared with K–x facing the same holding.

Two or more high cards in the same suit can be often worth more than cards of similar rank in different suits. This is easily demonstrated: K–x–x opposite Q–x–x will win a trick, but on a bad day K–x–x and Q–x–x in different suits may not.

Even better is to have high cards in the same hand as well as in the same suit. K–Q–x may now win two tricks, and there is a much better chance of establishing a trick with Q–J–x opposite three small than with Q–x–x facing J–x–x.

When strength is combined with length

There is clear advantage in having high cards in long rather than short suits, if only because you cannot win more tricks in a non-trump suit than you have cards in it: A–Q–J–x–x opposite K–10–x is worth five tricks: A–Q–J opposite K–10–x is worth three.

Also, it is easier to develop long cards. A holding of A–x–x–x–x facing K–x–x is soon established, but J–10–x–x–x opposite 9–x–x takes forever.

Best of all is to have high cards in a suit your partner has bid: he will (you hope!) have high cards as well as long cards that yours can combine with. Now you must be flexible: when your partner opens 2♣ and you have almost a bust, you should dote on any smidgeon of strength – as little as J–x – in a suit he subsequently bids. Conversely, when you open 2NT and your partner shows a string of hearts, don't throw your hat in the air just because you have the king. He will expect no less.

When opponents enter you may revalue or devalue your hand according to the expected lie of the cards. After a vulnerable overcall on your right, K–x of the overcaller's suit ought to be worth a trick. The converse is also true.

Suppose that you have to value your hand for a bid in notrumps, RHO having overcalled earlier in spades. On one occasion you have ♠A–x–x; on another, ♠J–10–x–x. Which is the better holding? The second, by far: you are spending only one of your points on a guaranteed stopper.

A holding of x–x–x in a suit that both opponents are bidding vigorously is splendid when you and your partner have a big trump fit. Nothing is wasted, so your high cards – and your partner's – are sure to be 'working'. But beware a doubleton in the enemy suit: your partner may have the same holding, known as duplication of values.

Duplication occurs also when the partnership hands contain too many high cards in one suit:

North	South
1♣	1◇
1NT	?

♠ K Q J   ♡ 9 7 4 3   ◇ Q 9 8 3   ♣ 8 2

North has shown 15–17, so South would normally raise to 2NT. Here, however, North is likely to have the ♠A, so there will be ten points in spades but only three tricks. At duplicate, especially, South may elect to pass 1NT.

The precise number of cards held in partner's main suit is always germane: the more the merrier. If a notrump contract depends on establishing a non-solid 5-card suit, your partner will look much more kindly on x–x–x in your hand than on x–x:

(1)   A Q 5 4 3   (2)   A Q 5 4 3

      7 6 2   6 2

Mathematicians tell us that the first combination is twice as likely to produce four tricks as the second. This is because there are eight cards in (1), seven in (2).

The finer points of valuation are well worth absorbing, as they lead directly to better contracts.

Quiz on opening bids

(1) ♠ K J 10 2   ♡ 7   ◇ K 10 8 7   ♣ A Q J 4
(2) ♠ K 10 9 3 2 ♡ A 4   ◇ A Q 9 6 3   ♣ 7
(3) ♠ A Q 8   ♡ K Q 8 4 ◇ A J 10 9 6 ♣ 4
(4) ♠ K J 9 3   ♡ A J 10 8 4 ◇ K J   ♣ 7 4
(5) ♠ Q 7 2   ♡ K J   ◇ K 8 6 3   ♣ K 9 5 2
(6) ♠ K Q 6 4   ♡ A Q J 4 ◇ 8 2   ♣ J 10 2

(1) 1♣. With 4–4–4–1 and a red singleton, the normal opening is 1♣, making it easy to find a fit in any suit. To open 1◇ risks missing a club fit, with no compensating advantage.

(2) 1♠. It is normal to open with the higher-ranking of two 5-card suits, with some exceptions when they are clubs and spades.

(3) 1◇. With 5–4 suits the longer is opened regardless of rank. Here, with 16 points and two good suits, you intend to follow a reverse sequence. Thus, over 1♠, 1NT or 2♣, you would bid 2♡, indicating a strong opening with longer diamonds than hearts.

(4) 1♡. Again you open in the longer suit, even though the hand is about three points short for a reverse sequence. This is because you do not now intend to reverse; if the response is 2♣ or 2◇ you will rebid 2♡. If your partner has a spade suit he will not fail to show it at some stage.

(5) Pass. Your points are of the number of the tribes of Israel, which means that normally you would open the bidding, and indeed there are many players who would open 1NT on tactical grounds. But the hand is not really worth an opening on values: no aces, and a K–J bare combination.

(6) 1NT. If there were any exceptions (other than the club-spade type) to the rule that 4–4–3–2 patterns in the 12–14 range should be opened with 1NT rather than one of a suit, this would be one. But there aren't: 1NT is the only sound opening to avoid subsequent problems even though your strength is concentrated in two strong major suits.

Chapter 2

RESPONSES TO SUIT OPENINGS

The raise of opener's suit – The response in notrumps – The response in a new suit – Responding with a passed hand

Over a 1♣, 1♢, 1♡ or 1♠ opening the Acol player looks first for a single bid that will express the full strength and character of his hand and may allow his partner to select the final contract.

The calls most likely to achieve this end are a raise of opener's suit to any level and a bid of notrumps at any level. These are limit bids: that is to say, there is only a narrow limit between the strongest hand on which they may be made and the weakest.

A limit bid is never forcing unless a game-forcing situation was already in being when it was made and game has still not been reached.

When no suitable limit bid can be found, the responder bids a new suit. This is forcing and has no upper limit of strength.

THE RAISE OF OPENER'S SUIT

When the opening is 1♡ or 1♠ and responder has four or more cards in the suit, he seeks no other contract: the only question is how high to raise. That question, however, is critical, for he must usually decide right now how many tricks his hand is worth with his partner's suit as trumps.

Many experienced players value their hands in the way I am about to discuss, using judgment to strike a balance between point count and distribution. There is also a radically different method, called the Losing Trick Count (LTC), which is described in Chapter 6. It covers all situations where a player has to value his hand for a known 4–4 or 5–3 or better trump fit and is helpful also in many other phases of the bidding process. Many good players use both methods, and this is very effective.

The direct raise of a major

With 4–4–3–2, which is much the most common of all patterns, a single raise is made with about 6 to 9 points, a double raise with 10–11. These figures are scaled down when a singleton is held.

A straight raise to game is based not on points but on playing strength: very powerful trump support with a singleton or void. The honour strength is always less – often distinctly less – than that of an opening bid. Hands that are worth a raise to game but have too many high cards to fit this description are expressed by indirect methods, using two or more bids. (See Chapter 6.)

Opposite a 1♠ opening, the following are typical raises to 2♠, 3♠ and 4♠ respectively:

(1)	♠ J 9 7 3	♡ J 4	◇ A J 9 4	♣ 10 5 2
(2)	♠ K J 7 2	♡ A 8 6 2	◇ K 10 4	♣ 10 5
(3)	♠ K J 9 8 6	♡ 5	◇ K 10 9 3 2	♣ 9 7

Thus, with 4-card or better support for opener's major you always raise immediately (unless your hand is strong enough for one of the special sequences described in Chapter 6) and do not bid another suit, not even the other major. Partner opens 1♡ and you hold:

$$\spadesuit\ Q\,J\,8\,3\,2 \qquad \heartsuit\ J\,10\,9\,7 \qquad \diamond\ K\,6 \qquad \clubsuit\ 9\,7$$

This is a common type and a little awkward: topweight for a raise to 2♡, weakish for 3♡. Nevertheless, you should bid one or the other. It is wrong to say, 'I am really worth two-and-a-half hearts, so I will bid 1♠ and see what happens.' If you do, your partner will never subsequently believe that you hold 4-card heart support and he will value his hand on a wrong basis. Unless your vibes tell you otherwise, you could do worse than to select the cautious option when playing duplicate, the optimistic one at other forms of scoring.

A double raise of opener's suit promises at least four trumps but a single raise may be made with three to an honour and a doubleton outside.

Raising a 1♣ or 1◇ opening

In response to a minor suit the approach is sharply different. It is by no means automatic to raise with four trumps: game in a minor is hard to make, and although the tactical advantage of a raise is still there it must often take second place to the search for a more achievable game.

New suits are introduced freely, not only to discover a fit but also to see whether the necessary guards are held for 3NT:

♠ J 10 8 2   ♡ A 3   ◇ A J 10 4   ♣ J 6 2

In response to 1◇ this hand is worth a raise to 3◇ on values but a better bid is 1♠. If opener rebids 2♣ or raises to 2♠, then you support diamonds. If instead he rebids 1NT, denoting 15–17, you raise to 3NT, not mentioning diamonds at all.

However, the straight double raise of a minor is not without a place in the scheme of things:

♠ 8 3   ♡ A 6   ◇ K 8 7 4 3   ♣ J 10 7 4

A 1♣ or 1◇ opening would be raised to three with this hand. Notwithstanding that the double raise may be partly pre-emptive in intention, as it is here, opener will often bid 3NT on anything better than a minimum, as he expects to run the suit.

On weaker hands with no new suit to bid and few if any ruffing values, a response in notrumps is often better than a raise:

♠ K 8 3   ♡ Q 10 4   ◇ 9 8 3 2   ♣ Q 7 5

Over a 1◇ opening, bid 1NT, the strain with more future. There is one type of responding hand where experts differ. The opening is 1◇ and you hold:

(1)   ♠ 8 5   ♡ J 10 7 3   ◇ A J 7 2   ♣ 10 6 2
(2)   ♠ A 9 8 3   ♡ 9 6 4   ◇ K Q 7 3   ♣ 8 2

With the first, one school would raise to 2◇, arguing that the hand is worth only one bid: if they were to respond in hearts and opponents contested in spades, it would no longer be possible to show diamond support. The other school would respond 1♡, being more impressed by the fact that a heart fit might be missed if opener had 4–4 in the red suits and was not strong enough to proceed over 2◇.

Hand (2) is stronger and the problem does not arise: it is clear to respond 1♠ and support diamonds on the next round.

THE RESPONSE IN NOTRUMPS

All responses in notrumps, whether at game level or below, are non-forcing limit bids.

The response of 1NT

This is in the nature of a catch-all: you respond 1NT on all 6–9 hands where you cannot raise opener's suit and have no suit that can be bid at the one level. The hand does not have to be of notrump character. Your partner opens 1◇, 1♡ or 1♠ and you hold:

♠ Q 2   ♡ 10 4   ◇ 10 8 6   ♣ K Q 7 4 3 2

You have too much to pass and too little to bid 2♣, which would suggest 10+. 1NT is all that is left.

The response of 2NT

This shows 11–12, or perhaps 10 with a good 5-card minor and plenty of nines and tens. You do not go out of your way to make this call on hands of borderline strength. To go down in 2NT when opener has an unsuitable minimum is bad, as presumably you could have made a part-score in a different strain.

Some partnerships therefore no longer use 2NT as a limit response, preferring the conventional Baron 2NT response over a minor-suit opening and the Jacoby 2NT over a major.

The Baron response shows 16+, balanced, and has no upper limit. The auction is developed along standard lines. The convention works well but the opportunity for its use is infrequent.

The Jacoby 2NT response to 1♡ or 1♠ is described in Chapter 6. It is equivalent to a game-forcing raise of the major.

The response of 3NT

This is natural, showing 13–15 and a 4–3–3–3 pattern with no major suit that could have been bid at the one level. With 4–4–3–2 an exploratory approach is preferred on a hand of this strength, for if opener is above-minimum a slam will be at least borderline and a 4–4 fit may be the clincher. Your partner opens 1♣ and you hold:

(1)	♠ K 8 3	♡ K J 7	◇ J 9 8 6	♣ A Q 2
(2)	♠ K 10 4	♡ A 2	◇ A 10 9 7	♣ K J 4 2

Hand (1) is flat and is well expressed by an immediate 3NT. With (2) the chances of a slam are not to be ignored: a response of 1◇ will allow opener to disclose his type.

THE RESPONSE IN A NEW SUIT

This is forcing but the count can be anything from 5 or 6 points up. Responder may merely be keeping the bidding open in case opener has a powerhouse or he may have a big hand and be planning an exploratory sequence leading to game or slam.

One-level response in a new suit

The search for a major-suit fit is paramount and on even the
weakest type the responder should show a major suit if he can
do so at the one level. Your partner opens 1◇:

♠ 10 8 5 3   ♥ A 7 2   ◇ 10 4   ♣ K J 8 2

The indubitable response is 1♠, not 1NT: when you bid
1NT over your partner's minor-suit opening he will take it as
gospel that you have no 4-card major. Few rules on bidding
are sacrosanct but this one is rarely broken. Incidentally, if
you ever encounter a partner who thinks that bidding a suit at
the one level shows a stronger hand than bidding 1NT you
should take him aside and gently explain that this is somewhat
old hat.

When more than one 4-card suit is held, it is usual to bid 'up
the line', as the expression has it:

♠ A J 8 3   ♥ 10 7 6 2   ◇ 8 5   ♣ Q 7 3

Over partner's 1♣ the response is 1♥, not 1♠.

It is quite normal to bid a 4-card major suit at the one level
ahead of a 5-card minor when too few points are held for a
two-level response:

♠ Q 8 7 3   ♥ J 4   ◇ 8 2   ♣ A Q 7 6 5

Over a 1♥ or 1◇ opening, a response of 1♠ is preferred to
2♣, even though you are only a point shy for this call. Indeed,
it is sometimes correct to bid a 4-card major ahead of a 5-card
minor with a stronger hand:

♠ A 10 9 7   ♥ 10 6   ◇ A 2   ♣ Q 10 9 5 3

Suppose that your partner opens 1♥ or 1◇: you have the
values for a bid of 2♣, but if opener were then to rebid his
suit, suggesting a limited hand, you would not want to continue with 2♠ as this would force opener to bid again. As it is

so important not to miss a major-suit fit, it is better to respond 1♠ initially.

Now suppose that your partner gets the show on the road with 1♢ and you have this hand:

♠ 10 4   ♡ K Q 7 3   ♢ J 6   ♣ A K 7 5 4

This time you willingly bid 2♣. If opener rebids 2♢, you are strong enough to bid 2♡. Thus the general idea is that when you have a 5–4 minor-major with, say, the equivalent of opening strength, you arrange to show both suits. When you are not that strong, you give priority to the major.

Two-level response in a new suit

There is nothing at all against showing a 4-card minor suit, but the particular response of 2♡ over 1♠ always promises at least five hearts. With 4–4 suits you respond in the more economical one:

♠ 10 4   ♡ Q J 8 5   ♢ 8 6 3   ♣ A K 7 3

Bid 2♣ over 1♠, but 1♡ over 1♢.

With two 5-card suits, the first response depends on whether you propose to show both. The opening is 1♠ and you hold:

(1)   ♠ Q   ♡ Q 2   ♢ K 10 7 6 4   ♣ A 10 7 5 3
(2)   ♠ 4   ♡ K 3   ♢ A Q J 8 2   ♣ K 10 9 8 6

With (1) you respond 2♣ initially, intending to pass a rebid of 2♠ by partner as you do not expect a game to be there. If instead your partner rebids 2♡, you still do not introduce diamonds but this time you continue with 2NT, which is not forcing, as the possibility of game is still open.

With hand (2) you respond first with 2♢, as you are strong enough to bid clubs on the next round, intending to reach game.

A two-level response may sometimes be made on marginally fewer than 10 points: but only with a long, strong suit that can be bid again to show discouragement on the next round.

New-suit response with a game-going hand

With a decent 12 points or more the responder expects to reach game. There may be a slam if opener is strong and the hands fit well, so with some types responder may plan a sequence of several rounds.

The strongest response, with no upper limit, is the jump shift: that is, a jump bid in a new suit, which is forcing to game. A sound minimum is about 16 points with a good 5-card suit.

However, it does not follow that one must always force with such a hand. 'I had to force because I had 16 points,' is a remark often heard, but there are many hands where a jump shift is not best: in particular, the two-suiter, by which is meant not a freak hand but any 5–4 or longer pattern where you propose to bid both suits. Your partner opens 1♡ and you hold:

♠ A Q 10 4 2   ♡ 7 4   ◇ A K Q 2   ♣ Q 10

With this type you want to show both suits, but without going beyond 3NT, which may be the best contract. If you respond 2♠ this may not be possible, but it is unnecessary to use up so much space, as a simple change of suit on the second round will keep things moving.

There is sometimes a different, and perhaps surprising reason for avoiding a jump shift: your hand may be too strong! A responder with a very great number of points – say, 19 or more – may find it difficult to limit his hand, even on the second round, and it may be more convenient to allow – or rather, to oblige – opener to limit his own hand. It is a fact that opener's rebid is apt to be more informative over a simple response than over a jump shift:

(1)	*Opener*	*Responder*	(2)	*Opener*	*Responder*
	1♣	2♠		1♣	1♠
	3♠			3♠	

In each sequence responder holds:

♠ K 8 5 4 2   ♡ A K 7   ◇ A Q 8   ♣ K 4

Clearly he is better placed after the second sequence than after the first, as he knows for sure that opener has 4-card support and an above-minimum opening with only six losers. (In the first sequence, opener cannot show this type by bidding 4♠: the jump raise over a force shows good trump support but denies extra values.)

There are in fact only two types of responding hand on which an immediate jump shift is a necessity: the powerful one-suiter and the hand with strong support for partner and another suit on the side:

♠ K Q 9 7 3   ♡ Q 6   ◇ A 10   ♣ A Q 10 5

When your partner opens 1♣ you should bid 2♠ and then support clubs; similarly, jump to 3♣ if he opens 1♠.

What is your call on these hands over an opening 1♡?

(1)	♠ A K J 8 6 3	♡ J 4	◇ A 6 3	♣ K 7
(2)	♠ K Q 6	♡ 10 7 4	◇ A J 8 4	♣ A J 6
(3)	♠ K 5	♡ K Q 10 2	◇ J 10 4	♣ A K 10 8
(4)	♠ 8	♡ K 7	◇ A Q 7 4 3	♣ A K J 9 3

With (1) the features are: a fine 6-card suit, fair controls and tolerance for opener's suit. This fits the classic description of a jump shift: an immediate 2♠ will express the strength and character and allow you to leave any slam initiative to your partner.

With (2) a limit bid of 3NT reflects the all-round strength and balanced character.

Hand (3) qualifies for a bid of 3♣. It is unusual to make a jump shift in a 4-card minor but it is an acceptable move when primary support for opener's major is held.

With (4) there are four possible contracts: hearts, notrumps and the minors. If you were to make a jump response you would not be able to cover all options, so the preferred bid is 2◇. Then 3♣ will be forcing over partner's 2♡ or 2NT.

In general, when you have an extremely powerful responding hand, and a slam is possible, you should consider whether you are likely to have to take the final decision yourself. If you are, then it may be better to issue a series of forcing bids than to make an immediate jump shift.

RESPONDING WITH A PASSED HAND

Opener may now pass a response in a new suit, so there is a tendency for responder to raise the opening with 3-card support, or to respond in notrumps. Your partner opens 1♠ in third position and you hold:

(1)	♠ A 7	♡ A 10	◇ Q J 10 8	♣ 10 7 4 3 2
(2)	♠ Q 10 7	♡ 10 9 2	◇ A 7 5	♣ A 9 7 6

Were you not a passed hand, you would bid 2♣ in each case. As it is, you cannot risk being left in so moderate a suit and should respond 2NT with the first hand, 2♠ with the second.

Jump shift by a passed hand

This is a well-focused bid, forcing for one round and logically implying three-level support for opener's suit; otherwise the jump would be unsafe on a hand that was not strong enough to open:

♠ Q 6 4 2   ♡ 7 2   ◇ 10 4   ♣ A Q 8 6 3

Over your partner's third-hand 1♠, a response of 3♣ is more definitive than a raise to 3♠, since game may depend on whether opener has a fit for clubs. Opener may now go straight to game in his suit; not only when he has extra values but whenever he has a fit in the side suit. A rebid of 3♠ by opener is therefore a sign-off.

Quiz for the responding hand

Your partner opens 1♡ as dealer and next hand passes.

(1)	♠ K J 8 4 3	♡ K J 10 8	◇ 9 6	♣ 8 4
(2)	♠ 7 4	♡ Q 7 3 2	◇ 9 6 2	♣ Q 8 7 3
(3)	♠ A 6	♡ Q J 8 7 4	◇ 5	♣ A Q J 5 3
(4)	♠ 10 7 3 2	♡ 10 8 7	◇ K 5	♣ K J 7 3

(1) 3♡. When the hand is suitable for a limit raise of opener's major, you look no further. If you were to bid 1♠, you might never persuade your partner that you held such strong heart support.

(2) 2♡. This hand is not really worth a raise on values, but on tactical grounds one should almost always support opener's major suit with four trumps and a likely ruffing value. If your partner bids some more and goes down, you will probably be saving at least a part score.

(3) 3♣. With strong support for opener's suit and a fine side suit, a jump shift may be made with less than the usual high-card strength. 3♣ is game-forcing and suggests a slam if partner has key cards.

(4) 1♠. This is preferred to a raise of hearts, which would, however, be perfectly sound. A 'weakness' response of 1NT, concealing both of your useful features, is not to be contemplated.

Your partner opens 1♠ and next hand passes.

(5)	♠ 10 4	♡ J 3	◇ Q J 9 5 3 2	♣ K 8 2
(6)	♠ Q J 8 6 3 2	♡ 9 4	◇ 4	♣ K 10 8 5
(7)	♠ K J 5	♡ 8 5 3 2	◇ Q 8	♣ A J 10 3

(5) 1NT. This is the only sound response on 6–9 with no suit that can be bid at the one level and no support for opener's suit. 2◇ would suggest at least 10 points.

(6) 4♠. The direct game raise shows very strong trump support but less than opening strength. It is in no way a slam invitation and is aimed partly at shutting out opponents. Opener passes unless his hand is very rich in controls.

(7) 2♣. A raise to 3♠ would require four trumps, so you respond in clubs with the intention of supporting spades on the next round.

Your partner opens 1♣ and next hand passes.

(8)	♠ K 8 7 4	♡ A 10 8 3	◇ K Q 4	♣ 10 2
(9)	♠ Q 10 5 3	♡ J 3 2	◇ 6 4	♣ A K J 7
(10)	♠ J 8 4 2	♡ Q 9 5 3	◇ A 7 3	♣ 9 5
(11)	♠ A 3 2	♡ 9 7 4 2	◇ J 7 6 4	♣ 5 2
(12)	♠ K 9	♡ K J 5 4	◇ A 10 8 7	♣ K J 2

(8) 1♡. With two 4-card suits that can be bid at the one level, you bid first the lower-ranking.

(9) 1♠. You have the values for a jump raise in clubs, but the minor suits are low in the pecking order. Show the major suit, and if your partner rebids 1NT, do not show club support at all but raise to 3NT.

(10) 1♡. The reader who has led a sheltered life may be surprised to learn that there are players at large who will bid 1NT with this hand ('I had only seven points, partner'.) To find a 4–4 major-suit fit is a prime objective and a response of one of a suit promises no greater strength than 1NT.

(11) Pass. The danger in bidding with such a weak hand when you cannot raise opener's suit is not that your partner may have a weak opening but that he may have a strong one. If you make it a habit to bid with such skimpy values you will sometimes do very well but will more often incur a minus.

(12) 1♦. To bid 3NT with such a strong hand is to risk missing a slam when there is a 4–4 fit and opener has anything more than a minimum. Also, 3NT may not be the best game: 4♡ on a 4–4 fit could easily be superior. If opener rebids 1♠, a bid of 3NT will then be O.K.

Chapter 3

OPENER'S SECOND BID

Responder has raised opener's suit – Responder has bid notrumps – Responder has bid a new suit – Responder has made a jump shift

The challenge facing opener at his second turn differs according to whether his partner has made a limited response or an unlimited bid in a new suit.

Over a limited response, opener is put firmly in charge. He knows the combined strength within close limits and can often select the final contract. If he needs further information he has ways of getting it. The two types of limited response are a raise of opener's suit to any level and a bid of notrumps at any level.

RESPONDER HAS RAISED OPENER'S SUIT

The simplest case is where responder raises a major and opener is satisfied that the hand should be played in this suit. It is then a matter of straight valuation:

	Opener	Responder
	1♠	2♠
	?	

♠ A 10 7 3 2   ♡ K Q 6   ◇ A J 3   ♣ J 4

After such a start, how can opener tell whether he should continue? A rough guide is that he should be able to take away an ace and still have a sound opening. He can't do that here.

A better guide is the Losing Trick Count, described in Chapter 6. To bid game after a single raise you need a five-loser hand. Only an optimist would count this hand as six losers, so the single raise won't be enough, even if responder is maximum.

Now suppose that 1♠ is raised to 3♠. Responder will be close to opening values, so now you should bid game whenever you have anything more than a minimum. The hand above meets the test and stands well with the LTC also.

The only types on which opener is likely to pass a double raise of a major are a minimum 5–3–3–2 and a sub-minimum 5–4–2–2. Other types will either be balanced and therefore 15+, or will include a singleton which, together with the guaranteed fit, will justify a shot at game.

When opener has a second suit this will have a bearing on how he should continue after a raise:

Opener	Responder
1♠	2♠
?	

♠ A Q 8 6 3   ♡ 8 4   ◇ A J 8 2   ♣ K 4

Opener has six losers and responder is expected to have nine – on the face of it, one too many. However, if responder has 4-card support there will be nine trumps. Opener also has two aces. These are very positive features.

This is a case where responder's holding in opener's second suit, diamonds, will be the decisive factor. If he has fitting cards, or a shortage and plenty of trumps, a low point-count game may be there. The standard move is a trial bid of 3◇, saying: 'Bid game if you have a fit (singleton or high honour) in diamonds, even if you are not maximum.'

The best suit in which to make a trial bid is an empty holding with a high card and two or three losers. Avoid a suit where you need no help, unless you intend to bid game regardless of partner's response and are making a trial bid merely to mislead opponents.

The responder to a trial bid goes to game when he has a high honour or a shortage in the suit and four trumps. With a poor holding he bids game only when he has a blown-in-the-glass maximum.

Next, what does it mean when opener avoids a trial bid in a sequence like this?

Opener	Responder
1♡	2♡
3♡	

Two styles are popular. In the recommended one, favoured especially by tournament players, the 're-raise' by opener is not a game try but a shut-out. Responder is expected to pass, even with a maximum. The theory is that if 2♡ is all that can be made, opponents will not let you play there. The other style is to treat the re-raise as natural, saying, 'Bid game if you are maximum.'

Inasmuch as the single raise of a major may be based on three trumps, there is sometimes a need for this sequence:

Opener	Responder
1♠	2♠
2NT	

Opener is showing 17–18, fairly balanced. Responder reverts to the suit when he has 4-card support, bidding game when his raise was sound.

Responder has raised a minor suit

A single raise in a minor offers little hope for eleven tricks, so when opener is strong he will usually explore other contracts. Game in a major is still a possibility, but not a very likely one: responder will have hidden a 4-card major only when his hand is very weak. Game in notrumps is therefore more promising.

After 1◇–2◇ you hold:

♠ K Q 3   ♡ K 6   ◇ A J 7 5 2   ♣ A 8 6

The raise of your broken suit is good news and you are well worth a bid of 2NT.

Over a double raise, opener needs very little to take a punt at 3NT when he has extra length:

Opener	Responder
1♣	3♣
?	

♠ A 2   ♡ J 4   ◇ K 10 4   ♣ A J 8 5 3 2

Go straight to 3NT despite the heart weakness. It is often better to take a chance on an unguarded suit than to draw attention by showing side features. This is a type where points hardly matter: you hope to rattle off nine fast tricks when you get in.

RESPONDER HAS BID NOTRUMPS

Opener now has a good idea of which suits are still potential trump suits. If responder has bid 2NT over 1♡, there won't be a spade fit, and so on.

A key question is, which of opener's rebids will be forcing, which invitational and which sign-offs? The answer depends on the level of the notrump response.

Responder has bid 1NT

Opener should decide first whether he still has hopes of reaching a game, either in notrumps or in his main suit when this is a major:

	Opener	*Responder*
	1♡	1NT
	?	

(1)   ♠ Q J 10 6   ♡ A J 10 8   ◇ Q J   ♣ A J 10
(2)   ♠ J 10   ♡ K Q 10 8 7 3   ◇ A 10 9   ♣ A 6

Hand (1) is a minimum for a raise to 2NT, justified partly because RHO may find it hard to make a good lead through these sequential holdings. Hand (2), with six losers and a suit that can play opposite x–x, is a minimum for a jump rebid of opener's suit, non-forcing.

Suppose next that the opener decides to settle for a partscore. He does not rebid his suit merely because it is rebiddable:

	Opener	*Responder*
	1♠	1NT
	?	

(3)   ♠ A K J 8 3   ♡ A 9 2   ◇ J 10   ♣ J 9 6
(4)   ♠ K 9 7 5 4 2   ♡ A 6   ◇ 8 6 3   ♣ A 9

In neither case is a game conceivable and the only question is whether 2♠ is likely to be safer than 1NT. With (3) opener should pass, since 1NT may have chances even when the spade suit cannot be brought in. With (4) opener should bid 2♠. This holding may survive a poor division when it is the trump suit but may be little use at notrumps.

With 5–4–3–1 it is usually right to take partner out of 1NT, but with 5–4–2–2 the test is whether the 1NT bidder may be expected to have length in the second suit. After 1◇–1NT you hold:

♠ 9 2   ♡ 7 4   ◇ K Q J 8 2   ♣ A K 9 7

Responder's failure to show a major suit means that there is sure to be a playable contract in one minor or the other, but it also means that opponents are probably queuing up to bid the majors. If you bid 2♣ there will be two opponents who can chip in, so it may be better to let partner fail in 1NT. You just have to weigh matters up, taking account of vulnerability and your opponents' psychology.

When taking responder out of 1NT, it is usually right to bid a secondary suit, even a weak minor, rather than to rebid a 5-card suit, even a strong major. After 1♠–1NT you hold:

♠ A Q J 8 6   ♡ Q J 8   ◇ 6   ♣ A 10 5 3

Bid 2♣. This denotes a 5–4 pattern and is much more definitive than a bid of 2♠, which in the best circles would carry at least a faint adumbration of 6-card length.

A takeout in a higher-ranking new suit, as in 1♡–1NT–2♠, is forcing for one round. Opener probably does not expect to play in the second suit, as responder has denied a 4-card major, so the sequence tends to be exploratory. A jump bid in a lower-ranking suit ('jump-shift') is forcing to game.

Opener	Responder
1♡	1NT
3◇	

♠ K Q 6   ♡ A Q J 9 4   ◇ A K J 8   ♣ 4

After partner is able to respond, you do not want to play in less than game, but which game is best is not clear yet. 3◇ creates a game-forcing situation. Responder can show strong heart support with 3♡ and weaker support with 4♡.

Responder has bid 2NT

A simple rebid of opener's suit is a sign-off with a 6-card suit. With anything more than a minimum, opener pushes on to game. When he has a 5-card major he should preferably allow responder the opportunity to show support, as the best game is so often in a 5–3 major:

Opener	Responder
1♠	2NT
3♣	

♠ A 9 7 3 2   ♡ J 4   ◇ K J   ♣ A J 8 6

Had the response been 1NT, you might well have passed rather than bid 2♣, but here it is clear to bid 3♣ because if responder cannot support spades you still have the values for 3NT.

Responder is unlikely to raise a minor in this type of sequence unless he is wide open in one of the unbid suits, and even then he should preferably show a feature, staying within range of 3NT. Responder would much sooner support the major suit on three cards than raise the minor with four.

When giving preference for the major suit, responder should distinguish between two types:

Opener	Responder
1♠	2NT
3◇	?

(1)	♠ Q 10 3	♡ A 8 7 2	◇ K 6	♣ Q 9 5 4
(2)	♠ K 8 3	♡ Q J 9	◇ J 8 7	♣ Q J 10 8

With each hand responder shows delayed support, but with (1), eminently suitable, he gives jump preference to 4♠. With (2) he bids 3♠ because if opener now goes to 3NT he intends to pass.

Responder has bid 3NT

This is an uncommon response, based on a precise type: 13–15, 4–3–3–3. A rebid of opener's major is now a sign-off, but a takeout into a minor, whether a new suit or not, is a slam try. After 1♠–3NT, you hold:

♠ A J 9 4 3   ♡ K 6   ◇ K 7   ♣ A Q 10 4

Bid 4♣. You can count on 30+, so a fitting dummy may produce a slam. 4◇ or 4♡ from partner will be cue-bids, accepting the slam try; perhaps with clubs as the suit, perhaps with spades. 4♠ will be a sign-off.

RESPONDER HAS BID A NEW SUIT

We have been dealing with sequences where responder's strength is known within narrow limits, but now only the lower level is known. Opener therefore aims to limit his own hand so that one partner, at any rate, will know the combined strength.

Rebid in notrumps by opener

When opener is 4–4–3–2 or 4–3–3–3, or 5–3–3–2 with a minor suit, he will necessarily be in the range of 15–19; otherwise he would have opened 1NT or 2NT. Now:

Over a one-level response he rebids 1NT with 15–17. 2NT with 18–19.

Over a two-level response he bids 2NT regardless. This is forcing. (To jump to 3NT merely to show that you are in the upper range is not a good use of space.)

(1) ♠ K 9 3   ♡ A J 7   ◇ Q J 8 6   ♣ K J 2
(2) ♠ A 4   ♡ K J 8 3   ◇ A Q J 2   ♣ K 7 5

With (1) you open 1◇ and over a response of 1♡ or 1♠, rebid at 1NT, 15–17. Over a response of 2♣, you bid 2NT, which is forcing to game, 15–19.

With (2) you again open 1◇, this time rebidding 2NT, 18–19 but not forcing, over 1♠. A response of 1♡ would be raised to 3♡. Over 2♣ you bid 2NT, 15–19 and game-forcing.

Opener does not rebid in notrumps if he can show a 4-card major suit at an economical level:

Opener	Responder
1♣	1♢
?	

♠ 10 9 7 2   ♡ A K 3   ♢ Q 4   ♣ A Q 8 6

The recommended rebid is 1♠, not 1NT, despite the balanced character. But this practice is not universal: devotees of Second-round Stayman (see next chapter) may prefer to rebid 1NT, defining the strength. According to this convention the responder, if strong enough to invite game over 1NT, may then bid 2♣ to inquire for an undisclosed major.

The raise of responder's suit

With 4-card support for responder's major suit, opener always gives a direct raise unless he is strong enough for game and can show a feature *en route*:

Opener	Responder
1♣	1♡
?	

(1) ♠ A Q 7 4   ♡ J 10 3 2   ♢ 2   ♣ A Q J 5
(2) ♠ K Q 7   ♡ A J 10 2   ♢ 8   ♣ A Q 10 9 2

Hand (1), with six losers, is worth a raise to 3♡. A bid of 1♠ is not on the menu: thereafter, responder would never credit you with four hearts.

Hand (2) has only five losers so is worth game, but as you have a singleton the best bid is 4♢, a splinter. (Chapter 6.)

A single raise is often made with 3-card support and a ruffing value. In the same sequence you hold:

♠ 6 4   ♡ K J 8   ♢ A K 5   ♣ K J 10 3 2

Had partner responded 1♠ you would have bid 1NT. As it is, a raise to 2♡ is more likely to encourage partner.

Opener rebids his suit

A simple rebid suggests at least a 5-card suit with minimum or near-minimum points and no other suit that could have been shown economically.

With even the weakest opening hand, a 5-card suit is not rebid when a new suit can be introduced without raising the level:

	Opener	Responder
	1♡	2♣
	2◇	

♠ 5 ♡ A K 9 8 7 ◇ J 10 8 5 ♣ K 10 8

To bid 2♡ would be very poor, not only because opener does not wish to sound discouraging after such a favourable response but also because by bidding 2◇ he effectively shows five hearts also.

It is, however, usual to rebid a 6-card major suit before introducing a 4-card minor: when the secondary suit follows, the 6–4 pattern is defined.

A single raise of responder's spade suit with 3-card support is often preferred to a rebid in opener's 5-card heart suit:

	Opener	Responder
	1♡	1♠
	?	

♠ K 7 3 ♡ K Q J 8 3 ◇ 4 2 ♣ A 8 6

2♠ is more descriptive than 2♡, which in this sequence would hint at a 6-card suit. But suppose responder's bid had been 2♣: should opener raise to 3♣? Not on this hand, because the heart holding is strong, but the raise is an option when opener's suit is weaker.

Finally, a jump rebid of opener's suit over a one-level response is invitational. Over a two-level response it is forcing to game. Two types may be distinguished:

	Opener	Responder
	1♠	2♣
	?	

(1)	♠ K Q J 9 8 4	♡ 10	◇ K Q 7	♣ Q J 4
(2)	♠ A J 8 7 3 2	♡ J 3	◇ A K 2	♣ K 7

With (1) the most sensible bid is 4♠ (a vestige of the good old Acol slogan, 'Bid what you think you can make'). There is nothing to be gained by going slowly, as you have nothing else to say.

With (2) you bid a game-forcing 3♠, saying: 'I have a hand of quality. There may be a slam, or even an alternative strain.'

Such are the ways in which opener may limit his hand over responder's new suit. When none is available, opener's recourse is to bid a new suit.

Opener bids a new suit

Before discussing the forcing quality of a bid in a new suit by opener over responder's new suit, it will be convenient to define what is meant by a reverse.

(1)	Opener	Responder	(2)	Opener	Responder
	1◇	1♠		1♠	2◇
	2♡			3♣	

Each of these is a reverse sequence. That is to say, opener has not bid his suits in the most economical order and the responder will have to go to the three level if he wants to return to opener's first suit.

A reverse sequence always shows a strong opening, presumptively 16+. The first suit is always of at least 5-card length and when the reverse occurs at the two level, the first suit is always longer than the second.

Now we consider the meaning of different rebids in a new suit by opener.

i) A simple change of suit by opener is not forcing after a response at the one level:

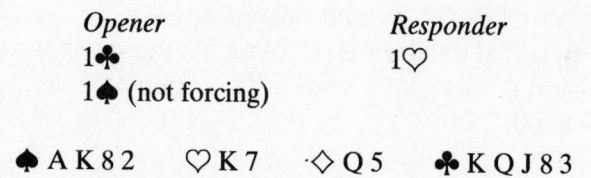

Opener   *Responder*
1♣   1♡
1♠ (not forcing)

♠ A K 8 2   ♡ K 7   ◇ Q 5   ♣ K Q J 8 3

This is about a maximum: with any better hand, opener would bid 2♠, a jump shift. Here, however, opener has no clear vision of where a game might be made if responder is minimum.

ii) A reverse by opener after a response at the one level is forcing for one round:

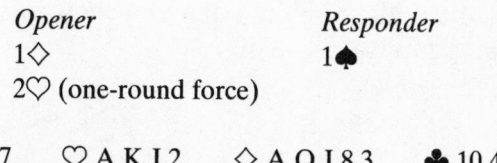

Opener   *Responder*
1◇   1♠
2♡ (one-round force)

♠ J 7   ♡ A K J 2   ◇ A Q J 8 3   ♣ 10 4

This hand is about a minimum. There is no upper limit.

iii) A simple change of suit by opener after a response at the two level is forcing for one round:

Opener   *Responder*
1♠   2♣
2♡ (one-round force)

The forcing quality of this sequence derives from responder's holding of at least 10 points, not from extra values in opener's hand, which may be a minimum.

iv) A reverse by opener after a response at the two level is game-forcing:

Opener   *Responder*
1♡   2◇
2♠ (game force)

Here, the game-forcing quality of the sequence is imparted

by the responder's 10+ and opener's 16+.

A new suit at the three level – a high reverse – shows similar values and is also game-forcing. It is often made in a strong 3-card minor:

Opener	Responder
1♠	2♡
3♣	

♠ A Q 10 6 2   ♡ A 6   ◇ 8 4 3   ♣ A Q 9

Over 2♡ opener expects to reach 4♡, 4♠ or 3NT, so a game-forcing 3♣ is clearly best.

v) Finally, a jump bid in a new suit shows a rock-crusher and is game-forcing:

Opener	Responder
1◇	1♡
2♠ (game force)	

♠ A Q J 4   ♡ A J 6   ◇ A K 10 9 3   ♣ 4

Here the jump is necessary as a bid of 1♠ would not be forcing. Had responder bid 2♣ over 1◇, a reverse bid of 2♠ would have sufficed.

RESPONDER HAS MADE A JUMP SHIFT

This is a response that never fails to charm the ear. A slam may be on the cards whenever opener is above minimum or has a fit.

A rebid in notrumps by opener will indicate the same range as over a simple response:

Opener	Responder
1♡	2♠
2NT (15–17)	

With a balanced 18–19, there is nothing against opener's rebidding 3NT when he has nothing else to say, but the same principle does not extend to rebids in a suit:

Opener	Responder
1♡	2♠
?	

♠ J 4   ♡ A J 10 9 8 3   ◇ A Q 4   ♣ K 2

Over 1♠ opener would have rebid 3♡ with this six-loser quality hand. Here, he still bids 3♡, not 4♡. This is partly because a jump rebid of a suit by either player in a forcing sequence has a special meaning:

Opener	Responder
1♠	3♣
4♠	

4♠ guarantees a solid suit, at least A–K–Q–J–x–x, and may set the stage for a slam. A negative inference is that when, in a forcing sequence, a suit is rebid without a jump, it probably is not solid.

After a jump shift both partners should avoid bidding weak suits. One of the worst of all disasters is to end in a slam with an inadequate trump suit when slam could have been made in a different strain.

Quiz on opener's second bid

You open 1♡ and your partner responds 1NT.

(1)	♠ A 8	♡ K J 10 8 5 2	◇ A 10 7	♣ K J
(2)	♠ J	♡ A Q 6 5 4	◇ K Q 3	♣ K 9 8 6
(3)	♠ 4	♡ A K 10 8 7	◇ A Q 9 8	♣ A 10 5

Quiz on opener's second bid follows on p. 56.

(1) 3♡. This shows a good 6-card suit in an above-minimum hand. Game is possible if responder is maximum, as you will have about 25 points.

(2) 2♣. It is seldom right to pass 1NT with a singleton. Responder evidently has fewer than four spades, so there is sure to be a fit somewhere.

(3) 2◇. Not quite enough for 3◇. If partner passes, no game is likely to succeed. If responder bids 2♡, bid 3♣ to complete the description of your shape. This allows partner to bid 3NT with strong spades or downgrade secondary spade honours for a heart contract.

You open 1◇ as dealer and your partner bids 2NT:

(4)	♠ Q 7 4	♡ 2	◇ Q J 8 6 4 2	♣ A K 2
(5)	♠ 6 4	♡ A Q J 3	◇ A K 7 6 4	♣ A 5

(4) 3◇, a sign-off. If hearts are led your partner may be unable to establish diamonds in time to make 3NT – or even 2NT.

(5) 3♡. Game should be icy. A slam may be there if partner has fitting cards, but any further initiative must come from his side of the table.

You open 1♣ and your partner bids 1♠:

(6)	♠ K J 4	♡ Q 3	◇ A 10 4	♣ A J 10 8 4
(7)	♠ K	♡ A 8 5 3	◇ K Q J	♣ A J 8 4 3
(8)	♠ K 10 9	♡ A J 10 8	◇ 4	♣ A K 10 9 3

(6) 1NT, showing 15–17. This is a close decision, as a raise to 2♠ is a sound alternative even though it could also be made on fewer points. The deciding factor is that you would quite like to be the declarer: ♡Q–x may be a more effective holding when held in the closed hand than when your hand is dummy at a spade contract.

(7) 2NT. You have the formal requirements for a reverse bid of 2♡ but this would place too much emphasis on two moderate suits. The jump rebid in notrumps, showing 18–19, is descriptive.

(8) 2♡. You have nothing to spare in high cards but the two suits are strong and responder's spade call is very favourable. Also, while the hand is overweight for a raise to 2♠, you have not enough trumps for a raise to 3♠.

You open 1♡ and your partner bids 2◇:

(9)	♠ 6 4	♡ A Q 9 8 7 2	◇ K J	♣ A 10 8
(10)	♠ 10 8 7	♡ A Q J 6 3	◇ J 10	♣ A K J
(11)	♠ Q 5	♡ A K J 5 4	◇ K 10 5	♣ Q 3 2
(12)	♠ K 5	♡ K Q J 9 8 6	◇ K Q 5	♣ 8 6

(9) 3♡. Over the two-level response this is forcing to game. You owe partner a point, perhaps, but the 6-card major and fitting diamond holding are positive factors.

(10) 3♣. A high reverse in a 3-card suit, forcing to game, is sometimes the most convenient way to express a hand of this quality.

(11) 2NT. Even with no sure spade stopper, this is the most accurate call. A raise to 3◇ would suggest a less balanced hand and could be made with fewer high-card values; as too could a simple rebid in hearts.

(12) 4♡. The distinction between this hand and the type on which you would bid 3♡ is that here the suit is stronger and the hand weaker.

You open 1◇ and your partner bids 2♠:

(13)	♠ A 4	♡ K 10	◇ A Q J 10 2	♣ Q 8 4 2
(14)	♠ Q 9 6	♡ A Q	◇ A 10 5 3 2	♣ Q J 2
(15)	♠ 10 4	♡ 8 3	◇ A K Q J 10 7	♣ K 10 2

(13) 2NT. 3◇ would be a reasonable choice but 2NT expresses the strength of the hand and shows stoppers in the unbid suits. 2NT also allows responder to indicate the nature of the jump-shift, rebidding 3◇ with diamond support or 3♠ with a one-suiter. If responder rebids 3◇, you can continue with a 3♠ cue-bid and over 3♠, you can cue-bid 4◇.

(14) 3♠. The jump-shift shows an excellent five-card or longer suit and Q–x–x or better rates as primary support. To bid 2NT would show the balanced pattern and at least 15 points but would imply weaker spades, such as a doubleton or three low spades. Your side has over thirty points and it is wise to agree on the trump suit as early as possible.

(15) 4◇. In a forcing situation the jump rebid guarantees a solid suit and does not imply extra values.

Chapter 4

THE LATER AUCTION

*Opener has rebid in notrumps – Opener has raised
responder's suit – Opener has rebid his suit – Opener
has bid a new suit – Fourth suit forcing – Misfits*

On many hands opener's second bid is meant to end the
auction, and does. A responder who intends to bid further
may focus his mind by asking these questions:

Does the hand belong in no more than a part-score? If so,
how can I make this clear with my next bid, so that we do not
get too high?

Does the hand belong in game or slam? If so, can I already
determine the best strain or do I need to know more about
opener's hand?

The answers come easiest in these cases:

  i) Opener has rebid in notrumps.

 ii) Opener has raised responder's suit.

iii) Opener has rebid his own suit.

In each case opener has made two descriptive bids and has
limited his hand. There is therefore a good chance that the
responder can now pick the contract.

The fourth case is where opener has bid a new suit, which is
unlimited. It is logical for responder to assume that the
opener is in the lower range for his sequence and to select a
contract on that basis if he can. If opener holds undisclosed
strength, he will take it from there.

OPENER HAS REBID IN NOTRUMPS

As we have seen, this is specific as to points and says much
about the opener's pattern. He definitely does not hold four
cards in responder's major and he is very unlikely to have

hidden a major suit of his own that could have been shown at the one level.

Opener has rebid 1NT

Opener has shown 15–17, so responder may raise to 2NT on about nine. Opener, if he accepts the invitation, may show delayed support for responder's suit or rebid his own major suit:

Opener	Responder
1♡	1♠
1NT	?

♠ K Q J 4 3   ♡ 10 7 4   ◇ J 4 2   ♣ Q 3

A thruster might raise straight to 3NT and this would be an acceptable gamble if the long suit were a minor. As it is, 2NT is better as it keeps open three possible game contracts.

A simple bid in a new suit is not forcing or even invitational when lower in rank than responder's first suit:

Opener	Responder
1♣	1♠
1NT	2◇ (or 2♡)

Responder is at least 5–4 and may be quite weak. Opener may pass, but a raise with four trumps is not ruled out. Here and in all similar situations, opener should prefer his partner's first suit, with 2-card support, to the second suit with 3-card support. A 5–2 trump suit usually plays better than a 4–3.

A bid in a higher-ranking new suit – a reverse – by responder is forcing for one round. A jump rebid in any suit, including a suit already bid by either partner, is forcing to game:

Opener	Responder
1♥	1♠
1NT	3♥

3♥ is forcing. Responder is very likely to hold this type:

♠ A 10 7 4 2   ♥ Q 10 8   ♦ 8 7   ♣ A J 5

The practice described is eminently workable but this is a critical area and any gain in accuracy is welcome. A convention called Stayman on the Second Round has its devotees. Over opener's rebid of 1NT, 2♣ is artificial, even when the suit has been bid by opener. The 2♣ rebid is used for all game-invitational hands, over which opener's 2♦ reply is artificial, showing an abject minimum, other two-level bids are natural with medium values and three-level bids are natural and game-forcing with maximum values.

Another version in known as New Minor Forcing. Two of an unbid minor suit suggests about nine points or more and is at least game-invitational. Comprehensive schemes of rebids can be devised.

The Crowhurst convention

This allows opener to rebid 1NT on a wider range than usual: for example, 12–16:

Opener	Responder
1♥	1♠
1NT	2♣

2♣ asks opener to clarify his hand. 2♦ from opener is artificial and shows an absolute minimum, 12 points. 2♥, 2♠ and 2NT are natural within the context of the auction and show medium values, 13–14 points. In the above sequence, 2♥ would be a 5-card suit, 2♠ shows three-card support and 2NT would deny both of these features. A three-level bid is natural, showing 15–16 points.

Responder does not bid 2♣ with fewer than about 11 points, because if he finds opener with an unsuitable minimum the bidding may already be too high.

Some pairs use the convention also when responding to a balancing, or protective, 1NT; where indeed a wide range is very convenient.

Opener has rebid 2NT

The points shown by opener depend on whether he has or has not jumped:

(1)	Opener	Responder	(2)	Opener	Responder
	1♡	2♣		1♣	1♠
	2NT			2NT	

In (1) opener's range is 15–19. Responder is expected to have 10 or more, so the sequence is game-forcing.

In (2) the range is 18–19 but nevertheless 2NT is not forcing as responder may have no more than five or so points. In standard bidding 3♠ now by responder is a sign-off, but some partnerships treat all bids over 2NT as forcing, and this no doubt is the better practice.

Opener has rebid 3NT

A player who opens with 1♣ or 1♢ and goes to 3NT over his partner's response is normally bidding on a long minor: otherwise he would have been strong enough to open 2NT. Responder therefore continues in his own suit at his peril: opener may have no support at all. After 1♣–1♡–3NT, responder should pass with this type:

♠ K 9   ♡ J 8 6 5 3 2   ♢ Q 10 6   ♣ 8 4

If, however, over 3NT, responder does bid game in his own suit, this is to play. Anything else will be slam oriented:

Opener	Responder
1◇	1♠
3NT	4◇

Responder will seldom remove 3NT to a minor suit unless he hopes for a slam.

OPENER HAS RAISED RESPONDER'S SUIT

Responder should always feel a warm glow when his suit is raised: especially when this is a straggly 5-card or longer suit in a hand where game may initially have seemed problematical:

Opener	Responder
1♣	1♡
2♡	?

(1) ♠ A Q 3   ♡ K 10 7 5 4   ◇ 4 2   ♣ Q 10 5
(2) ♠ K 8   ♡ Q 8 6 4 3 2   ◇ A J 10   ♣ 7 2

These are types that improve dramatically when the suit is raised. Both are minimum in points, but responder should push on to game.

When responder's minor suit is raised he may return to opener's major to show 3-card support:

Opener	Responder
1♠	2♣
3♣	?

♠ K 10 7   ♡ 9 4   ◇ K 8 2   ♣ A J 9 5 2

3♠ now by the responder will be invitational only. With any slightly stronger hand the responder may bid 4♠ with the assurance that opener has a 5-card suit; or he may bid a new suit at the three-level (forcing) to show a stopper for 3NT.

OPENER HAS REBID HIS SUIT

Opener's simple rebid denotes at least a 5-card suit, but its strength may vary widely. There are some sequences that hint at a good suit or extra length:

Opener	Responder
1♡	1♠
2♡	?

Responder holds:

♠ A K 5 4 2   ♡ Q 9   ♢ J 10 3 2   ♣ 7 4

Here, if opener held five hearts and three spades he would raise to 2♠ unless the hearts were strong. If he held a moderate 5-card heart suit and two spades he would probably open 1NT, or rebid in a strong 3-card minor. A raise to 3♡ is therefore a satisfactory solution to a rather awkward problem.

It is sometimes expedient to pass opener's rebid with a singleton when the bidding might otherwise get out of hand. In the same sequence responder should pass with this hand:

♠ Q 9 7 4 3   ♡ 9   ♢ K Q 7 5   ♣ Q 10 2

2NT may well be a better contract than 2♡. Unfortunately, 2NT here would not mean, 'This is where I want to play,' but, 'I have 11 or so points and am still hopeful of game.'

A new suit by responder is forcing for one round. It is sometimes not a genuine suit but feature-showing and a move towards 3NT:

Opener	Responder
1♣	1♠
2♣	?

♠ A K 10 5 4   ♡ 7 2   ♢ K Q 6   ♣ Q 10 2

2♦ is safe, as opener will not persist in raising the suit even in the unlikely event that he does so initially.

Opener has made a jump rebid in his suit

Over a two-level response this is forcing to game. Over a one-level response it is not, but responder should still bid game when the suit is a major and he has one or two useful features:

Opener	Responder
1♡	1NT
3♡	?

♠ Q 9 3   ♡ 6 5 2   ♦ A 7   ♣ J 10 7 4 3

Here South has three trumps, a quick trick and a ruffing value, which add up to a very sound raise to 4♡. With an only slightly stronger hand, two of these features would suffice.

Suppose that opposite your partner's jump rebid you are not short of points but have no ruffing value. It does not follow that you must bid 3NT:

Opener	Responder
1♠	2♦
3♠	?

♠ 7 3   ♡ K 6 4   ♦ A J 9 5 2   ♣ A 6 3

With this good hand there will surely be a sound play for both 4♠ and 3NT, but you want to be in the superior contract. It is close, but the preferred bid is 4♠. Opener will be quite short in one suit, possibly in two. If you bid 3NT and the most hostile lead is found, you will very likely have only one stopper. In that case 3NT may depend on running the spade suit, but at 4♠ declarer can probably comfortably afford a trump loser.

From that example arises a principle of wide application. When the choice is between supporting partner's 6-card major and bidding 3NT, you should bid notrumps when you think the suit can be run without loss. When you expect a loser, go for the trump contract.

Over opener's jump rebid in a minor, a feature-showing bid in a 3-card suit may be responder's best move:

	Opener	*Responder*
	1♣	1♠
	3♣	?

(1)	♠ K 10 8 7 2	♡ 8 5 2	♢ A 10 8	♣ Q 6
(2)	♠ A 10 8 6	♡ Q 4 3	♢ Q 10 6	♣ J 9 5
(3)	♠ A K 5 3 2	♡ 7 2	♢ 6 5 3	♣ J 10 8

With (1) responder is prepared for 3NT if opener has a heart guard and for 5♣ if he has not. For the moment, 3♢ is best.

With (2) the red-suit holdings warrant a direct 3NT. With Q–x–x there is better than an even chance that opponents cannot run five tricks.

With (3) a bid of 3NT does not appeal, as one of the red suits is likely to be wide open. However, with eight losers the hand is worth a raise to 4♣. Opener will bid 4♠ now if he holds delayed support.

OPENER HAS BID A NEW SUIT

When this is not a reverse, opener's hand will be in the 12–18 range: with more he would have forced. When game seems unlikely responder may pass or sign off:

	Opener	*Responder*
	1♣	1♡
	1♠	?

(1)	♠ 10 8 2	♡ Q J 8 5	♢ 8 4 2	♣ Q 5 4
(2)	♠ 10 4 3	♡ A J 6 4 3	♢ 4 2	♣ K J 3
(3)	♠ K 7	♡ K J 9 4	♢ 9 8 6	♣ K 10 7 3

With (1) the ceiling is 23 points and there is no evidence of a fit. If you could give preference for opener's first suit without raising the level, you would do so. As it is, it may be prudent to pass 1♠. Admittedly, over a 1♠ opening you would have bid 1NT, but that does not mean it is logical to do so now, as you have learned that opener's maximum is 18.

With (2) you bid 2♣; simple preference. The call has a relatively wide range and this hand is close to a maximum: if opener makes any kind of effort, you intend to co-operate. On hand (3) with similar values plus a fourth club you bid 3♣; jump preference.

Preference and jump preference

Whether jump preference should be treated as forcing in a sequence such as the following is a critical question:

Opener	Responder
1♠	2♣
2♡	?

♠ Q J 8   ♡ Q   ♢ A 8 7 4   ♣ A J 8 5 4

Some pairs treat it so and in that case it will certainly be convenient to bid 3♠ now. But in standard practice, 3♠ is not forcing, and as the responder has game-going values he should bid either 3NT or, better, 4♠.

When jump preference is not forcing responder can cope efficiently with this type:

♠ Q 8 3   ♡ J 2   ♢ J 9 4   ♣ A K 10 9 7

In the same sequence responder has too promising a hand for a simple 2♠ so he gives non-forcing jump preference by bidding 3♠.

Which method is better? Like many questions in bridge it cannot be decided because it rests upon imponderables. But since there are many experts in both camps, neither method can be too bad.

With a doubleton in opener's known 5-card suit and three cards in his second suit, responder normally shows preference for the first suit:

Opener	Responder
1♠	2♣
2♡	?

♠ Q 6   ♡ J 5 2   ♢ 10 9 2   ♣ A K 8 6 5

Bid 2♠. If opener is 5–5 and intends to proceed, he will rebid hearts.

Here is an extreme, but not precious, example of 'false preference':

Opener	Responder
1♠	1NT
2♢	?

♠ Q 6   ♡ 8 4   ♢ Q J 10 5   ♣ J 9 7 5 3

Against decent opposition you won't buy the contract by passing 2♢, but if you bid 2♠ it may be difficult for opponents to contest.

When responder holds primary support for opener's second suit, a raise will be equivalent to a first-round raise to the same level:

Opener	Responder
1♣	1♡
1♠	?

♠ K 9 8 4   ♡ A Q 10 2   ♢ J 4 3   ♣ 10 6

Responder would have raised a 1♠ opening to 3♠, so 3♠ is the right bid now.

The choice between two trump suits of equal length proffered by the opening bidder is often close. Suppose that the opener has bid two suits and the responder, also with equal length, intends to raise. He should not necessarily select the suit in which he holds high cards. At game level and below, solid suits make good side suits but non-solid suits make good trump suits. Here is a contrived but convincing example:

	West	East
♠	A K Q J 4	8 7 5
♡	10 9 7 5 2	J 8 3
◇	K 4	A J 2
♣	5	A 8 6 2

4♠, despite the solid trump suit, cannot be made against repeated club leads, as West cannot bring in the heart suit. He runs out of trumps while defenders still have a heart stopper and a club or so.

At 4♡ West cannot be beaten if hearts are 3–2. He wins the club lead, plays a heart, ruffs the return and plays a second heart. Again he is forced to ruff but now he switches to spades, leaving the defenders to make only the master trump.

Opener has shown reversing values

A reverse by opener suggests 16+. It is forcing for one round over a one-level response; to game over a two-level response.

Opener	Responder
1◇	1♠
2♡	?

(1)	♠ Q 9 6 4 3	♡ J 5 2	◇ J 7	♣ K Q 8
(2)	♠ Q J 9 8 6 5	♡ 10 4 3	◇ Q 4	♣ 9 2
(3)	♠ A 8 7 3 2	♡ 7 5	◇ 10 6 3	♣ J 10 6

With (1) responder bids 3NT, as 2NT would be a forced bid that could be passed. With (2) he bids 2♠ and with (3), 3◇; discouraging each time.

The advantage of treating opener's reverse as game-forcing after a two-level response is seen here:

Opener	Responder
1♡	2♣
2♠	?

♠ Q 4 3   ♡ 10 6 2   ◇ 7   ♣ A K Q 10 6 5

If game only were under consideration, responder's ♡10–x–x would constitute nourishing support, but here there is an aroma of slam so the emphasis should be on trump solidarity.

If opener's 2♠ were not game-forcing, responder would be in some difficulty: as it is, he may bid either 3♡ or 3♣, confident that this will not be passed. 3♣ is perhaps better: if opener accepts the suit it must surely be the right one.

The next sequence features a high reverse:

Opener	Responder
1♠	2♡
3♣	?

♠ 5 3 2   ♡ K Q J 8 2   ◇ A 4 3   ♣ 10 7

Responder has already indicated five hearts and should not rebid the suit. ('Do not tell partner the same thing twice' is a maxim that applies across the board.) The best spot may be 4♠, but it is sufficient to bid 3♠. If opener has an independent diamond guard and bids 3NT, responder will be happy to pass, knowing that his side entry is protected.

Opener has made a jump shift

Game must be reached, under penalty of boiling in oil. A slam may be there when responder has 10 points or more, and in that case he should avoid a bid that may end the auction prematurely:

Opener	Responder
1♡	1♠
3♣	?

♠ Q 10 8 3 2   ♡ Q 6   ◇ A K 10   ♣ J 9 4

3NT would be an underbid, as a slam is possible in several denominations. For the moment the best call is 3◇.

FOURTH SUIT FORCING

Charles Goren, who was bridge guru to a whole generation of Americans, used to remark that some hands are so difficult to bid that they should be quietly dropped on the floor so that they can be redealt, saving everyone a headache. Goren may have had in mind this type:

Opener	Responder
1♣	1♡
1♠	?

♠ A Q 2   ♡ K 10 9 7 4   ◇ 10 8 3   ♣ A 8

To bid this hand is not difficult: it is impossible. Game should clearly be reached – but in what strain?

The only solution is to bid 2◇, 'fourth suit forcing,' a style first codified by the present writer in an early book with Terence Reese and now almost universal.

A bid of the fourth suit conveys no promise of strength in the suit named but sends a simple message: 'I would like to hear more.' The loss of the natural meaning is no great hardship, for when three suits have been mentioned the partnership will seldom wish to play in the remaining one.

Opener now makes the most natural bid. He does not call notrumps unless he himself has a guard in the fourth suit.

To what level should the fourth suit be forcing? For simplicity, some partnerships treat it as forcing to game and this is a playable method, but a more common practice is this:

1. When the responder bids the fourth suit at the level of one or two, he may pass a minimum rebid in notrumps from opener. He may also pass a minimum rebid in opener's suit. When opener has anything more than a minimum, he must find a stronger bid:

Opener	Responder
1◇	1♡
1♠	2♣
?	

♠ K J 9 4   ♡ Q 7   ◇ A J 7 4 3   ♣ A 10

Responder will want to hear first and foremost about opener's guard in the fourth suit, but the correct bid is 3NT, not 2NT which could be passed.

2. When the fourth suit is bid at the level of three and the opener does not immediately go to game, the fourth-suit bidder must bid at least once more. This is necessary because of the shortage of space:

Opener	Responder
1♠	2◇
2♡	3♣
?	

♠ A K J 5 4   ♡ A Q 10 2   ◇ Q   ♣ 8 7 4

Here it is not clear whether responder has strong diamonds or intends to play in a major suit. Opener has a good hand but has no new feature that he can introduce. This is not fatal as a simple 3♠ will be forcing and is best at this point.

A raise of the fourth suit below the level of 3NT is no guarantee of length or a stopper. It is simply a forcing bid for hands that offer no convenient limit bid.

A refinement proposed by perfectionists takes care of one of the few situations where the partnership may actually wish to play in the fourth suit; the case where the suit is bid at the level of one:

Opener	Responder
1♣	1♦
1♡	1♠

1♠ is now treated as natural, showing a spade suit. Responder may have no more than six points.

Opener	Responder
1♣	1♦
1♡	2♣

This is not natural and not a jump shift: it is fourth suit forcing. Responder has 11+ and he denies a spade suit.

MISFITS

On misfit hands the best of players may come unstuck, but sometimes the danger ought to be foreseen. Players who are quick to bid the limit when they scent a good fit may fail to adjust when the clues point the other way.

Recognition of fit, good or bad, can begin on the first round. You open 1♠ with this hand:

♠ K Q J 9 7 3   ♡ –   ♢ J 10 2   ♣ A J 10 5

If the response is 2♡ you should, for the moment, presume a misfit and bid only 2♠. If the response is 2♢ you should boldly bid 3♠. This might horrify your bank manager but you are counting on strength opposite in diamonds to cover your weakness in this suit.

Commonsense decrees the cautious option not just when a misfit is likely but when it is possible:

Opener	Responder
1♣	1♠
2♣	2♡
?	

♠ 2   ♡ 7 6   ♢ A K 5 2   ♣ K J 9 8 7 5

Responder's change of suit is forcing and his hand is unlimited. Perhaps he has 'tops' and a club fit, and perhaps the sky's the limit. But it is also possible that responder has no more than he has promised, in which case you are going nowhere. It is logical to make the most discouraging bid, 3♣. The suit is nothing to crow about but: (a) the 9–8–7 are important cards: (b) a long broken suit is often useless unless it is trumps.

In this sequence 2NT would also be a weak bid, but the strength in diamonds is in the form of quick tricks and you have no points at all in responder's suits. These are considerations that favour a trump contract. If partner has a fit in clubs and needs only a diamond stopper for 3NT, he can still bid the fourth suit.

Partners, too, are capable of recognising a potential misfit and some high-class inferences may flow from this:

Opener	Responder
1♡	1NT
2♣	2◇
2NT	?

♠ 6 4   ♡ 9 2   ◇ A Q 10 8 6 3 2   ♣ 7 4

The response of 1NT with such a lopsided hand may surprise some readers but experts today dislike bidding two-over-one with fewer than 10 HCP.

As the bidding has gone, when opener bids 2NT you as responder should place him with the ◇K and should bid a confident 3NT!

Why? Because he places you with a long diamond suit and nothing else, and if he held nothing in diamonds he would recognise the misfit and pass. Next:

Opener	Responder
1◇	1NT
3◇	?

♠ Q 10 4   ♡ J 7 3   ◇ 9 5 4 2   ♣ A 8 2

If you were to think only in terms of points you might pass, but you should take account of the fact that you have four cards in partner's 6-card suit. These will be a positive factor if the suit is less than solid. Opposite A–K–x–x–x–x, for example, there will be six very likely tricks, so, bid 3NT.

On misfits with plenty of points, notrumps are often the best strain. A player who can see this must avoid forcing his partner into a position where 3NT may be by-passed:

Opener	Responder
1♡	1♠
2♢	?

♠ A J 10 8 7 3   ♡ 2   ♢ J 7 4   ♣ A K J

3♠ would be forcing and has its attractions: opener may have a useful, not too unbalanced, hand, with which even 6♠ may be on. But he may also have a moderate two-suiter with a singleton or void in spades, in which case 3NT may be the only makeable game.

If you were to bid 3♠, opener might have to go past 3NT for lack of a club guard: therefore the best move is 3♣. There may still be problems to come. If opener can show spade support, fine, but he is more likely to bid 3♡ or 3♢. Now you should bid 3NT, relying on your partner to catch the inference that your reason for bidding 3♣ was not to discover whether he held a club guard but to see whether he could support spades.

In competitive auctions, especially, misfits are notorious death-traps. The danger is greatest when only one opponent has bid. His partner, who has remained silent, is the one who will put the boot in. He will have a better idea of what each pair can or cannot make than anyone else.

Quiz on the later auction

Your partner opens and the bidding begins: 1♣–1♡–2♡.

(1)	♠ 4 3	♡ K J 8 3 2	♢ 9 5 2	♣ A Q 7
(2)	♠ K 10 3 2	♡ A Q 7 5	♢ A 8 2	♣ 10 3
(3)	♠ 7 5 3	♡ K Q 10 8	♢ K Q 10	♣ 6 3 2

(1) 3♣. This is bold but not rash. Perhaps you are a point shy, but the fine holding in opener's suit is compensation. 3♣ suggests that you have high cards but not necessarily length in the suit. You have been raised in a major and can hardly want to play in partner's minor, so this is a try for game in hearts.

(2) 3NT. With 13 points it is normal to bid game. To bid 4♡ would be precipitate, as you cannot be sure your partner has four hearts. A temporising bid of 3♢ would confuse the issue, but by bidding 3NT you keep open your options.

(3) Pass. You have less than the equivalent of opening values and there is no redeeming feature such as there was in hand (1). Game will be there only in the event of a perfect fit.

Your partner opens and the bidding begins: 1♣–1♠–1NT.

(4)	♠ A Q 8 7 2	♡ Q 10 9	♢ J 9 8	♣ 7 4
(5)	♠ A 9 5 3 2	♡ 10 7 6 5	♢ K J 6	♣ 4
(6)	♠ J 10 9 7 3	♡ K J 8 3 2	♢ 7	♣ K 2

(4) 2♣ Checkback. If opener bids 2♢, artificial, minimum, you can rebid 2♠. Over other rebids you will play in game, 4♠ if opener shows three-card support, 3NT otherwise.

(5) 2♡. 3NT is unlikely to be there, as you have minimum points and a singleton in partner's suit. Game in a major is just possible if there is a sufficient fit. If opener bids 2♠, you advance to 3♠. If he raises hearts, you bid game.

(6) 4♡. With your shape, this is strong enough for game. The jump to game in a new suit promises a five-card suit and asks opener to choose between 4♡ and 4♠. Opener should be able to support at least one major.

Your partner opens and the bidding begins: 1♣–1♡–1♠.

(7)	♠ K 8 2	♡ K J 9 6	♢ J 4 3	♣ Q 4 3
(8)	♠ A 3	♡ A Q 8 5 4	♢ 10 5 4	♣ K 9 2
(9)	♠ 6 4 3	♡ A Q 7 5 2	♢ 8 3	♣ Q 10 4
(10)	♠ 10 7 4	♡ K Q 8 5 3	♢ 8 6 5	♣ 9 6

(7) 1NT. An effort is warranted as opener could have as many as 18 points. 1NT in this sequence suggests a balanced 7–10. The lack of a full guard in the unbid suit is not a

deterrent as any hand on which your partner raises notrumps is likely to include a diamond honour.

(8) 2◇. You have game-going values but are completely stuck for a bid; you can neither support partner strongly enough, rebid your own suit strongly enough, nor bid notrumps. Rather than break up the game you should bid the fourth suit. This does not promise strength in diamonds but ensures that the bidding will continue.

(9) 2♣. A tolerable fit is known to exist in this suit. A rebid of 2♡ would be unspeakable: your partner may hold no support at all.

(10) Pass. You have a bare minimum, you prefer spades to clubs, and opener's simple change of suit is not forcing. To bid 2♡ you would need either a longer or a stronger heart suit.

Your partner opens and the bidding begins: 1♠–2◇–2♡.

(11) ♠ J 8	♡ K 2	◇ A J 7 6 4	♣ J 8 4 2
(12) ♠ K	♡ 10 8 3	◇ K J 8 3 2	♣ A 10 9 6
(13) ♠ Q 4	♡ J 5 3	◇ A Q 8 5 2	♣ A 6 3

(11) 2♠. You showed 10 points by responding at the two level, so simple preference is sufficient. If opener passes you will be in the right spot.

(12) 2NT. Now that opener has bid spades, the ♠K is awarded almost its full value. 2NT defines your strength more accurately than 3♣, which would be unlimited.

(13) 3♣. Before the fourth-suit style came in, this was the kind of sequence that used to age players prematurely. You need to know more about opener's hand: can he rebid one of his suits or show an independent guard in clubs?

Your partner opens and the bidding begins: 1♠–2♡–3◇.

(14) ♠ Q 9 8	♡ K Q 8 7 4	◇ K 4	♣ 8 3 2
(15) ♠ K 10 2	♡ A K 7 5 4	◇ Q J 9	♣ 4 3
(16) ♠ 10	♡ K Q J 5 4	◇ 10 8 5	♣ K Q J 9

(14) 4♠. Opener's high reverse shows 16+ and at least five cards in his first suit. 3♠ from you would be forcing, but the jump to 4♠ is expressive, suggesting genuine support, no more than these values, satisfaction with partner's second suit and a probable absence of controls.

(15) 3♠. A slam is probable, so you must avoid a bid of game. 3♠ allows opener to cue-bid clubs or diamonds, but your hand is so strong and so suitable that even if he signs off in 4♠ you should make a further effort by bidding 5♡.

(16) 3NT. With plenty of points but no vestige of a fit, this is likely to be the best contract.

Your partner opens and the bidding begins: 1♠–2♠–2NT.

(17)	♠ 10 9 3 2	♡ J 9 7	◇ K J 10	♣ J 8 4
(18)	♠ K J 6 4	♡ 5 2	◇ 9 7 4	♣ A 10 8 4

(17) Pass. Opener is expected to have a balanced 17–18. You have no ruffing values, so eight tricks in notrumps may be easier than nine in spades.

(18) 4♠. This hand is close to maximum for a single raise and has good features. In accepting the game invitation you should pick the trump contract as you have a ruffing value and four trumps.

Chapter 5

NOTRUMP SEQUENCES

The standard responses to the 12–14 1NT – Rebids by the 1NT opener – The Stayman convention – Transfers – When 1NT is doubled – The 2NT opening — The 3NT opening

The presence of 25 points in the partnership hands does not endow the success of a 3NT contract with any degree of inevitability, but it is a good start. Almost all notrump sequences take this figure as a datum. However, if you are of a cautious disposition and prefer to make it 26, I will not try to talk you out of it.

The only hands where you might deliberately stop short of 3NT with 25 points are those where you suspect duplicated values, such as K–Q bare opposite A–x, or where an unfavourable lead seems certain. Against that, when you have a 5-card or 6-card minor suit and expect to run it, you should be willing to bid 3NT with 23 or 24 points.

Whatever the range of the 1NT opening, the questions are the same. Can you count on 25 points? If so, be sure to reach game, either in notrumps or in a known major-suit fit. Can you compute that 25 points are not present? Then drop the bidding at the lowest possible level. Might there be 33 points or more? In that case a slam should be favourably considered, so now you should launch an exploratory sequence.

There is one convention without which life as we know it would be impossible. The Stayman 2♣ is central to the scheme of responses now discussed.

THE STANDARD RESPONSES TO THE 12–14 1NT
(Transfers not in use)

Response	Meaning
2♣	Responder has at least one 4-card major and usually 11+ HCP, with no upper limit. *Exception:* With both majors, 5–4 or longer, there is no point-count requirement.
2◇,2♡,2♠	A sign-off that must be respected, based on at least a 5-card suit and a maximum of 10 HCP.
2NT	Invitational to 3NT. 11–12 HCP, no 4-card or longer major.
3♣,3◇	Game force, invitational to slam. 18+ HCP with no upper limit. At least a 5-card suit.
3♡,3♠	Forcing to 3NT or game in the suit named. 13+ HCP with no upper limit. At least a 5-card suit.
3NT	Natural.
4♣	Gerber convention asking for aces.
4◇	A rare pre-emptive response.
4♡,4♠	Sign-off, at least a 6-card suit.
4NT	Natural, no 4-card major unless the hand is flat, 19–20 HCP.
6NT	21–24 HCP.
7NT	25+ HCP.

For a notrump opening other than 12–14 the same meanings apply, with suitable adjustments.

Whether to take out into 2♡ or 2♠ with a weak hand and a 5-card suit is a recurring question. It is usually right to do so on a 5–4–3–1 pattern and often on 5–4–2–2. On 5–3–3–2, it is common to take out with a spade suit, rare with diamonds, and borderline with hearts.

It is worth remembering that if you pass 1NT, only one opponent has a chance to contest, whereas if you make a weak takeout, both opponents have the opportunity.

(1)	♠ 7 4	♡ A J 10 5 3	◇ 7 4 2	♣ Q J 2
(2)	♠ Q J 9 8 7	♡ 7 2	◇ Q J 9	♣ 8 4 3
(3)	♠ 10 4	♡ J 6	◇ K Q 8 4 3	♣ Q 7 6 4

With (1), pass 1NT, expecting opener to be able to bring in the 5-card suit. When opponents have a spade fit they may find it more difficult to commandeer the auction if you pass than if you bid 2♡.

With (2) bid 2♠: this suit may be hard to establish at 1NT, as there is no sure entry. Moreover, 2♠ shuts out opponents.

With (3) pass 1NT. Opponents are likely to have a spade or heart fit and if you were to bid 2◇ you would be laying out the 'Welcome' mat.

A response of 3♡ and 3♠ is an almost automatic move when a 5-card suit and game values are held. Opener normally accepts the suit with 3-card support and always accepts when he has a ruffing value. With a maximum, and suitable, hand he may cue-bid an ace.

Responses of 3♣ and 3◇ are seldom made unless slam is at least a possibility. When opener's hand is unsuitable for slam he rebids 3NT.

REBIDS BY THE 1NT OPENER

Opener should pass a response of four of a major and two of any suit but clubs. Over three of a major he chooses between 3NT and game in the suit. He prefers the suit always with four trumps, and always with three trumps and a ruffing value. With three trumps in a flat hand a raise is usual but not obligatory.

	Opener	Responder
	1NT	3♠
	?	

(1)	♠ 10 9 2	♡ A K 4	◇ Q J 8 7 3	♣ K 2
(2)	♠ K Q 2	♡ Q 10 8 5	◇ Q J 3	♣ Q J 4
(3)	♠ K 10 4 2	♡ A 7	◇ J 10 9 3	♣ A J 10

Hand (1), with 3-card support and a ruffing value, is a type where the raise of partner's major is virtually automatic.

Hand (2) is a comparatively rare case where opener might rebid 3NT with good 3-card support: his spade honours will allow the suit to be run quickly and he has guards in the other suits. If responder is 5–3–3–2, 3NT is likely to be safer than 4♠.

Hand (3) invokes a principle of wide application. Opener's hand is so suitable in every way that he should bid not 4♠ but 4♣, a cue bid agreeing spades. If responder is borderline for slam, this will give him the assurance he needs to proceed further.

THE STAYMAN CONVENTION

All bidding systems lay emphasis on the search for a 4–4 or better major-suit fit – and with good reason. At notrumps a 4–4 holding can take no more than four tricks, but at a trump contract it may win the same four tricks in one hand and one or more ruffs in the other. When game in either strain is likely, you will often be better off in the suit contract, especially at duplicate.

The classic type for the use of Stayman is one that is playable in notrumps if the 2♣ inquiry fails:

♠ Q 10 9 3   ♡ A K 8 2   ◇ A 8 4   ♣ 4 2

Responder has the values for a raise to 3NT, but first he bids 2♣, which is artificial and says nothing about clubs. Opener bids his lower 4-card major, or 2◇ if he has neither: he may make no other call. With the hand above, the responder raises a major suit to game and bids 3NT over 2◇.

The 2♣ bidder always has at least one major suit and opener may rely on it in this sequence:

Opener	Responder
1NT	2♣
2♡	3NT
?	

♠ 10 8 5 3   ♡ K J 7 5   ◇ A 6   ♣ K Q 7

Opener's spade holding is very weak but he must still bid 4♠. A fit is guaranteed, and responder is not inviting him to exercise discretion.

The normal minimum for a Stayman 2♣ is 11 points. The Staymanite is then able to continue with a normal invitational 2NT if no fit is found:

Opener	Responder
1NT	2♣
2♠	2NT

Responder holds:

♠ 6 4   ♡ Q 10 6 3   ◇ A Q J 2   ♣ Q 8 2

Had opener bid 2♡, responder would have raised to 3♡. He would have passed 1NT with any lesser hand as he could not have coped with an unfavourable response to 2♣.

With a 5-card major, responder does not normally use Stayman: he bids three of the suit. The only exception is this:

♠ Q 9 7 3 2   ♡ 8 3   ◇ A K 2   ♣ Q 7 3

This hand is not quite strong enough for a game-forcing 3♠ so responder (unless playing transfers) cannot find out whether opener has 3-card support. However, game may still be there in spades if opener has four spades, or in 3NT if he is maximum. So responder bids 2♣, raising a 2♠ response to game, as his hand is improved by the 9-card fit. If the response is 2◇ or 2♡ he bids 2NT.

Stayman with a weak hand

When responder is 5–4 or longer in the majors he may bid 2♣ with a weak hand as now he can play in the longer suit in the event of a 2◇ response:

♠ K 10 9 7 3   ♡ J 10 7 2   ◇ 4   ♣ J 9 4

Two of a suit by the Staymanite is always a sign-off, so if opener rebids at 2◇, responder will bid 2♠.

Concerning the next sequence there are two schools of thought:

Opener	Responder
1NT	2♣
2◇, 2♡ or 2♠	3♣

Traditionally 3♣ is a sign-off with a 6-card suit. However, the need for the sequence does not often arise, and when it does, the opposition will often be active, allowing you to compete if you wish.

Many players, therefore, prefer to treat 3♣ by the Staymanite – and 3◇ also – as natural and game-forcing. A strong 5–4 pattern, if it includes a major, can then be introduced with 2♣ followed by a forcing bid at the three level if no immediate fit is found. Over 1NT you would bid 2♣ with each of these:

(1)   ♠ 8   ♡ K Q 3 2   ◇ A Q J 9 7   ♣ A J 2
(2)   ♠ A Q 6 3 2   ♡ K 10 9 7   ◇ A 8 2   ♣ 7

On (1) you hope to reach slam if partner has an ace and either a heart suit or a diamond fit. Over a response of 2♠ or 2◇ you would continue with 3◇, forcing. This time you do not intend to go beyond 3NT unless opener shows interest in a diamond slam. You would follow a parallel sequence if the 5-card suit were clubs.

On (2) you intend to bid 3♠ over a response of 2◇. Here you are interested only in game but you would launch the same sequence if you held slam-going values.

With a non-solid 5-card major, game values and a 5–3–3–2 pattern it is normal to avoid Stayman and bid three of the suit direct:

♠ K 10 8 7 3   ♡ K 10 7   ◇ 3 2   ♣ A Q 9

Over 1NT, bid 3♠, asking partner to choose the contract.

This jump bid may even be made with a lesser suit. When game is borderline and the 1NT bidder has a ruffing value, a 5–3 fit in a weak major suit is often best.

When responder's suit is likely to produce five fast tricks, a raise in notrumps comes more prominently into the reckoning:

♠ K Q   ♡ A K Q 8 3   ◇ 6 5 2   ♣ 8 7 2

Bid 2♣, and if opener does not show hearts continue with 3NT. The suit will probably run and you have no great wish to play the contract from your side, as the opening lead will come through your partner's minor-suit holdings.

After 2♣, 4NT by the Staymanite on the next round is not Blackwood:

Opener	Responder
1NT	2♣
2◇, 2♡ or 2♠	4NT

4NT is natural, showing the values of a direct raise to 4NT. If the responder wishes to inquire for aces he must first bid a new suit at the three level. Then 4NT will be Blackwood. When responder wishes only to know how many aces are held he uses the Gerber convention.

TRANSFERS

The reader who has yet to come to grips with transfer bids is recommended to do so without delay; not just because they bring great accuracy to the sequences that follow an opening bid in notrumps but because they are a joy to use. Over a 1NT opening:

2◇ by responder shows at least five hearts and requires opener to bid 2♡;
2♡ by responder shows at least five spades and requires opener to bid 2♠.

The bidding continues on natural lines. When responder wishes to play in two of the major he passes the forced bid:

♠ 10 8 7 6 4 3   ♡ 6   ◇ A Q 2   ♣ 9 7 3

If transfers were not in use, responder would simply bid 2♠ over 1NT with this hand. Playing transfers, he bids 2♡ and passes opener's 2♠. In that case the only advantage conferred by the transfer is that the contract is played with opener's hand concealed.

It is on hands that merit a constructive sequence that transfers have their finest hour, as suit patterns and shades of strength can be expressed with great precision. Your partner opens 1NT, you respond 2♡, and he transfers to 2♠:

(1) ♠ K Q 10 3 2   ♡ 7 2   ◇ 10 9 4   ♣ A Q 6
(2) ♠ A Q 10 3 2   ♡ A 2   ◇ 10 9 4   ♣ A 9 6
(3) ♠ K 10 9 7 4   ♡ A J 3   ◇ 5   ♣ A K 7 4

With (1), where you have a typical invitational hand, you continue with 2NT, indicating the values for a direct raise to 2NT but with the advantage of having shown a 5-card spade suit and a likely 5–3–3–2 pattern. Opener may pass, raise to 3NT, or bid 3♠ or 4♠. Clearly this is super-efficient.

With (2), where you have game values, you bid 3NT over 2♠, showing this precise type and leaving opener to pass or bid 4♠.

With (3), over opener's forced 2♠ you continue with 3♣, natural and game-forcing. The sequence not only allows opener to redefine his hand without going beyond 3NT but also may establish whether a slam in spades or clubs is a possibility. Thus, when opener bids 3NT you stop there: opener has no fit and may be minimum. When he jumps to 4♠, again you pass, as that is where he wants to play.

When, however, he bids 3♠ he is confirming the suit and showing a very suitable hand. If you are interested in slam you have space for cue-bidding.

Finally, when, over 3♣, opener has good support for the

minor suit, he can signify this below the level of 3NT by bidding a new suit.

An alternative practice is to treat responder's new suit at the three level as two-way: it may be game-going or merely game-invitational. It is a playable method but the treatment described is more popular.

Next, suppose that the question is whether to make a weak takeout or to leave opener in 1NT. When playing transfers you follow the same practice as when transfers are not in use: take out always with 5–4–3–1 and often with 5–4–2–2. With 5–3–3–2, think it over.

Transfers also gain heavily when responder has a long major where the hand belongs indubitably in the suit but game may be borderline. Responder now follows this sequence, which always shows a 6-card or longer suit:

Opener	Responder
1NT	2◇ (transfer)
2♡	3♡ (natural)

This hand would be typical:

♠ 6   ♡ Q J 9 7 4 3   ◇ A Q J   ♣ 7 3 2

Next, a direct response of three in any suit, avoiding transfers, shows a one-suited hand with slam interest:

♠ A Q 10 7 3 2   ♡ K 4   ◇ Q 6   ♣ A Q 5

After 1NT–3♠, opener may cue-bid freely with a suitable hand.

Opener breaks the transfer

Opener will sometimes have such a good fit with the responder's suit that he may envisage a game even when responder has in mind only a part-score:

Opener	Responder
1NT	2◇ (transfer)
?	

♠ 8 3   ♡ K Q J 8   ◇ A J 7 3   ♣ K 7 6

There could well be a magic fit and a low point-count game, so opener bids not 2♡ but 3♡, breaking the transfer. If responder is weak and 3♡ fails, an opposing part-score will surely have been saved, as opener has so much of his strength in his partner's suit.

Other transfer sequences

The methods described are called simple transfers and they may be enough for many partnerships. (More than enough, some diehards may think!) However, theorists abhor a vacuum and have found a new use for virtually all the calls made redundant by the use of transfers. To avoid cerebral overload I put forward only one, which is both popular and efficient.

When simple transfers are in use, a response of 2♠ to 1NT is no longer needed in a natural sense:

Opener	Responder
1NT	2♠

This response is therefore used to ask opener to bid 2NT with minimum points and to show a maximum by bidding his lowest-ranking 4-card or longer suit.

Responder may now express two different types. The hand he is most likely to have is a balanced 11–12 with which he would normally have raised 1NT to 2NT. With this type, if opener bids 2NT over 2♠, responder passes. If instead opener shows a maximum by bidding a suit, responder goes to 3NT.

In each case the same contract is reached as if transfers had not been in use, but 2♠ may be used for a second type also, and moreover, the natural response of 2NT over 1NT is released for a valuable purpose.

The second type with which the responder may bid 2♠ over 1NT is one that is borderline for slam but has no long suit. Now the twelfth trick may depend on whether opener is maximum and whether there is a fit. By bidding suits in ascending order the partnership can establish, below the level of 3NT, whether there is a 4–4 fit in any suit:

Opener	Responder
1NT	2♠
3♣	3♢
3NT	

3♣ is natural, showing clubs and a maximum. 3♢ is natural and forcing. 3NT shows that opener has no suit other than clubs.

With this scheme the natural response of 2NT over 1NT is no longer needed, so is used to initiate a minor-suit sign-off:

Opener	Responder
1NT	2NT (transfer)
?	

Opener must bid 3♣. Responder may pass or bid 3♢ to play.

Transfers may also be used when the 1NT call is not an opening but an overcall. Transfers, and Stayman too, are abandoned if 1NT is doubled: responder is free to retreat to any suit.

WHEN 1NT IS DOUBLED

Suppose that your partner opens 1NT and next hand, pawing the ground, doubles for penalties. With a weak hand and a 5-card or longer suit you should remove, partly because the takeout may not be doubled.

With no 5-card suit it is sometimes possible to issue an SOS redouble:

West	*North*	*East*	*South*
	1NT	Dble	?

♠ 9 7 5 3   ♡ J 8 6 5   ◇ Q 7 6 4   ♣ 10

With this hand South bids 2♣ and when doubled, he redoubles, SOS. On a bad day opener's only suit will be clubs and he will have to bid a 3-card suit.

Duplicate players have developed some ingenious mechanisms that improve on this tactic. In one of the less Byzantine, over a double of 1NT:

2♡ and 2♠ are natural and weak with a 5-card suit;

2♣ initially shows clubs and the 1NT bidder passes. If 2♣ is doubled, a redouble shows diamonds and hearts, while a bid of 2◇ shows diamonds and spades;

2◇ initially shows diamonds. If doubled, a redouble shows spades and hearts while 2♡ shows hearts and spades.

When the doubler has chosen the wrong moment and you have 10 points or more it is standard to redouble unless you think you might get a better score in 1NT doubled than from doubling opponents when they run from the redouble.

THE 2NT OPENING

All fairly balanced hands from a good 20 to 22 are opened with this call, which therefore has to be used flexibly. An unguarded suit, a 5-card major, or both may be present:

♠ A Q 10 8 3   ♡ 9 2   ◇ A Q 10   ♣ A K J

There is no better call than 2NT. If you were to make a practice of opening one of a suit with such strong hands, responder would have to keep the bidding open on the smell of an oil rag, which is not desirable. Moreover, after 1♠–1NT–3NT, game will be played from the wrong side, which may be disastrous.

Responding to 2NT

3◇ and 3♡ are transfers and are especially effective when they lead to game in responder's weak 5-card major suit. The powerful hand is concealed and the trump suit provides entries to the weak hand. Responder therefore should not fail to bid 3◇ over 2NT with this type:

♠ 4   ♡ 9 7 6 4 3   ◇ K 8 7   ♣ J 10 6 3

A 3♠ response to 2NT shows interest in the minor suits, at least 5–4, and is a slam try. Opener may sign off in 3NT.

Stayman over 2NT

3♣ over 2NT is simple Stayman. There is also an improved version, called 5-card major Stayman, with these responses:

3♡ or 3♠ = 5-card suit;
3◇   = no 5-card major, at least one 4-card major;
3NT   = no 5-card or 4-card major.

The Baron 3♣ was once a popular alternative to Stayman, initiating a sequence in which partners bid their lowest suits until a fit is found or 3NT is reached. A 4–4 fit in any suit, including a minor, can be located, but the convention has slipped out of favour as it too often leads to the strong hand becoming the dummy in a major-suit game.

THE 3NT OPENING

This is conventional, showing a solid minor suit and no outside ace or king:

(1) ♠ 6 2   ♡ 10   ◇ A K Q J 9 3 2   ♣ 8 7 4
(2) ♠ J 5   ♡ 8   ◇ Q 9 3   ♣ A K Q 10 7 5 4

Hand (1) is a non-vulnerable 3NT opening, hand (2) a vulnerable opening.

The responder is always in charge: if the contract is doubled, he decides whether to run, usually by bidding 4♣ which allows opener to pass or bid 4◇. With a slam-going hand, responder may bid a conventional 4◇ over 3NT, asking opener to name any singleton.

Notrump bidding quiz

Your partner opens a 12–14 1NT. You are playing Stayman and transfers.

(1)	♠ 10 9 3	♡ 10 7	◇ A 3	♣ A K 10 8 3 2
(2)	♠ J 4	♡ Q J 9 8 2	◇ A Q 3	♣ Q J 4
(3)	♠ Q 9 8 4	♡ K 10 7 3	◇ A J 10 2	♣ J
(4)	♠ A 10 9 4 3	♡ K Q 7 2	◇ A 8 7	♣ 2
(5)	♠ J 9 8 6 4 2	♡ 10 7 2	◇ 6	♣ 8 5 4
(6)	♠ K Q 10 2	♡ A J 3	◇ 6	♣ A K J 8 4

(1) 3NT. With such a fine club suit and good intermediate cards this hand will probably play as well as a normal 13 points.

(2) 2◇. Over partner's obligatory 2♡ you intend to bid 3NT, leaving him to pass or bid 4♡.

(3) 2♣. If opener bids 2♡ or 2♠ you are worth a raise to game with this 7-loser hand. If he bids 2◇ you are worth no more than 2NT.

(4) 2♡. Transfers are seen at their most efficient with 5–4 patterns. Over opener's 2♠ you intend to continue with 3♡, natural and forcing.

(5) 2♡. Here the transfer initiates a normal sign-off as you propose to pass partner's 2♠.

(6) 2♣. If opener rebids 2♠ you will want to be in 6♠ if he has an ace. You would therefore continue with 3♣, forcing: then 4NT on the next round will be Blackwood. If opener does not bid 2♠, you still bid 3♣, but this time you are willing to settle for 3NT unless there is a dynamic reaction.

In the remaining problems you are the opener.

Opener	Responder
1NT	2♢
2♡	2NT
?	

(7) ♠ Q 7 3   ♡ K Q J 3   ♢ J 6 2   ♣ K 8 4
(8) ♠ K Q 7 5   ♡ J 5   ♢ K J 8 2   ♣ K 4 2
(9) ♠ A 7 6 4   ♡ K 10 2   ♢ A 4   ♣ K 10 8 2
(10) ♠ Q J 2   ♡ K Q 4   ♢ K 9 8 3   ♣ Q J 7

(7) 3♡. This is a sign-off. The trump holding looks impressive but this is a rather poor hand: minimum values and no aces. However, 3♡ in the 9-card fit is likely to be a safer contract than 2NT.

(8) Pass. With only median values and an uninspiring holding in responder's 5-card suit, this hand does not warrant a raise to 3NT.

(9) 4♡. You have a sprightly maximum, highly suitable for a heart contract.

(10) 3NT. Again a maximum, but this time with no ruffing value. Your fitting cards in hearts suggest a likely five quick tricks in the suit.

(11)	Opener	Responder
	1NT	2♢
	2♡	3♡
	?	

♠ A Q 5   ♡ 7 4 3   ♢ K J 7 5 4   ♣ K 2

(11) 4♡. Responder is showing a 6-card suit. With three trumps and a ruffing value you support almost automatically. The fact that your hearts are small is no reason to prefer notrumps; quite the opposite.

(12)   *Opener*   *Responder*
        1NT   2♠
        ?

♠ A J 10 7   ♡ Q 4   ◇ Q J 10 8   ♣ K 10 9

(12) 3◇. Responder's 2♠ is artificial, and you should respond on the basis that he has the values for an invitational raise to 2NT. (If he has a different type, this will show up.) 2NT from you would be sign-off. Here, however, you gladly accept the game invitation because your strong intermediates bring the hand almost into the 14-point category. You signify this by bidding your lowest-ranking suit.

Chapter 6

POWERHOUSE HANDS

*The Losing Trick Count (LTC) – Splinters –
Overall scheme for strong supporting hands – Cue
bids and other slam tries – 2♣ opening and Acol
twos – Benjamin 2♣ and 2♢ openings –
Multicoloured 2♢ – Blackwood and other slam
conventions*

To be a winner you must score big on your big hands. Players
settling for game when a slam was there have been heard to
remark that it is never wrong to take a sure profit, but there is
a certain lack of logic to this. If you don't bid your cold slams
and opponents do bid their cold slams, where is the sure
profit?

There are two steps in slam bidding. First, to be sure you
have twelve winners, then to be sure you have not two quick
losers.

In the case of low point-count slams that depend not on
overwhelming high cards but on a trump fit, the first step is the
more difficult. But it is a whole lot easier when the Losing
Trick Count is in use.

THE LOSING TRICK COUNT (LTC)

Just occasionally, your partner may let up on his habit of
bidding only the suits you are short of and may name one that
you can support strongly. Once in a while he may even admit
to holding powerful support for your own suit. When that
happens you must be capable of judging precisely how high to
bid with this suit as trumps. Your partner opens 1♠ and you
hold:

♠ K Q 9 4   ♡ 10 9 3   ◇ A Q 10 7 2   ♣ A

Clearly you expect to make a lot of tricks, but the question is, how many?

In each suit, including the trump suit, you should count one loser for each missing high honour (A, K or Q). Count no more than three losers in a suit. And count no more losers than you have cards in the suit.

This hand has five losers: one in spades, three in hearts, one in diamonds, none in clubs. Next, add your total of losers to opener's expected total.

A sound minimum opening normally has seven losers and this is what you place your partner with. Now comes the gizmo. Deduct the total, twelve, from 24 (a constant) and the answer, twelve, is the number of tricks you may expect to make. 24 = the total losers, 12 each, in the partnership.

Now you develop the bidding according to your lights. What the LTC has told you is that opposite a sound minimum you have the material for twelve tricks.

The LTC may be used by either partner at any stage of the auction when a 4–4, 5–3 or better trump fit is known to be present. As may be seen from the many allusions to it in this book, it is helpful in other ways also.

Refinements to the LTC

For the avoidance of doubt: a small doubleton is two losers; A–x is one loser; Q–x is two and the singleton king one.

The extra trump in a 5–4 fit is an asset. When there is a 10-card fit and other features are good a whole loser may be deducted for 'super fit'. A 5–3 suit should be viewed with some caution: if other features are poor, you might count an additional loser.

A–x–x in any suit is obviously a better holding than Q–x–x, although each has two losers. When both combinations are present they cancel out but when you have Q–x–x and no ace you should take a conservative view. With two such holdings and no aces, add a loser. With two aces not balanced by queens, deduct a loser if the rest of the hand is up to snuff.

The queen is not devalued when supported by the jack: Q–J–x counts as two losers. Nor is the 10 to be entirely ignored in the combination Q–10–x. The holding A–J–10 is usually worth at least as much as A–Q–x and is counted as one loser.

Use of the LTC by responder

Many players use the LTC as their primary method of valuation. Those who do not may still use it to resolve a close decision. Partner opens 1♡:

(1)   ♠ A 10 2   ♡ Q 9 8 3   ◇ K 10 9 6   ♣ 7 4
(2)   ♠ 3   ♡ Q 10 9 8 6   ◇ K Q 6 3   ♣ 10 4 2

By ordinary standards, hand (1) is strong for 2♡, weakish for 3♡. Which call is better? The LTC says you have eight losers so you should raise to 3♡.

On (2) the choice is between 3♡ with sub-minimum honour strength and a pre-emptive 4♡. You have seven losers and the 9-card fit is a plus factor, so you should certainly raise to game.

Responder may also use the LTC when his own suit is raised:

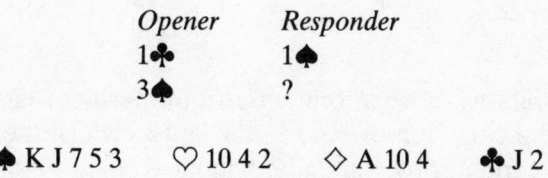

Opener	Responder
1♣	1♠
3♣	?

♠ K J 7 5 3   ♡ 10 4 2   ◇ A 10 4   ♣ J 2

Responder has an extra trump and an outside ace with no queen to balance against it. He therefore deducts a loser, leaving eight. Opener has shown six losers: with an average opening containing seven losers, he would have raised to 2♠. Responder subtracts 14 from 18 and bids 4♠.

Other uses of the LTC

Even before a trump fit is identified, the LTC may be used to see whether a hand is good enough for certain bids.

A reverse by opener is normally based on no more than five losers, or six with a high point count. A jump rebid by opener in his suit, as in the sequence 1♡–1♠–3♡, shows six losers.

A 12–14 notrump normally has seven or eight losers. If seven, you should be strongly inclined to accept any invitational bid your partner may make in a Stayman or transfer sequence. If eight, you should resolve any close decision in favour of caution.

When raising an overcall, assume that at the one level the overcall shows eight losers or fewer; at the two level, seven or fewer.

The LTC is in no way dependent on partnership understanding: it can be used in a cut-in game with a partner who has never heard of it.

SPLINTERS

A splinter is a double jump in a new suit – one more than is needed for a force:

(1)	*Opener*	*Responder*	(2)	*Opener*	*Responder*
	1♠	4♣		1♣	1♡
				4♢	

The splinter shows strong support for partner's last-named suit and a singleton or void in the suit in which the jump is made. A splinter by responder will have no more than seven losers, and very likely six.

A splinter allows the player opposite to value his hand with exceptional accuracy. Suppose that in sequence (1) opener has this hand:

♠ A K J 4 3   ♡ K Q J 9   ♢ 7   ♣ 10 8 3

With at least a 5–4 fit and the assurance of no more than one loser in clubs, opener counts his hand as five losers. He is therefore already willing to bid 6♠ if responder has two aces: ideal conditions for the use of Blackwood.

Obviously, x–x–x or similar is an ideal holding in the suit of partner's splinter. So is A–x–x. But don't throw your hat in the air when you have K–Q–x; the high cards may be of little account.

When a simple change of suit would be forcing, a single jump can be treated as a splinter.

Opener	Responder
1♠	2♡
4♦	

3♦ by opener would be forcing, so 4♦ is a splinter with strong heart support.

The same applies on the responder's side of the table:

Opener	Responder
1♠	2♦
2♡	4♣

Responder holds:

♠ 8 3   ♡ K Q 7 2   ♦ A J 9 4 3 2   ♣ 6

Here the splinter is ideal on a hand that would otherwise be difficult to express.

After a 2♣ or other artificial strong opening and a negative response, splinters may be used by the responder on the second round when opener has shown his suit.

Splinters allow not only low point-count slams that are otherwise unattainable but also the avoidance of poor slams when wasted values are present.

OVERALL SCHEME FOR STRONG SUPPORTING HANDS

When partner opens 1♡ or 1♠ and you hold strong trump support with game-going values, this scheme will cater for most types:

A *direct raise to game* shows very strong trump support – usually 5+ – but less than opening strength.

A *simple response in a new suit followed by a jump to game in opener's suit* is a delayed game raise: opening values, 4+ trumps, and a side suit that is strong but not necessarily long. (When you have this type, but with 3-card support facing a known 5-card suit, there are two styles: either give a DGR straightaway, or first make a temporising bid and support opener's suit on the next round.)

A *jump shift* followed by support for opener's suit on the next round is a stronger version of the DGR.

Many partnerships supplement this scheme with 'Jacoby' or 'Swiss'.

The forcing 2NT raise ('Jacoby 2NT')

This has won popularity with players willing to forgo the traditional use of the 2NT response as a natural limit bid. 2NT over 1♡ or 1♠ is a forcing raise: 13+ points, too balanced for a splinter, unsuitable for a DGR or jump shift.

Opener now clarifies his hand. The scheme proposed by Oswald Jacoby is this:

three of a new suit = a singleton or void in that suit;
three of opener's major = 16+;
3NT = 14–15;
four of opener's major = a minimum opening;
four of a new suit = five cards in that suit, including two of the top three honours.

When the use of the Jacoby 2NT is extended to hands suitable for a DGR, an important advantage is gained: the traditional DGR sequence now shows specifically three trumps.

The Swiss convention

This has fallen in public esteem as splinters and the Jacoby convention have risen:

4♣ over 1♡ or 1♠ shows at least opening values, strong trumps and either two aces and a singleton or three aces.

4♢ over 1♡ or 1♠ shows similar values but fewer controls.

(1)	♠ A J 8 3	♡ 6	◇ A 10 8 4	♣ K J 7 3
(2)	♠ K Q J 4	♡ A J 3	◇ Q J 4 2	♣ 10 5

After a 1♠ opening, hand (1) qualifies for 4♣; (2) for 4◇.

Playing Swiss, you cannot use 4♣ and 4◇ as splinters in direct response to an opening but other splinters remain in force.

CUE BIDS AND OTHER SLAM TRIES

When a trump suit has been agreed and the partnership is committed to game, a bid in a new suit by either partner is a cue bid, saying: 'I have first-round control of this suit, the ace or void, and am at least mildly interested in slam. Can you co-operate?'

Opener	Responder
1♣	2♠
3♠	4◇

4◇ is a cue bid. The partner may respond by making a cue bid of his own, by bidding 4NT, or by bidding slam direct. The weakest move by either player is to return to the agreed trump suit at the lowest level.

In the next example 3◇ is not a cue bid as the sequence is not game-forcing:

Opener	Responder
1♡	2♡
3◇	

3◇ is a normal trial bid, asking for help in diamonds. Game in hearts is the objective but the sequence may still end in 3♡.

A cue bid is not made just because the cue-bidder has extra values but only when in his estimation a slam is at least possible:

Opener	Responder
1◇	1♠
3♣	?

♠ K Q 10 9   ♡ 10 3   ◇ 8 7 4   ♣ A Q 6 3

Responder has more than enough for game but it does not follow that he should cue-bid the ♣A. Opener has indicated six losers and responder, with seven, has no reason to think that more than eleven tricks can be made; so he simply bids 4♠.

A player may make a cue bid, receive an encouraging response, and then sign off! This is not illogical: he is saying that he has nothing to add and that his partner will have to make the running if slam is to be reached.

It is normal to cue-bid first the cheapest control, but this is not written in stone:

Opener	Responder
1♣	1♡
3♡	3♠
?	

♠ 9 2   ♡ K J 6 3   ◇ A 4   ♣ A K 9 8 3

Responder's 3♠ is a cue bid and opener has a fine 6-loser hand. Which ace should he show?

4◇ is likely to be more helpful, since opener has bid clubs and responder may be ready to assume that there are not two quick losers in the suit.

After a cue bid either player may bid 4NT:

Opener	Responder
1♠	2♣
4♣	4◇
4♡	4NT

♠ K Q 10 5 3   ♡ A 6   ◇ J 4   ♣ A Q 9 4

4◇ and 4♡ are cue bids with clubs as trumps, and 4NT is

Blackwood. Aces already shown are still counted, so opener bids 5♡.

Second-round controls

A second-round control, the king or singleton, may be shown without ambiguity when first-round control has already been disclosed by either partner:

(1)	Opener	Responder	(2)	Opener	Responder
	1♢	2♡		2♣	2♠
	3♡	3♠		3♠	4♢
	4♣	4♠			

In (1), 4♠ shows second-round control and implies that the responder has no feature in diamonds that could have been shown instead. He obviously has a very sound force, as he has gone beyond game in hearts.

In (2), 4♢ purports to show the ace or void, but responder could have this hand instead:

♠ A J 9 5 2   ♡ Q J 7   ♢ 7   ♣ Q 10 9 2

Over 3♠ responder is worth an effort and 4♢ is the most suitable move. A player with a rock-crusher should allow his partner leeway for helpful efforts of this sort.

The advance cue bid

When there is no room to agree trumps below the level of game and still make a cue bid, the cue bid may be made in advance:

Opener	Responder
2NT	3♡ (transfer)
4♣	

Opener would never bid clubs here in a natural sense, so 4♣ means: 'I like spades and have the ♣A.'

'The perfect minimum'

A slam try that takes the bidding beyond game is not to be lightly made: it puts a lot of points on the line. A test proposed by Ely Culbertson never caught on but is of more than historic interest:

Invite a slam when a perfect minimum from partner will make it a laydown.

Partner's hand will seldom if ever be perfect but, equally, slams are not required to be laydown. So there is a trade-off, and it is probably a fair one:

Opener	Responder
1♠	2♡
3♡	?

♠ Q 4   ♡ A Q 10 8 6 3   ◇ 6   ♣ A 9 7 4

From responder's angle a perfect minimum for opener to hold could be something like this:

♠ A–K–J–x–x   ♡ K–x–x–x   ◇ x–x   ♣ x–x

6♡ will be icy, so the rule of the perfect minimum says that responder is worth a slam try.

The minor-suit takeout of 3NT

An accepted way to make a slam try is to remove 3NT to 4♣ or 4◇ in a sequence where this can make no sense unless you have hopes of slam:

Opener	Responder
1♣	1♡
1♠	3NT
?	

♠ A K 4 2   ♡ 8   ◇ A 4   ♣ A Q 10 7 3 2

If responder has one or two key cards a slam may be laydown, so opener bids 4♣. Here and in similar sequences the sign-off for partner is 4NT.

2♣ OPENING AND ACOL TWOS

2♣ is the Acol system's mega-bid; artificial, and game-forcing except in this one sequence:

Opener	Responder
2♣	2◇
2NT	

Opener has a balanced 23–24 and responder may pass with a bust. All other rebids by opener insist that the bidding be kept open until game is reached.

Requirements for 2♣

Two types qualify for 2♣:

  (i)   23+, balanced or not;
  (ii) 20+ with a pattern that makes a game almost certain:

(1) ♠ K Q 10 9 5   ♡ A Q 7   ◇ A K Q 4   ♣ A
(2) ♠ A   ♡ A K J 10 7 5 3 ◇ K 4   ♣ A Q 8

With (1) you open 2♣ and rebid 2♠, game-forcing. Hand (2) has fewer points but you are willing to take your chances in 4♡ if partner has thirteen cards. The hand is too strong for an Acol two, so you force to game with 2♣.

The response to 2♣

2◇ is a negative, showing 0–7. All other responses are positive, but poor suits are avoided on good hands since you do not want to reach slam with an inadequate trump suit. With a poor suit, you might try 2NT or bid 2◇ and hope to catch up later:

(3)	♠ Q 7 3 2	♡ 8 4	♢ K 6 5 3	♣ A 9 6
(4)	♠ K 4	♡ K 7 3	♢ J 8 7 5 4	♣ K J 2

Over 2♣, bid 2NT with each, showing 8+. With (4) you have points to spare, but to bid 3NT would be wasteful and to bid 3♢ would be wrong because the suit is too weak to mention in a sequence that is sure to reach slam level.

Opener's rebid after 2♣–2♢

A suit call by the 2♣ opener is based on a strong suit and sets up a game-forcing situation. A jump shows a solid suit: thereafter, a bid in a new suit by either player is control-showing. After 2♣–2♢–2NT, Stayman and transfers come into use.

Responder's rebid after a positive response

A second-round bid in notrumps is a denial of support for opener's suit rather than strength-showing in the unbid suits:

Opener	Responder
2♣	2♡
2♠	2NT

Responder may hold:

♠ 8 5   ♡ A K 9 7   ♢ 8 5 4 2   ♣ J 7 4

2NT means that responder has nothing more to contribute. Players often fail to distinguish slight shades of strength in a weak responding hand facing a 2♣ opening. After a 2♢ negative, responder may portray three different types:

	Opener	Responder
	2♣	2♢
	2♠	?

(1)	♠ J 9 7 3	♡ 6 4	♢ Q 10 6 5	♣ Q 7 3
(2)	♠ Q 9 3	♡ 6 4	♢ A 10 6 5	♣ 8 7 3 2
(3)	♠ J 9 3	♡ 10 6 4 3	♢ 10 6 5	♣ 8 7 3

With (1) he jumps to 4♠, showing trump support but no ace, king or void.

With (2) he raises to 3♠, this time promising an ace, king or void. With four trumps and a singleton or void he would splinter.

With (3) responder intends to support spades but first he indicates the bombed-out nature of his hand by bidding 2NT, a 'second negative'.

When responder, having bid 2◇, cannot support opener's suit on the next round, he should still show any useful feature that may spell the difference between game and slam:

♠ 7 2   ♡ K 6 3   ◇ Q 7 5 3   ♣ J 8 4 2

Opener	Responder
2♣	2◇
2♠	?

The constructive bid is 3NT, not 2NT. In the same sequence the responder may introduce any potentially useful suit on the second round.

Acol twos

An Acol two is forcing for one round and shows at least eight playing tricks. It is based usually on at least 16 points and a strong 6-card or longer suit; sometimes on 5–5; exceptionally on 5–4 when both are majors.

A defining feature is that if you were to open one and responder passed, a game might be missed:

(1)   ♠ 8   ♡ A K Q J 8 7 3   ◇ 6 4   ♣ A Q 2
(2)   ♠ A K 10 9 7   ♡ A Q J 9 2   ◇ 6   ♣ A 7

With each of these, responder could well pass a one opening with a hand that offered a play for game, so the openings should be respectively 2♡ and 2♠.

Responding to Acol twos

The traditional denial is 2NT but a better method is 'Herbert', an artificial negative in the next higher suit. Thereafter, a rebid of opener's suit is not forcing but may be raised with very little.

For a positive response about eight points are needed unless responder has support for opener's suit. This scheme is followed:

With trump support and an outside ace: raise to three, guaranteeing an ace. Opener's next move will indicate whether he is interested in a slam. Q–x of trumps or x–x–x constitute good support.

With trump support but no outside ace: raise to four, denying an ace.

Lacking trump support: show a good 4-card suit at the two level or a 5-card suit at the three level; or jump to 3NT with the side suits held.

The Acol two is the bridge equivalent of the battering ram. It is still favoured by those who prefer frontal assault and has been given a new lease of life by the Multi 2$\diamondsuit$, which takes care of weak twos and leaves 2$\heartsuit$ and 2$\spadesuit$ free.

BENJAMIN 2$\clubsuit$ AND 2$\diamondsuit$ OPENINGS

These have a certain following as they allow weak two openings in the majors to be used without forgoing the benefits of the Acol two.

Benjamin 2$\clubsuit$ opening

This shows an Acol two in any suit. The negative is 2$\diamondsuit$: any other response is forcing to game. Over 2$\diamondsuit$ a simple rebid by opener is not forcing. In the case of a 2$\heartsuit$ or 2$\spadesuit$ rebid, therefore, the bidding will be one range lower than after an Acol two and a negative response.

Benjamin 2◇ opening

This means the same as an Acol 2♣ and is likewise forcing to game except when the rebid is 2NT. The negative response is 2♡.

The scheme of notrump rebids

The Benjamin convention allows for a complete range of notrump rebids on balanced hands. One schedule is this:

A 2NT opening shows 20–22 points;
2♣–2◇–2NT	23–24, not forcing;
2◇–2♡–2NT	25+, game-forcing;
2♣–2◇–3NT	Long, solid minor;
2◇–2♡–3NT	Similar but stronger.

A plus factor is that Stayman and transfers can still be used below the level of 3NT even when opener is 25+.

MULTICOLOURED 2◇

This convention is a favourite with the nimble minded. A 2◇ opening denotes either a weak two in a major or a quite different strong type or types. Many versions of the Multi are in use. In one of the most popular, an opening 2◇ may be based on:

i) A normal weak two-bid in hearts or spades;
ii) An Acol two in clubs or diamonds;
iii) A balanced 23–24. (This allows the standard sequence, 2♣–2◇–2NT, to be played as forcing, 25+, leaving space for exploratory bidding.)

The responder always assumes initially the first meaning, a

weak two. His responses have the following meanings:

2♡ 'Pass if you have a weak two in hearts. Otherwise disclose your type: that is to say, bid 2♠ with a weak two in spades, 2NT with 23–24, 3♣ or 3♢ with an Acol two.'

2♠ 'Pass with a weak two in spades. With a weak two in hearts, bid 3♡ or 4♡, according to strength. Otherwise disclose your type.'

2NT 'With a minimum weak two, bid 3♡ or 3♠; with a maximum, bid 3♣ or 3♢. Otherwise disclose your type.'

3♣,3♢ 'Good suit, forcing, even if you have a weak two.'

3♡,3♠ These are usually played as pre-emptive: 'Pass or correct.'

Defensive schemes by the opposing pair can be as labyrinthine as the convention itself. One of the simplest is this:

Action by second hand over 2♢

Suit overcall = Good suit, 15 points maximum;
Double = 16+, any pattern;
2NT = 19–21, balanced; 3NT = 22–24.

Action by fourth hand

The most common sequence will be this:

West	North	East	South
2♢	Pass	2♡	?

South should double when his hand is suitable for a takeout double of hearts. With a takeout double of spades he should pass, expecting to double next time. 2♠ and 2NT overcalls are natural.

When the response to 2♢ is 2♠, a double by fourth hand is takeout and 2NT is natural.

BLACKWOOD AND OTHER SLAM CONVENTIONS

Blackwood, the best known of all conventions, allows a player to find out how many aces his partner holds by bidding 4NT. In reply:

> 5♣ shows no ace or four;
> 5◇ shows one ace;
> 5♡ shows two aces:
> 5♠ shows three aces.

If the 4NT bidder now calls 5NT, he asks for kings in the same way. 5NT affirms that all four aces are held in the two hands: a void is not enough.

The attraction of Blackwood lies in its apparent simplicity, but the impression is false, as serious thinking is often needed to use it properly. A player should bid 4NT only when three conditions are met:

(1) It must already be clear that the material for twelve tricks is present. To know that there are not two quick losers is not the same as knowing that there are twelve winners.

(2) There must be no risk that the response to 4NT, when too few aces are held, will take the bidding past a safe level.

(3) It must suffice to know how many aces partner holds, rather than which ones:

Opener	Responder
1♠	2♡
3♣	3NT
4♡	?

♠ Q   ♡ K 10 7 6 4 3   ◇ J 10 8 6   ♣ A 2

4NT is O.K. as all conditions are met. (Opener had indicated shortage in diamonds.) In the next sequence they are not:

Opener	Responder
1♠	3♡
4♡	?

♠ K 2　　♡ A K J 8 5　　◇ Q J 7　　♣ A Q 2

If responder bids 4NT and opener shows one ace, it will not be clear whether there are two losing diamonds. Responder should bid 5♣.

When 4NT is not Blackwood

4NT is never Blackwood when suits have been bid only in a conventional sense:

(1)	Opener	Responder	(2)	Opener	Responder
	1NT	2♣		2♣	2NT
	2◇	4NT		4NT	

4NT is always Blackwood when a trump suit has been agreed:

(1)	Opener	Responder	(2)	Opener	Responder
	1♠	2♡		1♠	3♡
	3♣	4♣		3NT	4♠
	4NT			4NT	

When opponents obstruct Blackwood

Opponents may sometimes interfere with a Blackwood sequence:

West	North	East	South
1♡	Pass	3♡	4◇
4NT	5◇	?	

One solution is to bid one step up for each ace held. Here, 5♡ shows one ace, 5♠ shows two, and so on. A pass says: 'Either I have no ace or the bidding has made it unwise to show how many I have.' A double is for penalty.

Two other methods are popular. One is called DOPI –

Double with 0 aces, Pass with 1. The other, DIPO, reverses the meanings. Using either, a bid in the next available suit shows two aces.

Showing a void suit

The responder to 4NT shows the number of aces held, but at the six level instead of the five level. This is done only when the void is in a suit that the 4NT bidder will be able to identify. Other methods are also in use.

Stopping at 5NT when not enough aces are held

When willing to play in 5NT in the event that your partner has not enough aces, you may bid 4NT and if the response is unfavourable, continue with five of a new suit. Partner – on the heroic assumption that he is familiar with this esotericism – then bids 5NT, which can be passed.

Roman Key-card Blackwood

Many attempts have been made to improve on Blackwood and this is one of the few that are of more than trivial advantage. The king of the agreed trump suit is counted as a fifth ace, or key card, and the responses to 4NT are:

5♣ 0 or 3 key cards;
5♦ 1 or 4 key cards;
5♡ 2 or 5 key cards *without the trump queen*;
5♠ 2 or 5 key cards *with the trump queen*.

The 4NT bidder may continue with 5NT to ask for kings, but only when all five key cards are held. In responding to 5NT the king of trumps is excluded. The convention may be further elaborated.

Gerber convention

When partner's last bid was in notrumps, a jump to 4♣, provided the suit has not previously been mentioned, asks for aces. The responses are:

4♢	no ace or four aces;
4♡	one ace;
4♠	two aces;
4NT	three aces.

The 4♣ bidder may now bid 5♣ to ask for kings. The convention fills the gap in sequences where Blackwood cannot be used:

(1)	Opener	Responder	(2)	Opener	Responder
	1NT	4♣		2NT	4♣

(3)	Opener	Responder	(4)	Opener	Responder
	1♡	2NT		1♡	1♠
	4♣			2NT	4♣

4♣ is Gerber in each case.

Grand slam force

5NT asks partner to bid seven of the agreed trump suit if he holds two of the top three honours (A,K,Q); otherwise he signs off in six of the suit. The convention may be used only when not preceded by 4NT.

Such is the original version which, because of its simplicity, is still *en vogue* in cut-in circles. It is often called Josephine after Culbertson's wife, who launched it.

When Roman Key-card Blackwood is in use, 'Josephine' is hardly needed and most partnerships use versions that achieve greater disclosure. Some are elaborate but the following scheme is simple and effective. Over 5NT:

6♣	shows the ace or king of trumps (when clubs are not the agreed suit);
6♢	shows the queen of trumps (when the agreed suit is not a minor). In most sequences it is safe to treat x–x–x–x–x as equivalent to the queen.

Six of the agreed suit denies the ability to make either of the above responses. Seven of the agreed trump suit shows two of the top three honours.

Quiz on powerhouse hands

Your partner opens 1♠. How many losers have you and what is your call?

(1)	♠ Q J 7 3 2	♡ 5	◇ K 10 8 7 4	♣ 8 6
(2)	♠ A 10 6 4 3	♡ A Q 7	◇ J 8 6 3	♣ 4
(3)	♠ K J 9 4	♡ Q 7 2	◇ J 4	♣ A J 8 3

(1) 4♠. You have seven losers: two in trumps, one in hearts, two in diamonds and two in clubs. If opener has a sound minimum with the expected seven losers, you should make four-odd.

(2) 4♣. This is treated as a six-loser hand as you have at least a 5–4 fit and two aces. A splinter bid is in order, showing typically six or seven losers with 11+ points.

(3) 3♠. This may seem a cautious response on a hand where you have opening values, but there are no grounds for counting it as other than a straight eight-loser hand.

You open 1♣ and your partner bids 1♠.

(4)	♠ Q J 7 2	♡ A 6	◇ 8 2	♣ K Q J 4 2
(5)	♠ K 9 8 6	♡ 4	◇ A Q 10	♣ A K J 6 2

(4) 3♠. You have six losers and responder is expected to have nine if he is minimum. 15 from 18 means that you expect to make at least three-odd. However, your high-card strength is moderate for the double raise and you should reflect this in any further bidding.

(5) 4♡. You have five losers, warranting a contract of 4♠. A splinter is the right move, as a direct raise to 4♠ would imply that you had no singleton or void.

What is your call as responder after the sequence
1♣–1♠–3♠:

(6)	♠ K Q 5 4 3 2	♡ A Q 8 4	◇ 7	♣ Q 10
(7)	♠ A Q J 7 4	♡ 8 3	◇ A J 5	♣ K 9 4
(8)	♠ A Q J 10 2	♡ 8 7 4	◇ 10 6	♣ A J 2

(6) 4NT. Opener has shown six losers. You have five, but with a known 10-card trump holding a loser may be deducted. You also have a feature in partner's suit. The hand is ideal for Blackwood, since all you need for 6♠ is two aces and it does not matter which ones.

(7) 4◇. This hand is stronger in high cards than the previous one but even an optimist would count it as six losers after deducting a loser for two aces and nine trumps. However, 6♠ may still be there if opener has good clubs and a heart control. The hand is just about worth a cue bid of 4◇.

(8) 4♠. This hand does not merit a cue bid as you have seven losers opposite partner's presumed six. A cue bid is made only when a slam is seen as at least a possibility.

Your partner opens and the sequence goes: 2♣–2◇–2♡.

(9)	♠ 8 4 3	♡ J 9 5 4	◇ 9 8 6	♣ 10 5 3
(10)	♠ J 10 8 5	♡ 9 7 4 3 2	◇ 5	♣ Q 10 2
(11)	♠ J 8 2	♡ Q J 9 3	◇ 7 6 3	♣ J 9 5

(9) 2NT. This is a 'second negative'. If you support hearts straight off, your partner may get delusions of grandeur.

(10) 4◇. With 5-card support and a feature in every suit, this hand is well worth a splinter, which may allow opener to go on to slam.

(11) 4♡. The direct raise to game after a negative shows trump support but no first or second round control.

Chapter 7

PRE-EMPTIVE BIDS

*The opening three-bid – Responding to three-bids –
Doubles and overcalls of a three-bid – Responding
to doubles and overcalls – Weak twos – Other pre-
empts*

The object of a pre-empt is to prevent opponents from getting
their act together. Bridge of course would be a better game if
opponents could be persuaded to stay out of the auction
altogether, but pre-empts are the next best thing. Pre-empts
swing a lot of points and are easy to mis-use.

THE OPENING THREE-BID

Beginners are told to open a vulnerable three with seven
playing tricks, a non-vulnerable three with six tricks; always
with less than opening values. This is the Rule of 500.
Experienced players regard this as too restrictive, especially
when not vulnerable. Life has taught them that when they
have plenty of playing tricks and few high cards, opponents
will also have plenty of playing tricks – and high cards as well.
Left alone, they are apt to reach lucrative contracts.

Players therefore take great liberties with the 500 Rule, and
indeed, at 'green' vulnerability may open three with nothing
but a tatty 7-card suit or a fairly decent 6-card suit. The idea is
to float like a butterfly and sting like a bee. If sometimes they
lose more than they bargained for, or concede a penalty when
the opposition could not have made a game, they hope to
come out on the right side in the long run.

The profits come when opponents land in the wrong contract and a game is saved at no cost at all. When this happens
the gain is very large, although only 50 or 100 may appear on
the score-sheet. Also, a pre-empt will sometimes save not just
a game but a slam.

In first or second position it is more important that a three-opening should conform to type than that it should contain a particular number of playing tricks. You do not want to hold poorly guarded honour cards in side suits where they are likely to be useless in attack but may produce unexpected tricks in defence:

(1)　　♠ Q J 9 7 6 3 2　　♡ 7 5　　♢ 10　　♣ 9 8 3
(2)　　♠ K 10 8 6 5 4 3　　♡ Q 4　　♢ J 2　　♣ J 6

Hand (1) is a lightweight but purposeful three bid as you have no defence whatever. Hand (2) is not mint specimen: the isolated high cards may combine with partner's to produce one or more defensive tricks, upsetting calculations of what the enemy can make.

When pre-empts are made only on the proper type, the pre-emptor's partner is in the favourable position of being better able to judge who can make what than anyone else at the table.

From this we develop a rule that covers all auctions where a pre-emptive bid has been made: the *partner* of the pre-emptor is the captain. He decides how high to bid, whether to save, and so on. He will assume that your three-bid is of this kind:

Less than the strength for a one-bid;
a maximum of six tricks when not vulnerable, not far short of seven when vulnerable;
no secondary major suit.

The reason for this last stipulation is that it can be hard for responder to assess the potential of either side if he has to allow for the possibility of four cards in an unbid major in the pre-emptor's hand. Your partner opens 3♡ at 'green' and you hold:

♠ 9 4　　♡ J 9　　♢ A K 8 7 3　　♣ K 7 4 3

You probably compute that nine tricks, and no more, may be there for your side. However, after a pass by RHO a pre-emptive raise to 4♡ seems tactically right, as opponents may have game in spades. This diagnosis is safest when the pre-emptor can be relied on not to have four spades. The rule against a secondary 4-card major is not the Eleventh Commandment, but it does make sense.

A pre-empt in a minor suit is less effective than in a major but the risks are the same, so one does not rush to open a borderline 3♣ or 3◇.

In counting tricks one takes a fairly optimistic view:

(1)   ♠KQ107632   ♡72   ◇104   ♣J5

(2)   ♠4   ♡AKJ8653   ◇83   ♣1074

Hand (1) would be counted as six tricks, hand (2) as seven, qualifying for a non-vulnerable 4♡.

Neither side vulnerable, you hold these hands in first or second position. What is your call?

(3)   ♠AQ109542   ♡73   ◇4   ♣K109

(4)   ♠QJ3   ♡Q7   ◇KJ76532   ♣4

(5)   ♠10963   ♡AKJ983   ◇94   ♣5

On hand (3) there are three calls you might make, but 3♠ is not one of them, as you are too strong in high cards. In order of preference the options are 1♠, 4♠, and pass.

Hand (4) is light on playing tricks and, more important, is apt to produce a trick or two in defence, so should be passed.

On (5), you have four cards in spades, so again you should pass. In third position you would be much more willing to risk partner's wrath by opening 3♡.

Three-bids in third position

If, after two passes you are weak enough in high cards to consider pre-emptive action, fourth hand is very likely to have an opening bid. You should therefore be willing to take risks, especially at 'green', and perhaps even to pre-empt on hands that are slightly offbeat. In third seat after two passes you hold:

(1)	♠ Q J 9 7 6 4 3	♡ 7	♢ 10	♣ Q J 8 2
(2)	♠ 6	♡ K 10 8 7 5 4 2	♢ Q J 3	♣ 8 4
(3)	♠ A 8	♡ 5 4	♢ J 2	♣ A Q J 8 6 4 3

Each hand is worth a three-bid. With (1) you hope that the long suit will produce five tricks and that if fortune smiles, the club holding may be worth something.

With (2), if the suit were spades the pre-empt would be a stand-out, despite the possible defensive value in diamonds. In hearts it is a minimum under the most favourable circumstances.

Hand (3) would be too strong for a three-bid in first or second position, but in third hand the pre-empt makes sense. You will be happy to make 3♣, whether opponents have a contract or not.

Three-bids in fourth position

Three-bids are now made only when you expect to make the call if your partner has a fair share of the outstanding strength and where competition would be unwelcome. It may then pay to open three when in first or second hand you would have opened one:

| (1) | ♠ 8 3 | ♡ 9 4 | ♢ A K J 10 6 2 | ♣ K J 7 |
| (2) | ♠ 5 | ♡ Q J 10 9 7 4 | ♢ A Q J 4 | ♣ 8 2 |

With (1), after three passes, your partner will clearly have some values but opponents may be able to compete in hearts or spades. An opening of 3♢ is not a bad move. Partner is expected to pass, but a response of 3NT is not ruled out. On (2), considering the spade weakness, an opening 3♡ may be best.

RESPONDING TO THREE-BIDS

Opener's hand is presumed useless unless played with the long suit as trumps, so responder with a good hand and two

small trumps or a singleton honour should be strongly inclined to accept the suit. Your partner opens a non-
vulnerable 3♡:

♠ A 7 5 4   ♡ 4 2   ◇ A Q J 2   ♣ A Q 6

Raise to 4♡, which will have good chances if partner has
five or six trump tricks and one of the finesses succeeds. To
bid 3NT would be horrible: you might make no more than one
trick in the dummy hand.

3NT in response to a three-bid makes little sense unless you
hope to make nine tricks in your own hand or expect to bring
in opener's suit with no outside entry to dummy. Your
partner opens 3♣, not vulnerable:

(1)   ♠ K 10 2   ♡ A Q 3   ◇ A K Q J 9 2   ♣ 7
(2)   ♠ K J 7 5   ♡ Q J 9 3   ◇ K Q 3   ♣ 8 4

With (1) you hope to make 3NT all by yourself. With (2)
you cannot expect to come close to nine tricks unless you can
bring in your partner's club suit, which on the whole is
unlikely. Opener is not expected to have four cards in a major
so you pass.

When assessing the defensive prospects, responder counts
on only the tricks in his own hand: the pre-emptor is not
depended on for a single trick. Your partner opens 3♡, next
hand overcalls with 4♠ and you hold:

♠ A 7   ♡ K 8 3   ◇ K Q J 8 5   ♣ 10 4 3

Bid 5♡. You do expect to beat 4♠ all by yourself and
should rely on no help from partner. 5♡ will not be expen-
sive, and if opponents go to 5♠ you are willing to try to beat
them.

When as responder you are very short in your partner's
suit, he may make fewer tricks than he expected. Your
partner opens 3♡:

♠ Q 10 4   ♡ 7   ◇ A Q 5 3   ♣ A K 8 4 2

Not vulnerable, the pre-emptor's maximum is six tricks and you have either three or four. If you had two hearts you might bid game: as it is, you should pass. Vulnerable, you would raise to 4♡ despite the singleton.

The defensive raise

There are many hands where a three-bid should be raised defensively or semi-defensively, not expecting to make. Your partner opens a non-vulnerable 3♠:

(1)	♠ Q 10 6	♡ 4 2	◇ K Q 7 5 2	♣ J 8 3
(2)	♠ J 9 4 3	♡ Q 8 7 4 3	◇ K Q	♣ A 7

With (1) opponents will have at least an 8-card fit in hearts, so you raise to 4♠, forcing them to take a decision at a high level. Much of the profit from pre-emptive openings comes fron anticipatory moves of this kind.

With (2) you expect to make 3♠ but are by no means certain you can make four. However, a raise to game can hardly be wrong: opponents can surely make four of a minor, perhaps five.

When it is clear that opponents are very strong, a faked response to a pre-empt may muddy the waters. East-West are vulnerable:

West	North	East	South
	3◇	Pass	?

♠ Q 7 4   ♡ Q 6 2   ◇ J 9 7 2   ♣ A 5 3

Nine tricks may be the limit for your side, so it would not be wrong to pass. Moreover, East has passed and if the strength is divided West may do the same. But on the whole it is likely that West will re-open, and in that case opponents will reach game and very probably make it.

There is something to be said for bidding 3NT, the least transparent way of furthering North's pre-emptive action. Of course, if doubled you stand not upon the order of your going.

When opponents intervene

Over a three-bid, opponents will be to some extent in the dark, so you should not help them by doubling prematurely. Your partner opens 3♡, next hand bids 3♠ and you hold:

♠ K Q 10 3   ♡ 4   ◇ Q 8 7 4 2   ♣ A K 2

In such situations, do not double unless confident of beating any take out – and sometimes not even then. Here, you cannot be sure of defeating 4♣ or 3NT. Moreover, if you pass in normal tempo you may have the chance to double 4♠, as fourth hand may be faced with an awkward bid and may be constrained to raise with poor trumps.

After a three-opening it is never necessary to double to warn the pre-emptor against contesting further. A player who pre-empts should seldom bid again, even when he has been supported.

DOUBLES AND OVERCALLS OF A THREE-BID

A popular defence to three-bids is to treat them as one bids: a double is for takeout, 3NT is natural and a simple overcall is a one-suiter. The cue bid in opener's suit is a special case: it shows always a strong two-suiter.

This scheme is applied with some spirit: to wait for a big hand would allow the pre-emptor to succeed in his object, so you operate on the basis that your partner has a fair share of the high cards.

A non-vulnerable three will be based, on average, on six or seven points. Suppose that over RHO's 3♡ you have this hand:

♠ A J 3   ♡ A 5 4   ◇ K 10 7   ♣ K J 9 8

You have 16 points, RHO has about six, and the other two hands 18. If your partner has half you will have 25, so you boldly bid 3NT. If your partner has unwisely chosen this moment to hold a bust, is that your fault?

With this approach you will be no stranger to shaky contracts but you will be able to play them with even more than your usual brilliance, having a good idea of the lie of the cards.

Similarly, you do not need a rock-crusher to double a three-bid: your hand should be such that if partner has his fair share you can either make game or comfortably beat the contract if he elects to pass for penalties. A 6-loser hand is a sound minimum. Double 3◇ with these cards:

♠ A J 7 2   ♡ K Q 6 3   ◇ 7   ♣ K 10 9 3

With a one-suited hand, however strong, you do not double, as you might a one bid, since at this level you may have no opportunity to clarify your hand. Instead, always bid the suit. Again, six losers is about the mark. Bid 3♡ over 3◇ with this hand:

♠ A K   ♡ A Q J 6 4 2   ◇ 6 5   ♣ 8 7 3

If you had this hand with an extra ace or king you would go straight to game.

When you have a two-suited hand not strong enough for a cue bid, you either double or overcall. The choice often depends on the rank of the suits. RHO opens 3♡ and you hold:

♠ K Q 7 4 3   ♡ 6 5   ◇ K 2   ♣ A K J 4

Bid 3♠. If you double and partner with a moderate hand responds in diamonds, you are out of your depth. Now, suppose that the opening is 3♠ and you hold:

♠ A 2   ♡ K Q 8 3   ◇ A Q 9 4 2   ♣ 10 7

This time a double may be the only way to reach a heart fit and it is fairly safe because if your partner responds in clubs you can continue with 4◇.

For a cue bid in opener's suit a typical hand would be this:

♠ A K J 10 3   ♥ 6   ♦ A K 10 9 7   ♣ A 2

Over RHO's 3♥ the bid is 4♥.

Over a pre-empt, 3NT is often the best contract, as the pre-emptor may have no card of entry. RHO opens 3♠ and you hold:

♠ K 8 3   ♥ 7 4   ♦ A K J 8 6 2   ♣ K 8

Do not bid 4♦. If 3NT is the only makeable game, how can you reach it unless you bid it now?

When a pre-empt is followed by two passes, the fourth player, as in all balancing situations, may re-open with less than the usual values.

RESPONDING TO DOUBLES AND OVERCALLS

Remember that the doubler is already counting on you for about nine points, or two tricks. When you have no more, you should make a minimum response unless you have a good pattern or an assured fit:

	West	*North*	*East*	*South*
	3♦	Dble	Pass	?

(1)	♠ Q 10 8 7 2	♥ 10 6	♦ 9 7 4	♣ A K 10
(2)	♠ K 10 5 2	♥ Q 9 8 7	♦ A 6	♣ 8 7 4

With (1), bid 4♠. You have only nine points but they are 'top colour' and you expect North to have at least tolerance for spades.

With (2) also your hand should be enough for game, as you can count on a fit in either spades or hearts. This time the bid is 4♦.

WEAK TWOS

A weak 2♥ or 2♠ opening describes a hand with a fair 6-card suit and about 6–10 points:

♠ Q J 9 7 6 3   ♡ 8 3   ◇ 7 2   ♣ K 10 4

This hand is a minimum, but it is of distinctly the proper type and 2♠ is an acceptable opening at any vulnerability. Lighter two-bids have a certain vogue among players who place emphasis on pre-emption, but a disciplined approach is more usual, treating the weak two as semi-constructive as well as pre-emptive.

A minimum weak two will have eight losers; a maximum, seven. Opener is expected not to have four cards in the other major. A popular scheme of responses is this:

1. A direct raise to any level is pre-emptive.
2. A new suit is natural and forcing.
3. 2NT is a one-round force, opener rebidding as follows:
   3♣ – minimum, poor suit.
   3◇ – minimum, good suit.
   3♡ – maximum, poor suit.
   3♠ – maximum, good suit.

A simple and effective defence to weak twos is to treat them as one openings.

OTHER PRE-EMPTS

A four-opening should be at least a trick stronger than a three, as it is more likely to be doubled for penalties. This is especially true of 4♡ and 4♠.

(1)	♠ A K J 10 6 4 3 ♡ 7	◇ 9 6	♣ Q 10 4
(2)	♠ 7 ♡ A Q J 10 8 3 2	◇ K Q 9	♣ 6 2

(1) is a typical 4♠ opening, not vulnerable. (2) is worth a vulnerable 4♡, hoping to shut out their spade suit.

Transfer pre-empts

By using transfers it is possible to show a 'good' 4♡ by opening with 4♣ and a good 4♠ by opening 4◇. Responder accepts the transfer by calling the true suit, but with a strong hand he may bid the intervening suit as a slam try.

When transfer pre-empts are used, a direct 4♡ or 4♠ says that no useful high cards are held outside the long suit.

Pre-emptive overcalls

A double-jump overcall when an opponent has opened the bidding is pre-emptive:

♠ K J 10 8 7 4 2   ♡ 7   ◇ 9   ♣ J 10 5 2

Not vulnerable, bid 3♠ over any opening bid of one on your right.

A single jump overcall is also used as a pre-empt by many tournament players. See Chapter 9: weak jump overcalls.

Pre-emptive responses to one openings

A double-jump response, such as 3♡ over 1◇, is pre-emptive only when splinter bids are not in use. The values are about the same as for a non-vulnerable three-opening but the hand should conform more closely to type: K–Q–J–10–x–x–x and no other high card would be fine. It is pointless to pre-empt with the wrong kind of hand when there is no reason to think that the opponents can outbid you.

Pre-emptive bidding quiz

Neither side vulnerable, you are the dealer:

(1) ♠ Q J 10 9 7 6 5 2 ♡ 8   ◇ 9 4   ♣ J 3

(2) ♠ Q 4   ♡ A K J 8 7 3 2 ◇ A 10 ♣ 9 6

(3) ♠ A 8   ♡ 7 4   ◇ K 3   ♣ Q J 10 9 4 3 2

(1) 3♠. With less than the values for a one bid and six tricks with spades as trumps, this is an ideal non-vulnerable three. As the hand is so defenceless you might even make the same

128

bid at game all, for if you go down 800 you may be saving a slam.

(2) 1♡. In third or fourth seat, a 4♡ opening would be perfectly sound but in first or second seat, you have too much outside strength for a pre-empt. Partner might easily pass 4♡ when 6♡ is on.

(3) 1♣. To open three with so many high cards may lead partner to take a phantom save.

Neither side vulnerable, your partner opens 3♠ and next hand passes:

(4)	♠ 7	♡ K J 2	◇ K J 8	♣ K J 10 8 4 2
(5)	♠ J	♡ A K 9 6 3	◇ A 9 7 3	♣ A J 3
(6)	♠ K 5 2	♡ K Q 10	◇ Q J 9 3	♣ A J 9

(4) Pass. Your partner is expected to have no more than six tricks with spades as trumps. By no stretch of the imagination is your hand likely to provide four more.

(5) 4♠. You have four sure tricks and your spade support is only slightly sub-standard: a jack has its value when facing a 7-card suit. To bid 3NT with no expectation of bringing in the pre-emptor's suit would be unspeakable.

(6) 3NT. The spade holding is such that you may expect to bring the suit in, and your stoppers in the plain suits are bomb-proof. At a spade contract there could be four losers.

Neither side vulnerable, RHO opens 3♠.

(7)	♠ 7	♡ A J 10 6	◇ K Q 10 7	♣ A Q 9 3
(8)	♠ Q J 5 4	♡ 8 3	◇ K 8 3	♣ A K J 2
(9)	♠ A Q 8 3	♡ 10 4	◇ A J 10	♣ K Q 9 2

(7) Double. With 16 points and support for three suits, this is a model hand. If your partner elects to pass for penalties your defensive tricks will not disappoint.

(8) Pass. A double would invite partner to bid any suit, and you would not be comfortable with a response in hearts. As you are under strength for a bid of 3NT it is better to pass in the hope your partner may re-open with a double, which you would pass for penalties.

(9) 3NT. With 16 points in high cards you should pick up the gauntlet, even though 3NT is likely to fail if partner has less than his fair share of points.

Neither side vulnerable:

West	North	East	South
3♣	3♡	Pass	?

(10)	♠ K Q 9 3	♡ 10 8	◇ A J 6 2	♣ 8 6 4
(11)	♠ J 10 8 4	♡ J 9 6	◇ A Q	♣ K J 8 2
(12)	♠ K Q 5	♡ A Q 3	◇ K J 10 6 4 2	♣ 4

(10) 4♡. North will have at least opening values and at least a good 5-card suit. A bid of 3♠ would suggest a longer suit. Moreover, if North held spades as well as hearts he might have doubled for takeout.

(11) 3NT. With a hand of this strength the only problem is to pick the sounder game contract. At 4♡ a club opening lead through your hand might be damaging, but 3NT must be safe.

(12) 4NT. Since North is missing two high honours in his trump suit it is reasonable to assume that he has appreciable length. There must surely be a play for 6♡ if he has two aces.

West	North	East	South
3♣	Dble	Pass	?

Your side is vulnerable.

(13)	♠ J 7 2	♡ Q 8 4 3	◇ 5 4	♣ Q 10 6 4
(14)	♠ K 8 7 2	♡ J 8 6 4	◇ 10 6 5	♣ K 4
(15)	♠ K J 7 3	♡ 8 5	◇ A Q 10 8 4	♣ 9 8

(13) 3♡. Sitting under the pre-emptor, your club holding is quite unsuitable for a penalty pass. You also have too much in the major suits, where partner is likely to have length.

(14) 3♡. To bid 4♣, inviting the doubler to name his better major, would be a touch optimistic. It is sounder to bid the more economical suit and hope partner will make a move.

(15) 4♣. You expect to make game in either 4♠ or 5◇. If partner bids 4♡ over 4♣, you remove to 4♠. The sequence hints at four spades only, and longer diamonds.

Chapter 8

THE TAKEOUT DOUBLE

*The doubler's hand – Responding to a double – The
doubler's rebid – The balancing double – Takeout
double by the opening bidder*

The takeout double is the defending side's surest way of
finding a fit, which is their most important goal. The double is
now used with more exactness than previously, partly because new ways have been found of expressing certain types
that used to come under its aegis but were not really suitable.

A double shows at least opening strength, has no upper
limit and promises support for all unbid suits. Sometimes the
doubler cannot deliver on this promise, but he then has extra
values and can take care of matters in one way or another.

The standard takeout double is distinguished from a
penalty double by this rule:

*A double of a suit call below the four level is for takeout
when made at the player's first opportunity of doubling, provided that the doubler's partner has not bid.*

An immediate double of a suit call is therefore always for
takeout:

West	North	East	South
		1♡	Dble

When both opponents have bid, an immediate double is
still for takeout:

West	North	East	South
1♣	Pass	1♡	Dble

Next, a double is for takeout when opener's suit is raised
below the four level:

West	North	East	South
1♠	Pass	3♠	Dble

Still takeout. Moreover, the rule holds good when the doubler has passed initially:

West	North	East	South
			Pass
1♣	Pass	1♡	Dble

This is South's first opportunity of doubling, so it is for takeout.

Such are the standard uses of the takeout double. In no case had the doubler's partner entered the auction. However, in Chapter 11 it will be seen that competitive players extend its use to many more situations.

THE DOUBLER'S HAND

A double is always the favoured way of contesting when support is held for all unbid suits: the best patterns are 5–4–3–1, 4–4–4–1 and 5–4–4–0, but 4–4–3–2 is acceptable when the high-card values are sound:

(1)	♠ 4	♡ K J 10 3	◇ K 10 9 4 2	♣ A 10 9
(2)	♠ 8	♡ Q 10 5 2	◇ A Q 8 5	♣ K J 7 4
(3)	♠ 7 3	♡ A Q 9 7	◇ Q J 7	♣ K J 9 2

You would double 1♠ with each of these at any vulnerability, though at 'red' each would be an irreducible minimum.

There are two more types on which a takeout double may be made. The first is the balanced 19+, overweight for a 1NT overcall:

(4)	♠ A Q 3	♡ K 10 4	◇ K 9 8 3	♣ A Q J

With this or any stronger balanced hand you double a suit opening and bid notrumps at a suitable level on the next round.

The remaining type is the strong one-suiter:

(5)   ♠ A Q 10 7 3   ♡ K 2   ♢ A 6 4   ♣ K Q 2

This hand is about a king above the upper limit for a simple overcall, so you double and over partner's response bid spades at minimum level. The sequence shows typically no more than five losers.

It used to be common to double also on fairly strong two-suited hands, 5–4–2–2 or 5–5–2–1, but this is no longer done. It is now a firm principle that a double followed by a takeout shows a one-suited hand.

The double of a major suit always highlights the other major: only when you have extra strength and there is no other suitable call should you double without it. Thus, while 5–4–3–1 is normally a fine shape for a double, when the 3-card suit is the only unbid major you might think twice about it. RHO opens 1♠:

(6)   ♠ 4   ♡ A J 2   ♢ Q J 8 6   ♣ K Q J 7 3
(7)   ♠ 7   ♡ A K 6   ♢ K 10 7 5 3   ♣ K Q 8 5

With (6) an overcall of 2♣ is best as you do not want partner to respond to a double in a moderate 4-card heart suit. With (7), however, you would double because the diamonds are too weak for an overcall.

When both opponents have bid

A distinction is made, according to whether RHO has raised – in which case you should be even more eager to compete – or has responded in a new suit:

West	North	East	South
1♡	Pass	2♡	?

♠ K 9 6 2   ♡ 8 3   ♢ K J 10 5   ♣ A J 3

When opponents have found a fit the chances are good that your side has a fit also. Therefore you should be willing to double on these limited values. Much of the time you will compete effectively, and even when you choose a bad moment, opponents may find it hard to make a penalty double stick.

When opponents have bid two suits there are no grounds for presuming, initially, that either side has a fit. The question now is whether you should pass, accepting the risk of being shut out:

	West	North	East	South
	1♣	Pass	·1♡	?

(1) ♠ A Q 10 8 ♡ 9 7 4 ◇ A K 10 8 ♣ 8 4
(2) ♠ K 9 5 3 ♡ A 3 2 ◇ A J 7 3 ♣ J 5

In each case you want to double if West is going to raise hearts but not if he is going to bid spades. A double is more worthwhile with (1), where all the strength is in the unbid suits and a game is not impossible. With (2) a double on the first round would be contemplated only at duplicate.

When RHO's response is 1NT, again there is no presumption that either side has a fit, but this time there may not be a second round. Therefore you have to be more willing to double on a borderline hand. A double of a 1NT response is now played as a takeout double of the opening bid.

Double by a passed hand

To double now on a wing and a prayer is safe in the limited sense that your partner will not be misled, but unless there is a live chance of competing effectively, the double may help the opponents more than your side. You deal and after three passes your RHO opens 1♠:

(1) ♠ 9 3 ♡ A 10 7 6 ◇ K 10 2 ♣ K 10 7 3
(2) ♠ 7 ♡ K Q J 3 ◇ Q J 10 7 ♣ J 10 4 3

With (1) a double is a poor idea as you have a defensive type. Only if the bidding is still at a low level on the next round should you compete. With (2) you might double at favourable vulnerability as this is essentially an attacking-type hand.

RESPONDING TO A DOUBLE

Doubler's partner never passes just because he is weak, but only in infrequent cases where he holds blown-in-the-glass trump tricks:

West	North	East	South
1♠	Dble	Pass	?

♠ Q J 10 9 6 2   ♡ 4   ♢ 9 4 3   ♣ 8 5 2

This is the classic type: you pass, not because you are stuck for a bid but because 1♠ doubled will be your best contract. Now suppose that you hold this type:

♠ 9 6 4 3   ♡ 10 7 2   ♢ 6 3 2   ♣ 10 7 5

This time you may not pass, under penalty of excommunication. Nor is there any conventional way to tell partner you are busted. You just have to make the cheapest bid; in this case 2♣. But this nightmare scenario is rare: when you are so weak, third hand may be expected to arise in his might, probably with a redouble. Then of course you pass. (In the best circles, not with indecent haste.)

In general, hands with fewer than about 9 points are not a problem: you simply make a minimum bid, giving precedence to a major suit. Indeed, a major may be chosen when it is neither the cheapest nor the longest suit:

	West	North	East	South
	1♠	Dble	Pass	?

(1)	♠ 8 3 2	♡ J 8 5 2	♢ 10 5	♣ A 9 8 3
(2)	♠ J 7	♡ Q 9 8 3	♢ K 7 6 4 3	♣ 9 2

With each hand the best response is 2♡, partly because this is a more likely route to game if North is strong, but still more because a fit is almost assured.

Responding on medium hands

With 9–11 the challenge is to express just the right degree of encouragement, as game may be there if the fit is good or the doubler has extra strength.

Responder looks first for a jump bid in a suit, which is invitational and shows typically eight losers opposite the doubler's expected seven. LHO opens 1♡ and your partner doubles:

♠ 10 8 2   ♡ 7 4   ◇ Q J 7 5 3   ♣ A K 2

Bid 3◇. If the doubler is minimum he will pass. If he bids 3♠, which is forcing, he will be happy for you to raise on three.

For a jump response a 5-card suit is not indispensable, as the doubler is presumed to hold support. When the presumption is strong, as in the case of the only unbid major, even a moderate 4-card holding may suffice. Again your partner doubles 1♡:

♠ Q 9 6 3   ♡ 7 4 2   ◇ A 3   ♣ K 10 9 6

Bid 2♠. If the doubler lacks 4-card support he will have extra strength and will not pass.

The response of 1NT

This is natural and constructive, 6–10, and is preferred to a response in a minor suit. Your partner doubles 1♠:

| (1) | ♠ Q J 9 2 | ♡ 10 7 | ◇ Q 9 8 4 | ♣ A 8 6 |
| (2) | ♠ K J 9 4 | ♡ 8 3 2 | ◇ 10 8 5 | ♣ 6 5 2 |

Hand (1) is archetypal for 1NT. So, what is the best call with hand (2)? Purists will bid 2♣, pragmatists 1NT. The lack of definition is unsatisfactory, but so is anything else.

Responding on strong hands

With 12+ and seven losers you either bid game direct or cue-bid the enemy suit. You do not make a jump bid below game, as this may be passed.

The responder is expected to bid imaginatively, as he knows quite a lot about the hand opposite. LHO opens 1♡, your partner doubles, and next hand passes:

(1)	♠ 2	♡ Q J 3	♢ A Q 9 6 3 2	♣ J 6 4
(2)	♠ J 9 3 2	♡ 8 7 4	♢ A 4	♣ A Q J 3

With (1), go straight to 3NT, expecting your partner to come up with a diamond picture and a spade stopper as well.

With (2) you have eight losers but may deduct one as you have two aces and four cards in the unbid major. You expect to make 4♠ but, rather than go for broke, you should cue-bid 2♡, to cover possible contracts of 3NT and 5♣.

Responding in competition

When your RHO bids over your partner's double you may pass, but you should be reluctant to do so when there is any chance that you can force opponents to the three level:

West	North	East	South
1♠	Dble	2♠	?

♠ 8 4 2   ♡ J 9 7 2   ♢ K 10 8 3   ♣ Q 4

At any vulnerability, bid 3♡. All the points are working and you do not expect to go down more than one trick.

The responsive double

When you have competitive values but are not sure what suit to play in, the solution is to double responsively:

West	North	East	South
1♣	Dble	3♣	Dble

♠ Q 8 7 2   ♡ K 9 8 2   ♢ K 7 6   ♣ 8 6

South's double says: 'I am strong enough to compete at this level. Please choose the suit.' Here, South is minimum and will pass a three-level call from North.

The responsive double is used only when stuck for a bid. Therefore the original doubler will often be able to work out the responsive doubler's pattern. He will not have a 5-card suit, and when he has doubled a major he will not have the other major. Over a minor he will have both majors: with only one, he would have bid it. All these are reliable inferences.

Responsive doubles are usually played through 3♠.

When third hand redoubles

(1)   *West*   *North*   *East*   *South*
     1♠   Dble   Rdble   ?

This sequence means war. The redoubler is stating that his side holds the balance of strength. More than likely, he hopes to double for penalties, so you must seek a fit at the lowest level.

When you have length in the next suit up from the suit doubled, you must bid it, no matter how weak your hand, lest the suit be lost:

(2)   *West*   *North*   *East*   *South*
     1♦   Dble   Rdble   ?

  ♠ 8 3   ♡ 9 8 5 3 2   ♦ 8 7 5   ♣ J 8 3

Bid 1♡, otherwise North may bid 1♠. The same applies when your only strength is in the enemy suit and 1NT seems the least objectionable contract. Suppose that in sequence (1) you have this hand:

  ♠ Q J 8 5 3   ♡ 6 2   ♦ 9 7 4   ♣ 6 5 3

You are probably not going to enjoy playing in 1NT

doubled but if your partner, having no 5-card suit, leaves you there it may be the least of evils.

When you pass the redouble you are not saying that you wish opponents to play in the redoubled contract; only that your partner should make his own arrangements.

THE DOUBLER'S REBID

The doubler's rebid comes easiest when his partner is strong enough to cue-bid the enemy suit: now the bidding is standard and straightforward. Lesser hands require careful handling.

Doubler's partner makes a minimum response

Responder could, as we have seen, be busted, but when there has been no backlash from the opening bidder it is much more likely that he has a few points, perhaps as many as eight.

When a good trump suit is found it is always right for the doubler to raise with a hand that could at best produce a game, even when at worst not even a part-score may be safe. Such a hand will normally have five losers:

West	North	East	South
		1♡	Dble
Pass	1♠	Pass	?

♠ K Q 10 3   ♡ 6   ◇ A J 10 8   ♣ K Q 9 2

Bid 2♠. You cannot tell whether you are going to reach a thin 4♠ – if North was almost worth a jump response – or go down in 2♠ if he is very weak. In this last case opponents were never going to let you play in 1♠.

If North makes a move over 2♠, you should accept, but this hand is the least you could have.

In the same sequence, with four losers and strong support you should raise to 3♠:

♠ A K J 3   ♡ 4   ◇ K Q 8   ♣ K Q 10 8 5

A bid in a new suit by the doubler suggests a 5-loser hand with 16+ and a strong 5+ suit. A jump in a new suit shows a

4-loser hand but is not forcing: to force you have to bid the enemy suit.

A 1NT response to a double is presumed to be 6–10. There is no cast-iron guarantee. When you think the cards lie well, don't hesitate to reflect this:

West	North	East	South
	Pass	1♡	Dble
Pass	1NT	Pass	?

♠ A Q 10 9 2   ♡ 10 3   ◇ A Q 9   ♣ K J 6

Your hand offers scope for a lot of finesses – and they are likely to succeed. So, raise to 2NT. To bid 2♠ would depict a hand of this strength, but would send the wrong message. You do not want to steer away from notrumps, as your hand is suitable. Nor do you want West to be able to lead his partner's suit through the dummy against a spade contract.

Doubler's partner makes a jump response

This is a limit bid, based on the expectation of a fit. A raise by the doubler is also limit, but a bid in a new suit is forcing for one round:

West	North	East	South
		1◇	Dble
Pass	2♡	Pass	?

(1)	♠ J 8 7 5	♡ A K J 8	◇ 6 4	♣ A Q 4
(2)	♠ A Q J 5 3	♡ K 9 8	◇ 8 2	♣ A K 4

With (1) do not bid game on the strength of the impressive heart holding: when the pattern is 4–4–3–2, 15 points are little more than a minimum. The hand is just about worth a non-forcing raise to 3♡.

With (2) South bids 2♠, forcing, and raises three of either major to game.

The opening is raised and the doubler's partner passes

In this common situation the question is not whether the doubler can still hope to secure the contract but whether he can push opponents a little higher at not too great a risk:

West	North	East	South
		1♡	Dble
2♡	Pass	Pass	?

(1)	♠ K 10 7 3	♡ Q 4	◇ A J 7	♣ K J 9 3
(2)	♠ A J 8 7 5	♡ 9 2	◇ A Q 5	♣ K Q J

With (1) it looks perhaps as though you should pass: North may have four spades, or a few points, but not both. Against that, opponents have found a fit, so the chances are good that you have a fit also: North will surely have four cards in a black suit or five in diamonds. In the best circles a second double does not promise extra values and tigers would consider it routine.

With (2) South competes with 2♠. This is not without risk: North may expect a better suit. But you may not pass, and a second double would incur the greater risk of losing a 5–3 fit.

THE BALANCING DOUBLE

A double now may be made on about three points fewer than an immediate double. There is a slight reluctance to double on hands that lack defensive tricks, since second hand may have passed with strength in opener's suit and may be eager to pass a balancing double:

West	North	East	South
1♠	Pass	Pass	?

(1)	♠ 8 3	♡ A 8 5 2	◇ J 10 3	♣ A 7 3 2
(2)	♠ 6	♡ 10 8 7	◇ K J 7 3	♣ K Q J 5 2

Hand (1) is a fair minimum double. Hand (2) is stronger in playing tricks but weak in defence. South would still double if he had four hearts, but as it is, 2♣ is better.

In response to a fourth-hand double, a handy rule is to deduct a king and then respond as if to a direct double:

West	North	East	South
		1♣	Pass
Pass	Dble	Pass	?

♠ K J 8 3   ♡ K 6   ◇ K Q 10   ♣ 10 4 3 2

Over a direct double South, with opening values, would be worth a cue bid. As it is, he deducts a king and bids 2♠.

TAKEOUT DOUBLE BY THE OPENING BIDDER

A partner who failed to respond to an opening bid may sometimes be galvanised on the second round by a double. There are two radically different sequences:

(1)	West	North	East	South
				1◇
	2♣	Pass	Pass	?

(2)	West	North	East	South
				1◇
	Pass	Pass	2♣	?

In (1) North may have passed with as many as eight or nine points, so South may re-open with a hand no stronger than this:

♠ A Q 2   ♡ K 9 4 3   ◇ A J 9 8 3   ♣ 7

Despite North's pass there is a good chance that the hand belongs to your side. There is also the possibility – enhanced when playing the negative double – that North is poised for a penalty pass.

In (2) North's upper limit is at most five points, so South would need at least a queen more for a double.

Takeout double quiz

RHO opens 1♡. You are vulnerable.

(1)	♠ Q J 7	♡ K J 6 2	◇ A 10 8 2	♣ K 5
(2)	♠ K J 6 3	♡ 6 4	◇ A K 5 3	♣ Q 8 2
(3)	♠ K 10 7	♡ A Q 7	◇ A Q 6 4	♣ K Q 2

(1) Pass. With a balanced pattern and strength in the enemy suit, second hand should pass unless his hand is worth a 1NT overcall.

(2) Double. 4–4–3–2 is not the most attractive pattern for a double but this hand is adequate in high cards and possesses the important requirement of four cards in the unbid major suit.

(3) Double. This hand is too strong for 1NT, so first you double. Over a suit response a minimum rebid in notrumps will denote 19–21.

West	North	East	South
1♡	Pass	3♡	?

East–West are vulnerable.

(4)	♠ A 8 7 3	♡ 7	◇ K 10 5 4	♣ K Q 7 3
(5)	♠ A J 5	♡ Q 3	◇ A 5	♣ Q 8 7 6 5 4

(4) Double. The double of a raised suit is for takeout through 3♠. Opponents have found a good fit, so there is a strong probability that your side has one also. In that case, even if your partner has a weak hand you cannot be badly hurt.

(5) Pass. To double with minimum high-card values and only three spades would be asking for trouble. A bid of 4♣ holds little appeal as you are not sure that you wish to suggest either a save or a club lead against 4♡.

West	North	East	South
1♡	Dble	Pass	?

Neither side vulnerable.

(6)	♠9753	♡103	◇108432	♣97
(7)	♠8	♡K9742	◇Q973	♣Q83
(8)	♠K1087	♡64	◇AJ83	♣Q107
(9)	♠QJ3	♡A104	◇KQ753	♣J4
(10)	♠94	♡AQ3	◇J3	♣QJ7432
(11)	♠82	♡QJ10953	◇A72	♣82

(6) 1♠. With a weak responding hand it is better to show a 4-card major suit at the one level than a 5-card minor at the two level. To pass would be high treason.

(7) 1NT. For starters, a penalty pass should be crossed off the list of conceivable calls: this empty trump holding will be less than the dust beneath West's chariot wheels. Next, a bid of 2◇ is rejected as it would not show values. 1NT, suggesting up to 10 points, is O.K. despite the singleton in spades: the doubler will surely hold strength in this suit.

(8) 2♠. A jump response in a 4-card suit is a satisfactory move when this suit is the only unbid major. It is not forcing but it does state that prospects are rosy if the double is sound.

(9) 2♡. With opening values opposite a double you should head for game unless there is clear evidence of a misfit. Here you expect to make 3NT, 5◇, or perhaps 4♠.

(10) 2NT. If the doubler has an honour in clubs your hand will produce a lot of tricks – and quickly. A response of 3♣ would not be wrong, but a bid in notrumps normally takes precedence over a minor suit.

(11) Pass. This heart holding is ideal for a penalty pass and 1♡ doubled is likely to provide your best score. Partner will lead a trump if he has one.

West	North	East	South
1♡	Dble	2♡	?

Both sides vulnerable.

(12)	♠ 6 2	♡ K J 2	◇ Q 7 4	♣ A Q 10 5 4
(13)	♠ Q 9 8 2	♡ 7 6 2	◇ A 8 4 3	♣ 6 2
(14)	♠ A 8 3	♡ 9 5	◇ K 8 4 3	♣ J 9 6 2

(12) 3NT. The deciding factor between 2NT and 3NT is not the precise number of points held but the fifth card in clubs, a suit that you expect to scamper off with.

(13) 2♠. You should not let opponents play in a low part-score when your side is highly likely to have a 4–4 spade fit and cannot be very badly out-gunned in terms of points.

(14) Double. This is a responsive double, saying that you have the values for a response at this level but would prefer your partner to name the suit. The double indicates that you have both minors, for if you held four spades or only one minor, you would bid the suit.

West	North	East	South
1◇	Dble	3◇	?

Both sides vulnerable.

(15)	♠ K 2	♡ 10 7 5 4 3	◇ 7 5 3	♣ K 10 8
(16)	♠ K J 7 2	♡ 10 9 8 5	◇ A 7 3	♣ Q J
(17)	♠ K Q 10 8 4	♡ 10 7 4	◇ 7 3	♣ A 10 8

(15) 3♡. To pass would not be unreasonable but your partner would need a strong hand to re-open. 3♡ is perhaps a touch frisky, but you can point to two key kings and no wasted values in diamonds.

(16) 4◇. This cue bid is tenable as you have four cards in both major suits and the unguarded club honours are counted at full value opposite the double. A responsive double is a sound alternative, but a direct bid of game might hit the wrong suit.

(17) 4♠. You may not make ten tricks, but if you bid 3♠ your partner may be in a quandary, as he may have a decent hand with only 3-card support for spades.

West	North	East	South
		1♠	Dble
Pass	2♡	Pass	?

Neither side vulnerable.

(18)	♠ 4	♡ K J 10 2	◇ A J 7 5	♣ A K 8 2
(19)	♠ A J 2	♡ A 10	◇ A J 9 7 3	♣ K Q 10
(20)	♠ J 2	♡ A Q J 8	◇ Q J 7 3	♣ K 10 4

(18) 3♡. Opposite a partner who may be very weak, this single raise is very forward-going. If North has as many as two useful cards in the unbid suits he should bid game.

(19) 2NT. The sequence shows 19–21; too strong for an overcall of 1NT. A bid of 3◇ would not send a clear message.

(20) Pass. To bid 3♡ would be a game try in more senses than one. You have a minimum double and your partner was forced to bid. The strong heart holding is merely a part of the original double.

Chapter 9

THE ART OF THE OVERCALL

*The simple overcall – Responding to an overcall –
Jump overcalls, strong and weak – The cue-bid
overcall – The Michaels cue bid – Overcalls in
notrumps – The unusual notrump – Overcalls in the
balancing position*

To dignify a chapter on the overcall with this title is not over-
egging the custard. Overcalls are not just a rather breezy way
of making one's presence felt. They have serious purpose.

Also, there is much more to think about when contemplat-
ing an overcall than when opening the bidding. To give just
one example: when you have an opening, you open, but on
many hands that have the superficial requirements for an
overcall, it can be better to stay out of the auction.

West	North	East	South
	Pass	1♣	?

♠ 10 4   ♡ K J 8 7 5   ◇ K Q 10   ♣ 9 6 4

There can be little hope of competing effectively, but
perhaps the lead is a consideration: if LHO is poised to bid
spades, a heart from your partner might be good. So it might –
but a diamond could be better. Why bid?

The four main overcalls are these:

Simple overcall: Normally one-suited, occasionally
two-suited. The likely maximum is 15, exceptionally 16:
perhaps as few as eight.

Jump overcall: A good 6-card suit with the high-card
values of at least a sound opening. (Many tournament
players prefer the weak jump overcall.)

Cue-bid overcall: Traditionally a game force: for modernists, a Michaels cue bid. The two cannot, or at any rate should not, be combined.

1NT overcall: Natural and strong.

THE SIMPLE OVERCALL

The most valid purpose of a simple overcall is competitive, catering to the possibility that the deal belongs to the overcalling side or that they can at any rate compete strongly enough to prevent opponents from making an easy part-score. It may also be lead-suggesting, or it may be a mild attempt at obstruction: and it may of course combine these motives.

The hand will be unsuitable for a takeout double, a jump overcall or a 1NT overcall, as these calls are normally chosen ahead of a simple overcall.

The net effect of modern techniques is to put more emphasis on constructive overcalls and less on obstructive calls.

Overcalls with competitive purpose

An overcall that does not rob opponents of space will be construed by partner as either competitive or lead-suggesting. RHO opens 1♣:

♠ A J 4   ♡ 10 3   ◇ A J 9 8   ♣ A 5 3 2

You should not double with so little in the majors, but nor should you pass when it is not clear that opponents have the better hands. So, bid 1◇.

You might make the same call with, say, ◇A–K–J–x and a bust, and at this stage your partner cannot tell which you have; but at any rate he will presume that you do not have a load of rubbish, as your call has no obstructive value.

With this type you do not necessarily expect to secure the contract in the suit of your overcall, but you hope that by showing signs of life you may get partner to enter into the spirit of things.

Most experts today will overcall on certain strong types that previously were introduced with a double. RHO opens 1♡:

♠ K Q 7 6 3   ♡ A 8   ◇ K 7 2   ♣ K J 5

The modern style is to bid 1♠ but to reopen with a double if LHO raises to 2♡ and this comes back to you.

When opponents' bidding takes a suitable course, a second-round double may be used to define a 5–4 hand:

West	North	East	South
Pass	Pass	1◇	1♡
1♠	Pass	2◇	?

♠ J 3   ♡ A K 7 4 2   ◇ K 2   ♣ Q J 10 4

An immediate double with no support for spades would have been hazardous, but now that West has bid the suit a reopening double will denote this pattern.

Overcalls with obstructive purpose

To put a spoke in the opponents' wheel is a fine idea, but it is not as easy as it used to be: countermeasures such as those described in Chapter 11 have become more efficient. Still, the more space you take away, the more effective the overcall must be; or so the theory goes:

♠ K 9 2   ♡ 8 5   ◇ 8 4   ♣ K J 7 6 4 3

Not vulnerable, after 1◇ by RHO, an overcall of 2♣ may be as weak as this. LHO may not exactly be transfixed, but on many hands you cause a minor problem. Over a major-suit opening the overcall would hold less advantage.

Because of its superior rank an overcall in spades may combine obstructive and competitive intent:

♠ Q 10 9 4 2   ♡ 6 4   ◇ A Q 3   ♣ 9 8 2

Over 1♣ or 1◇ this hand is worth a 1♠ overcall, shutting out hearts, at any vulnerability. When the opening is 1♡ the overcall is still purposeful at equal vulnerability as you may be able to compete for the part-score against opponents who have slightly the stronger hands. At favourable vulnerability there is the additional prospect of a cheap save.

Overcalls to invite a lead

Overcalls with only this motive are not common, but they can pay bumper dividends. RHO opens 1◇ and you hold:

♠ 7 4 3   ♡ A Q J 8   ◇ 10 6 4   ♣ 5 3 2

A heart lead from partner can hardly be bad against any contract, and a bid of 1♡ may also keep opponents out of a makeable 3NT, as they will expect a longer suit.

Lead considerations may also swing the issue when other factors are not decisive:

West	North	East	South
	Pass	1◇	?

♠ J 8 7 6 3   ♡ 8 6   ◇ Q 7 3   ♣ A Q 6

At 'green', the chance of competing with a 5–3 spade fit may justify an overcall, even though you do not want partner to go out of his way to lead the suit. At equal vulnerability this last consideration might swing you in favour of a pass.

RESPONDING TO AN OVERCALL

The overcaller is presumed to be one-suited, so his partner does not go to a lot of trouble to bid a new suit. In only two cases is game likely to be reached: either the responder can support the overcaller's suit or he has opening values and a hand that can play in notrumps.

A minimum one-level overcall has typically about eight losers. It may be made on a 4-card suit, so a jump raise requires four trumps. A two-level overcall suggests seven losers and a 5+ suit.

When raising, the overcaller's partner faces a basic problem: he might want to make the same raise with two quite different types, constructive and pre-emptive. But there is a solution.

The unassuming cue bid

This term was coined by Terence Reese and the present author when putting forward a more profitable use for the cue bid than was then current:

	West	North	East	South
	1♣	1♠	Pass	?

(1)	♠ Q J 9 5	♡ 5 3	♢ Q J 10 6 3	♣ 9 2
(2)	♠ A 9 8 2	♡ 8 6 4	♢ A J 10 2	♣ 9 5

On (1) a pre-emptive raise to 2♠ is a competitive necessity. On hand (2) you also want to bid 2♠, but this time you want to tell partner that you have a quality raise and some defence.

The unassuming cue bid allows you to distinguish. With (1) you make a normal pre-emptive raise to 2♠, showing trump support and not much else.

With (2) you cue-bid 2♣, saying: 'I have a sound raise to 2♠. Unless you have overcalled on rubbish, this is our hand.' Obviously, 2♠ from the overcaller now will be a sign-off.

The same style is followed on stronger hands:

	West	North	East	South
	1♢	1♡	Pass	?

(3)	♠ 9 8 2	♡ Q 9 8 7	♢ 3	♣ K J 9 6 4
(4)	♠ A Q 5	♡ K 8 7 2	♢ A 7 6 4	♣ 6 3

With (3) you raise pre-emptively to 3♡. With (4), where you hope for game if partner is good, and where you expect to be safe at 3♡ if he is not, you cue-bid 2♢. This time, however, if partner bids only 2♡, you raise to 3♡, showing these values. The cue bid may also introduce a hand worth a raise to game. In short:

A direct raise of an overcall to any level is always pre-emptive. All constructive raises are preceded by a cue bid.

When third hand raises opener's suit you may still cue-bid:

West	North	East	South
1♡	1♠	2♡	?

♠ K J 6 3   ♡ A 2   ◇ 8 7 4   ♣ A 9 8 2

You have a sound raise to 3♠ with high-card values, so over 2♡ you can bid 3♡.

The cue bid can still be used as a traditional game-force when game may be elsewhere than in the overcaller's suit:

West	North	East	South
1♣	1♡	Pass	2♣
Pass	2♡	Pass	2NT

♠ A J 10   ♡ 8 3 2   ◇ K J 8 7   ♣ K Q 10

Initially, North presumes 2♣ to be an unassuming cue bid, but on the second round, by making any call other than a raise, South discloses a normal game force.

The new-suit response to an overcall

This is not forcing and denies direct support for the over-caller's suit, but suggests that there is still a chance of game. A typical hand will have opening values and a fair suit.

West	North	East	South
1◇	1♠	Pass	?

(1)	♠ K 7	♡ K Q 10 8 7	◇ A J 2	♣ 7 6 4
(2)	♠ 6 2	♡ 9 3 2	◇ J 6 5	♣ K Q J 9 2
(3)	♠ 8 4	♡ A J 8	◇ 10 9 4	♣ A 8 6 4 3
(4)	♠ 7 5	♡ K 10 4	◇ Q J 8 3	♣ K 10 9 2

With (1) South has a sound response of 2♡. If North bids 2♠, South is just worth a raise to 3♠, for if North had a moderate suit in a moderate hand he would have passed 2♡.

Some theorists contend, not unreasonably, that if a new-suit response is to be as strong as this, it might as well be defined as a one-round force.

On hand (2) South would like to bid 2♣ to rectify the contract, but he is about an ace short of a new-suit bid and should pass.

With hand (3) South sees no prospect of game so he passes but now he is willing to bid 2♠ on the next round if necessary. The spade holding does not warrant an immediate raise.

Hand (4) is expressed by a bid of 1NT but this time South, having shown his values, would not continue with 2♠ if West reopened.

When an overcall is doubled for penalties

Before rescuing, one should ask this question: 'Is my hand likely to be more useful to partner in his contract than his hand to me in my contract?'

West	North	East	South
1♡	2♣	Dble*	?

*Double for penalties

(1)	♠ 7 4 3	♡ J 10 2	◇ A K 10 5 3	♣ 7 3
(2)	♠ J 10 9 8 7 5	♡ J 7 3	◇ 9 2	♣ 7 3

Hand (1) will be worth two tricks to North, so 2♣ doubled cannot be too awful. North's hand may not be of the slightest use to you in 2◇, so you should not rescue.

With (2) it is hard to see even your illustrious partner doing much with your spade holding in a contract of 2♣ doubled. You should therefore bail out, especially as opponents are usually less eager to double a contract that gives game.

JUMP OVERCALLS, STRONG AND WEAK

The standard use of the jump overcall is to show opening values and a good 6-card suit, typically in a 6-loser hand. The maximum is about 16 points: on stronger hands you double.

♠ 6 5   ♡ A J 10 8 7 5   ◇ A K 10   ♣ 9 7

Over 1♣ or 1◇ from RHO, this is about rock-bottom for a bid of 2♡. Over 1♠ you would still bid 2♡, not 3♡.

A doubleton honour constitutes good support. Two small will do under pressure. A change of suit is a one-round force:

West	North	East	South
1♣	2♠	Pass	?

(1)	♠ 9 4 3	♡ K 8 7 2	◇ Q J 9 4	♣ A 6
(2)	♠ J 2	♡ J 5 3	◇ A Q J 8 2	♣ J 10 4

With (1) South raises to 4♠, not 3♠: he has eight losers and North is expected to have six. With (2) South is willing to play in 4♠ but first should see whether North can bid 3NT. 3♣ is all right but a bid of 3◇ is more expressive.

When the jump overcall is in a minor, the responder with a fit and likely guards in two suits should not hesitate to bid 3NT:

West	North	East	South
1♠	3♣	Pass	3NT

♠ J 10 7 2   ♡ 10 8 4   ◇ A 8 7   ♣ K 3 2

With this type you romp home on a 23 count, or even less if partner has ♠x–x ♡A–x–x ◇K–x ♣A–Q–10–9–x–x.

The weak jump overcall

This call has risen sharply in the popularity ratings. It is disruptive, based on a 6-card suit and only a few points; certainly less than opening values.

♠ K J 8 7 4 3   ♡ 8 6   ◇ Q 10 2   ♣ 7 4

Competitive players will overcall with 2♠ at anything other than 'red' vulnerability, when a stouter suit would be preferred.

In response, all direct raises are pre-emptive: a cue bid is the only force.

Some partnerships seek the best of both worlds by playing weak jump overcalls when not vulnerable, strong when vulnerable.

THE CUE-BID OVERCALL

In standard bidding this is a game force, promising no particular pattern and no particular holding in opener's suit. Over 1◇ from RHO you might bid 2◇ with any of these:

(1)	♠ AK108432	♡ 7	◇ 86	♣ AKJ
(2)	♠ AK1094	♡ KQJ92	◇ −	♣ KQ8
(3)	♠ A83	♡ A2	◇ 74	♣ AKQJ62

With (1), a minimum, you start with a cue bid because a direct bid of game would suggest you held little strength outside the long suit. When slightly weaker you would double and jump to 3♠ over partner's response.

With (2) you cue-bid because you want to show both suits and cannot afford to be passed out in a simple overcall or a double.

With (3) you hope your partner will be able to bid notrumps, either on the first round or the next; otherwise it may be possible to stop in 4♣, as in this sequence.

West	North	East	South
		1◇	2◇
Pass	2♡	Pass	3♣
Pass	4♣	Pass	?

North would be expected to bid 3NT over 3♣ with ◇J–10–x–x and a blizzard. He should also bid 5♣ over 3♣ with any genuine support. As the bidding has gone, South may pass.

It is possible to handle this type in a different way. A direct bid of three in opener's suit says: 'I have a long running minor with about seven or eight tricks. Bid 3NT if you have a stopper.'

Hands suitable for the cue-bid overcall are infrequent and can be expressed in other ways. The traditional version is therefore increasingly being displaced by the Michaels cue bid.

THE MICHAELS CUE BID

Two-suited hands can be a problem. If a simple overcall is made, there may be no opportunity to show the second suit; a double can lead to complications best avoided. The Michaels solution is this:

Over 1♣ or 1◇: a cue bid shows typically at least 5–5 in the majors; exceptionally 5–4 when the 4-card suit is strong.

    ♠ K 10 7 5 4   ♡ A J 9 5 3   ◇ 8   ♣ 10 4

Bid 2♣ over RHO's 1♣, 2◇ over 1◇.

Over 1♡ or 1♠: a cue bid guarantees five cards in the unbid major and five cards or a strong 4-card holding in an unspecified minor.

    ♠ Q J 9 3 2   ♡ 7   ◇ 8 4   ♣ K Q 10 6 2

Bid 2♡ over 1♡. You cannot make a Michaels cue bid over a minor suit with this type.

The strength will be either 6–11 or 17+; the next round will clarify. Responder always presumes the weak type. On intermediate hands you either overcall or double.

One of the advantages is that when there is a known fit the responder may be able to take heavy pre-emptive action:

West	North	East	South
1◇	2◇	Dble	?

    ♠ Q J 3 2   ♡ 7 5 4   ◇ 9 7 3 2   ♣ Q 6

Suppose that East's double is explained as strength-showing: at 'green' vulnerability South, even with this weak hand, would bid 3♠, where there is a known 9-card fit. Now suppose that in the same sequence South had high-card values:

♠ A 8 6 2   ♡ Q 7   ◇ A 9 5 4   ♣ J 8 3

South has nine losers in support of spades and North probably has seven. This apparently leaves South well short of game. But there is a known 9-card fit and he also has two aces. Moreover, the holding of Q–x in North's known 5-card heart suit is a considerable asset. Game could be a fair bet if North has a sound average, and South can find this out by bidding 3◇, a one-round force. If North is minimum he bids 3♡ and South signs off in 3♠. If North makes any other bid South will reach 4♠.

A simple response to Michaels in a major shows 3+ trumps but posts a warning: 'My hand does not fit well enough for pre-emptive action and I have no interest in game.'

Over a 2♡ or 2♠ cue bid the responder may bid 2NT to ask for the cue-bidder's minor. 3NT is always to play.

Rebids by the Michaels bidder

When one of his suits is supported the cue-bidder usually does not bid again unless the pattern is stronger than 5–5. Raises are then pre-emptive:

West	North	East	South
		1♡	2♡
Pass	2♠	3♡	3♠

South is likely to be 6–5 in spades and a minor suit, but the sequence shows no extra high-card strength. He might still have raised pre-emptively if East had passed 2♠.

When the cue-bidder is in the rare 17+ bracket he says so by making a bid inconsistent with a weak two-suiter: he may bid a suit he cannot have, or bid notrumps, or make a repeat cue bid in opener's suit. In a competitive auction he may double.

When the opening side has bid two suits

How Michaels should be used now is a matter for partnership agreement:

West	North	East	South
1♠	Pass	2♣	2♠

One scheme is to let the cue bid retain its usual strength, showing the other two suits, while an unusual 2NT denotes an intermediate two-suiter, neither weak enough nor strong enough for Michaels.

Various refinements of and extensions to the Michaels cue bid are used by aficionados.

OVERCALLS IN NOTRUMPS

1NT directly over an opponent's opening is equivalent to a strong 1NT opening. It is an efficient call and is used freely, as Stayman and transfers can be deployed just as if the opponent's bid had not been made. RHO opens 1♠ and you hold:

(1)   ♠ K 4   ♡ K 7   ◇ 10 8 7 2   ♣ A K Q J 5
(2)   ♠ A Q 10   ♡ 3 2   ◇ K Q 9 5 3   ♣ K Q 10

Bid 1NT in each case, despite the 5–4–2–2 pattern in (1) and the heart weakness in (2), which represents a still greater objection to a takeout double.

The 2NT overcall

For most players this is 'unusual', since a strong balanced hand is introduced with a double. However, when played as natural, 2NT suggests a running minor suit in a hand too strong for 1NT but not quite in the same league as a 2NT opening:

♠ K 10 3   ♡ 8 4 3   ◇ A K Q 10 3   ♣ A Q

Over RHO's 1♣ or 1♠ you could bid 2NT with this hand: with an additional diamond the call would be 3NT.

THE UNUSUAL NOTRUMP

A direct 2NT over an opponent's 1♡ or 1♠ shows at least 5–5 in the minor suits. The high-card strength may vary widely, according to vulnerability and whether the 2NT bidder has passed.

The responder assumes initially that the overcaller is weak. Simple preference for one of the overcaller's suits is a sign-off and may be based on three cards or even a doubleton.

West	North	East	South
1♠	2NT	Pass	?

♠ 10 7 4   ♡ K 10 8 7 4   ◇ Q 5 2   ♣ K 3

Here South bids 3◇, confident of at least a 5–3 fit. The doubleton king in partner's second suit is an encouraging feature, and if the ♡K were the ace South would bid 4◇, invitational, although he would prefer to have a fourth trump. A direct 5◇ would be pre-emptive.

Such is the original form of the convention, but many partnerships now use more efficient versions. It is proposed to describe one that fits in well with the Michaels cue bid.

Unusual 2NT over any suit opening

A direct 2NT over a suit opening of one shows the two lowest unbid suits. These will always differ from those shown by Michaels:

over 1♣: 2NT shows at least 5–5 in the red suits;
over 1◇: at least five hearts and five clubs;
over 1♡ or 1♠: at least 5–5 in the minors.

Like Michaels the high-card strength is two-way: 6–11 or 17+. When weak, all or nearly all the points should be in the two suits. At 'red', when weak you would bid 2NT only with two very good suits or a freakish distribution.

Responses to 2NT are along the same lines as in Michaels and so are the 2NT bidder's rebids.

Other unusual notrump sequences

Any overcall in notrumps by a player who has passed and who therefore cannot have a strong balanced hand is self-evidently 'unusual':

(1)	West	North	East	South
	Pass	Pass	1♣	Pass
	1♠	1NT		

(2)	West	North	East	South
	1♢	Pass	1♠	Pass
	2♠	2NT		

In (1) North is showing the red suits, in (2) clubs and hearts. However, a bid of notrumps is never unusual if it can logically be genuine:

West	North	East	South
Pass	1♠	Pass	Pass
1NT			

Here it will be normal for West with a balanced hand just short of an opening to protect his partner's pass, so 1NT is natural.

Further sequences include the showing of weak two-suited hands over opponents' strong two bids. Always there is the drawback that if opponents play the hand they will know the distribution. In any form, Michaels and the unusual notrump are best used only when there is a fair chance of securing the contract or forcing opponents too high.

OVERCALLS IN THE BALANCING POSITION

When a suit opening is followed by two passes, some bids by fourth hand may be made on about two or three points less than the usual strength. The rationale is that third hand must be very weak to pass and second hand may have passed with fair values.

West	North	East	South
1♡	Pass	Pass	1♠, 1NT or Dble

1NT now shows 11–14 while a double can be as weak as 10, but still with no upper limit. Overcalls, however, are not now made for obstructive reasons and are likely to be 9–13.

1NT can be the best move even when no guard is held. This is because you are usually better off with the lead coming from the opponent who opened the bidding than from his partner:

West	North	East	South
1♠	Pass	Pass	?

(1)	♠ Q 6	♡ A 7 4	◇ Q 8 6 3 2	♣ A J 5
(2)	♠ K 4	♡ K 10 9 3	◇ A J 7 5	♣ Q 10 3

Bid 1NT in each case. With (1) there are various holdings where West will be able to lead his suit only at the cost of a trick. With (2) the pattern is suitable for a double but you do not want North to be declarer with the lead coming through your ♠K–x.

In the balancing position a wide-range notrump – say, 11 to 16 – used with the Crowhurst convention, has some popularity.

Weak jump overcalls are redundant in fourth position, so jump bids are made freely on hands such as these:

(1)	♠ K Q J 5 3 2	♡ 8 7	◇ A 10 6	♣ 9 7
(2)	♠ A 7	♡ J 9 6	◇ 8 2	♣ A K J 10 3 2

Balancing bids may also be made on a later round when opponents stop at a low level:

West	North	East	South
		1♡	Pass
1NT	Pass	2♢	Pass
2♡	Pass	Pass	?

♠ 10 7 5 4 3   ♡ 7 4 2   ♢ A 7   ♣ K J 2

South's two passes were well chosen – now it will be sound tactics to bid 2♠. North should not expect a stronger hand.

In all such situations the rule is not to allow opponents to play in their best contract at the level of one or two.

Overcalls quiz

(Unassuming cue bids not in use.)

Neither side vulnerable, RHO opens 1♣. What is your call?

(1)	♠ Q 10 8 7 3 2	♡ 5	♢ A 6	♣ 9 7 4 2
(2)	♠ K J 2	♡ K 6	♢ K J 9 4	♣ A J 9 3
(3)	♠ 4 3	♡ A K J 6	♢ A J 2	♣ J 9 8 2

(1) 1♠. With so few high cards this overcall is sound only because the suit is spades. Playing the weak jump overcall the hand would qualify for 2♠.

(2) 1NT. This shows the equivalent of a strong 1NT with the adverse suit well held. To double with no length in either major suit would be wrong.

(3) 1♡. Partner may not initially expect so much in high cards, but you cannot double with such weak spades, nor should you let yourself be shut out when you have opening values and a suit worth showing.

Neither side vulnerable, RHO opens 1♡.

(4)	♠ 10 4	♡ Q J 2	♢ Q 5 2	♣ K Q 7 5 3
(5)	♠ 8 4	♡ K 6 3	♢ A K 7 4	♣ K 8 6 3
(6)	♠ A J 5 4 3	♡ 10 5	♢ 8 2	♣ A K Q 3
(7)	♠ K Q J 9	♡ J 4	♢ 9 2	♣ A J 6 4 3

(4) Pass. This would be a poor 2♣ overcall because you have too little in clubs and too much in defence. Players who make such calls have been heard to describe them as nuisance bids, a term their partners readily endorse.

(5) Pass. No form of immediate intervention is safe. This type is best handled by backing in later if the bidding suggests that there is a fit.

(6) 1♠. The snag with a double is that if partner responds in diamonds you have to take out into spades, a sequence for which neither the values nor the spade suit are quite strong enough.

(7) 1♠. An overcaller is allowed more rope than an opening bidder, who is expected to bid his longest suit first. Here, given that you may end up defending, the need to attract a good lead comes into the reckoning. An overcall on a 4-card suit can be logical when it serves this purpose.

West	North	East	South
1◇	Pass	1♡	?

Both vulnerable, South holds:

(8)	♠ Q 8 4 3 2	♡ K 8 4	◇ K 6	♣ K J 2
(9)	♠ J 9 8 6	♡ K 4	◇ 8 3	♣ A K J 8 5
(10)	♠ Q 8 4	♡ K Q 7 3	◇ A Q	♣ Q 8 7 2

(8) Pass. If your partner is short in spades and has a weak hand as well, an overcall could fail dismally. But if the bidding peters out at the two level you should certainly compete in spades.

(9) Double. This is much more likely to animate your partner than an overcall of 2♣ as it brings into play the unbid major, your best chance of competing successfully.

(10) Pass. With so much strength in the enemy suits, a plus score is more likely to be gained by remaining silent than by doubling or bidding 1NT.

West	North	East	South
1◇	1♠	Pass	?

Neither side vulnerable, South holds:

(11)	♠ 6 2	♡ K J 6 4	◇ K J 10	♣ J 8 7 2
(12)	♠ Q 9 8	♡ J 4	◇ 9 8 4 3	♣ A K 10 8
(13)	♠ J 5	♡ A Q J 3	◇ J 10 2	♣ A K 8 7

(11) 1NT. The hand is minimum for this forward-going bid and if North can raise only to 2NT you should pass: North's strength is limited by the failure to double.

(12) 2♠. You have solid values and intend to go to game if North makes a try. Playing unassuming cue bids, you would bid 2◇. 2♣ is not an available bid as it would not be forcing.

(13) 2◇. With 16 points and tolerance for partner's suit, you should aspire to game, but the best contract is not clear. It may be 4♠ (if North has six spades); 3NT (if he has a diamond stopper); or 4♡ if he has a secondary heart suit.

West	North	East	South
1♠	Pass	Pass	?

Both sides vulnerable, South holds:

(14)	♠ 6 4	♡ 8 3	◇ A 8 7	♣ K J 9 8 3 2
(15)	♠ Q 6 4	♡ K 10 8 2	◇ A Q 8	♣ J 5 4
(16)	♠ Q J 8 7 6	♡ A 5	◇ K 2	♣ J 10 7 4

(14) 2♣. With this useful 6-card suit you should compete for the partial even though not well endowed with points.

(15) 1NT. You could double, but 1NT is better as you wish to protect your tenace holdings.

(16) Pass. The object of bridge is to score points and this may best be achieved by passing. Opponents are surely in their worst spot.

West	North	East	South
		1♠	Pass
Pass	2♢	Pass	?

Neither side vulnerable, South holds:

(17) ♠ K Q 4   ♡ A 9 7   ♢ K 8 7   ♣ Q 9 8 2
(18) ♠ J 7   ♡ Q 10 4 ♢ J 8 3   ♣ A K 8 5 3

(17) 2NT. In the balancing position North is likely to be bidding partly on the strength of your hand. Had he over-called in second position you would have bid 3NT.

(18) 3♢. The knowledge that you have diamond support and a fair hand may allow North to bid 3NT if he has a 6-card suit and a spade guard.

Chapter 10

STANDARD MOVES IN THE CONTESTED AUCTION

The response in competition – Opener's rebid in competition – Opponents have doubled for takeout – Sacrifices – Penalty doubles and redoubles – Part-score bidding – Psychic bids

Enemy intervention does not always work to the disadvantage of the opening side. There is a loss of space, which may or may not be valuable space, but in return you gain two opportunities, the double and the cue bid. Plus, you can value your hand more precisely, as you have an idea of how the cards lie.

By no means, then, does the opening side reconcile itself to a less accurate auction when opponents have chipped in.

THE RESPONSE IN COMPETITION

It is no longer necessary to make a courtesy response to keep the bidding open, but it is good tactics to respond with even the slenderest values when there is a fair chance to compete effectively:

West	North	East	South
	1◇	1♡	?

(1)	♠ J 7 5 3 2	♡ 7 5 4	◇ K 10 5	♣ J 2
(2)	♠ J 8 4 3	♡ J 5 4	◇ 6 2	♣ K 8 6 5

With (1), do not fail to bid 1♠. If your partner has 3-card support you may be able to outbid opponents even when they have slightly the stronger hands; but only if you bid the suit now.

Hand (2) is different and should be passed. There is probably no future unless opener himself has four spades and at least median values. In that case he can reopen and you may still compete successfully, but without the risk of bidding such a weak suit, which could be raised on three. (A duplicate player might be willing to accept this risk.)

With a weak hand that is barely worth any form of action, it may be better to support opener's minor than to bid a weak 4-card major:

West	North	East	South
	1♣	1♡	?

♠ 10 8 3 2   ♡ 6 4   ◇ Q 10 4   ♣ K 10 8 7

If you bid 1♠ you may never get to mention your club support. Suppose next hand raises to 2♡ and this comes back to you: perhaps your partner could have competed with 3♣ if you had raised, but as it is, a bid of 3♣ now would be consistent with a stronger hand. If you bid 2♣ on the first round, limiting your hand, you may be able to compete later with 2♠.

The thrust of these examples is that you do not need extra values for a response in competition. A response of 1NT, for example, might be based on A–Q–x in the overcaller's suit and nothing else. But you do need a fair chance of competing effectively, and moreover, you might well make a different bid from the one you would have made in an uncontested auction:

West	North	East	South
	1♡	2◇	?

♠ Q 9 5 3   ♡ 3 2   ◇ A J 7   ♣ K J 10 3

With no butt-in you would have bid 1♠ but this does not mean that you should bid 2♠ now: the values are adequate, but the suit isn't, as your partner could raise on three. A negative double would be fine; next best is 2NT.

The negative double, described in the next chapter, can by partnership agreement be limited to just one sequence:

West	North	East	South
	1♣(1◇)	1♠	Dble

This shows a heart suit and 6–9 points, not strong enough for a two-level response.

The general-purpose cue bid

This is a catch-all for hands where responder has game values but where the correct game is not obvious:

West	North	East	South
	1◇	1♠	2♠

♠752　♡K983　◇KQ7　♣AJ2

South can force with a hand no stronger than this because North, playing the 12–14 notrump, will have either 15+ or distributional values.

OPENER'S REBID IN COMPETITION

After an overcall by his LHO, opener's obligation to rebid remains in force but, like the responder, he does not necessarily make the same call:

West	North	East	South
			1♡
1♠	1NT	Pass	?

♠83　♡AKJ82　◇AK4　♣QJ10

Without the butt-in South would raise to 2NT. As it is, he is willing to finish in 3NT, since North's spade holding will be well placed and if there is a finesse in clubs it is likely to succeed. However, the best call at this point is 2♠, to see if

North holds heart support. Again:

West	North	East	South
Pass	Pass	Pass	1♡
1♠	2♢	Pass	?

♠ K J 4   ♡ Q J 9 8 6 3   ♢ A   ♣ A 8 2

Without the overcall you would have a clear rebid of 3♡, but this time you have a close decision. As you expect the spade honours to be badly placed, you might devalue the hand and bid only 2♡.

The meaning of opener's rebid in notrumps is unchanged except in a sequence where LHO's overcall may have robbed him of a suit rebid:

West	North	East	South
			1♣
1♠	2♡	Pass	?

♠ A Q 8 3   ♡ 7 5   ♢ A 2   ♣ Q 9 6 4 3

Now that South cannot rebid in spades, the only satisfactory call is 2NT, which in this sequence suggests a 5–4 pattern with minimum points. It follows that when opener has a balanced 15+ he should, after a two-level response, rebid 3NT or make a forcing bid.

At a lower level the problem does not arise:

West	North	East	South
			1♣
1♡	1♠	Pass	1NT

Here nothing has happened to change South's intentions. He always intended to rebid 1NT over a 1♠ response and he has a balanced 15–17.

Opener's rebid when RHO overcalls

Opener may now pass, but he should not do so merely because he is low in points:

West	North	East	South
			1♠
Pass	2♣	2♡	?

(1) ♠ A J 10 8 7 3   ♡ 8 4   ◇ K 10 4   ♣ K 2
(2) ♠ Q 10 6 5 2   ♡ 4 2   ◇ A K 6   ♣ A 3 2

With (1) opener has only 11 points but he still bids 2♠: he is eager to stress a suit that can play opposite x–x. With (2) he passes, not because he is minimum but because the pass is descriptive: it can only mean that he is 12–14 with a suit he does not wish to emphasise.

No matter how poor his hand, opener should always show 4-card support for responder's major suit if this can be done at a low level:

West	North	East	South
			1♣
Pass	1♠	2♡	?

♠ J 6 4 3   ♡ A 2   ◇ Q 4   ♣ K J 9 8 2

A pass as dealer might have escaped censure, but now that you have got lucky you must of course follow through and bid 2♠. To open light and fail to exploit when things turn out well is folly.

OPPONENTS HAVE DOUBLED FOR TAKEOUT

New-suit responses keep their normal meaning – and their normal forcing or non-forcing quality – but direct raises are pre-emptive and are stretched to the limit. A raise to three suggests the values for a raise to two and a half, and so on.

A normal sound raise to three of opener's suit is shown by bidding 2NT:

West	North	East	South
	1♡	Dble	2NT

2NT is forcing and shows at least a raise to 3♡ with high-card values.

1NT still shows 6–9 and is used freely to prevent fourth hand from bidding a major suit at the one level. A bid in a new suit by a non-passed hand is forcing but denies a hand suitable for a redouble.

The redouble

This shows a defensive 10+, probably with the potential to double at least two suits:

West	North	East	South
	1♠	Dble	?

♠ 5 2   ♡ Q 10 9 3   ◇ A 9 8   ♣ A 10 8 5

This is a minimum but sound redouble. It will hardly ever be left in, but if it is, you get good odds, as the contract is quite likely to be made.

Opener's rebid after a redouble

When the opener has a long suit and does not wish to play for penalties he may distinguish between a quality opening and a sub-standard one:

(1)	West	North	East	South
				1♠
	Dble	Rdble	Pass	2♠

The immediate 2♠ says: 'I'm not interested in doubling the opponents. I have a moderate tactical opening with a long spade suit.' If East bids over the redouble, the message is similar. In each case opener shows this type:

♠ K J 9 7 6 3   ♡ 8 5   ◇ K J 7   ♣ K 2

In the next sequence the opener still does not want to play for penalties but this time his opening is sound:

(2)

West	North	East	South
			1♠
Dble	Rdble	Pass	Pass
2♡	Dble	Pass	2♠

♠ A Q 10 9 6 5   ♡ 2   ◇ A Q 4   ♣ 10 8 5

The delayed removal says: 'Your double of 2♡ doesn't suit me but I have a respectable opening.' Here South would have been willing to stand a double of 2♣ or 2◇.

With other types the opener follows a similar principle; that is, with sound values he does not take immediate action:

West	North	East	South
			1♠
Dble	Rdble	2♣	?

The sequence is forcing, so South may double 2♣ or may pass with any hand on which he is willing to defend 2♣ doubled. A bid in a new suit will show a weak two-suiter: with a respectable two-suiter South would pass and show it on the next round.

SACRIFICES

Your opponents bid laughing and splashing to a game but you also have found a fit. Will a save be cheap or could it be a phantom?

When you think you have enough tricks to hold opponents to their contract, you should not save, as an extra trick may come unexpectedly from a holding such as J–x in a side suit, especially when your partner has the ace or king. But when you are sure opponents can make their contract and that there are no holes in your trump suit, you should save, even when you think it may cost 500. If it does, this will certainly be nothing to cheer about, but the big profits come when opponents bid one more and go down.

Now suppose that you have the balance of strength and opponents are doing the pushing: you should be willing to take 300 rather than bid an uncertain 5♡ or 5♠. (At duplicate a different assessment is made: see Chapter 12.)

To save at unfavourable vulnerability is rare and requires pinpoint accuracy:

West	North	East	South
		1♡	1♠
2♡	3♠	4♡	?

♠ K Q J 8 6   ♡ A 7 3   ◇ K 8 2   ♣ 10 5

You are playing unassuming cue bids, so North's raise is known to be pre-emptive. To save profitably you must be able to make nine tricks and opponents ten. Clearly the second condition is met: you have no chance of four defensive tricks, as one opponent or other will have a singleton spade.

As you have nine trumps, and close to a fair share of the high cards, your own expectation is nine tricks. (See next chapter.) You should therefore bid 4♠. To be held to eight tricks would be rather unexpected, but the overall loss would still be small (except at duplicate). The gilt on the gingerbread is when opponents press on and go down.

The double fit

It has been repeatedly urged that when your side has a fit, opponents are likely to have one also. This is still more true with a double fit, where you and your partner have length in the same side suit as well as in trumps. You must go all out to buy the contract, whether hoping to make it or as a save:

West	North	East	South
	1♣	1♡	1♠
3♡	3♠	4♡	4♠
5♡	Pass	Pass	?

♠ 10 8 7 5 3   ♡ 7 4 3   ◇ 10   ♣ K Q 10 5

At any vulnerability, bid 5♠: your attacking power is great, but in defence your hand could be worse than useless. Even if you had a sure defensive trick you would still bid 5♠, as the opponents will also have a double fit and as many playing tricks as you.

When you have a straggly two-suiter, be very careful: the quality of your partner's trump holding will be crucial. Did he support at the first opportunity, or reluctantly? If the latter, do not be carried away by a two-suiter such as K–x–x–x–x and A–Q–x–x–x–x, especially if partner has merely given forced preference. When suits break badly, weak two-suiters are death traps.

PENALTY DOUBLES AND REDOUBLES

To be a good doubler you have to draw every possible inference from opponents' bidding as well as from your partner's. It is also legitimate to take note of an opponent's tempo or mannerism, though not of course of your partner's. You yourself can do much to avoid hesitations by doing your thinking in advance while others are meditating over their calls.

A double will often allow declarer to save a trick by deducing what you have doubled on, so you must consider whether you can afford this.

Doubles of overcalls

Doubles at a low level are usually more profitable than doubles after several rounds of bidding, for by then opponents have found their best suit and have a good idea of what they can make.

When your partner opens and your RHO overcalls, a double should be considered when the following conditions are met:

1. You have at least two tricks in high cards and at least four trumps. (The best trump holding is not a combination such as A–K–x–x but one that is bad news for declarer, like Q–J–x–x or J–10–x–x with top cards elsewhere.)

2. You have no more than two cards in your partner's suit. (When you have more, his high cards may not live to take tricks.)

3. It is not obvious that your side has a safe game contract. (The more distant your game prospects, the more attractive the penalty.)

4. You have a sound opening lead. (Before doubling, consider what you will lead. If you are at all uncomfortable with the answer, don't make a close double.)

Finally, do not double an overcall unless you have at least some hope of doubling any removal. If either opponent takes out, your partner must feel free to double readily with a suitable hand, relying on you to have some defence.

Your partner opens 1♠ at love all and next hand bids 2♣:

(1)	♠ 5 3 2	♡ 9 6	◇ Q 9 8	♣ K J 9 4 2
(2)	♠ 9 7	♡ K 10 4	◇ A 8 7 4	♣ J 10 5 4

With (1), pass. You can be happy to let RHO play here undoubled. A double when the only real feature is a long trump holding is apt not to end the auction.

With (2), double. You have an 'unexpected' trump trick and two high cards outside. Whether the double is left in or not, your hand will not disappoint.

A double is sometimes made with four small trumps, especially when strength is held in declarer's second suit. This holding then has considerable nuisance value: a declarer who has to develop a side suit will hate having to draw four rounds of trumps first.

Doubles with three trumps are not made at the one level, but are not entirely *verboten* at higher levels when a ruff as well as a trump trick is likely and when there is no reasonable alternative. Your partner opens 1♠ and next hand bids 2◇:

♠ Q   ♡ J 8 6 2   ◇ K 8 2   ♣ A 8 7 5 4

Neither 3♣, 2♡ or a pass is very attractive, nor are you very eager for your partner to reopen in spades. With two defensive tricks and a likely ruff, a double is likely to net at least a small plus; but this double is made only for want of better.

The holding in opener's suit

This is almost as critical as the trump holding itself. A singleton or doubleton is better than a void, as a lead from you may be needed to develop your partner's high cards.

Generally, the less you have in your partner's suit, the less certain are your game prospects. When your hand is such that a game seems assured, you should not double unless you hope for a really big penalty. Remember that if you can see a game, your partner, whose strength is wide-ranging, may be able to visualise a slam.

All these considerations apply also to a double by opener when fourth hand overcalls.

When opener should remove the double

With three likely defensive tricks, two or more trumps, and a fairly ordinary pattern, a pass is automatic. With anything different, you have to exercise the bean:

West	North	East	South
			1♠
2♡	Dble	Pass	?

(1)	♠ A Q 7 4 2	♡ 6 3	◇ K Q 10	♣ J 6 2
(2)	♠ K J 9 8 6	♡ 5	◇ Q 7 5 3	♣ A Q 3

With (1) or any better defensive hand you can leave the double in and watch your savings grow. Your partner's hand is expected to be sound, as the double would give game if made.

With (2), Your hand is far less suitable and the decision is borderline. Suppose first that your side is vulnerable and the opponents not: your partner knows this too, so you can be sure that the double seemed attractive. You should just about pass, but hardly with a gay tra-la. At 'green' vulnerability a takeout might be safer, as now there is not such a strong presumption that the double was clear cut.

When much of your strength is in a secondary suit, there is danger. If your partner has length in the same suit, both you and he may see your defensive tricks evaporate:

West	North	East	South
			1♡
2♢	Dble	Pass	?

East–West vulnerable.

♠ K Q J   ♡ 10 8 6 5 3   ♢ 5   ♣ K Q J 8

This is not a healthy situation. You do not have three defensive tricks, and the ones you do have may clash with those of your partner who, being short in hearts, is likely to have at least some length in clubs or spades. It only needs him to lead an unsupported heart honour and dummy to go down with a singleton club, and you will be paying out overtricks at 200 a time.

At 'green' vulnerability, if you remove to 2NT this will be understood as weakness. At 'red' you would have to try something else, as your partner might think you were more interested in reaching for a vulnerable game than for a non-vulnerable penalty.

Doubles of freely bid game contracts

These are not recommended as a source of untapped wealth except against opponents who have not heard of sign-offs. The arithmetic is all wrong: minus 290 instead of 120 is poor odds against an extra 50 or 100.

When either opponent is unlimited, speculative doubles are off the menu altogether:

West	North	East	South
1♠	Pass	2♢	Pass
2NT	Pass	3NT	?

♠ 2   ♡ A J 6 3   ♢ K J 8 2   ♣ Q J 4 2

Pass. You have dummy's suit sewn up and your partner might have a spade holding. Against that, dummy is un-limited and could have enough to redouble. Moreover, if you double the declarer will play for the cards to lie badly.

For a double of game to be at all attractive, both opponents must be limited and there must be no lead problem:

West	North	East	South
1♣	Pass	1♠	Pass
2♠	Pass	2NT	Pass
3NT	Pass	Pass	?

♠ 3   ♡ A 5 3   ♢ Q J 10 4 2   ♣ Q 10 5 4

In this kind of sequence, declarer does not expect to get home unless the cards lie reasonably well: if they lie badly, he expects to go down. Here, you should ensure that he goes down doubled.

Suppose that in the same sequence you hold this hand:

♠ 9 3   ♡ A K 7 5 4   ♢ 7 6 2   ♣ A 4 3

This time East's suits appear to be breaking well, but you can double for a different reason. If East were 5–4 in the majors he would not have bid 2NT, and if West held four hearts he too would have bid differently, so declarer will surely have no more than one heart stopper. It is unlikely that he can make nine tricks without letting you in with the ♣A, so a double is fairly safe.

SOS redoubles and business redoubles

A redouble is SOS when it is clear that the player would pass if he thought the contract could be made:

(1)

	West	North	East	South
	1♠	2♣	Dble	Rdble

(2)

	West	North	East	South
	1♠	2♣	Pass	Pass
	Dble	Pass	Pass	Rdble

(In the second auction East–West are playing negative doubles and East has passed West's double for penalties.) South holds in each case:

    ♠ 8 5   ♡ J 10 7 5 3   ◇ Q 10 9 6 2   ♣ 7

Common sense will tell North that the redouble is SOS, for if South thought his partner could make 2♣ doubled he would pass. (But cut-in players inscribing 2800 on the score sheet have been heard to remark that the trouble with common sense is that it is not common enough.)

A redouble is also SOS when it is logically impossible for the redoubler to be sure of making the contract:

West	North	East	South
	1♡	Pass	Pass
Dble	Pass	Pass	Rdble

This is for rescue. South was too weak to respond to his partner's opening, so how can he be sure of making 1♡ after East has shown that he is on the warpath? North must remove; if necessary into a 3-card suit.

A redouble at game level is always business and should be favourably considered when the contract will be no worse than borderline, provided that you expect a big penalty if opponents remove. The odds are generous, but you must be sure you have a secure trump suit.

PART-SCORE BIDDING

What is the notional value of a part-score? Howard Schenken, a killer at rubber bridge, put it at about 150 points. When playing opposite a weak partner with whom he did not wish to prolong the rubber he would reduce the figure; and vice versa.

When trick value is added to the equity value it works out that, not vulnerable, a safe part-score should not be jeopardised for a doubtful game unless the game has at least an even chance. Vulnerable, slight odds against are acceptable.

This applies to *safe* part-scores. But suppose that you reach the level of, say, 2NT and are wondering whether to press on to a risky 3NT. It may be that 2NT and 3NT depend on the same thing, and in that case you should bid the game.

Opening the bidding when either side has a part-score

It is good tactics to open light when you have a partial, not just because you might convert it but because opponents may defend. Always be willing to accept a 300 that might turn out to be 500, as you will still have the part-score.

It follows that the side that has a part-score should be willing to take risks to preserve it: to go down 500 to save a game and still have a part-score against opponents who have not is good business.

PSYCHIC BIDS

A psychic is a bid that either names a suit that is not the true suit or pretends to non-existent values or both.

The vogue for out-and-out psychics in the early days of contract did not last long, as it proved ever more difficult to persuade opponents they did not have the cards they could see they did have. For some players psychics still add spice, but the serious fraudster is more subtle. He psyches not on weakness but on strength, and his objectives are limited and realistic. He hopes to gain a favourable lead or cause defenders to misread the hand:

♠ A 8 3   ♡ Q J 9 3   ◇ K Q 10 4   ♣ A 2

His partner having passed, the psychist opens 1♣, and over

1♠ he rebids at 1NT. Opponents will, he hopes, hurl themselves in vain against his red suits.

Some psychics are virtually risk-free. For example, when you know to what contract you are headed, you may bid a non-existent suit to inhibit a lead or confuse opponents.

In a competitive auction it can be a good ploy to bid a non-existent suit when you intend to play in a higher-ranking suit and want to buy the contract cheaply. East–West are vulnerable:

West	North	East	South
1♡	1♠	2♣	?

♠ Q J 8 7 3   ♡ 4   ◇ 10 7 4   ♣ 8 5 3 2

To bid 2◇ is not a bad idea. Later in the auction, opponents may double prematurely or value their hands wrongly.

To conceal a giant fit for as long as possible is another ploy with a proven record:

West	North	East	South
1♡	1♠	?	

♠ 7   ♡ K 10 7 5 4   ◇ 8   ♣ A 8 7 4 3 2

Very likely the opponents have as good a fit as you have – and theirs is in spades. So you bid simply 2♡, willing to be pushed to whatever level is necessary.

Quiz on the standard contested auction

West	North	East	South
	1♡	2♣	?

Neither side vulnerable.

(1)	♠ K Q 10	♡ A J 7 5 3	◇ Q J 10 4	♣ 7
(2)	♠ K 9 6	♡ J 5 4	◇ J 10 6 4	♣ K Q J
(3)	♠ 10 4	♡ Q 10 9 7	◇ K 8 5	♣ A J 9 7
(4)	♠ J 8 5 4 3	♡ K 10 2	◇ K 7 2	♣ 8 3

(1) 4♣. A splinter bid can be made in the suit of an enemy overcall: here, 4♣ shows a singleton club and strong trump support with six or seven losers. A direct 4♡ would come nowhere near expressing these values, and 4NT is no solution since if an ace is missing it will not be clear whether there are two diamond losers. If you were not playing splinters, a game force would be best.

(2) 2NT. This is not the type on which to double, as you have no 'unexpected' trump trick.

(3) 3♡. With four cards in opener's major you make a normal raise, no matter how strong your holding in the enemy suit. Opponents are almost sure to have a fit in spades or diamonds, and by doubling you would help them find it.

(4) 2♡. Had East passed, you would have bid 1♠, but as it is, a bid of 2♠ would show at least a king more than you have.

West	North	East	South
			1♣
1♠	2♡	Pass	?

Both sides vulnerable.

(5)	♠ A K J 2	♡ 7 3	◇ K 6	♣ Q 7 5 3 2
(6)	♠ A 4	♡ K Q 7	◇ 9 6 3	♣ A K 10 7 6
(7)	♠ K 7	♡ 5 3	◇ A Q 3 2	♣ K Q J 10 8

(5) 2NT. Without the butt-in you would have rebid in spades, but here your intended rebid has been stolen. A bid of 3♣ would be nauseating, and you cannot raise hearts, so only 2NT remains. North is expected to read you, for if you held a genuine notrump rebid of 15+ you would bid 3NT.

(6) 4♡. This is no overbid, as North will have at least 10 points, more likely 11, and 5+ hearts. If you had a weaker hand you would still have to bid 3♡, so with these values you must distinguish.

(7) 3NT. If you were to bid only 2NT North would place you with the type of hand in problem (5). A slightly under-strength reverse of 3◇ is a reasonable alternative, as North can cue-bid spades if he is interested in 3NT.

West	North	East	South
			1♣
Pass	1♡	1♠	?

Neither side vulnerable.

(8)   ♠ 7 2   ♡ 9 7 4 2   ♢ A 10   ♣ A K 10 9 7

(9)   ♠ A K 3   ♡ 7   ♢ 8 4 2   ♣ A 9 5 4 3 2

(8) 2♡. When RHO enters you are allowed to pass, but 4-card support for partner's major is a vital asset and should be shown on even the weakest of opening hands.

(9) Pass. You opened with a minimum and the early exchanges have not made your hand any better, as most of your points are in the enemy suit. The pass is in fact a good descriptive call: you did not open 1NT, so must have a shapely minimum with 5+ clubs.

West	North	East	South
			1♡
1♠	2♣	2♠	?

Neither side vulnerable.

(10) ♠ K Q 10   ♡ K 8 6 4 2 ♢ K 10 4 ♣ K J

(11) ♠ 8 2   ♡ K Q J 8 5 ♢ Q 10 4 ♣ A J 8

(10) 2NT. This sequence is different from that in problem (5). Here you are not obliged to bid at all, so 2NT shows the full 18–19 with which you would have rebid in notrumps over a two-level response in an uncontested auction.

(11) 3♣. A raise of responder's suit is normally preferred to a rebid of opener's suit. Moreover, in this sequence the raise virtually guarantees 5+ in your own suit. What you should not do is pass, as you have an attacking type.

West	North	East	South
	1♠	Dble	?

Neither side vulnerable.

(12)	♠ 10 6	♡ J 8 4	◇ K 7 6 3	♣ Q 9 7 5
(13)	♠ J	♡ K 10 7 4	◇ A J 8 6 3	♣ J 8 7
(14)	♠ Q J 8 3	♡ 8 4	◇ K 10 3	♣ A 10 8 7

(12) Pass. This is borderline. Had North opened in a lower-ranking suit, you would have bid 1NT over the double, shutting out a one-level bid by West. Duplicate players would bid 1NT anyway.

(13) Redouble. This states that your side has the whip hand and that opponents should not be allowed to secure the contract unless they can profitably be doubled.

(14) 2NT. Over a takeout double this is conventional, denoting a sound raise to three of opener's suit or better. A direct 3♠ would be pre-emptive.

West	North	East	South
	1♠	2◇	?

Neither side vulnerable.

(15)	♠ 8 3	♡ 9 2	◇ K J 7 6 4 2	♣ Q 6 3
(16)	♠ K J 9	♡ 8 6 4	◇ A 8 6 2	♣ Q 6 3
(17)	♠ 4	♡ A 8 7 5	◇ Q 5 4 3	♣ A 10 4 3

(15) Pass. You have so many diamonds that if you double, someone is sure to take out. The hand has no future for your side and you could be happy to defend 2◇ undoubled.

(16) 2♠. This perhaps does not fully express the values but the alternative, a double of 2◇, is unlikely to be good business when you have too many cards and too many points in opener's suit.

(17) Double. This is a good double. You have defensive tricks but no clear vision of where a game might be made. Your trump holding should be worth a natural trick and a ruffer too.

(18)

	West	North	East	South
		1♠	Pass	2♣
	2♡	Dble	Pass	?

Neither side vulnerable.

♠ K Q 9   ♡ 8 2   ◇ Q 4 3   ♣ A 8 7 4 2

(19)

	West	North	East	South
		1♠	2♡	3♣
	3♡	3♠	Pass	3NT
	Pass	Pass	4♡	?

North–South vulnerable.

♠ 4   ♡ K 6 2   ◇ K J 7   ♣ A Q 8 5 3 2

(20)

	West	North	East	South
			1♠	2♣
	Dble	Rdble	Pass	?

Neither side vulnerable.

♠ 7 3   ♡ A J 7   ◇ 8 2   ♣ A 10 8 4 3 2

(21)

	West	North	East	South
				1♠
	Pass	1NT	Pass	Pass
	Dble	Rdble	Pass	?

East–West vulnerable.

♠ A K 8 7 2   ♡ J 10 4   ◇ 8 5   ♣ A 10 7

(18) 3♣. This is close, but you have too much in spades to stand the double with any enthusiasm and your cards are a shade too good for a bid of 2♠.

(19) Double. These proceedings have gone far enough. 4NT would be natural, but would be an act of conspicuous gallantry: the deal is an obvious misfit and even your previous call of 3NT might have been hard to make. Take the money.

(20) 2♡. North's redouble is for rescue: if he thought you could make 2♣ doubled he would pass. He probably has a void in clubs and length in the red suits.

(21) Pass. A redouble is assumed genuine if it can logically be so. Here, North probably has a maximum and is hoping to extract a penalty if opponents take out. You have a fine defensive hand and can stand a double of any suit.

Chapter 11

THE HIGHLY COMPETITIVE
AUCTION

The negative double ('Sputnik') – Competitive doubles – The Law of Total Tricks – The forcing pass – Opponents overcall your 1NT – You overcall their 1NT

Progress in competitive bidding has been dominated by the onward march of the takeout double, which now covers many new situations.

In a book on tournament play, Terence Reese and the present author remarked that a double has the special merit of consuming no space and leaving open every option. We put forward some new ideas, including what we called competitive doubles.

The caravan has moved on. All those doubles and more besides are now treated by keen partnerships as competitive – that is, primarily for takeout. In addition a new type has emerged, the support double.

The present situation is that, for players who use the methods described in this chapter, all first-round doubles and most second-round doubles at a low level are for takeout. A double is for penalties only when logic says it can be nothing else. To clear the decks for the main thrust of the chapter, it will be convenient to discuss these sequences first.

A double is for penalty:

1. *After a redouble:*

West	North	East	South
1♠	Dble	Rdble	2♣
Dble			

Any double by the opening side is for penalties, for that was the intention of the redouble.

2. *When the same suit could have been doubled at a lower level:*

West	North	East	South
1◇	1♠	Pass	Pass
2♣	2♠	Dble	

East's double of 2♠ is for penalties, as he could have doubled 1♠ for takeout.

3. *When there has been a previous penalty double or when a double has been passed for penalties:*

West	North	East	South
1◇	2♣	Pass	Pass
Dble	Pass	Pass	2♡
Dble			

West's first double is for takeout. East's pass is for penalties: therefore, so is any subsequent double by East or West.

All other doubles except the support double carry this message: 'I have the values to contest at this level but there is no suitable bid I can make.' Thus these doubles are defined by a negative criterion: it is the inability to make a natural bid that fixes the character of the doubler's hand.

THE NEGATIVE DOUBLE ('SPUTNIK')

In a competitive auction the side that does not find its fit, and quickly, is dead in the water. For the opening side, sequences such as this used to be a torment:

West	North	East	South
	1♣	1♠	?

♠ 9 7 5   ♡ Q J 7 2   ◇ A 7 6 3   ♣ 10 4

To pass with these values is no way to win a contested auction but South's hand is too weak for 2♡ or 2◇ and unsuitable for 1NT. In this and other sequences there is no solution unless you play the double of an overcall as takeout.

The negative double was proposed by Alvin Roth and it swept the tournament world, first in the U.S., then in Europe. A popular modern version is this:

1. A double by opener's partner of an overcall is for takeout through 3♠. At a higher level a double is similar to the double of a pre-empt at that level.
2. The minimum strength for a one-level double is 6+; for a double that invites opener to bid at the three level, 9+.
3. The double denies support for opener's suit: a doubleton or singleton is a likely holding. The pattern is seen in these examples:

West	North	East	South
	1♣(1♢)	1♡	Dble

Most play that this double shows exactly four spades and 1♠ would have five or more spades. Some experts play this double to deny four spades.

West	North	East	South
	1♣(1♢)	1♠	Dble

South has 4+ hearts and some support for the unbid minor or for opener's minor.

When both major suits have been bid, a double promises 4+ in both minors; correspondingly when both minors have been bid.

When responder has a normal penalty double

The responder will usually pass, but it does not follow that the overcaller will go unpunished.

West	North	East	South
1♡		2♣	?

♠ K 62   ♡ 83   ♢ A 632   ♣ Q J 82

South cannot double for penalties so he passes, but if West

passes too, North is expected to reopen, even on a minimum. Suppose that North holds these hands:

(1)	♠ A 8 5	♡ A J 9 4 2	♢ K J 5	♣ 7 6
(2)	♠ Q J 4	♡ K Q 9 7 6 4	♢ Q J 7	♣ 3
(3)	♠ 10	♡ A Q 7 6 5	♢ K J 7	♣ K J 5 4

With (1) North doubles; this is the preferred way to reopen when opener's hand is such that he would have passed a normal penalty double of the overcall.

With (2) he 'removes' to 2♡, just as he would if South had made a penalty double of 2♣. Hand (3) is the only type where opener may pass: his length in the enemy suit is such that South cannot have a penalty double. South must have made a normal pass on weakness, so North passes too.

Opener's rebid in response to a negative double

Opener's rebid is always 'limit', expressing the doubler's values as well as his own. He may – indeed should – bid a weak major suit when he knows the doubler has 4-card support. All reverse-bid requirements are off: opener may reverse into a known fit on a complete minimum. The only forcing call is a cue bid.

	West	North	East	South
			Pass	1♣
	1♠	Dble	Pass	?

(1)	♠ 4	♡ Q 8 6 5	♢ Q 10 3	♣ A K J 8 2
(2)	♠ 10	♡ J 10 4 2	♢ A K 2	♣ A Q J 7 3
(3)	♠ K 10 4	♡ 10 3	♢ A Q 9	♣ A K Q 10 4

Over the one-level double, South should rebid as though North had responded at this level. On (1) South bids 2♡, which does not imply reversing values and will normally be passed when responder is minimum. With this sound hand, however, South will accept any invitation.

On (2) he bids 3♡, just as if North had responded 1♡ in an

uncontested auction. Had East raised pre-emptively to 3♠, South would have had to accept the challenge and bid 4♡, even on this very weak suit.

On (3) South may bid a confident 3NT, expecting hearts to be stopped by his partner.

Opener may pass a negative double for penalties, but this is a rare occurrence as he is sitting under the call and may not rely on trump tricks from the doubler.

The doubler's rebid

With 6–9 the doubler normally passes, but if he dislikes opener's rebid he may return to the first suit or bid a new 5+ suit. This is not forcing and does not show extra values, for with 10+ and a 5-card suit he would not have doubled.

However, responder may have doubled with 10+ and no 5-card suit, and in that case he may raise opener's rebid, or make an encouraging move such as 2NT, or give jump preference.

The negative double seems likely in the fullness of time to displace the penalty double almost as completely in rubber bridge circles as it already has in the tournament world.

COMPETITIVE DOUBLES

All doubles through 2♠, no matter by whom, are for takeout except those noted at the start of this chapter. Some doubles at the three level are also for takeout.

When no fit has been established a double always says: 'I am unwilling to sell out but I have no suitable call.' The inability to make a natural bid defines the doubler's hand to some extent.

First-round double by fourth hand

When the opening side has bid two suits the doubler is likely to have a doubleton in his partner's suit – a holding typical of 'awkward' hands – and length in the unbid suit:

West	North	East	South
1♣	1♠	2♡	Dble

♠ Q 7   ♡ 7 3 2   ◇ K 10 6 4 3 2   ♣ A 6

South wants to compete, and double, which always asserts that there are at least two options apart from a penalty pass, is the most satisfactory call.

When the opening side has bid only one suit, the doubler may have various types, defined always by the fact that he has no suitable natural bid:

West	North	East	South
1♠	2♡	2♠	Dble

♠ 8 5   ♡ 9 4   ◇ K Q 7 2   ♣ A 7 6 4 3

South is willing to play in 3♡ if necessary – but not if his partner has a secondary minor suit.

Second-round double by opener

At the one level opener has less need than other players of the competitive double, as he will have opened with a prepared rebid.

To know precisely how many trumps your side has is a great advantage in a competitive sequence. It is therefore useful to have the understanding that a double by opener of a simple overcall over partner's major suit response shows specifically 3-card support. A direct raise then shows 4-card support and any other call suggests fewer than three.

West	North	East	South
			1◇
Pass	1♡	1♠	?

(1) ♠ J 5   ♡ K 10 2   ◇ K J 8 7 5 4   ♣ A 7
(2) ♠ 7   ♡ J 5 3   ◇ A K 8 6 5   ♣ A Q J 2
(3) ♠ 10 8   ♡ K 6   ◇ K Q 7 3 2   ♣ A 10 6 4

With (1) you double, showing 3-card support for hearts: on

a good day this may enable partner to go to game. This is called a support double. No extra values are needed: a competitive double at a low level promises no greater strength than the original opening.

With (2) also you double but this time if partner can do no more than bid 2♡ you are strong enough to continue with 3♣, a sequence that will be highly descriptive.

With (3) you pass, just as you might without competitive doubles. North now knows that you have no more than two hearts and he will be better able to judge in what strain to continue.

Second-round double by responder

When opener passes on the second round and the responder has a hand with options, a double may be the most comprehensive move, even with slender values:

West	North	East	South
	1♡	1♠	2♡
2♠	Pass	Pass	Dble

♠ 8 6   ♡ K J 2   ♢ J 10 8 4   ♣ A 9 8 3

The double says that South has supported on only three hearts and he is willing to play in at least one of the minors.

Second-round double by the overcaller

A player who has overcalled on a good hand may animate his partner on the second round by doubling:

West	North	East	South
		1♣	1♠
2♣	Pass	Pass	Dble

♠ A Q 7 5 3   ♡ A 8 4   ♢ K J 7   ♣ 8 2

With this type, on the first round the overcall is preferred to a double, but on the second round, if the bidding goes like this, a double will be very satisfactory.

The game-try double

A double by a player whose side has bid and supported a suit
is equivalent to a game try in the agreed suit:

West	North	East	South
			1♠
2♡	2♠	3♡	Dble

♠ A Q 9 5 4   ♡ 8 4   ◇ A 7 2   ♣ K Q 9

This double says: 'If your raise is sound we can make
game.' If instead South bids 3♠ he is merely contesting the
part-score. The difference is crucial.

THE LAW OF TOTAL TRICKS

To survive in the fast lane one must contest vigorously, never
allowing opponents to play at a low level in easy contracts.
But how can one tell how far to push? All competitive
measures depend ultimately on the player's being able, most
of the time, to gauge within about one trick how many tricks
his side can make.

A handy guide was proposed by the French theorist, Jean-
Rene Vernes, but attracted little attention at first:

*When both sides have found a fit and the points are not too
unequally divided, you should bid for as many tricks as your
side has trumps.*

This works because of an underlying safety net, peculiar to
the contested auction: when both sides can make a part-score,
if you go down a trick you do not necessarily lose in a real
sense.

A fit means at least eight trumps, so when both sides have a
fit, both can bid for at least eight tricks. Already, then, you
know you should compete to the three level if you are
prepared to go one down.

With nine trumps you should usually bid 3-over-3. If the
cards lie reasonably well you expect to make the contract and
if they don't you can be fairly sure that the opponents were
going to make theirs:

West	North	East	South
			1♠
2♣	2♡	3♢	?

♠ A 10 9 8 4   ♡ Q 10 7 3   ♢ K Q   ♣ 6 4

South has a distinctly sub-standard opening but he knows of at least nine trumps so should contest with 3♡, especially as he has no reason to think opponents will fail in their contract.

The rule sometimes gives an accurate result, no matter whether a vital card is well placed or not:

West	East
♠ A 7 4	♠ 8 2
♡ 7 4	♡ K 8 3 2
♢ Q J 8 7 3	♢ 10 9 5 2
♣ A K J	♣ Q 10 7

West	North	East	South
1♢	Dble	2♢	2♠
3♢	3♠	Pass	Pass
?			

As West you are willing to contest with 4♢ if this will be down no more than one trick, provided opponents can make 3♠.

However, you have nine trumps, so presumably should stop at 3♢, and this is borne out. For you to make nine tricks, the ♡A will have to be with North, which means that the opponents probably won't make 3♠. If they *can* make 3♠, the ♡A being with South, there will be only eight tricks for you in 4♢. Don't bid.

Vernes' main thesis was not the tip just described, which he saw as having some practical value, but his Law of Total Tricks:

When playing in a suit contract, the total of tricks that can be made by the two sides, each in its best suit, is equal to the total of trumps held in these two suits.

Thus, if one side has eight spades and the other ten hearts, there are 18 tricks to be made. The Law does not say how they will be divided. It has been found surprisingly accurate, but its usefulness is limited. A great number of refinements and adjustments can be made, but always the stumbling block is that the number of trumps held by opponents can seldom be reliably estimated.

THE FORCING PASS

A very convenient move is to pass an enemy call when you know your partner will have to take action. In this way you may avoid, or at any rate defer, a difficult decision:

West	North	East	South
			2♣
Pass	2♢	3♡	?

North–South vulnerable.

♠ A K 9 3   ♡ A   ♢ K Q J 9   ♣ A K Q 2

South could cue-bid 4♡ but a forcing pass has to be better, for if North can bid 3NT South will let him play in what may be the only makeable game. If North doubles, the cue bid can still be made.

A pass is always forcing when the sequence was already game-forcing before the enemy call was made:

West	North	East	South
			1NT
Pass	3♠	4♡	?

Here South can distinguish between various types:

(1)	♠ 9 4	♡ K 8 7 3	♢ A K 8 2	♣ Q 6 5
(2)	♠ Q J 3	♡ 8 4 2	♢ A K 3	♣ A 8 5 3
(3)	♠ J 8 3	♡ K 10 2	♢ A 9 6 4	♣ A J 2

In (1) South doubles. He has a moderate hand, but it is well suited to defence. North can be sure the double is a good one, as South could have made a forcing pass.

With (2) a bid of 4♠ is automatic: South has good support and no strength in the enemy suit. With (3) the choice between a double and 4♠ is close and a forcing pass allows South to say as much.

A pass is also forcing when it is obvious that your side has the superior cards and would not wish to let opponents play the hand unless they could profitably be doubled:

West	North	East	South
			1♡
1♠	2♣	2♠	Pass
Pass	3♡	Pass	4♡
4♠	Pass	Pass	?

North–South vulnerable.

♠ 4 2   ♡ A 9 5 4 3   ◇ A K 9 2   ♣ Q 6

After North's two-level response, this hand belongs to your side, so North's pass to 4♠ is forcing. Here you should double as you cannot be sure of making 5♡: you have a bad holding in the enemy suit, your partner may have the same and there may very well be a trump loser in addition.

OPPONENTS OVERCALL YOUR 1NT

Your partner opens 1NT and next hand bids two of a suit. In standard bidding, a new suit from you is natural and non-forcing. A double is for penalties. A raise of notrumps is natural but does not promise a stopper. A cue bid is a game-force.

Not bad, but the loss of space means that there may still be problems:

West	North	East	South
	1NT	2♣	?

(1)	♠ 7 2	♡ Q 10 8 5 3 2	◇ A 6	♣ J 10 4
(2)	♠ 8 2	♡ A J 7 4 3	◇ K Q 3	♣ K 7 3
(3)	♠ 9 4	♡ K Q 4	◇ A J 9 3	♣ K J 10 3

With (1) and (2) the snag is that South wants to bid 3♡ both times: on (1) as a part-score sign-off and on (2) as a force, offering a choice between 3NT and 4♡. With (3) he would like to raise to 3NT, but does not know whether spades are wide open. There is a neat solution to these problems.

The Lebensohl convention

With (1) South bids 2NT, which always requires opener to bid 3♣. South would pass 3♣ if this were his suit. Here, over 3♣, South bids 3♡ and North passes. Mission accomplished.

With (2) South bids 3♡ over 2♠. The direct three-level bid in a new suit over intervention is natural and forcing, whether it is a jump or not.

The Lebensohl convention can end there, in which case hand (3) is still a headache, but it is more common to play the following extension, which is very productive:

2NT followed by 3NT over the forced 3♣ shows a stopper in the opponent's suit;
2NT, then a cue bid, is Stayman, also promising a stopper;
3NT is natural but denies a stopper;
A direct cue bid is Stayman and denies a stopper.

Accordingly, with hand (3) South bids a direct 3NT. North passes only when he has a stopper in opponents' suit.

Lebensohl gives up the natural response of 2NT after an overcall, but there is a considerable net gain. In some sequences the responder can even fit in an invitational bid:

West	North	East	South
	1NT	2♡	2NT
Pass	3♣	Pass	3♠

South may hold:

♠ Q J 7 4 3 2   ♡ 8 5   ◇ K 3   ♣ K 10 6

If South had wanted to sign off he could have bid 2♠ over 2♡. If he wanted to force he would have bid 3♠ over 2♡. Therefore in the actual sequence 3♠ is invitational.

Double of an overcall of 1NT

When Lebensohl is in use a double of a two-level overcall, whether natural or two-suited, is for penalties and shows general strength, about 10+. When the overcall is artificial, the doubler will usually have four cards in at least one of the overcaller's true suits.

Against a natural overcall at the three level it is more usual to play a double as negative.

Lebensohl in a modified form can also be used after an artificial overcall of partner's 1NT opening.

YOU OVERCALL THEIR 1NT

If only to show that you are serious people, you have to have a conventional way of entering the auction over an enemy 1NT when you hold competitive values and a hand playable in two or more suits.

Simplest is the Landy 2♣, showing about 12–14, at least 5–4 in the major suits. All other overcalls are natural. In response, 2NT is natural: the only force is 3♣.

Ripstra is similar but has two artificial overcalls: 2♣ to show club tolerance and both majors; 2◇ to show diamond tolerance and both majors.

The Astro convention also has two overcalls: 2♣ to show hearts and a minor suit, at least 5–4; 2◇ to show spades and any other suit. Responder normally bids the anchor suit when he has 3-card support or better; otherwise he may bid the cheapest suit as a relay. If he bids 2NT, this is artificial and forcing.

The Cansino convention uses 2♣ to show clubs and two other suits, 2◇ to show a major two-suiter.

All these conventions may be used also in fourth position. It is also standard to play 2NT over an opponent's 1NT as a game-forcing two-suiter.

The double of 1NT

A penalty double of a 1NT opening shows at least as many points as the upper limit of the opening. Unless third-hand redoubles, fourth hand is expected to pass with a balanced hand, no matter how weak.

However, it is by no means automatic to double just because the hand is strong enough: 1NT can be hard to beat, even with plenty of points. When sitting over the 1NT opening the doubler's cards are in theory well placed, but he may be in danger of giving a trick away each time he leads. So, before doubling you should project the play:

West	North	East	South
		1NT(12–14)	?

(1)	♠ A Q 5 2	♡ K J 8 2	◇ Q 7 6	♣ K 3
(2)	♠ K J 3	♡ A J 6	◇ A J	♣ 9 7 5 4 2

With (1), suppose that you lead a heart, finding dummy with 10–9–x and declarer with A–Q–x. Three rounds of diamonds put you back on play. Already you wish you had passed.

Hand (2) is a much better hand on which to double as you intend to beaver away in clubs, forcing declarer to come to you in the other suits.

The double of 1NT by a passed hand may be used conventionally to show specific types, such as two touching suits. Some partnerships extend this to a double in any position when the opening 1NT is strong.

Double of a suit takeout of 1NT

When 1NT is doubled and next hand removes, the doubler's partner may double on any balanced hand with two or more defensive tricks:

West	North	East	South
1NT	Dble	2♣	?

♠ A 8 5 3   ♡ Q 9 6   ◇ 10 8 3   ♣ J 9 4

South should double not just 2♣ but any rescue by third hand, and North should normally leave in the double when his hand too is balanced. Often there will be no game and +300 will be very acceptable.

A player with a weak hand facing a 1NT opening will often remove without waiting for the axe to descend. After 1NT–Pass, third hand holds:

♠ J 7 5 4 2   ♡ 8 6 3   ◇ J 3   ♣ 10 4 3

1NT will surely be doubled by fourth hand so the player with this hand bids 2♠.

In this common situation, fourth hand should double with a strong balanced hand on which he would have doubled the 1NT opening. The double may be left in when second hand, too, is balanced.

It is possible, and simple, to use Lebensohl against an opponent's removal of 1NT:

West	North	East	South
1NT	Dble	2♠	?

South proceeds as though East's bid were an overcall of *North's* 1NT opening: 2NT asks North to bid 3♣; a direct three of a suit is forcing; double is penalty-oriented.

Contesting over a Stayman or transfer response to 1NT

A double by fourth hand shows strength in the suit of the artificial call; in principle with the values for a simple overcall.

A bid in the true suit shown by a transfer is equivalent to a takeout double of that suit and may be no stronger than a minimum double of a suit opening.

The pass of a transfer, followed by a double on the next round is usually played as a strong balanced hand on which fourth hand would have doubled 1NT:

West	North	East	South
1NT	Pass	2♡	?

(1)	♠ 6	♡ K J 8 2	♢ A K 8 7	♣ Q 10 9 4
(2)	♠ 10 7 4	♡ A Q 8	♢ K Q 3 2	♣ A J 10

With (1) or a type close to it you bid 2♠. With (2) you pass and double next time if 2♠ from West comes round to you.

West	North	East	South
1♢	1♠	Dble	2♠
?			

In such auctions it is sensible for opener to bid to the three level only with 16 points or better. This enables responder to judge whether game is likely. With less, it is safe to pass opposite a competent partner who will not let the bidding die out at the two level when the opponents have a trump fit.

Quiz on the highly competitive auction

(1)	West	North	East	South
		1♢	1♠	?

	♠ 10 2	♡ Q 8 7 4	♢ J 7 3	♣ A J 7 2

(2)	West	North	East	South
				1♠
	2♣	Pass	Pass	?

	♠ K 8 7 6 4	♡ A 8 3	♢ K Q 2	♣ 5 2

(3)

West	North	East	South
		Pass	1♢
1♡	Dble	2♡	?

♠ Q 9 7 3   ♡ 8   ♢ K Q 10 7 5   ♣ A K J

(4)

West	North	East	South
1♠	2♢	2♠	?

♠ 10 2   ♡ A K 7 3   ♢ J 5   ♣ J 9 8 6 3

(5)

West	North	East	South
	1♢	Pass	1♡
1♠	Dble	2♠	?

♠ 8 7 4   ♡ A Q 8 5 3   ♢ K 9 8   ♣ K 7

(6)

West	North	East	South
	1♡	1♠	2♡
2♠	Pass	Pass	?

♠ A 2   ♡ Q J 8   ♢ 9 7 5 3   ♣ J 10 8 4

(7)

West	North	East	South
	1♡	2♢	2♡
3♢	Dble	Pass	?

♠ Q 7   ♡ Q J 3 2   ♢ 9 8 4   ♣ K 7 3 2

(8)

West	North	East	South
	1NT	3♣	3♡
4♣	Pass	Pass	?

North–South vulnerable.

♠ K Q 7   ♡ K 8 7 5 3   ♢ A 10 4   ♣ 9 2

(1) Double. This is a negative double showing 4+ hearts and support for at least one minor suit.

(2) Double. Playing the negative double, you are expected to reopen (not necessarily with a double) in this sequence even on a minimum hand, as your partner may have been prevented from making a normal penalty double.

(3) 3♠. In general, when introducing a suit that your partner has indicated via a negative double, you should bid as though he had responded in the suit at minimum level.

(4) Double. This is a competitive double: 'I am strong enough to contest the auction but I have no suitable natural call.' With this hand you are willing to play in 3◇ if partner has no secondary heart or club suit.

(5) 4♡. North's double is a support double, denoting precisely three hearts. Your hand now assumes game-going stature and you must not bid 3♡, which might be passed out.

(6) Double. This again is competitive: you do not want to sell out to 2♠, but there may be a better spot than 3♡.

(7) 4♡. North has made a game-try double, asking you to bid 4♡ if your single raise was sound. It was, and in addition you have no wasted values in the enemy suit.

(8) Double. Your bid of 3♡ was game-forcing, whether playing Lebensohl or not. Therefore North's pass is also forcing: he wants you to choose between a double and a bid of 4♡. At this vulnerability you would normally prefer the game contract, but here your heart suit is moderate and it is evident that North's trump support cannot be overwhelmingly strong.

Chapter 12

THE BIDDING AT PAIRS

Competing for the part-score – The uncontested auction – Sacrifices – The double of a freely bid game – Competing against a 1NT opening – The mechanics of duplicate

Duplicate is by far the most popular form of tournament bridge. It is exciting and totally absorbing, and its appeal is enhanced by the fact that the scope for *post facto* discussion is rivalled in no other game. It is perhaps not the ideal recreation for those whose top priority is inner peace.

To survive at all the player must grasp that he and his partner are not trying to amass as many points as possible but to beat, on each separate deal, the pairs that hold the same cards at other tables.

This requires that in a contested auction one should often bid more competitively – sometimes, much more – than in a team event or rubber bridge.

A partnership needs to have a much closer understanding of the meaning of bidding sequences than is practicable at rubber bridge, but it is by no means essential to employ a great array of add-on conventions. Many partnerships do, of course, but one suspects that this is as much from the pleasure it gives as from an unalloyed faith in better results.

A brief account of the mechanics of duplicate appears at the end of this chapter: how it is scored, the procedure, and so on. The unacquainted reader may find it convenient to scan this section first.

COMPETING FOR THE PART-SCORE

When your opponents stop in a low part-score you should always contest unless you are sure they are much stronger than you. Small scores are just as important as big ones. It is almost true to say that, except at unfavourable vulnerability, you should never let opponents play in a low part-score without some attempt to push them to the three level.

This is especially so when opponents find a fit, for then you too are likely to have a fit, and should be willing to take risks to find it. The loss of an occasional 500 or 800 is acceptable if, rather more often, you wind up with +50 instead of −110.

Balancing

It follows that balancing is much more necessary at duplicate than at rubber bridge. When you think opponents have probably stopped in their best part-score, you can be fairly sure that if you pass you will get a poor result. Therefore, in the pass-out seat you should re-open not just on weaker hands but on patterns that may offer no more than a goodish chance of finding a fit and may occasionally come badly unstuck:

West	North	East	South
		1♠	Pass
2♠	Pass	Pass	?

(1)	♠ A 7 3	♡ 8	◇ J 9 7 6 4	♣ K Q 6 2
(2)	♠ 8 2	♡ A 10 9 2	◇ A J 8 6 2	♣ J 4
(3)	♠ A 7 6 3	♡ Q J 6	◇ 8 2	♣ K Q J 8

At rubber bridge many players would pass with each of these at any vulnerability. At duplicate you should be strongly inclined to re-open when not vulnerable. At game all, think it over. At 'red', pass.

Thus, with (1) you might introduce yourself with an unusual 2NT. Hand (2) is suitable for a takeout double, perfectly sound by duplicate standards. If your partner responds in clubs, you remove to 3◇, suggesting this two-suited type. Partner, if in sentient mode, knows you have not the strong one-suiter that the sequence would normally show, as you passed initially.

With (3), few rubber-bridge players would even dream of bidding 3♣, but there are many pairs specialists who would not hesitate to do so, hoping opponents will not have hands suitable for a double and may bid 3♠.

Of course, such bids sometimes cost heavily, but the pairs specialist maintains, correctly, that what matters is not how heavily but how often.

When contesting a part-score you need to have a fair chance of conceding no more than 100: you will then beat pairs who have a part-score made against them. It follows that when you can make a part-score and opponents are doing the pushing, you should be reluctant to accept 100: you should either bid one more, or double if you think you may get 200 or 300. Here, with neither side vulnerable, you face a typical decision:

West	North	East	South
			1NT
2♡	2♠	3♡	?

♠ A Q 9   ♡ J 10 2   ♢ K J 7 6 2   ♣ Q 7

North did not double 2♡ and you have a poor hand defensively, so you should not expect 3♡ to be more than one down, if that. You should also reckon that 2♠ would probably have been made, as you have a rather suitable hand. Therefore you must now bid 3♠, even though you cannot be sure of making it. To let opponents play in 3♡ undoubled is sure to be bad, while to double and take 100 would also be bad if other pairs were scoring 110 or 140.

Many players have the wrong idea about when to double. When the hand belongs clearly to opponents and you have succeeded in pushing them one level higher than they wanted to go, you should not double. If the contract goes down undoubled, you will get a good result. If it is made you may hope for an average. To double invites a zero when the contract is made and gains little when it fails.

THE UNCONTESTED AUCTION

In theory, when the hand belongs to your side and opponents allow you a clear run, you want to play in the highest-valued odds-on contract; an elusive concept, which some examples may clarify.

The part-score zone

On part-score hands some pairs will usually be too high, in which case any plus score will bring in at least some match points. A safe part-score is therefore preferred to an odds-against game. But when there is a choice of fairly safe part-scores you go for the higher-valued: an odds-on 110 or 140 is preferred to a guaranteed 90 or 120. There are, however, a number of ifs and buts. Your partner opens 1NT and you hold:

$$\spadesuit \text{K 9 8 7} \qquad \heartsuit \text{A 10 9 6} \qquad \diamondsuit \text{8 5 4} \qquad \clubsuit \text{6 2}$$

At rubber bridge this would be an automatic pass. At duplicate it is a fair gamble to bid 2♣: mathematically, you have better than an even chance of finding partner with a major suit, and if you land in a 4–3 fit a poor score is not inevitable.

The next sequence is one where you would select the safer part-score:

Opener	Responder
1♣	1NT
?	

$$\spadesuit \text{K Q 2} \qquad \heartsuit \text{Q 7} \qquad \diamondsuit \text{K 6} \qquad \clubsuit \text{Q J 10 8 6 2}$$

At all forms of scoring it is better to rebid 2♣ than to pass 1NT, as the club suit may not be readily brought in.

In the next sequence, too, you bid the same way at any form of scoring:

Opener	*Responder*
1♡	1♠
?	

♠ A 5   ♡ A Q 10 9 4   ◇ 9 4   ♣ A 9 8 6

To bid 2♡ merely because you are playing duplicate would be contrary to the partnership principle. Opener should show his 5–4 shape by bidding 2♣: responder is well aware that hearts score higher than clubs and will take appropriate action.

Game contracts

The arithmetic of rubber bridge says that you want to be in game when it is no worse than slight odds against. At duplicate the size of the game bonus is unimportant, so you need to have at least an even chance of success. Imagine that you are the only pair to reach game: you cannot gain in terms of match points unless you make it more often than not.

Still more is this true on hands where some pairs may be in the wrong strain:

♠ A 9 3   ♡ J 8 5 3 2   ◇ J 4   ♣ A K 6

After 1♡–3♡ you are faced with a close decision. At rubber bridge you would perhaps press on: the weak 5-card suit has received hormone treatment. At duplicate a game at even slight odds against is not attractive so you should pass, hoping that ten tricks cannot be made. Nor is it certain that every pair will have found the heart fit. Some players may open 1NT on your hand, and as you can be almost certain of beating pairs who play in a notrump partial, this is an additional reason for passing.

Invitational bids are also made cautiously. In general, when a forward move of any kind is likely to jeopardise a safe part-score, you should pass. When your partner opens with 1NT, do not raise to 2NT unless there is a solid chance of game. To play in 2NT is to incur extra risk for no extra reward.

When the values for game are clearly present there may be a choice between 3NT and game in a major. With a known 4–4 fit, many good players make it a rule always to select the trump contract, holding that this will usually produce an extra trick and that the exceptions are hard to distinguish. Your partner opens 1NT and you hold:

♠ K 6 3 2   ♡ J 9 5 3   ◇ A Q J   ♣ K Q

At rubber bridge you might well bid 3NT as this should be safe while a contract of 4♡ or 4♠ might be unluckily defeated by a ruff or a poor trump break. At duplicate, you must bid 2♣: an odds-on 620 or 650 is more attractive than a cast-iron 600 or 630.

However, to say that one should always play in a *known* 4–4 or better fit is not the same as saying one should always deploy the Stayman convention when there is a chance to do so. If no fit is found, defenders will have gained information:

♠ 9 7 6 5   ♡ K 7 4   ◇ K Q 2   ♣ A 8 5

When your partner opens with 1♠, then of course you expect to play in this suit, but when he opens 1NT you do not necessarily bid 2♣. This type is the rare exception where you would raise to 2NT: the 4-card suit is very weak and all the strength is in the 3-card suits. Moreover, game in either strain may be borderline, which means that you should go for the safer contract.

The player who bids game in a minor is almost a subject for a Bateman cartoon: you don't want to play in 5♣ or 5◇ unless you know there will be an unstopped suit at notrumps. It follows that when you know there will be a play for 3NT you do not go beyond it in a minor suit unless willing to be virtually committed to a slam.

The slam zone

If all competitors in a pairs contest were to bid perfectly, the criterion for slam would be the same as for game: 50% or better. In real life some pairs may reach the wrong slam and some may not reach slam at all. Therefore a slam should be reached only when it is at least slightly odds-on.

This applies even more to grand slams. Suppose that you can get 60 to 70% by bidding an icy small slam. To bid seven will probably give you 90% if you make it and 10% if you don't. This is not a good buy. In particular, when the only makeable slam is in a minor suit you should seldom go beyond six, as some pairs will stop in 3NT.

However, when you are sure that the field will be in a small slam it is reasonable, in theory at any rate, to bid a grand slam that depends on no more than, say, a 3–2 break, or a finesse with extra chances. But this assumes that all other pairs will be in six at least, and such an assumption is rarely justified.

SACRIFICES

A save at duplicate is a big decision. Suppose that you hope to go down 300 against 420, and it turns out to be 500. At rubber bridge this is neither here nor there. At duplicate it is a cause for weeping and wailing and gnashing of teeth.

Never save unless you feel sure that a game will be bid at most tables. Suppose that you are unlucky enough to be the only pair against whom an 80% game is bid: to save at a cost of 300 will guarantee you a zero! The only way you can score is by taking the 20% chance of beating the contract.

Still more is this true of saves against slams. Unless icy these are seldom bid at every table, so if a fairly decent slam is bid against you, you are headed for a poor score. Making a good save won't help, so you must hope to beat it.

THE DOUBLE OF A FREELY BID GAME

To make frequent small gains in exchange for infrequent big losses is a Good Thing, so one might think that close doubles would be common. If you can make 200 instead of 100 fairly often, you can laugh at an occasional 790.

However, a capable declarer will often save a trick when doubled, going one down instead of two. That means you have taken a risk and gained nothing. Moreover, if you can beat a game by two tricks you can expect to score fairly well without doubling, for now it will be the kind of game that some pairs stay out of. However, when a double gives declarer no advantage in the play, the odds are certainly more favourable at duplicate.

A different situation is when both sides are bidding freely for game and the question is whether to double or bid one more. At rubber bridge the solution is simple: because of the arithmetic you nearly always bid one more. At duplicate you should not cop out so easily, but should attempt to assess the chances. If you think the odds are against opponents making 4♠ and also against your making 5♡, you must double 4♠.

COMPETING AGAINST A 1NT OPENING

A duplicate partnership should have a conventional means of finding a fit over an enemy 1NT. Some of the more popular methods are described in the previous chapter. One reason why they are more necessary at duplicate is that while at rubber bridge a double may produce a nourishing penalty, at duplicate an occasional +500 does not compensate for a string of +100s – not to mention minus 180s – when your side could have made 110 or 140.

On semi-balanced hands the best strategy is not to double but to go for your own best contract, using one of the conventional overcalls. If you find a fit you are likely to score very well, as you will profit from knowing how the cards lie.

A double does not always work out, even when the contract can in theory be beaten. It is harder for defenders to cash all possible tricks in a low contract than in a high one.

THE MECHANICS OF DUPLICATE

The cards are not played into the centre of the table: each card is placed face down on the player's side of the table. When the hand is over the cards are put into a flat container called a duplicate board, permanently marked to show vulnerability and dealer.

The board is passed in turn to each other table, where each North player takes the cards that were held by North at the first table. The other three players do similarly. When the hand has been played at all tables it is possible to compare scores gained by pairs who held the same cards under the same conditions.

Each hand is a separate event: there is no carrying forward of part-scores or games. There is a 50-point bonus for bidding and making a part-score; 300 for bidding and making a non-vulnerable game; 500 for a vulnerable game. There are the normal penalties for undertricks. The score thus reckoned is converted to match points.

Match points

Suppose there are seven competing tables. The North–South pair with the highest score on a board receives 6 match points, one fewer than the number of competing tables. The pair with the second-best score receives 5 match points, and so on, the bottom pair receiving none. The East–West score is the complement of the North–South score: thus if the North–South pair score 2, the East–West pair score 4. When two or more pairs have the same score the points are shared.

It follows that even if the best score in the room is no more than, say, 140, the pair that gains this score (called a 'top') is rewarded with as many match points as if it had bid and made a grand slam not made by any other pair.

The fact that each board carries the same number of points, with part-score hands enjoying the same importance as slam hands, means that bidding and play are extremely keen, each pair striving for the slightest advantage.

In Britain and some other countries it is customary to double the match points as this avoids fractions, no matter how many pairs tie with the same score. The complete score sheet for a particular board might look therefore like this:

Pair No.		Contract	N–S Score	Match-points	
N–S	E–W			N–S	E–W
1 vs. 1		3NT by N	+430	6	6
2 vs. 3		3NT by S	+430	6	6
3 vs. 5		4H by N	+420	2	10
4 vs. 7		4CX by E	+500	12	0
5 vs. 2		3NT by S	+430	6	6
6 vs. 4		4S by S	+450	10	2
7 vs. 6		3NT by S	+400	0	12

Seven is a convenient number of tables for a small duplicate, but there may be hundreds, and in contests held simultaneously at different centres, perhaps thousands.

Quiz on bidding at pairs

1.

West	North	East	South
		Pass	1♣
Pass	3♣	Pass	?

Neither side vulnerable.

♠ Q 7   ♡ A J 10   ◇ A Q J   ♣ K Q 9 8 6

2.

West	North	East	South
1♡	1♠	3♡	Pass
4♡	Pass	Pass	?

East–West vulnerable.

♠ Q 4 3 2   ♡ 7 2   ◇ 9 8 4   ♣ Q J 10 8

3.

West	North	East	South
		Pass	1NT
Pass	2♣	Pass	2♡
Pass	2NT	Pass	?

Neither side vulnerable.

♠ J 10 8 2   ♡ K 8 7 3   ◇ K J 9   ♣ A Q

4.	West	North	East	South
				1♠
	2♣	2♠	3♣	3♠
	4♣	Pass	Pass	?

Both vulnerable.

♠ A K 8 7 4   ♡ K 10 2   ◇ 5 3   ♣ K J 6

1. 3NT. At rubber bridge you might set out to cue-bid your aces. (But you would have to take the bidding beyond 3NT, as new suits at the three level in this kind of sequence are played as showing stoppers, not as cue bids.) You would hope to reach a slam if partner had a suitable hand and would expect to be safe for eleven tricks if he had not.

At duplicate you cannot afford the risk of landing in 5♣, so it will be better to settle for a contract where you expect to make 430 or 460.

2. 4♠. Your chances of beating 4♡ seem dismal, and since there is nothing unusual about the bidding, this may well be the room contract. These are the prime conditions for a sacrifice and as you expect your partner to make seven tricks you should take the save.

3. 4♠. Partner's 2♣ guarantees a 4-card major. Since you have a maximum 1NT, you should accept the game invitation, but the choice between 4♠ and 3NT is not overwhelmingly clear, as your spade holding is moderate and your doubleton a strong one. Nevertheless, the odds favour making an extra trick in the 4–4 fit. You must of course bid 4♠, not 3♠, which is the call you would make with a minimum opening on which you wanted to stop in a part-score.

4. Double. This is a typical match-point double. South assumes that he would probably have made 3♠, but that he is unlikely to make 4♠. East–West will not push to the four level at all tables, so a number of North–South pairs will be making 140. The only way to beat them is to collect 200 against 4♣ doubled. If 4♣ is made, you were headed for a bad score anyway.

PART TWO

THE PLAY

Chapter 13

THE OPENING LEAD

The choice of suit against notrumps – The choice of suit against trump contracts – The choice of card – The lead against slam – Special lead conventions – Doubles of slams ('Lightner') and notrumps

It is a curious thing: even players who are keener than a barn rat in most areas of the game can be surprisingly lackadaisical in the matter of the opening lead. Perhaps they take the view that as there is sometimes little to go on, it does not reward concentrated thought.

They are right that the choice of lead is sometimes not much more than an informed guess but wrong if they conclude that it therefore does not warrant the most careful attention. The opening lead is of such overwhelming importance that any small gain in accuracy is worth having.

What, then, should be the basic approach? Sometimes a particular suit has to be led regardless of the cards held because strategy demands it. Sometimes the cards held in a suit make the lead so attractive that this factor alone is decisive. But usually there is a trade-off between the two.

It goes without saying that one leads partner's suit if there is nothing against it and one avoids a suit bid by opponents unless there is some reason for it. Beyond that, you have to start thinking.

THE CHOICE OF SUIT AGAINST NOTRUMPS

A notrump contract, when it is not open and shut, will usually depend on whether the defenders can establish their suit before the declarer can establish his. That is why we are told, 'Lead your longest and strongest suit.' It is good advice, although what it really means is, 'Lead the partnership's longest and strongest suit.'

There are a number of ifs and buts: a lead from a strong 4-card sequence such as Q–J–10–8 is usually preferred to fourth-best from a longer but weaker suit such as J–x–x–x–x. But when the choice lies between two 4-card suits, preference does not always go to the stronger suit:

♠ 10 8 7 4   ♡ 8 6 5   ♢ K 3   ♣ A J 4 2

There is a better chance to establish clubs quickly than spades, but a club lead is more likely to give away a trick. Suppose that the bidding goes 1NT–2NT–3NT: this contract may be borderline so you should play for safety and lead a spade, which is less likely to give a trick away, especially as Stayman has not been used.

Now suppose that in a similar sequence you hold a weak suit and a strong suit, each of 5-card length. This time you lead the strong suit. There is still the risk of giving away a trick but you hope to establish four tricks in return, not three.

There are many 4-card holdings from which one is not eager to lead, such as A–Q–x–x, K–J–x–x and K–Q–x–x. Again, with a fifth card the lead is attractive.

A–K–x–x in an unbid suit is a case by itself: you start with a top card, inspect the dummy and decide then whether to continue with a low card.

Always take note of how assured the opponents' bidding has been. After a fortissimo 1NT–3NT you have to lead from this hand:

♠ 10 9 6   ♡ J 5   ♢ 8 5 2   ♣ K 7 6 5 2

The club holding is empty and you have no side entry; partner will need to have good clubs to get the suit going. Still, against this confident sequence an attacking lead may be the only chance; so, lead a club.

Now suppose that the bidding is 1NT–2NT–Pass. The contract sounds shaky, so you make the relatively safe and possibly constructive lead of the ♠10.

Leading the opponents' suit

When it is clear that all suits are guarded you may have to lead a suit the opponents have bid. A lead from small cards in dummy's second suit often does no harm. But suppose that you have to lead from a non-solid honour combination: in that case you may be better off leading declarer's suit than leading dummy's. If you lead the 10 from K–10–9–8, finding declarer with A–J–x–x and dummy with Q–x, you have not lost a trick, only a tempo. When dummy has A–J–x–x and declarer Q–x, you lose a trick as well.

However, one does not often lead declarer's suit from non-solid holdings unless partner is expected to have entries and to be able to return the suit from his side.

Diagnosing partner's length

When you decide to play for partner's hand, the bidding may indicate which suit he is more likely to have. You are South:

West	North	East	South
	Pass	1◇	Pass
1♡	Pass	1NT	Pass
3NT	Pass	Pass	Pass

♠ 8 7   ♡ Q 10 5 3   ◇ K J 3 2   ♣ J 8 2

Lead the ♠8. North's failure to overcall in spades gives some credence to a club lead, but a more powerful indicator is that East is unlikely to have concealed a spade suit over 1♡. It is possible that West is 4–4 in the majors, but even then North will have at least four spades.

When leading from short suits with no clue to partner's length, strong preference is given to a sequence of spot cards such as 9–8–6.

The lead against a 3NT opening based on a long minor is a special case. You want to find a wide open suit before surrendering the lead, so you should lay down an ace if you have one. After 3NT on your right you hold:

♠ J 10 2   ♡ Q J 10 8 7   ◇ 7   ♣ A 6 3 2

Lead the ♣A to buy a look at dummy. If hearts or spades is your suit there may be time to switch. The lead of an ace will more often beat the contract than give away a vital trick.

THE CHOICE OF SUIT AGAINST TRUMP CONTRACTS

The best approach now is to consider whether a specific strategy is needed: should you play to cut down ruffs, to shorten declarer, or what? When no particular plan suggests itself, you look for a lead that gives nothing away and leaves declarer to find his own tricks.

When you have no strong combination such as K–Q–J, prefer a safe lead from low cards to an attacking lead from an unsupported high card, especially when the contract sounds borderline.

The most likely case for an attacking lead is where opponents have shown strength in a side suit and there is no reason to think this suit is breaking badly. You must then try to get at your high-card tricks before the side suit is established and losers discarded.

West	North	East	South
	Pass	1♠	Pass
2◇	Pass	3◇	Pass
3♠	Pass	4♠	All pass

♠ 8 7 6   ♡ A 7 5 4   ◇ 9 3 2   ♣ K J 9

Neither a heart nor a club comes high on the list of preferred leads, but South must lead one or the other as it is clear that declarer's suits are breaking favourably. The ♣9 is best, for unless North has the ace of this suit there is probably no way to take four tricks.

When opponents land in a trump contract after an exploratory sequence, the fact that they have not settled in notrumps suggests that there is a gap in at least one suit. It may then be right to lead from holdings such as J–x–x, K–x–x, K–J–x or even A–Q–x. The ace from A–Q–J–x can be an excellent attacking lead when the king is expected to be in dummy.

The ruffing game

A singleton or doubleton in an unbid suit is a fine lead: it may gain a ruff and is relatively safe. But don't play for a ruff when there is little chance that partner will have enough strength to obtain the lead. And beware the singleton lead in declarer's second suit: it may expose partner's holding and allow declarer to overcome a bad break. At the same time, watch out for the case where partner, not you, may have ruffing capability:

West	North	East	South
1♣	Pass	1♠	Pass
2♠	Pass	3♣	Pass
4♠	Pass	Pass	Pass

♠ A 7   ♡ J 10 4   ◇ A 8 6 2   ♣ 9 7 5 3

As South you can see that a lead of opponents' side suit will give away no trick and may lead to two ruffs if North has a singleton club and three trumps.

Forcing leads

A forcing defence, aimed at shortening declarer's trumps, should be considered by a defender who has trump length or can place his partner with length:

West	North	East	South
	Pass	1♠	Pass
2◇	Pass	2NT	Pass
3♠	Pass	4♠	All pass

♠ 9 7 5 2   ♡ K J 8 5 3   ◇ 7 4   ♣ A 5

The chances are that East has five trumps and dummy three. If declarer can be forced to ruff, South's four trumps will be a force to be reckoned with, so he should nail his colours to a heart lead. This lead would still be made if South held a singleton trump, for then North would be expected to have four.

Trump leads

When defenders have all-round strength it is natural to lead trumps with the object of imposing a notrump game on declarer. A trump is often a good lead when opponents are doubled for penalties after either defender has bid notrumps.

A trump lead is also considered when the bidding suggests that declarer intends to crossruff or that he has a two-suiter and will attempt to set up the second suit by ruffing:

West	North	East	South
		1♡	Pass
1♠	Pass	2♢	Pass
2NT	Pass	3♢	Pass
3♡	Pass	4♡	All pass

South holds:

(1)	♠ Q 7 4	♡ 6 2	◇ K J 9 5	♣ Q J 8 3
(2)	♠ Q 7 4 2	♡ 6 2	◇ K 5	♣ Q J 8 5 3

Some players are more inclined to lead a trump with (1), where there is a strong holding in the side suit, than with (2), but it should be the other way round. With (1), if East tries to ruff diamonds in dummy, North may be able to overruff. With (2), North will not be short in diamonds and dummy will be able to ruff with impunity.

There is one sequence where the only acceptable excuse for not leading a trump is that you haven't one. That is when a takeout double at the one level is passed for penalties.

THE CHOICE OF CARD

When the suit is settled, the card led is governed by convention: that is to say, you lead a particular card because it is customary to lead that card from that holding. If you lead anything else your partner may be put right out of his stride. The conventional leads are these:

(1) From a suit headed by three high cards in sequence, and from a broken sequence headed by two honours, lead the top card against both a suit contract and notrumps:

Lead the highest from all these:

K Q J x	Q J 10 x x	J 10 9 x x	10 9 8 x
K Q 10 x	Q J 9 x x	J 10 8 x	10 9 7 x

(2) From a suit headed by two high cards in sequence: against notrumps, lead fourth-best. Against a trump contract, think it over:

K Q x x	Q J x x	J 10 x x	10 9 x x

Against notrumps, in each case the fourth-best card gives the better chance of establishing long cards without a blockage.

Against a trump contract, where the object is to set up immediate winners, the top card is always led from K–Q, but other cases are not straightforward.

From Q–J–x–x the queen will obviously be best if partner has the ace over dummy's king. But it may cost a trick if he has a bare honour, and it may block the suit if he has a doubleton honour; so, if there is any likelihood that partner may be short in the suit, the fourth-best should be led.

The low lead is also likely to work better when dummy is not expected to have a high honour. For similar reasons most players also lead low from J–10–x–x and 10–9–x–x.

(3) From an interior sequence lead the top interior card against both a suit contract and notrumps:

K J 10 x	Q 10 9 x	K 10 9 x

Against a suit contract this does not apply to such holdings as A–Q–J–x and A–10–9–x. It is rare to underlead an ace at the first trick except as a deceptive measure.

(4) From a suit containing only one honour or honours not in sequence, lead fourth-best.

There are some exceptions, featuring the ace. Even against a notrump contract, when a sure side entry is held the ace may be better from A–Q–10–x–x: on seeing the dummy you may elect to continue with the queen, to pin a doubleton jack in either hand.

(5) From four or more small cards, it is usual to lead fourth best against notrumps in order to give partner a count. Some good players, however, prefer to lead the highest or second highest, to warn partner that no high card is held. Whatever your practice, you would normally do the same against a suit contract also, unless you have a sequence such as 9–8–7–x or 8–7–6–x, when most players would lead second highest.

(6) From three small cards, such as 7–5–4, the top card used to be standard: this shows that no honour is held and no more than three cards. (Some pairs lead the lowest of three small cards when partner has bid the suit and the leader has not supported.) On the second round the middle card is played, whether leading or following suit.

However, the top-of-nothing lead has slumped in popularity. To lead, say, the 9 from 9–3–2 may waste a significant card and moreover, one's partner may not know, even after a second round, whether the lead was from two cards or three.

It has therefore become increasingly common to play MUD (Middle, Up, Down). The opening lead from three spot cards is the middle one. On the next round, whether leading or following suit, you intend to play the top card unless to do so may cost a trick: from 9–6–2, for example, you lead the 6 but are not committed to squandering the 9 on the next round.

One advantage is that when your partner can recognise the card led as the highest outstanding spot card, he will know that it is a doubleton or singleton.

(7) From a doubleton, lead the top card.

(8) Finally, when leading a trump, the lowest is usually led, even from cards in sequence. To lead the 9 from 9–8–2 cannot gain and once in a while may allow declarer an extra entry to dummy by finessing against the 8 on the second round.

Similarly, the 8 should be led from J–10–8: the jack may be catastrophic if dummy has Q–9–x–x and partner the singleton king.

The lead from A–K and low cards

To lead the king equally from A–K–x and from K–Q–x, which for long was the traditional practice, is not efficient, especially when partner holds J–x–x and does not know whether to encourage. Most players now lead the ace from combinations headed by A–K: the king is then always from K–Q.

An ace lead may therefore be unsupported or from A–K–x, but uncertainty is rare. Unsupported aces are not often led, except in recognisable situations – and even then the king may be visible.

At notrumps, with A–K–x–x–x or longer, the normal lead is fourth-best. With A–K–x–x, as has been noted earlier, you usually start with a top card.

Once in a while, against a trump contract, you may hold a singleton in one suit and A–K–x in another. There is now a clever trick: first you lead the king, not the ace. When it holds your partner knows you have broken the convention – and that your next lead is going to be a singleton!

Avoiding a blockage

Suppose that you as South are on lead after this sequence:

West	North	East	South
	Pass	1NT	Pass
2♣	Pass	2♡	Pass
3NT	Pass	Pass	Pass

♠ J 5 2   ♡ Q J 10 4 3   ◇ A 7 3   ♣ K 2

Despite the bidding a heart lead is best but you must lead a low card. If you lead the queen and partner has K–x or 9–x, the suit will be blocked.

Sometimes there is a different way to overcome a blockage:

♠ A 2   ♡ K J 6   ◇ Q 10 9 8 5 3   ♣ A 5

You open 1◇, your partner passes, and the opponents bid briskly to 3NT. Realistically, the only useful card your partner can have is the ◇J: therefore you should lead the queen, lest it be singleton and declarer duck. This lead will also earn your partner's admiration if the singleton jack is in dummy. In the same way you might also lead high from K–J–10–9–x.

THE LEAD AGAINST SLAM

Against a grand slam, safety is the sole consideration: you do not try to establish a trick, for if you ever get in to cash it, you will already have beaten the contract.

At a small slam it is different. Against sound bidders it is often right to make an attacking lead, especially when the bidding gives evidence of a strong side suit. The reasoning is that declarer may have to force out a high card to make his slam, and you have got to be able to cash the setting trick at that point.

West	North	East	South
1♣	Pass	1♠	Pass
3♣	Pass	3♠	Pass
4♠	Pass	4NT	Pass
5♡	Pass	5NT	Pass
6◇	Pass	6♠	All pass

♠ Q 5 4   ♡ J 10 6 4 3   ◇ Q 6 2   ♣ 10 4

The bidding has been dynamic and you cannot hope to beat the contract unless the ♠Q is a trick and you can cash a winner when in with it. The best attacking lead is a diamond, as this will establish a trick if North has the king, whereas a heart may not.

The lead from a queen is usually less risky than one from a king, since a trick given away will less often be a vital one.

Whether to lead the ace of an unbid suit is a much-debated question. Sometimes it will set up declarer's K–x, but if declarer has plenty of tricks this may not matter. Perhaps you can take two tricks in this suit quickly: against bashers this is possible, against scientists, unlikely. When in doubt it is probably better to lead the ace, and clearly this should be done when you think that you have a sure trump trick.

A passive lead is likely to be preferred against a notrump slam when no suit has been bid strongly or when the bidding suggests lack of fit.

SPECIAL LEAD CONVENTIONS

Standard leads are good trick-builders but do not always convey needed information. The following conventions are more efficient in that respect.

Rusinow and Roman Leads

From touching honours the second highest is led: the king from A–K, the queen from K–Q, and so on down to the 9 from 10–9.

From three or more honours in sequence, the second honour is led and is followed usually by the third.

The main advantage is that when an ace is led it is known to be unsupported. A further gain is that when the touching honours are doubleton, such as Q–J bare, the initial lead can be the top card: then the lower card on the next round discloses that no more are held.

Rusinow leads apply only against suit contracts, only at the first trick, and only in a suit not bid by partner. Roman leads extend them to notrump contracts, with a useful addition: against notrumps only, the 10 is always a 'strong' card, from an interior sequence. Thus the 10 is led from K–J–10 or K–10–9, but the jack is led from J–10–9–x–x. Playing standard, third hand cannot tell whether the 10 is from 10–9–8–x or from a stronger holding such as Q–10–9–x. When Roman leads are in use, the lead from 10–9–8–x is the 9.

Journalist leads

These provide a comprehensive scheme for all opening leads. Against notrumps the lead from a long suit is not fourth best but 'attitude': the lowest if the leader wants the suit returned, a high spot card from a weak suit, such as the 6 from 9–6–5–3–2. Honour leads are Roman except that the king is led equally from A–K–x and K–Q–x, and the queen equally from Q–J–x and K–Q–10–9. Against a trump contract, honour leads are Rusinow.

When leading low, the third highest is led from an even number of cards, the lowest from an odd number. When no honour is held a high spot card is led.

DOUBLES OF SLAMS ('LIGHTNER') AND NOTRUMPS

The Lightner double, a brainwave of Theodore Lightner, has survived from the earliest days of contract. Its logic rests on two propositions: first, a slam is quite often made in comfort after a normal lead when it could have been beaten by an unusual lead. This is what you might expect, since if opponents thought a normal lead would beat the slam, they would not bid it.

Secondly, there is not much point to doubling a voluntarily bid slam for penalty, as it will rarely go down more than one trick. Therefore a double by the defender not on lead is conventional, asking for an unusual lead.

The player on lead, whose partner has doubled, should decide what would be a normal lead – and then avoid it. Whenever the bidding admits, the leader should assume that his partner is void of a suit and can ruff. Usually it will be clear which suit he is void of. When it is not he should lead dummy's first-bid suit. A suit bid by the defending side is never 'unusual', nor is a trump.

Here you are South and your partner will be on lead:

West	North	East	South
1♡	Pass	3♢	3♠
4♢	Pass	4♡	Pass
4NT	Pass	5♡	Pass
6♡	Pass	Pass	?

♠ Q J 8 7 6 4 2   ♡ 7 3   ♢ –   ♣ A 8 3 2

To beat the contract you will need an opening ruff. North's normal lead would be a spade, so you double to warn against this: from the bidding and his own hand, he may be able to deduce that a diamond is desired. The double would be just as sound without the ♣A, for now North is likely to have a trick; otherwise the opponents would have been looking for a grand slam.

When you want your partner to make his normal lead you do not double, even when you expect to beat the contract, as a double will deflect him. Of course, when you are confident of beating a slam on any lead, you double regardless.

The double of 3NT

A double of 3NT will often have lead-directing overtones, but these depend on the bidding. The clearest case is when the defending side has bid a suit: a double then asks for that suit.

When the defenders have bid different suits, a double asks not for the doubler's suit but for his partner's:

West	North	East	South
			1♣
1♢	1♡	1♠	1NT
Pass	2NT	Pass	3NT
Pass	Pass	Dble	All pass

The double asks for a diamond, not a spade. There is a logical basis for the rule: the player on lead would normally lead his partner's suit rather than his own, so if his partner is content with that, there is no need to double.

When the defenders have not bid, a double asks for dummy's first-bid suit.

West	North	East	South
1♣	Pass	1♡	Pass
1NT	Pass	3NT	Dble

This double asks for a heart lead. However it will sometimes be clear that although the doubler has strength in dummy's suit, he does not want it led. Here South is on lead:

West	North	East	South
1♣	Pass	1♡	Pass
2♣	Pass	2NT	Pass
3NT	Dble	All pass	

North has made a penalty double, based perhaps on opponents' tentative sequence. There is no doubt that he has a club holding, but declarer will have to bring in this suit, so South should not lead it.

When no suit has been bid by any player a double says: 'I have a strong suit and an entry. Try to find my suit.' The opening leader should often lead his shortest major suit, for if the declaring side held a major they might have looked for a fit. But he should avoid a suit that the doubler could have bid if he had it. However, the success rate for the guess-my-suit school is not impressive, and some pairs make it a convention to lead always a spade after such a sequence as 1NT–Pass–3NT–Double.

A double that will produce the right lead can be a fair speculation even when there is no certainty of beating the contract, as it can make a difference of several tricks.

A final thought. A defender often knows, well before the auction is over, that he is going to have to make the opening lead. If he has a problem he should do his thinking in advance, so that when the time comes he will be able to lead in normal tempo. It is quite remarkable how much an acute declarer can deduce, especially later in the play, when a defender huddles before leading.

Chapter 14

THE PLAY IN NOTRUMPS

Choices in suit development – Ducking to save entries – The hold-up – When not to hold up – The danger hand

How does an efficient declarer arrange his mind so as to contrive, most of the time, to come up with the right flight of thought? For many of us the neural pathways have become so well established that we have probably forgotten the answer to this question.

The tried and tested method is to count the winners readily available and make a plan for creating the additional winners needed for the contract. Next, look for the dangers: do opponents threaten to establish enough tricks to beat the contract? If so, how can they be prevented? We often think we need not do this – but sometimes we are wrong.

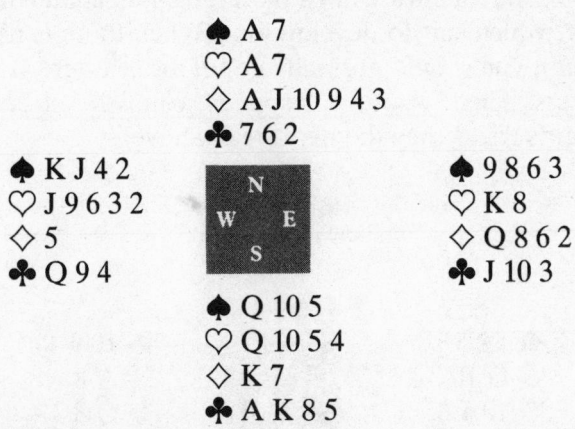

        ♠ A 7
        ♡ A 7
        ◇ A J 10 9 4 3
        ♣ 7 6 2

♠ K J 4 2   ♠ 9 8 6 3
♡ J 9 6 3 2   ♡ K 8
◇ 5   ◇ Q 8 6 2
♣ Q 9 4   ♣ J 10 3

        ♠ Q 10 5
        ♡ Q 10 5 4
        ◇ K 7
        ♣ A K 8 5

    South opens 1NT, North raises to 3NT and West leads the ♡3. 'This lead is most friendly,' South tells himself, and may decide without further thought that it can do no harm to let it run to his hand.

But it can. East wins with the king and is nasty enough to switch to a spade. South tries hard to guess the right card to play but fails. The ace is dislodged and, as the cards lie, South cannot establish diamonds without letting East in for another spade lead, with fatal results.

The methodical declarer counts his winners at the start. There are four top tricks in spades, hearts and clubs. On any lie of the cards, five more can be established in diamonds, so extra tricks in hearts are not needed.

South therefore puts up the ace, leads to the $\diamondsuit$K, and forces out the queen. The worst that can happen is that East gets in and returns a heart. In that case you cover his card. The defenders may make two heart tricks and a diamond, but declarer comes to nine tricks at least.

Even when you are sure that the play to the first trick needs no thought, you should still pause and crank up the grey cells by counting your tricks and the enemy's.

CHOICES IN SUIT DEVELOPMENT

When the defenders are not a threat, the immediate question may be, which suit to develop first. When there is no other indication you should normally go for a suit where you have top losers. Then, whatever happens, you will not be giving opponents tricks they did not already have:

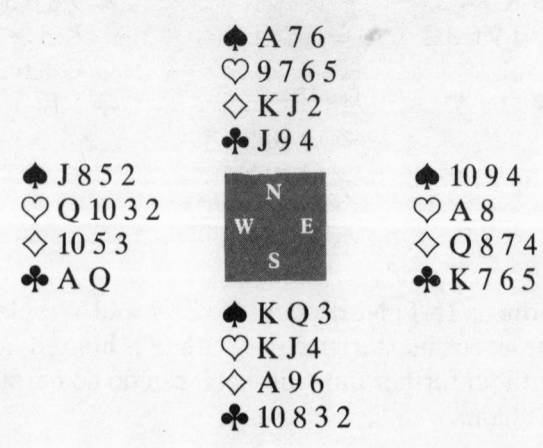

```
                  ♠ A 7 6
                  ♡ 9 7 6 5
                  ◇ K J 2
                  ♣ J 9 4
  ♠ J 8 5 2                      ♠ 10 9 4
  ♡ Q 10 3 2        N           ♡ A 8
  ◇ 10 5 3      W       E       ◇ Q 8 7 4
  ♣ A Q            S            ♣ K 7 6 5
                  ♠ K Q 3
                  ♡ K J 4
                  ◇ A 9 6
                  ♣ 10 8 3 2
```

Your 1NT opening is passed out and West leads the ♠2. There are only five winners, and somewhere along the line you will need to develop at least one trick in diamonds or hearts. However, if you tackle either suit now you may set up tricks for opponents, with no benefit for yourself. Therefore you should play on clubs, where you have top losers. Your chances in the red suits remain, and the defenders may open these suits themselves.

The same idea extends to suits that the defenders themselves could safely attack:

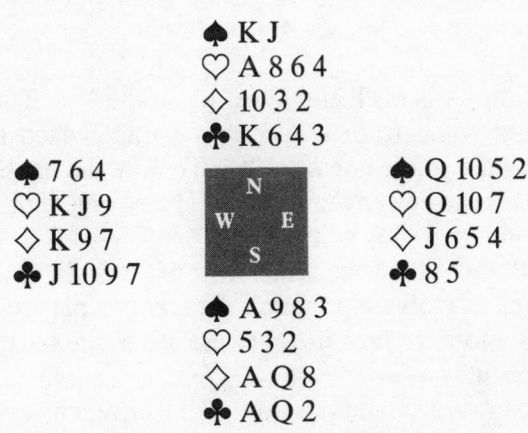

```
                    ♠ K J
                    ♡ A 8 6 4
                    ◇ 10 3 2
                    ♣ K 6 4 3
   ♠ 7 6 4             N          ♠ Q 10 5 2
   ♡ K J 9          W   E         ♡ Q 10 7
   ◇ K 9 7             S          ◇ J 6 5 4
   ♣ J 10 9 7                     ♣ 8 5
                    ♠ A 9 8 3
                    ♡ 5 3 2
                    ◇ A Q 8
                    ♣ A Q 2
```

After 1♠–2♣–2NT–3NT, West leads the ♣J. You have seven winners and there are chances in three suits. Which suit do you try first? It must be right to play hearts, as opponents can do so themselves if it suits them, but they may be unable to lead spades or diamonds without cost.

Combining the chances

To combine the chances in two suits it is often necessary to follow a precise sequence:

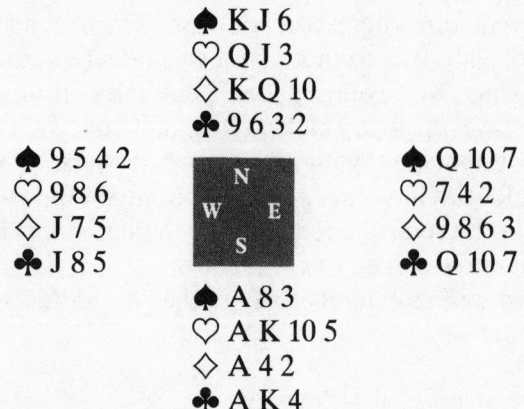

♠ K J 6
♡ Q J 3
◇ K Q 10
♣ 9 6 3 2

♠ 9 5 4 2
♡ 9 8 6
◇ J 7 5
♣ J 8 5

♠ Q 10 7
♡ 7 4 2
◇ 9 8 6 3
♣ Q 10 7

♠ A 8 3
♡ A K 10 5
◇ A 4 2
♣ A K 4

The contract is 6NT and West leads the ♡8. The twelfth trick could come from a 3–3 club break, which is a 36% chance, or the spade finesse, 50%. To take the finesse simply because it is the better chance would be wrong: if the chances can be combined they will be 68%. (36% plus 50% of 64%.)

If South takes the spade finesse and it fails, he cannot then try his luck in clubs. Nor should he start by playing the ace, king and another club: in that case he is set straight away when the suit is 4–2.

The first move should be a low club from each hand. Later, South cashes the ♣A–K, retaining all the chances.

It is also very common to duck for another reason.

DUCKING TO SAVE ENTRIES

When a trick has to be lost in developing a suit, it is usually right to concede it early rather than late:

(1)	*Dummy*	(2)	*Dummy*
	K 7 6 4 2		A Q 5 4 3
	Declarer		*Declarer*
	A 8 5		8 2

With (1), if you play off the ace, king and another, then, even if all goes well you will need an entry to dummy to cash the long cards. It is better to duck the first round, keeping an entry in each hand, or to cash the ace and duck the next.

With (2) you intend to play West for K–x–x. The best chance of running the suit without using an outside entry is to duck the first round completely, then finesse the queen.

When entries are crucial you may even duck at the cost of a trick:

(3)	A K Q 5 3	(4)	A Q J 6 2
J 9 8 4	1 0 6	1 0 5	K 9 7 4
	7 2		8 3

In (3) if dummy had plenty of entries you would play off the top cards and hope to make five tricks, but when you need only four and entries are short you duck the first round.

In (4), suppose that dummy has only one outside entry, but you need only three tricks. If you finesse the queen, East may be unsporting enough to duck, and you will make only one more trick. The way to prevent this is to duck the first round.

When entries are a problem, this will not escape defenders' notice, so declarer must anticipate their moves:

```
                    ♠ K 6
                    ♡ Q 6
                    ◇ K Q 5 4 3
                    ♣ 6 5 4 3

    ♠ 10 8 4 2          N          ♠ Q J 3
    ♡ 10 5 4 3 2    W       E      ♡ K J 9
    ◇ 9 8 6             S          ◇ A J 2
    ♣ 7                            ♣ K 10 9 8

                    ♠ A 9 7 5
                    ♡ A 8 7
                    ◇ 10 7
                    ♣ A Q J 2
```

West	North	East	South
Pass	Pass	1♣	1NT
Pass	3NT	All pass	

Opening lead: ♣7

East puts in the 8 and South wins with the queen. He must bring in the diamonds but even with a 3–3 break there will still be problems, as dummy has only one sure entry, the ♠K.

South foresees that if he plays a diamond to the queen, East will duck and the suit will wither on the vine. He therefore plans to duck the first round: then he can force out the ace and enter dummy in spades. This will not work if West is allowed to win the first diamond, as he will shift to a heart. So South must lead the ♢10, hoping to find East with precisely A–J–x.

We turn to what is sometimes declarer's most urgent task: to stop opponents from establishing enough tricks to set the contract. The supreme tactical weapon is the hold-up.

THE HOLD-UP

The advantage of holding up a stopper until one defender is out of the suit is that this defender will be unable to play the suit when he gets in:

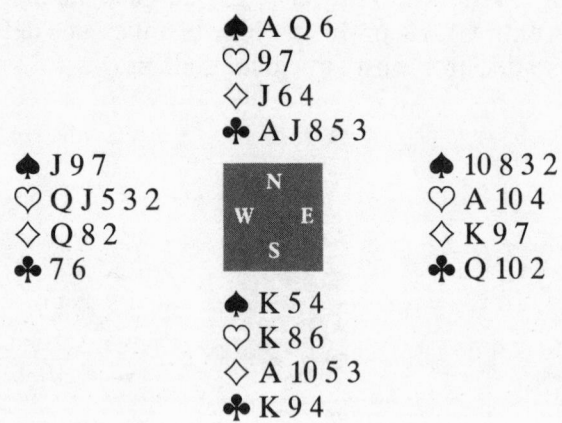

```
              ♠ A Q 6
              ♡ 9 7
              ♢ J 6 4
              ♣ A J 8 5 3
♠ J 9 7                        ♠ 10 8 3 2
♡ Q J 5 3 2      N             ♡ A 10 4
♢ Q 8 2      W     E           ♢ K 9 7
♣ 7 6            S             ♣ Q 10 2
              ♠ K 5 4
              ♡ K 8 6
              ♢ A 10 5 3
              ♣ K 9 4
```

After 1NT–3NT the ♡3 is led and East plays the ace, returning the 10. South holds up the king and on winning the third round attacks clubs. East has a club stopper but the contract is safe because he is out of hearts. If South does not hold up the ♡K he is defeated as East has a heart to lead when he comes in.

The hold-up with two stoppers

It is sometimes good play to hold up with two stoppers, but this must be done on the first round:

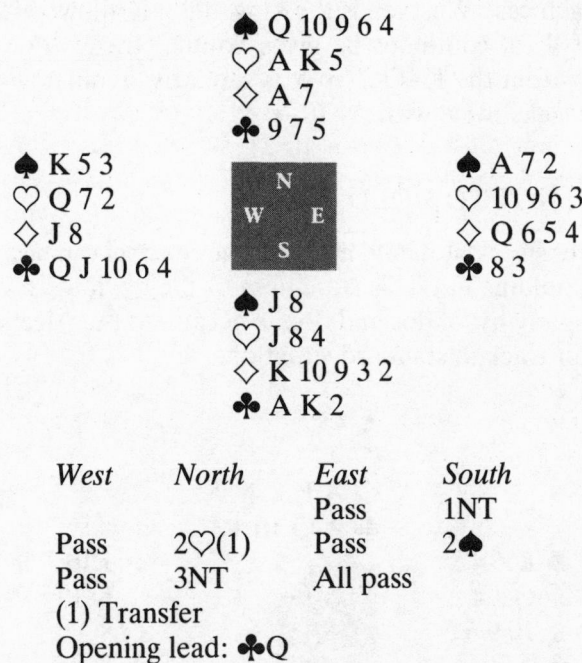

♠ Q 10 9 6 4
♡ A K 5
♢ A 7
♣ 9 7 5

♠ K 5 3
♡ Q 7 2
♢ J 8
♣ Q J 10 6 4

♠ A 7 2
♡ 10 9 6 3
♢ Q 6 5 4
♣ 8 3

♠ J 8
♡ J 8 4
♢ K 10 9 3 2
♣ A K 2

West	North	East	South
		Pass	1NT
Pass	2♡(1)	Pass	2♠
Pass	3NT	All pass	

(1) Transfer

Opening lead: ♣Q

South intends to establish spades, and if clubs are 4–3 he cannot be beaten, but if they are 5–2 he must not allow the suit to be run.

Suppose he wins the first trick: East will win the first round of spades and return a club. It does South no good to hold up now, for the suit will be established while West still has the ♠K.

By ducking the first club South makes sure of the contract unless West has both spade honours. He wins the next club and attacks spades. If East wins, he has no club to return. (If he had, clubs would be 4–3.) If West wins he can force out the remaining club stopper but has no re-entry for the long cards.

A hold-up is especially effective when it forces the defender to switch or give declarer an extra trick:

(1)   743   (2)   A 62
   K Q 10 8   965   K Q 10 8   954
          A J 2   J 73

In each case West leads the king and it is allowed to hold. Now if West continues he gives South a trick. A defender leading from the K–Q–J–x–x is similarly stymied when declarer ducks twice with A–10–x–x.

WHEN NOT TO HOLD UP

Declarer should not hold up when the contract can be assured by not holding up. This statement of the obvious is worth a place in any list of dos and don'ts because it puts declarer on the right track in standard situations:

♠ Q 2
♡ 9 2
◇ A K 7 4
♣ A Q 10 4 3

♠ K 6 4
♡ Q J 4 3
◇ 10 9 6 5
♣ 9 5

♠ J 10 7 5
♡ K 10 8 7
◇ 8 3
♣ K 8 7

♠ A 9 8 3
♡ A 6 5
◇ Q J 2
♣ J 6 2

After 1NT–3NT, West leads the ♡3 and East plays the king. At the table declarer may hold off, simply because this seems normal. East may then compute that three heart tricks and the ♣K will not beat the contract, and he may switch to a low spade. Now, if you duck, West wins and reverts to hearts. If you put on the ace the defenders make three spade tricks when they come in with the ♣K.

From the lead of the 3 South should conclude that hearts are 4–4. If he wins the first trick and attacks clubs, the most he can lose is three hearts and a club.

A situation difficult to assess is where the hold-up will afford the best chance if defenders continue the suit but not if they make the right switch. You just have to weigh things up:

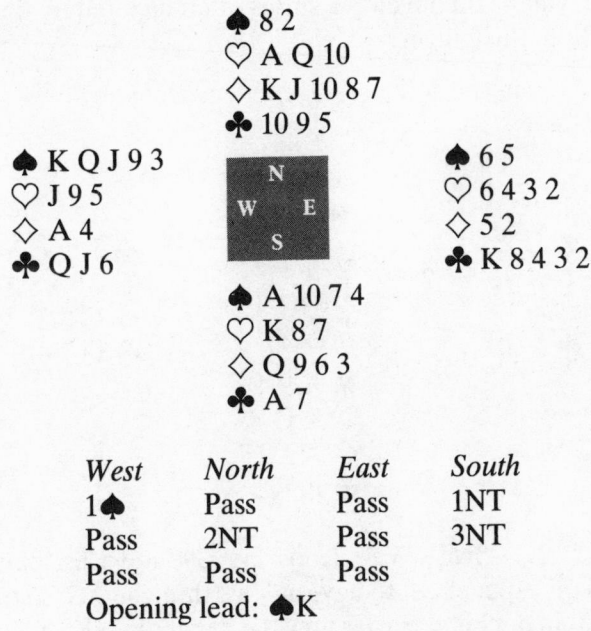

♠ 8 2
♡ A Q 10
◇ K J 10 8 7
♣ 10 9 5

♠ K Q J 9 3
♡ J 9 5
◇ A 4
♣ Q J 6

♠ 6 5
♡ 6 4 3 2
◇ 5 2
♣ K 8 4 3 2

♠ A 10 7 4
♡ K 8 7
◇ Q 9 6 3
♣ A 7

West	North	East	South
1♠	Pass	Pass	1NT
Pass	2NT	Pass	3NT
Pass	Pass	Pass	

Opening lead: ♠K

East contributes the 6, which you place as a doubleton. Suppose that you win the first trick: East, despite his pass, may have the ◇A, and in that case the spade return will mean curtains.

Suppose that you duck. If West leads a second spade you are safe, as you can win and force out the ◇A for nine tricks, with the spades still guarded. But if West switches to a club, curtains again.

From this you conclude that if East has the ◇A you may well go down whether you hold up or not. Therefore you should win the first trick and attack diamonds.

THE DANGER HAND

When one defender will be more dangerous than the other if he gains the lead, his hand is classed as the danger hand. The way in which you develop a suit is often dictated by the need to exclude this player:

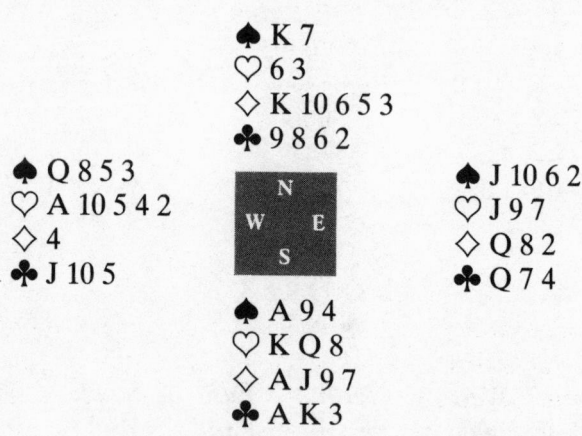

```
                    ♠ K 7
                    ♡ 6 3
                    ◇ K 10 6 5 3
                    ♣ 9 8 6 2
      ♠ Q 8 5 3                      ♠ J 10 6 2
      ♡ A 10 5 4 2      N            ♡ J 9 7
      ◇ 4            W     E         ◇ Q 8 2
      ♣ J 10 5          S            ♣ Q 7 4
                    ♠ A 9 4
                    ♡ K Q 8
                    ◇ A J 9 7
                    ♣ A K 3
```

After 2NT–3NT, West leads the ♡4 and East plays the jack. You expect East to have at least three hearts, so there is no point in ducking. East is now the danger hand, but you can easily take him out of circulation.

With this diamond combination you would normally play to drop the queen. Instead, needing only four tricks, you cross to the king and finesse against East on the way back. If West wins, the ♡Q is protected.

Applying a similar idea, consider this deal:

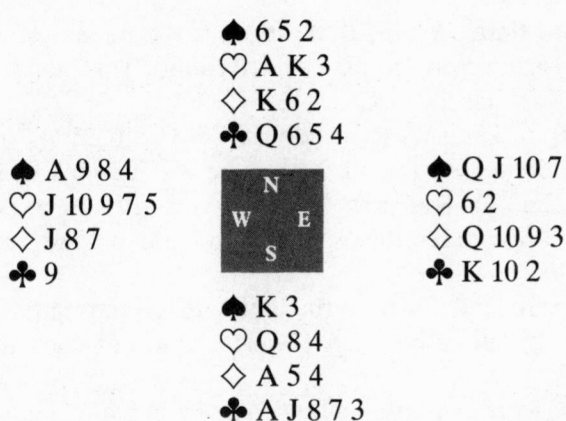

♠ 6 5 2
♡ A K 3
◇ K 6 2
♣ Q 6 5 4

♠ A 9 8 4   ♠ Q J 10 7
♡ J 10 9 7 5   ♡ 6 2
◇ J 8 7   ◇ Q 10 9 3
♣ 9   ♣ K 10 2

♠ K 3
♡ Q 8 4
◇ A 5 4
♣ A J 8 7 3

After 1NT–2NT–3NT, West leads the ♡J. Plan the play.

A spade switch from East could be fatal, so you identify him as Public Enemy No. 1. If you needed five tricks from clubs you would lead low from dummy and finesse the jack, but here four will be enough. The best chance of keeping East out is to win the first trick in dummy and lead the ♣Q. If East covers, you win, cross to dummy, and lead through him a second time. Only when East has K–10–9 does he get in.

Any play aimed at excluding a particular defender while declarer establishes his tricks may be termed an avoidance play. Examples are numerous and no attempt is made to memorise them. Often you manoeuvre in such a way that when the 'safe' opponent plays a high card, you can make him keep the trick.

(1)	Dummy		(2)	Dummy	
	A K 2			A 5 4	
Q 8		J 10 5	J 9 2		Q 8
	Declarer			Declarer	
	9 7 6 4 3			K 10 7 6 3	

In (1) East is the player to be avoided; in (2), which is more difficult, West. There is no shortage of entries.

In (1) you lead low from hand. If West plays the queen, you duck. If he does not, you win, re-enter your hand and lead low a second time. Again, if West plays the queen, you duck; otherwise you win and play a third round. This plan succeeds unless East has Q–x–x.

In (2), to keep West out, do not start with a top card from either hand: if East is on the ball he will unblock by playing the queen. To lead low from the closed hand is no good either: West plays the 9 and if you put on the ace, East unblocks.

Best is to lead low from the table: if East puts in the queen, you duck; and if he plays low you win and duck the next round.

These were examples of how to develop a single suit. When declarer has to develop two suits and may have to lose a trick in each, the question usually is not 'How?' but 'Which suit first?'

When defenders have entries in two suits

We now enter a wider field of strategy. Plan the play in 3NT on the lead of the ♢3.

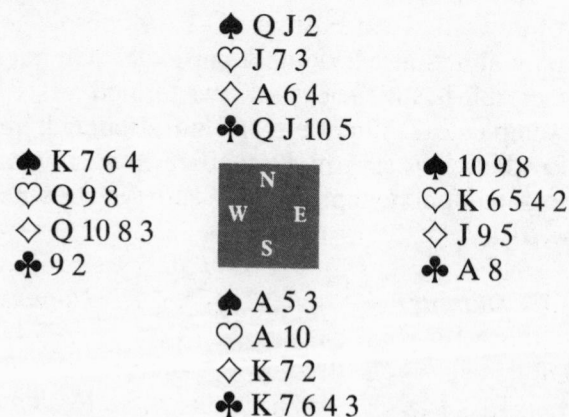

```
              ♠ Q J 2
              ♡ J 7 3
              ♢ A 6 4
              ♣ Q J 10 5
♠ K 7 6 4         N         ♠ 10 9 8
♡ Q 9 8      W       E      ♡ K 6 5 4 2
♢ Q 10 8 3       S         ♢ J 9 5
♣ 9 2                       ♣ A 8
              ♠ A 5 3
              ♡ A 10
              ♢ K 7 2
              ♣ K 7 6 4 3
```

South should work out before playing from dummy that it will be wrong to hold up, as he can afford to lose two diamonds, the ♣A and the ♠K. However, if he wins in either hand and tackles clubs, East may have the ace and return a heart. Now, as the cards lie, the contract fails.

Instead, South should take the first trick in dummy and lead the ♣Q. This is an avoidance play because it establishes a trick while keeping East out. On any return, South has time to establish clubs.

Attacking the danger hand

When a defender can make a damaging lead, you avoid him, but when he is dangerous because he threatens to establish long cards, you employ the opposite tactics and attack him:

```
              ♠ J 3
              ♡ 9 4 2
              ◇ A 7 6
              ♣ A J 9 4 2
♠ 10 9 5 4 2                  ♠ A 8 6
♡ A 8 6          N           ♡ 10 7 5 3
◇ Q 9 2      W       E       ◇ J 10 4
♣ 8 5            S           ♣ K 7 3
              ♠ K Q 7
              ♡ K Q J
              ◇ K 8 5 3
              ♣ Q 10 6
```

After 1◇–2♣–2NT–3NT, West leads the ♠4. East wins with the ace and returns the 8.

Suppose that you play on clubs: East wins, a spade comes back, and sooner or later you have to play a heart. West has the ♡A and the long spades, so you are smitten low.

In this standard situation declarer should attack the entry of the defender who has the long suit. Here, West's entry can only be in hearts, so the first move should be to lead a heart honour. If it is allowed to hold, you switch to clubs. If the heart is taken and a spade comes back, West will have no entry when the club finesse loses.

In the next type, equally common, the correct sequence does not assure the contract but it does improve the chances:

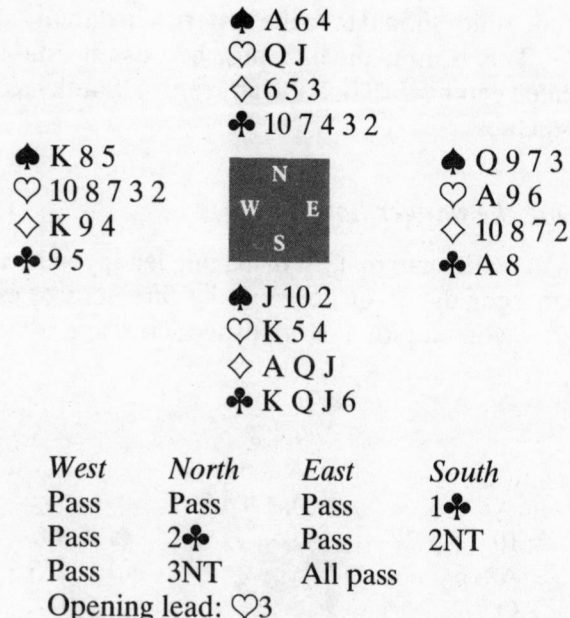

```
              ♠ A 6 4
              ♡ Q J
              ◇ 6 5 3
              ♣ 10 7 4 3 2
♠ K 8 5                        ♠ Q 9 7 3
♡ 10 8 7 3 2                   ♡ A 9 6
◇ K 9 4                        ◇ 10 8 7 2
♣ 9 5                          ♣ A 8
              ♠ J 10 2
              ♡ K 5 4
              ◇ A Q J
              ♣ K Q J 6
```

West	North	East	South
Pass	Pass	Pass	1♣
Pass	2♣	Pass	2NT
Pass	3NT	All pass	

Opening lead: ♡3

East wins with the ace and returns the 9 on which West plays the 2. You will need to play diamonds as well as clubs, so there is a danger of losing three hearts, a diamond and a club.

Suppose that you play clubs first. It does not matter who has the ace: your heart stopper is removed and when West has the ◇K, an even chance, you are defeated.

Suppose instead that you first take the diamond finesse. If it holds, you switch to clubs: if it loses, a heart comes back but you still get home when the ♣A is with East. With this sequence you need one of two cards, the ♣A or the ◇K, to be well placed, a 75% chance.

The principle is this: when there are two cards to force out and one can be held only by the defender who threatens to establish long cards, this card should be dislodged first.

Chapter 15

DEFENDING AGAINST NOTRUMP CONTRACTS

The play by third hand – Returning the lead – When to switch – When to cover an opposing honour – Protecting the entry of the key defender – Holding up a stopper

Strategy at notrumps is substantially the same for defenders as for declarer: they try to establish long cards and to prevent the opposition from doing likewise. The same thrusts and counter-thrusts are made. But of course the mental challenge is quite different, as a defender does not see his partner's cards and does see one of the enemy hands.

To assist each other the defenders exchange information in ways developed by players who have gone before us: they lead fourth-best from a long suit, the top card from a sequence, and so on and so forth. So familiar are these practices that we sometimes forget that they are intended to inform, and that high-class plays can be built upon them. You are East and your partner leads the ♡6 after 1NT–3NT:

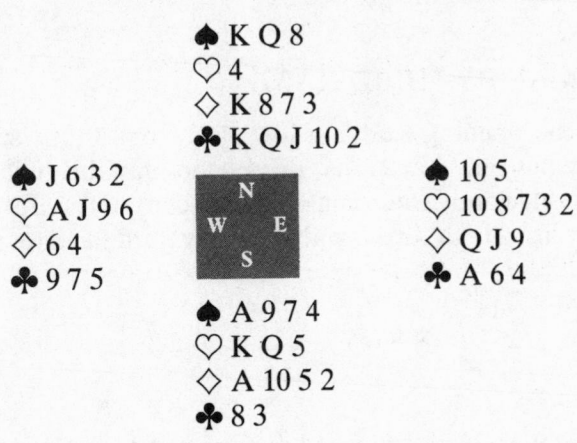

```
                    ♠ K Q 8
                    ♡ 4
                    ♢ K 8 7 3
                    ♣ K Q J 10 2
    ♠ J 6 3 2                        ♠ 10 5
    ♡ A J 9 6      N                 ♡ 10 8 7 3 2
    ♢ 6 4        W   E               ♢ Q J 9
    ♣ 9 7 5         S                ♣ A 6 4
                    ♠ A 9 7 4
                    ♡ K Q 5
                    ♢ A 10 5 2
                    ♣ 8 3
```

While South is admiring the dummy you should be doing some quick thinking. South will win and attack clubs, and the contract is likely to be made unless your side can take the setting tricks when you come in with the ace.

The only realistic hope is to take four heart tricks. So, precisely how are those tricks to be gathered in?

The opening lead is presumably fourth-best, so West will have three cards higher than the 6. One of these must be the 9; otherwise he would have something like A–Q–J–6 or K–Q–J–6 and would not have led the 6. Now it should occur to you that it will be entirely safe to play the 7 or 8, as the 10 may be your only card of entry when the ♣A has gone.

When you come in with the ♣A you return the ♡3, fourth best of your original holding. West takes the next two tricks with the A–J and on the fourth round you overtake the 9 to cash the setting trick. Had you played the 10 on the opening lead the contract would have been made.

Always extract the utmost from the opening lead. Try to work out the exact layout of the suit. Ask yourself such questions as, 'Has partner led his own longest suit?' If not, why not? Is dummy strong or weak for the bids it has made? Do the cards appear to lie well or badly for declarer? Why has declarer played whatever he did play from dummy? And so on. Even when these questions cannot be answered, they will help to kick-start the grey cells.

THE PLAY BY THIRD HAND

When the opening lead is a low card from a long suit and dummy has only low cards, third hand plays his highest, to prevent declarer from making a cheap trick. But when dummy has a high card it will often pay third hand to finesse:

```
(1)              Q 7 4
        K 9 6 5              A J 3
                 10 8 2
```

When West leads the 5 and dummy plays low, East puts in

the jack, retaining the ace to kill the queen. Frequently the finesse will allow declarer to win the current trick but prevent a second trick:

(2)   K 6 2   (3)   J 5 3
  J 9 7 3   A 10 5   Q 8 7 6 4   K 10 2
      Q 8 4   A 9

In (2) West leads the 3 and dummy plays low. By finessing the 10 East stops declarer from making two tricks. If South has the jack rather than the queen, the finesse neither gains nor loses.

In (3) East again finesses the 10 to prevent South from making two tricks. If this loses to the queen, South would have had a stopper however East played.

Often it is right to finesse a spot card:

(4)   A 10 3   (5)   K 9 3
  Q 9 6 4 2   J 8 5   10 8 6 4 2   A J 7
       K 7   Q 5

In (4) West leads the 4 and the 3 is played from dummy. To finesse the 8 will not please West if he has led from K–Q and declarer has the 9, but the risk is worth taking as it is more likely that West has the unsupported king or queen. Here the 8 holds South to two tricks.

In (5) when West leads the 4, and dummy plays the 3, the odds favour a finesse of the 7. As the cards lie, to play the jack gives South a double stop.

At a trump contract it is not automatic for third hand to finesse against a high card in dummy:

(6)   J 5 2
    K 10 6 3   Q 9 4
        A 8 7

At notrumps, when West leads the 3 and dummy plays low East saves a trick by finessing the 9. If declarer has A–10–x he always has a double stopper.

At a trump contract East has to consider which is more

important: to establish a trick quickly by putting up the queen, or to finesse the 9 and risk finding declarer with A–10–x.

When third hand has 'equals' – that is, two or more high cards in sequence – he plays the lowest:

(7)   10 8 2

     K 9 6 3   Q J 5

            A 7 4

West leads the 3 and East plays the jack, not the queen. When this brings forth the ace, West can deduce that East has the queen. If East were to play the queen on the first trick West would place declarer with the jack.

To play the lowest of equals is normal when playing third-hand high but not when signalling or when following suit to declarer's lead.

(8)   K 5 4

    7 2   Q J 10 9 3

       A 8 6

If West leads this suit and dummy's king is played, East should play the queen. Likewise, if South leads low from dummy, the queen is much more illuminating than the 9. In context, West will have no difficulty in realising that the queen is the top of an impregnable sequence. A defender might do the same with J–10–9–8–x or K–Q–J–x, and in this situation also:

(9)   9 7 3

    A 4 2   J 10 8 6

      K Q 5

South is in dummy and finds it convenient to tackle this combination. By playing the jack, East inspires West to make a devastating return of this suit when he captures South's king.

The Rule of Eleven

Third hand can sometimes work out the correct play to the first trick by a short cut known as the Rule of Eleven. When the lead is fourth highest, you subtract its rank from eleven to learn how many higher cards are held in the three hands other than the leader's:

<pre>
              K 10 4
     J 9 7 6 2   A Q 8
              5 3
</pre>

West leads the 6 and dummy plays low. If the queen is played, dummy will have a stopper, but by subtracting the card led from 11 East learns that there are only five higher cards in the second, third and fourth hands. He can see them all, so knows that the 8 will hold the trick. He could have worked it out anyway, but the Rule of Eleven allows him to do it more quickly.

When the opening lead is an honour

This lead is normally from a strong sequence, so when third hand has an honour and is short in the suit he should usually cover, to avoid a blockage:

<pre>
(1)   9 7 4   (2)   9 7 2
    K Q 10 5 3   A 6   Q J 10 8 5   K 3
            J 8 2   A 6 4
</pre>

In (1), when West leads the king East overtakes with the ace, otherwise the suit is blocked on the next round and the defenders take only two tricks quickly unless West has an entry. In (2), when the queen is led East puts on the king. If he ducks South will duck too, and will allow the king to hold the next trick.

Third hand may sometimes play a lower honour than the card led, not just to unblock but to assure his partner that the declarer does not have this card:

(3)   A 6 2   (4)   8 7 4

  Q J 9 5 3   10 4   K Q 10 6 2   J 5

         K 8 7   A 9 3

In each case West leads his highest and East judges that this is from a broken sequence. If he held a third card he might in some circumstances simply encourage: as it is he must play his honour, otherwise West may not continue.

Third hand does not play an honour if it will cost a trick:

(5)   9 6 4 2

    Q J 10 8 3   K 7

           A 5

On the lead of the queen East ducks, as he can see that if he unblocks, the 9 will become a stopper.

RETURNING THE LEAD

Suppose the declarer wins the first trick and third hand is the first defender to regain the lead: more often than not it is best to return partner's suit, and in that case it is essential to lead the right card, to show how the suit is distributed.

With three cards originally, third hand returns the higher remaining one. With more, he returns the original fourth best:

(1)   6

   K 10 7 4 3   Q 8 5 2

       A J 9

West leads the 4 to the queen and ace. When East gets in he returns the 2. West captures the 9 with the 10 and can safely lay down the king as he places East with four cards. Under the king East must play the 8, to avoid blocking the suit.

In theory the 2 could be from Q–2 doubleton, but at the table the bidding or the cards in dummy will rule that out. Here, for example, if East had Q–2 only, South would have A–J–9–8–5.

To avoid a blockage, third hand may have to return a card other than fourth best:

(2)   6   (3)   9

   A 8 7 5 2   K J 10 3   A J 6 5 2   Q 8 7 4

         Q 9 4   K 10 3

In (2) East wins the first trick with the king and returns the jack, not the 3. This is done to pick up the queen as well as to unblock.

In (3) West leads the 5 and the queen loses to the king. When East gets in he computes that to return the 4 will block the suit if South began with K–10–x or K–J–x. This is quite likely, for otherwise West would have A–J–10–x–x and might have led the jack.

Therefore, unless East knows that his partner has a quick entry he should return the 8. Now West, on winning the 10 with the jack, may be able to work out that East has been clever enough to do this and did not have Q–8–x originally (in which case South would still hold the guarded 7). West therefore continues with the ace and East clinches the laurels by unblocking with the 7.

WHEN TO SWITCH

Many contracts can be defeated only by a timely switch. The player who wins the first defensive trick should routinely ask himself, 'If I continue the suit led initially, will it produce enough tricks to beat the contract?'

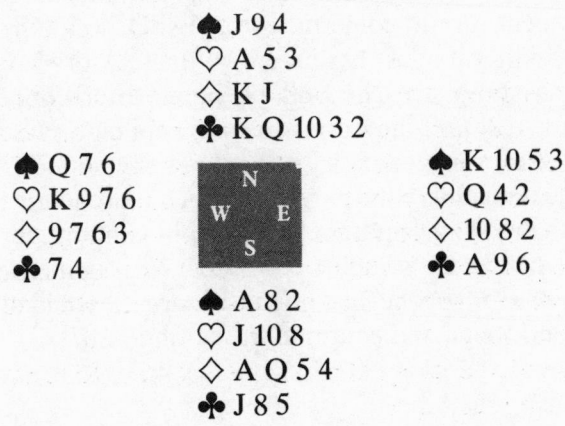

♠ J 9 4
♡ A 5 3
◇ K J
♣ K Q 10 3 2

♠ Q 7 6
♡ K 9 7 6
◇ 9 7 6 3
♣ 7 4

♠ K 10 5 3
♡ Q 4 2
◇ 10 8 2
♣ A 9 6

♠ A 8 2
♡ J 10 8
◇ A Q 5 4
♣ J 8 5

After 1NT–3NT, West leads the ♡6. If South knew that West had only four hearts he would put up the ace and force out the ♣A, but here he ducks. When the queen holds East places West with the king, which means that he can have no more than a queen outside. A heart return will produce at best three heart tricks and a club. To find West with the ♢Q will not help, so East switches to a spade, the killer.

Sometimes it will be right for a defender to return the suit led when the leader has a quick entry, but wrong when he has not. There may be a clue. You are East:

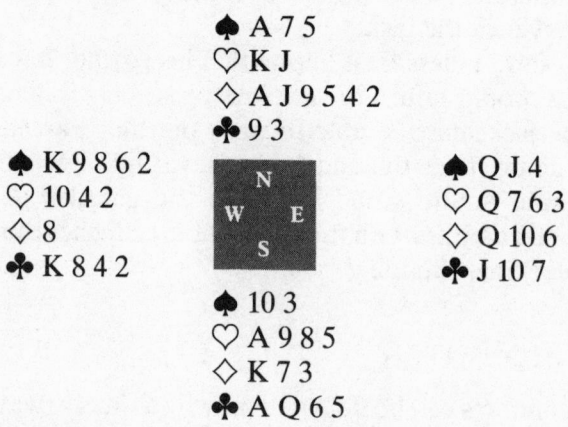

```
                  ♠ A 7 5
                  ♡ K J
                  ♢ A J 9 5 4 2
                  ♣ 9 3
  ♠ K 9 8 6 2                      ♠ Q J 4
  ♡ 10 4 2          N             ♡ Q 7 6 3
  ♢ 8          W         E        ♢ Q 10 6
  ♣ K 8 4 2          S            ♣ J 10 7
                  ♠ 10 3
                  ♡ A 9 8 5
                  ♢ K 7 3
                  ♣ A Q 6 5
```

After 1NT–3NT, West leads the ♠6. The jack holds the first trick and the queen the next, declarer following with the 3 and the 10. On the second round West plays the 2.

You seem sure to come in with the ♢Q, so a third spade will be a killer if West has an entry; the ♡A or ♣A. But if South has both aces he will be home after conceding a diamond trick and the only hope will be a club switch now, playing West for K–8–x or better. How can you tell?

Mathematically, your partner is much more likely to have an ace than to have a particular club combination, but nevertheless you should switch to the ♣J. West is marked with ♠K–9–8–x–x, so if he held an outside ace he would overtake the second spade and continue the suit himself.

WHEN TO COVER AN OPPOSING HONOUR

The advantage of covering the lead of an opposing high card is that you may win the trick, and if you don't, you are forcing the enemy to play two high cards to your one:

(1)	J 4		(2)	A J 10 9	
10 7 3		K 5 2	K 7 4 3		8 6 5
	A Q 9 8 6			Q 2	

In (1) declarer will normally lead the jack from the table, intending to take two finesses. East must cover; otherwise the defenders make no trick.

Of course, a defender does not cover when there is no chance of promotion. In (2) when South leads the queen West ducks, hoping that South will not be able to lead enough times to pick up the king.

Here and in most other cases there is advantage, when ducking, to do so in normal rhythm. If West does not hesitate before playing low, declarer will not know who has the king, even when the queen holds the trick.

Nor do you cover when there is danger of clashing with a high card in partner's hand:

(3)	J 5	
K		Q 9 4
	A 10 8 7 6 3 2	

If South has opened with a three bid or a weak two, East should judge there is danger in covering when the jack is led.

When the position is unclear, two rules are helpful, though not necessarily conclusive. First, when an honour is led from a sequence in dummy, *do not cover until the last of the sequence is led*:

(4)	J 10 9 4		(5)	Q J 8 3	
Q 5		K 7 3 2	10 6 2		K 7 4
	A 8 6			A 9 5	

In (4) if East covers an early lead he allows South to make three tricks. In (5), to cover the first honour will expose West to a second-round finesse through his 10, the defenders taking no tricks.

However, it is right to cover with a poorly guarded honour that will otherwise fall uselessly:

(6)		Q J 6 4		(7)		J 10 3	
	10 9 2		K 7		Q 8 7 5		K 2
		A 8 5 3				A 9 6 4	

In each case to duck the first honour will cost a trick, since dummy will lead low on the next round.

The second rule applies when an honour is led from the closed hand. The defender cannot tell whether this is from a sequence, but he will not go far wrong if he covers when there are two honours in dummy and ducks when there is only one.

(8)		A 10 8 5 2		(9)		A 8 6 5	
	K 7 4		Q 9 3		Q 4 2		K 9 3
		J 6				J 10 7	

In each case South leads the jack. In (8) there are two honours in dummy so West covers; in (9) there is only one so he ducks the first lead. In effect West is assuming that when there is only one honour in dummy, declarer will not lead an honour unless he has at least two in his own hand.

When the defender holds two honours

In the examples so far the defender has had one honour card. When he has two, he should cover the first high card from a sequence of two unless he can see that this will cost a trick.

(10)   A Q 6 4   (11)   J 10 7
   K J 5   8 3 2   4 3   K Q 8 6
          10 9 7   A 9 5 2

In (10) South tries to sneak the 9 through. If West lets it pass he takes no trick. In (11) the lead is in dummy. When an honour is led East covers first time; otherwise South makes three tricks.

Always the defender with the critical holding does well to ask himself, before the crunch comes, 'What am I going to do when an honour is led?'

PROTECTING THE ENTRY OF THE KEY DEFENDER

When the defender with a long suit has a winner in this suit, he can preserve this as an entry by ducking until the suit is established:

(1)   6 2   (2)   5
   K 10 7 5 3   A 8 4   Q 9 7 4 3   K 6 2
          Q J 9   A J 10 8

In (1) West leads the 5 and East wins with the ace, returning the 8. West ducks so that his partner will have a card to play if he comes in first.

In (2) West leads low and the king loses to the ace. When East is in he returns the 6, which South covers with the jack. West ducks and waits for East to lead again.

When the defender has a sure entry in a side suit it may be unnecessary to duck in the main suit and indeed it is sometimes a mistake. Consider West's problem:

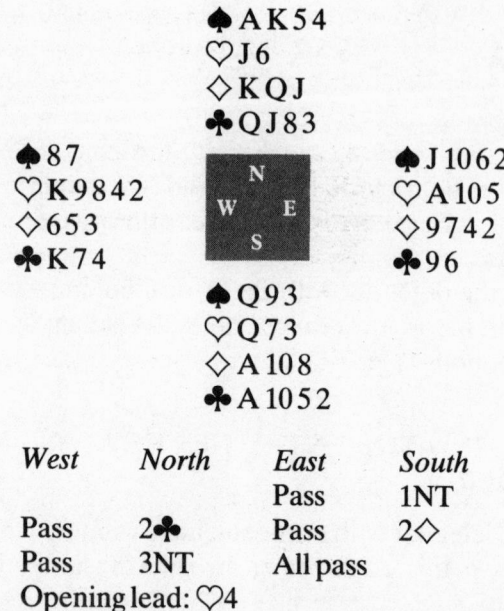

```
              ♠ A K 5 4
              ♡ J 6
              ◇ K Q J
              ♣ Q J 8 3
♠ 87                          ♠ J 10 6 2
♡ K 9 8 4 2       N           ♡ A 10 5
◇ 653         W       E       ◇ 9 7 4 2
♣ K 7 4           S           ♣ 9 6
              ♠ Q 9 3
              ♡ Q 7 3
              ◇ A 10 8
              ♣ A 10 5 2
```

West	North	East	South
		Pass	1NT
Pass	2♣	Pass	2◇
Pass	3NT	All pass	

Opening lead: ♡4

East wins with the ace and returns the 10, South following low. West can tell from the bidding that East has a third heart but he can tell too that East has no entry. There is therefore no point in ducking the second heart: West wins and clears the suit, relying on the ♣K to come in with.

If West were to duck the second round of hearts South, on finding spades 4–2, might decline to take the club finesse for his contract and instead cash three rounds of diamonds. He exits with a heart and West, after taking two more hearts, has to lead away from ♣K–x.

A finesse to prevent a hold-up

An effective way for the defenders to stay together is seen here:

```
              10 3
J 9 7 4 2           A Q 5
              K 8 6
```

Suppose first that West leads low and East wins with the ace, returning the queen. South will hold off if it suits him and West will need an entry in another suit.

At notrumps it is standard for East to play not the ace but the queen. South can hardly afford to duck, as West may have the ace. After South has released the king, the suit can be run no matter which defender gains the lead first.

To finesse the queen will also be good play when declarer has K–10–x–x, West having led from J–9–x–x. And a similar play may be made with A–J–x if the defender can afford to risk South's having Q–x–x:

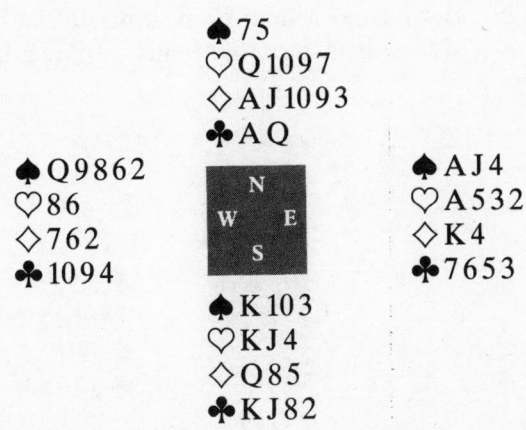

♠75
♥Q1097
♦AJ1093
♣AQ

♠Q9862
♥86
♦762
♣1094

♠AJ4
♥A532
♦K4
♣7653

♠K103
♥KJ4
♦Q85
♣KJ82

South opens 1NT, North bids 3NT after a negative response to 2♣, and West leads the ♠6. East can tell from the bidding that the contract must fail if South can be made to release his stopper, so he inserts the jack. If South held ♠Q–x–x he would gain a free trick but would still go down.

The duck by third hand

When the defenders' suit is held by third hand, he may duck in just the same way as a declarer would:

(1)	753		(2)	J73	
86		AK1042	62		KQ985
	QJ9			A104	

In (1) East has bid this suit and West leads the 8. East ducks with the 10 so as to leave West a card to lead.

In (2), suppose that East plays the queen on his partner's lead of the 6. South will duck if it suits him and now East will need two outside entries. If East has only one entry he should duck the first lead with the 8, obliging South to win with the 10. If West can get in and lead the suit again, the ace is removed while East still has his outside entry.

Protecting a side entry

When a defender has no winner in his long suit and his only entry is in a side suit, his partner must strive mightily to protect it:

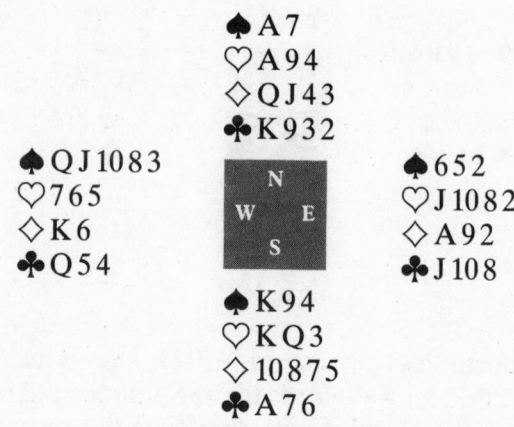

```
                    ♠ A 7
                    ♡ A 9 4
                    ◇ Q J 4 3
                    ♣ K 9 3 2
   ♠ Q J 10 8 3         N          ♠ 6 5 2
   ♡ 7 6 5        W         E       ♡ J 10 8 2
   ◇ K 6              S            ◇ A 9 2
   ♣ Q 5 4                         ♣ J 10 8
                    ♠ K 9 4
                    ♡ K Q 3
                    ◇ 10 8 7 5
                    ♣ A 7 6
```

West leads the ♠Q against 3NT. South cannot get home without using the diamond suit, so must hope not to lose too many spade tricks. He allows the ♠Q to hold and when West continues, leads a low diamond from dummy, hoping that East will duck. If he does, South succeeds in his mission, as West has to release the ◇K, after which the spade suit is dead.

East therefore must rise with the ◇A, accepting the risk that West may have the bare king. Now the spade return cooks South's goose. East has to defend in just the same way when he holds ◇K–x–x, a tougher assignment.

When the defenders each have a side entry and these are in different suits, the defender whose suit is under development must cling like a limpet to his entry:

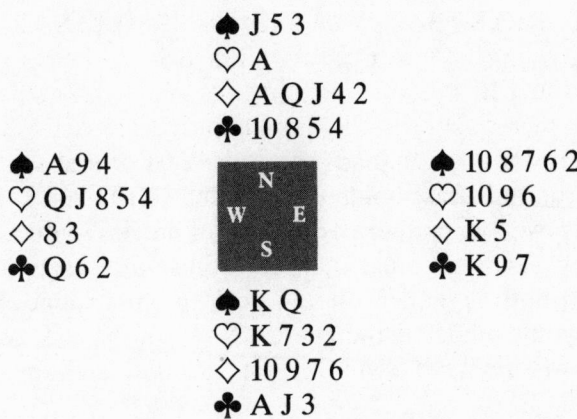

```
            ♠ J 5 3
            ♡ A
            ◇ A Q J 4 2
            ♣ 10 8 5 4
♠ A 9 4                      ♠ 10 8 7 6 2
♡ Q J 8 5 4                  ♡ 10 9 6
◇ 8 3                        ◇ K 5
♣ Q 6 2                      ♣ K 9 7
            ♠ K Q
            ♡ K 7 3 2
            ◇ 10 9 7 6
            ♣ A J 3
```

Against 3NT West leads the ♡5 and South sees that he will have to establish diamonds and make at least one trick in spades as well. From South's angle the dangerous situation is where East has the ◇K and West the ♠A: in that case West's entry must be removed first.

At the second trick, therefore, South leads a spade from the table. If West releases the ace the contract is made, as South holds up on the next heart. West however should refuse to part with his entry card, allowing the ♠K to hold.

As it happens, South is now out of court. If he plays a second spade, West wins and leads the ♡Q, which South is obliged to duck. Now West reverts to spades, establishing two tricks for East, who still has the ◇K.

West does not have to foresee this outcome when he ducks the spade: he ducks because he knows that without the ace his hand is dead. The rest is serendipity.

HOLDING UP A STOPPER

It is always a good idea to put pressure on declarer's entries, even when you cannot see what the effect may be. One of the commonest ways is by holding up a stopper in the suit he is trying to establish:

(1)   K Q 8 7 3   (2)   Q 10 8 3 2

  9 2   A 6 5   K 6 5   A 7 4

      J 10 4   J 9

In (1), when South leads the jack West echoes to show a doubleton and East holds up until the third round. This is routine, even when there are plenty of entries to dummy, as declarer may wish to use them for other purposes.

In (2) both defenders should duck the first round, just as South would if he held their cards. Now South needs two side entries to dummy. To win the first trick and duck the next is no good.

The next examples have already been seen from declarer's angle:

(3)   K Q J 9 3   (4)   A Q J 6 3

  8 5   A 10 4 2   8 2   K 10 7 4

     7 6   9 5

In (3) South leads low, West plays the 8 and dummy the king. East ducks routinely unless he is eager to get in. Now dummy will need a side entry to make a second trick and two entries to make three tricks.

In (4) also East should normally hold off when South leads low and finesses the queen. In both cases declarer can save an entry by ducking the first round completely, but he may be unwilling to forgo the chance of maximum tricks.

Chapter 16

THE PLAY IN TRUMP CONTRACTS

*Taking discards – Making use of dummy's trumps –
The crossruff – Establishment by ruffing – Dummy
reversal – Trump control – Nullifying the defenders'
ruffs*

The differences between trump contracts and notrumps are
worth reminding ourselves of. At notrumps, declarer cannot
establish a suit without conceding tricks to any stoppers the
defenders may have: with A–K–x–x–x opposite x–x, for
example, he must lose at least one trick. At a trump contract
he may establish the suit by ruffing, losing no trick at all.

At notrumps, declarer cannot win more tricks in a suit
than he has cards in the longer hand: A–K–Q–x–x opposite
J–10–x–x is worth five tricks, period. At a trump contract, by
ruffing in the shorter hand – or by ruffing enough times in the
longer hand – declarer adds to his harvest.

At notrumps, declarer cannot prevent the defenders from
cashing an established suit. At a trump contract an enemy suit
can be laughed at when declarer is out of the suit and has
plenty of trumps.

Declarer also has a resource not available at notrumps: he
may be able to put himself out of a suit by discarding a loser
from one hand on a winner in the hand opposite. This is
sometimes the first thing he must attend to.

TAKING DISCARDS

When dummy is exposed, declarer should count not just his
winners but his losers too. He may find that a discard is
needed before surrendering the lead:

After 1♠–4♠, West leads the ◇J. The queen loses to the ace, the diamond return takes the king; South sees that if he leads a trump he will lose the ♠A, another diamond and a club.

He is not yet a dead duck. At the third trick he finesses the ♡Q. If it fails he loses an extra trick but here the queen holds and a diamond can be thrown on the ace. Now trumps can be led.

When the threat of too many losers is less immediate, it may still be necessary to take immediate action:

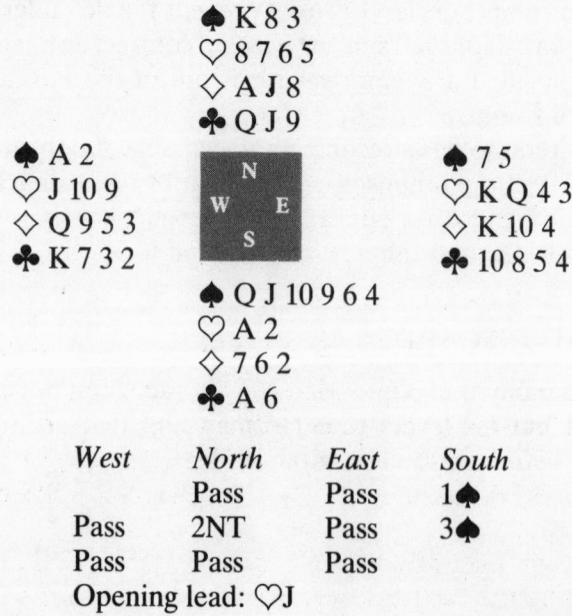

West	North	East	South
	Pass	Pass	1♠
Pass	2NT	Pass	3♠
Pass	Pass	Pass	

Opening lead: ♡J

Suppose that South elects to win the first trick and play a trump. The defenders may be clever enough to cash only one heart and switch to diamonds. Now, as the cards lie, if the club finesse fails so does the contract.

With the brain firing on all cylinders South should foresee this development and his very first move should be to play ace and another club. Then if diamonds are attacked a quick discard can be taken.

When taking a discard while trumps are out, the risk of a ruff is not to be ignored. To minimise it a precise sequence of play may be needed:

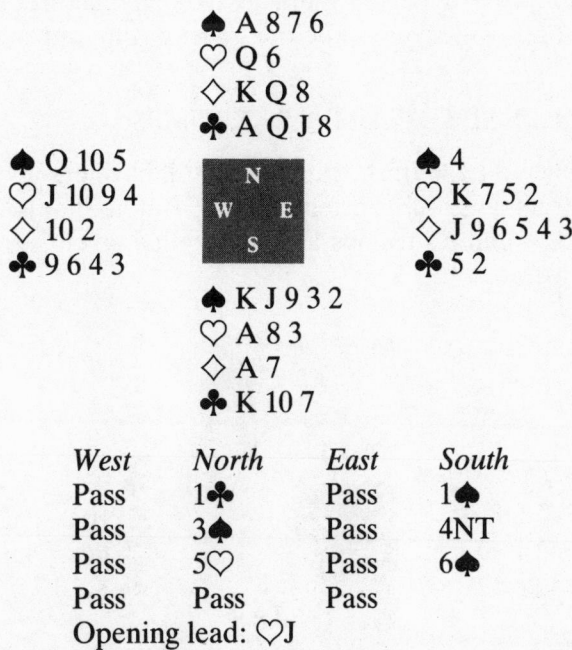

```
              ♠ A 8 7 6
              ♡ Q 6
              ◇ K Q 8
              ♣ A Q J 8
♠ Q 10 5                        ♠ 4
♡ J 10 9 4         N            ♡ K 7 5 2
◇ 10 2        W         E       ◇ J 9 6 5 4 3
♣ 9 6 4 3         S            ♣ 5 2
              ♠ K J 9 3 2
              ♡ A 8 3
              ◇ A 7
              ♣ K 10 7
```

West	North	East	South
Pass	1♣	Pass	1♠
Pass	3♠	Pass	4NT
Pass	5♡	Pass	6♠
Pass	Pass	Pass	

Opening lead: ♡J

This is a good slam, easily reached. North's double raise suggests six losers. South has seven but can safely deduct one as he has two aces, no queens, a fifth trump and a fit. There is no need for him to cue-bid as he does not need to know whether North has extra values and his hand is well suited to Blackwood.

However, the opening lead hits the target and the queen is covered by the king and ace. East shows out on the second round of trumps and now there is a problem. What is the safest way to take two heart discards?

Suppose that South plays three rounds of diamonds. This seems the natural thing to do, but it is not his day: West ruffs and cashes a heart. Think it through and you find that whatever happens in diamonds, you need West to follow to three rounds of clubs. You may then be struck by the thought that nothing can be lost by playing three rounds of clubs first. Once in a while East will show out, and in that case a fourth club can safely be taken. Now, when diamonds are led, West ruffs too late.

If clubs prove to be 3–3 South has to hope that three rounds of diamonds will stand up before he leads the fourth club.

MAKING USE OF DUMMY'S TRUMPS

When declarer can draw trumps and still have enough tricks for contract he should hasten to do so. But he should first be sure that dummy's trumps are not needed as entries or for ruffing losers:

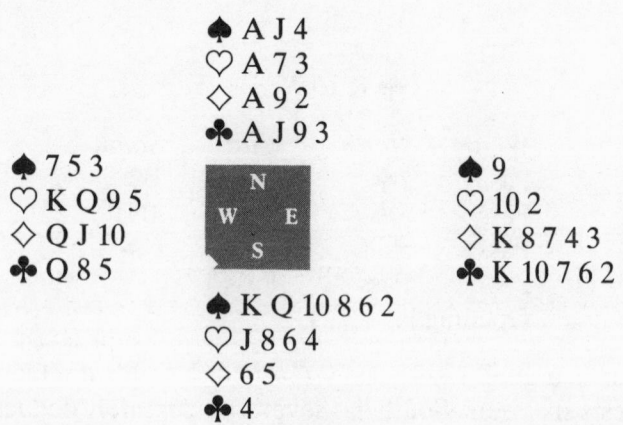

```
                  ♠ A J 4
                  ♡ A 7 3
                  ◇ A 9 2
                  ♣ A J 9 3
  ♠ 7 5 3                        ♠ 9
  ♡ K Q 9 5          N           ♡ 10 2
  ◇ Q J 10      W       E        ◇ K 8 7 4 3
  ♣ Q 8 5           S            ♣ K 10 7 6 2
                  ♠ K Q 10 8 6 2
                  ♡ J 8 6 4
                  ◇ 6 5
                  ♣ 4
```

West leads the ◇Q against 4♠. Immediate losers are not a problem but you should assess that if you draw trumps there may be only nine winners: six trumps and three aces.

Whenever a side suit is longer in the closed hand than in dummy, you should consider, before touching trumps, whether you wish to play for a ruff. Here a tenth trick can be made by ruffing the fourth heart, but only if you lead hearts before playing a single round of trumps; otherwise West will return a trump at every opportunity.

When a ruff in dummy will ensure the contract, other possibilities should be ignored if they may get in the way:

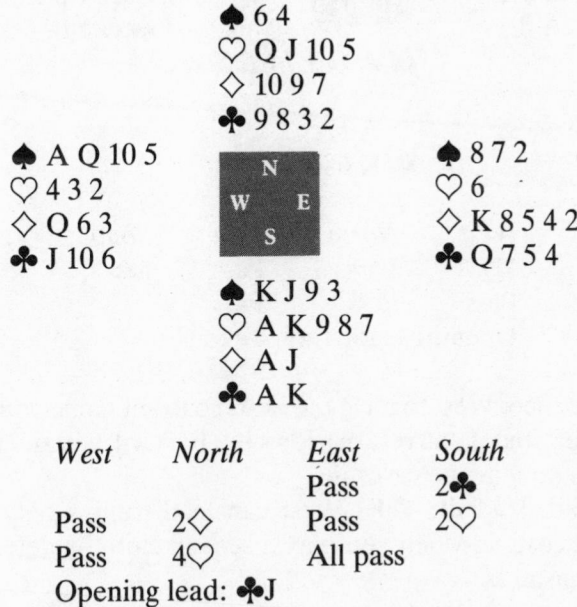

♠ 6 4
♥ Q J 10 5
♦ 10 9 7
♣ 9 8 3 2

♠ A Q 10 5
♥ 4 3 2
♦ Q 6 3
♣ J 10 6

♠ 8 7 2
♥ 6
♦ K 8 5 4 2
♣ Q 7 5 4

♠ K J 9 3
♥ A K 9 8 7
♦ A J
♣ A K

West	North	East	South
		Pass	2♣
Pass	2♦	Pass	2♥
Pass	4♥	All pass	

Opening lead: ♣J

North's raise to game shows trump support but little else so South, with a minimum, does not continue.

South has eight winners. Suppose that he tries to develop the spade holding. He crosses with a trump and leads a spade, but the jack loses to the queen and a trump comes back. A second spade is led from dummy but West repeats the dose. South is left with two losing spades and can ruff only one.

'This is unbelievable,' South tells his partner. 'West had all the spade honours and three trumps as well.' Yet two spade ruffs would have assured the contract, and they could have been gained by leading spades from hand instead of crossing with a trump and trying to develop a natural trick.

Defenders will try to kill a ruff if they can lead trumps without cost, but declarer may arrange that it *does* cost:

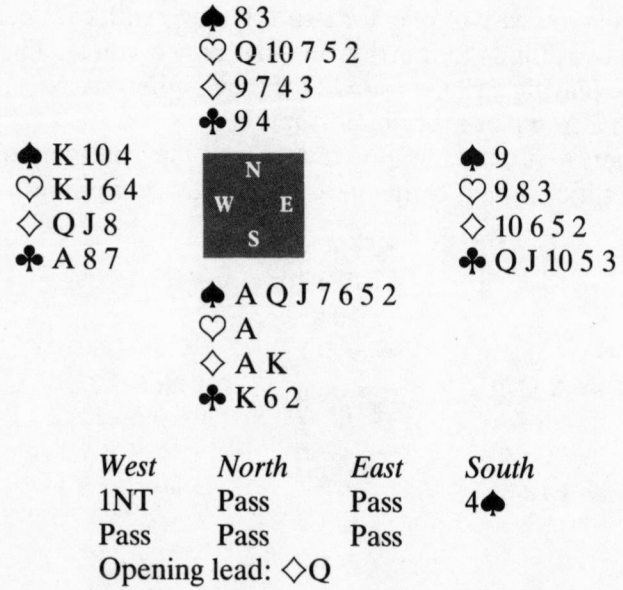

♠ 8 3
♡ Q 10 7 5 2
♢ 9 7 4 3
♣ 9 4

♠ K 10 4   ♠ 9
♡ K J 6 4   ♡ 9 8 3
♢ Q J 8   ♢ 10 6 5 2
♣ A 8 7   ♣ Q J 10 5 3

♠ A Q J 7 6 5 2
♡ A
♢ A K
♣ K 6 2

West	North	East	South
West	*North*	*East*	*South*
1NT	Pass	Pass	4♠
Pass	Pass	Pass	

Opening lead: ♢Q

You expect West to have the ♣A, so to get home you need a club ruff, but if you return a low club East will win and lead a trump – fatal as the cards lie.

Instead, lead the ♣K. West can lead trumps only once without cost, so when you play a second club the defence is out of business.

Trumps as entries

It is sometimes the case that a long card in dummy cannot be cashed unless declarer can remain in dummy as he draws the last trump:

```
              ♠ 10 5 4
              ♡ K Q 10
              ◇ K Q 8 7
              ♣ 6 3 2
♠ K 9 7 6        ┌─────────┐        ♠ J 8 3
♡ 6 3            │    N    │        ♡ 7 5 2
◇ J 6            │ W     E │        ◇ 9 5 4 3
♣ K Q 10 5 4     │    S    │        ♣ A 9 8
                 └─────────┘
              ♠ A Q 2
              ♡ A J 9 8 4
              ◇ A 10 2
              ♣ J 7
```

West	North	East	South
		Pass	1♡
Pass	2◇	Pass	2NT
Pass	3♡	Pass	4♡
Pass	Pass	Pass	

Opening lead: ♣K

Clubs are continued and South ruffs the third round. He draws two rounds of trumps and all follow.

If the diamond layout is favourable South may be able to avoid the spade finesse but as dummy has no side entries he should test diamonds before drawing the last trump. He plays a diamond to the king and a diamond back. As it happens, the jack falls and South continues with the ◇10. If this is ruffed, too bad: nothing would have been gained by drawing the last trump, and the spade finesse is still there. Here the 10 holds and now a trump to dummy allows the ◇Q to be cashed.

When a side suit has to be established by ruffing, several entries may be needed. Before drawing trumps declarer should work out whether he has enough:

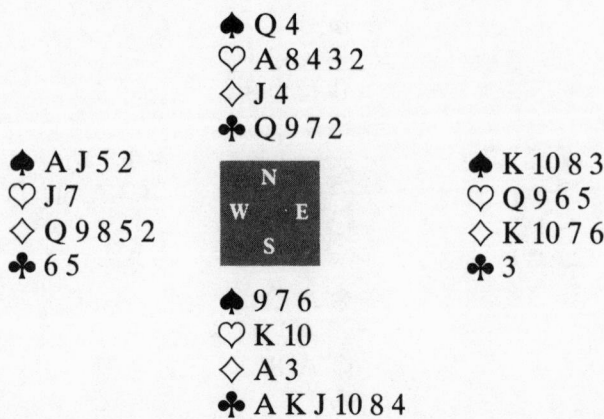

♠ Q 4
♡ A 8 4 3 2
◇ J 4
♣ Q 9 7 2

♠ A J 5 2
♡ J 7
◇ Q 9 8 5 2
♣ 6 5

♠ K 10 8 3
♡ Q 9 6 5
◇ K 10 7 6
♣ 3

♠ 9 7 6
♡ K 10
◇ A 3
♣ A K J 10 8 4

The contract is 5♣ and West leads a trump to which East follows. With any luck you may be able to establish the fifth heart and make game with three heart tricks, six trumps, the ◇A and a spade ruff. But are the entries sufficient?

Suppose you draw a second trump and play three rounds of hearts, ruffing. West shows out so you cross with a trump and take a second heart ruff.

The long heart is good but there is only one trump in dummy and this cannot be used for entry as it is needed to ruff a spade. You lead a spade, therefore, but a diamond comes back and you cannot get a discard in time.

The mistake was to play a second round of trumps. Instead, lead hearts straight away. After the first ruff you can enter dummy with the second round of trumps and ruff another heart. There are still two trumps in dummy, so you can enter with a trump, discard a diamond, and still get a spade ruff.

Thus the idea is that when entries are short you don't draw trumps as a separate operation but as part of your game plan, using them as entries.

THE CROSSRUFF

Declarer should consider a crossruff whenever he has no long suit to cash and no prospect of establishing long cards. A crossruff cannot be combined with these forms of play.

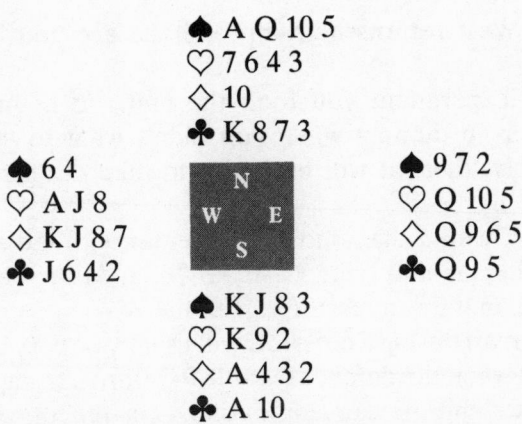

After 1♠–4♠ West hits a good lead, a trump. You have only three side winners so the best chance is to make all your remaining trumps by crossruffing.

There is no point to playing a heart from dummy, for even if East has the ace, a trump return will take away a ruff.

When crossruffing, it sometimes matters which hand you ruff in first. Do not try to luck your way through such a hand but first play it through mentally.

Suppose that you cash the ♣A–K and take a club ruff. Next, the ◇A and a diamond ruff, followed by club ruff, diamond ruff:

```
            ♠ A
            ♡ 7 6 4 3
            ◇ —
            ♣ —
♠ 6                       ♠ 7 2
♡ A J 8        N          ♡ Q 10 5
◇ K          W   E        ◇ —
♣ —              S        ♣ —
            ♠ K
            ♡ K 9 2
            ◇ 4
            ♣ —
```

By now you may have seen the writing on the wall. You are in dummy with a diamond still to ruff and are obliged to lead a heart. West returns a trump and the ace and king fall together.

In this experiment you took the first ruff in hand and finished up in dummy when you didn't want to be there. Presumably, then, it will be better to take the first ruff in dummy.

So, start with a diamond ruff, re-enter with the ♣A and take another diamond ruff. Cash the ♣K and ruff a club. Now the last diamond can be ruffed with the ♠A.

An overruff during a crossruff will usually be very harmful, especially when the defender is able to return a trump. There are ways to limit the damage. In one, declarer contrives that any overruff shall come only from a defender who was in any case due to make a trump trick:

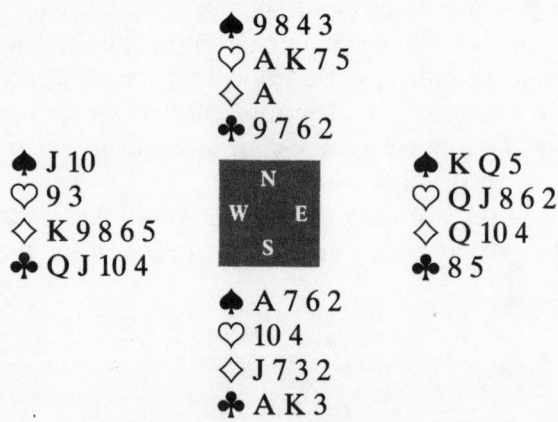

```
              ♠ 9 8 4 3
              ♡ A K 7 5
              ◇ A
              ♣ 9 7 6 2
♠ J 10                      ♠ K Q 5
♡ 9 3          N            ♡ Q J 8 6 2
◇ K 9 8 6 5  W   E          ◇ Q 10 4
♣ Q J 10 4     S            ♣ 8 5
              ♠ A 7 6 2
              ♡ 10 4
              ◇ J 7 3 2
              ♣ A K 3
```

South opens 1NT, the final contract is 4♠ and the ♣Q is led. South has to bank on a 3–2 trump break, but even then he will be a trick short if he draws three rounds of trumps. A crossruff, however, may hold defenders to their inescapable winners, a club and two trumps.

The wheeze with this type is to draw precisely two rounds of trumps before crossruffing: then you cannot be overruffed by the short trump hand, which here would be fatal. If the defender with three trumps overruffs, you do not mind, as he is ruffing with the master trump and has not been able to draw two trumps for one.

On winning with the ♣A, therefore, you do not play ace and another trump, which would allow East to draw a third round, but a low trump from each hand. Suppose the defenders play a second club: you win, cash the ♠A, ♡A, ♡K and ruff two hearts in hand, using the ◇A as entry for the second heart ruff. If this sequence is not followed, West gains a killing overruff in hearts.

The next deal shows a different way of preventing an overruff; simple, but often neglected:

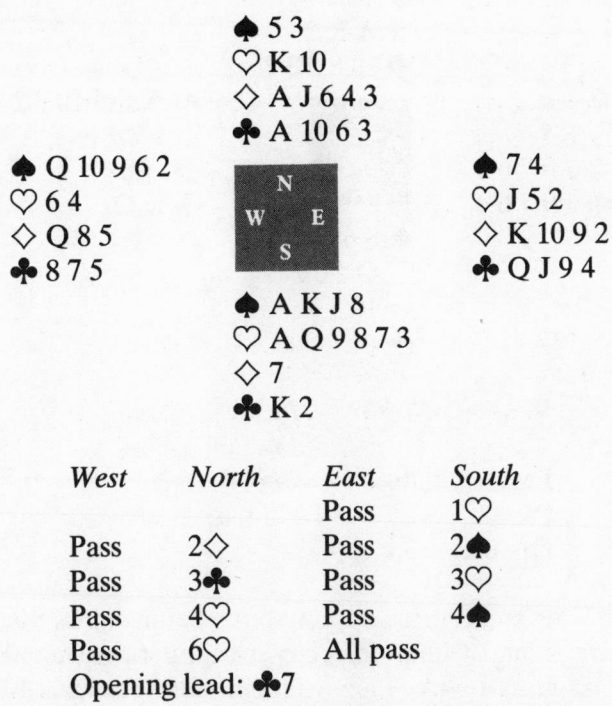

```
                        ♠ 5 3
                        ♡ K 10
                        ◇ A J 6 4 3
                        ♣ A 10 6 3
     ♠ Q 10 9 6 2          N           ♠ 7 4
     ♡ 6 4             W       E        ♡ J 5 2
     ◇ Q 8 5              S            ◇ K 10 9 2
     ♣ 8 7 5                            ♣ Q J 9 4
                        ♠ A K J 8
                        ♡ A Q 9 8 7 3
                        ◇ 7
                        ♣ K 2
```

West	North	East	South
		Pass	1♡
Pass	2◇	Pass	2♠
Pass	3♣	Pass	3♡
Pass	4♡	Pass	4♠
Pass	6♡	All pass	

Opening lead: ♣7

Dummy is pleasant to behold and the only challenge is to take care of the spade suit. So?

If you play two top spades and ruff a spade with the 10, East overruffs and takes out dummy's last trump. This would be very regrettable: you are trying to make twelve tricks, not thirteen, so should ruff the first spade with the king. The closed hand is re-entered with a diamond ruff and the next spade is ruffed with the 10. All you can lose is a trump trick.

When you cannot afford to ruff with a master trump, always ruff with the highest you can spare, to lessen if not to eliminate the risk of an overruff.

In a true crossruff the declarer cannot subsequently draw the enemy trumps, as they will have more trumps than he. Any winners in the side suits should be taken before the crossruff begins, for otherwise they may never be cashable:

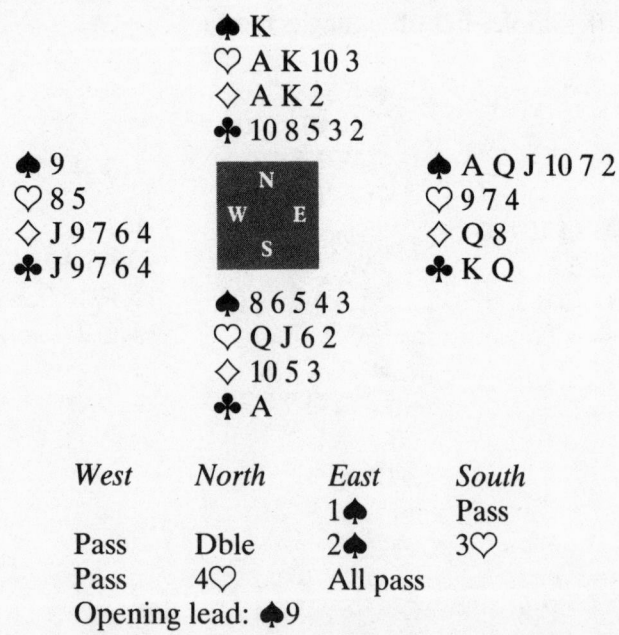

```
                    ♠ K
                    ♡ A K 10 3
                    ◇ A K 2
                    ♣ 10 8 5 3 2
   ♠ 9                                ♠ A Q J 10 7 2
   ♡ 8 5                              ♡ 9 7 4
   ◇ J 9 7 6 4                        ◇ Q 8
   ♣ J 9 7 6 4                        ♣ K Q
                    ♠ 8 6 5 4 3
                    ♡ Q J 6 2
                    ◇ 10 5 3
                    ♣ A
```

West	North	East	South
		1♠	Pass
Pass	Dble	2♠	3♡
Pass	4♡	All pass	

Opening lead: ♠9

East wins and returns a trump but a count shows that you still have enough trumps for a crossruff. First you should cash the ◇A–K and ♣A: then you can ruff spades and clubs alternately. If you don't, East will throw away diamonds as you ruff clubs and you will never make the ◇A–K.

ESTABLISHMENT BY RUFFING

Declarer should prefer to ruff a suit where there is a chance of establishing long cards than to ruff one where he gains only the immediate trick.

It has been noted that this form of play may impose entry problems and we have touched on the use of trumps to overcome them. There are other dodges:

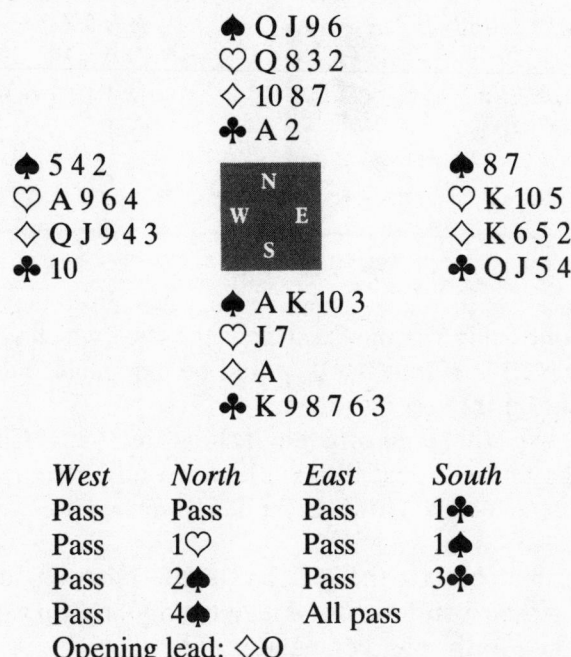

	♠ Q J 9 6	
	♡ Q 8 3 2	
	◇ 10 8 7	
	♣ A 2	
♠ 5 4 2		♠ 8 7
♡ A 9 6 4		♡ K 10 5
◇ Q J 9 4 3		◇ K 6 5 2
♣ 10		♣ Q J 5 4
	♠ A K 10 3	
	♡ J 7	
	◇ A	
	♣ K 9 8 7 6 3	

West	North	East	South
Pass	Pass	Pass	1♣
Pass	1♡	Pass	1♠
Pass	2♠	Pass	3♣
Pass	4♠	All pass	

Opening lead: ◇Q

First you take two rounds of trumps, for unless they are 3–2 you will have to bank on a favourable club division. Here, both opponents follow, so now you should consider whether you can beat a 4–1 club break.

Experiment will show that you have not enough entries to ruff two clubs and draw the last trump. So, how about taking only one ruff? After all, you can afford to lose a club and two hearts.

You must not risk having a club winner ruffed, so should cash the ♣A and duck a club! Then ruff the diamond return and ruff a club. Now you can re-enter your hand with the last trump and claim ten tricks.

The need to guard a 4–1 break in a side suit is very frequent:

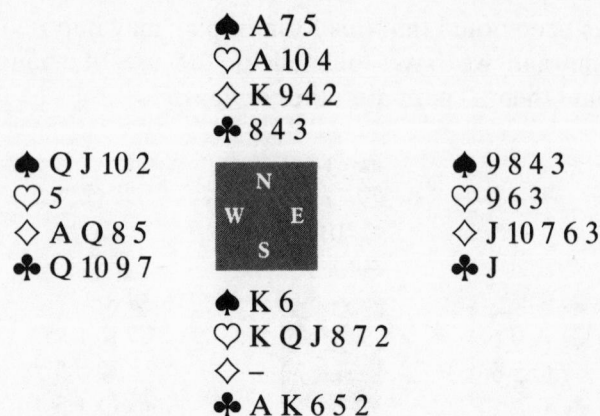

$\spadesuit$ A 7 5
$\heartsuit$ A 10 4
$\diamondsuit$ K 9 4 2
$\clubsuit$ 8 4 3

$\spadesuit$ Q J 10 2
$\heartsuit$ 5
$\diamondsuit$ A Q 8 5
$\clubsuit$ Q 10 9 7

$\spadesuit$ 9 8 4 3
$\heartsuit$ 9 6 3
$\diamondsuit$ J 10 7 6 3
$\clubsuit$ J

$\spadesuit$ K 6
$\heartsuit$ K Q J 8 7 2
$\diamondsuit$ –
$\clubsuit$ A K 6 5 2

The contract is 6$\heartsuit$ and West leads the $\clubsuit$Q, which you win in hand. A 2–2 trump break would be agreeable but West shows out on the second round.

There will still be no problem if clubs are 3–2. If East has four clubs you are a dead duck, as he will return a trump when you concede a club. However, if he has a singleton you can cope.

Cash a club, cross to the $\spadesuit$A, and lead a club from dummy. If East ruffs he is ruffing a loser and dummy's trump will take care of the fourth round of clubs.

If East discards on the second club you win and concede a club to West: the fourth club can then be ruffed with a master trump.

The reader will have noted how the club suit was tested: had the $\clubsuit$A–K been played off, the contract would have failed.

The next deal shows a form of play that is not widely recognised:

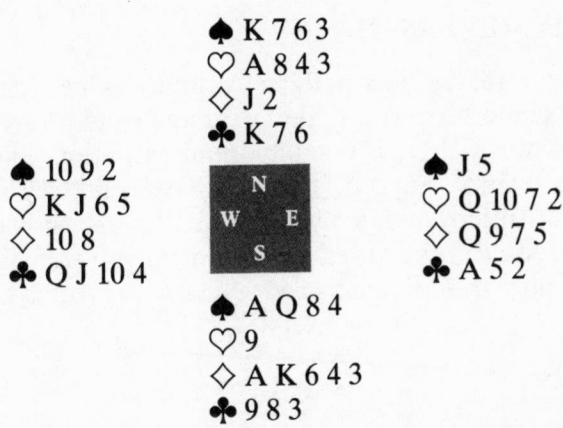

♠ K 7 6 3
♡ A 8 4 3
♢ J 2
♣ K 7 6

♠ 10 9 2
♡ K J 6 5
♢ 10 8
♣ Q J 10 4

♠ J 5
♡ Q 10 7 2
♢ Q 9 7 5
♣ A 5 2

♠ A Q 8 4
♡ 9
♢ A K 6 4 3
♣ 9 8 3

The contract is 4♠ and West leads the ♣Q, which is allowed to hold. He continues with the jack and South ducks again: the ace might be doubleton. But it isn't. West now leads the ♣4 and East wins with the ace, returning the ♡2.

Can you do better than to draw three rounds of trumps and bank on a 3–3 diamond break, which would allow you to get home with one ruff in dummy?

You might think of playing off only the ♠A–K before testing diamonds, hoping to ruff twice if necessary. This would be an improvement if you had enough entries, but you haven't. Even if you had, it would not work as the cards lie.

From the early play it seems that West may be 4–4 in hearts and clubs. In that case you cannot get home unless his remaining cards are 3–2. So, do not touch trumps: play off three rounds of diamonds. If the suit is 3–3, fine. Here, West can ruff the third diamond with the 9 but dummy overruffs with the king. Now trumps can be drawn with the A–Q and the fourth diamond ruffed with dummy's last trump.

If West elects not to ruff the third diamond you can still manoeuvre to take two diamond ruffs.

This form of play is worth considering when the defender in front of dummy can be placed with five cards in trumps and the side suit combined. Whether these are 3–2 or 2–3, the plan succeeds. If they are 4–1 the contract fails on any line.

DUMMY REVERSAL

Declarer normally gains nothing by ruffing in the long trump hand, usually his own, as these trumps would have made tricks anyway. There is one important exception, known as dummy reversal. Suppose that you have a holding such as Q–J–x of trumps in dummy and A–K–10–x–x in your own hand. If you can ruff three times in hand you will still have three natural trump winners and will make six trump tricks in all.

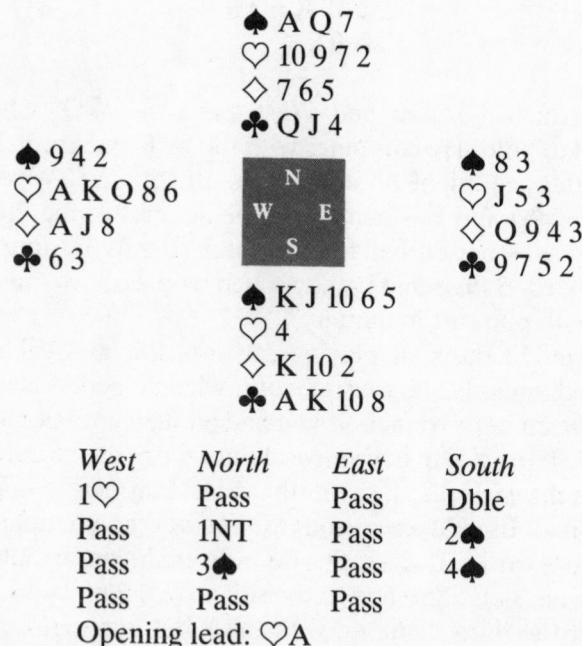

```
                    ♠ A Q 7
                    ♡ 10 9 7 2
                    ◇ 7 6 5
                    ♣ Q J 4
    ♠ 9 4 2                           ♠ 8 3
    ♡ A K Q 8 6           N           ♡ J 5 3
    ◇ A J 8          W         E      ◇ Q 9 4 3
    ♣ 6 3                 S           ♣ 9 7 5 2
                    ♠ K J 10 6 5
                    ♡ 4
                    ◇ K 10 2
                    ♣ A K 10 8
```

West	North	East	South
1♡	Pass	Pass	Dble
Pass	1NT	Pass	2♠
Pass	3♠	Pass	4♠
Pass	Pass	Pass	

Opening lead: ♡A

As South you ruff the heart continuation and note that there are only nine ready winners, with little chance of a trick in diamonds.

If you can ruff three times in hand, this will produce an extra trick, but only if trumps are 3–2. So, cash the ♠K and lead low to the queen. If someone shows out you must abandon the dummy reversal. Here, all follow, so you ruff a heart, cross with a club and ruff the last heart. Cross again with a club, draw the last trump and cash the clubs for game.

Defenders can often spike declarer's guns by attacking dummy's entries or by simply not leading the suit declarer can ruff. Had West switched to a club, the dummy reversal would not have worked.

A dummy reversal does not have to be based on solid trumps:

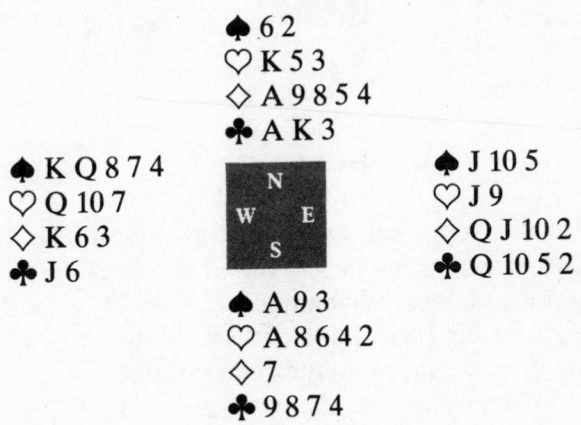

♠ 6 2
♡ K 5 3
♢ A 9 8 5 4
♣ A K 3

♠ K Q 8 7 4
♡ Q 10 7
♢ K 6 3
♣ J 6

♠ J 10 5
♡ J 9
♢ Q J 10 2
♣ Q 10 5 2

♠ A 9 3
♡ A 8 6 4 2
♢ 7
♣ 9 8 7 4

South reaches a shaky 4♡ and West leads the ♠K. Even with a favourable trump break and a spade ruff in dummy, there would be only nine tricks and South would need a club break as well. A dummy reversal offers a better chance.

Win the spade, cross to the ace of diamonds, ruff a diamond, cross with a club and ruff another diamond. Play off the ♡A–K and ruff diamonds once more. West cannot gain by overruffing, so you can cross with a club and lead the fifth diamond. This card or the ♡5 will provide the tenth trick.

TRUMP CONTROL

When a defender has the last trump, or is on lead when declarer has no more trumps, declarer is said to have lost control. This can be very bad:

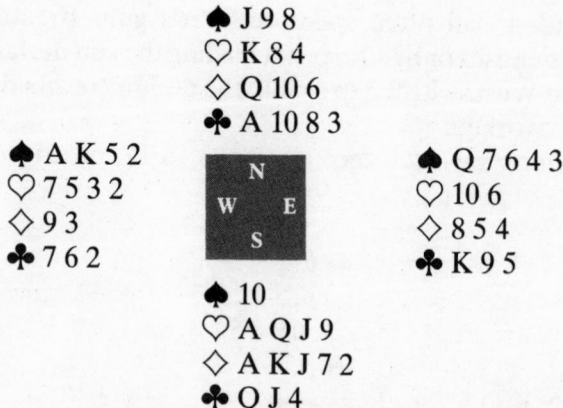

Against 4♡ West begins with two top spades. If South ruffs and tries to draw trumps he loses control. West is left with the last trump and when diamonds are played he ruffs, the defenders cashing their spade tricks for down two.

An effective counter is to refuse to ruff until the suit can be ruffed in dummy and declarer's trump length preserved. Here, on the second and third spades South should discard clubs, as he does not need to develop the suit. If a fourth spade is led it can be ruffed in dummy and four rounds of trumps drawn.

To avail himself of this strategy, declarer has to keep a trump in dummy until he is sure he will not have to lose the lead:

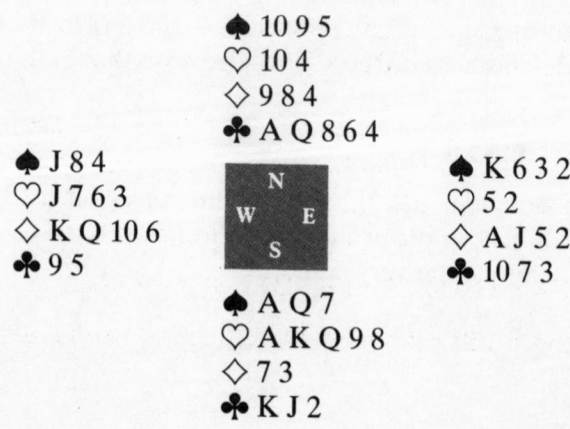

Against 4♡ the defenders begin with three rounds of diamonds. South has to ruff, for otherwise he might lose four tricks. The correct play now is the ♡9. South can afford to concede a trump trick as long as there is a trump in dummy to deal with a diamond return.

If instead South plays off the ♡A–K–Q he will be obliged to leave West with the jack and switch to clubs. Now West ruffs the third club and exits with a diamond.

Another counter to a forcing defence is to allow defenders to make trump tricks separately when normally you would try to drop them together:

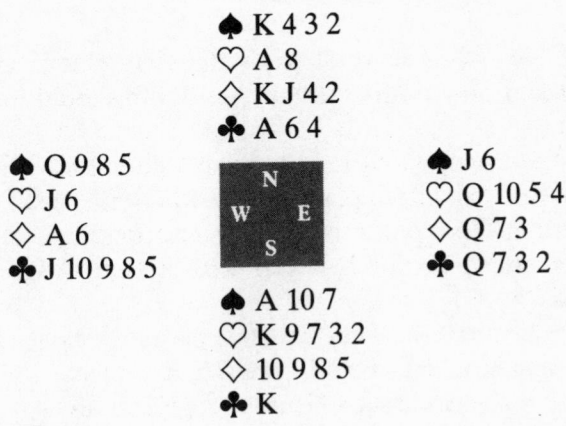

```
              ♠ K 4 3 2
              ♡ A 8
              ◇ K J 4 2
              ♣ A 6 4
♠ Q 9 8 5                      ♠ J 6
♡ J 6          N              ♡ Q 10 5 4
◇ A 6        W   E            ◇ Q 7 3
♣ J 10 9 8 5   S              ♣ Q 7 3 2
              ♠ A 10 7
              ♡ K 9 7 3 2
              ◇ 10 9 8 5
              ♣ K
```

The contract is 3♡ and West leads the ♣J. You take the ♡A–K and all follow. If you were in game you would play a third round, but as the cards lie East would cash his trump winners and force out the ♣A. With only one trump left you would never get the diamonds going.

As you can afford to lose two trump tricks you should play only the ♡A–K and then go for the diamonds. Now you are a jump ahead.

NULLIFYING THE DEFENDERS' RUFFS

Sometimes a ruff cannot be prevented but can be rendered harmless:

♠ Q J 8 5
♡ A 5 4 2
◇ 8 6 4
♣ K 10

♠ K 10 9 7 2
♡ K 7 6
◇ A 10
♣ A 7 3

After 1♠–3♠–4♠ West leads the ♡9. This is an easy contract and only a ruff can hurt, so South should focus on this.

He should realise that it may make a difference where he takes the first trick. Suppose that he wins with the ♡A and leads a trump. East puts on the ace and returns the ♡Q. West ruffs the king and South is left with a heart loser and a diamond.

'This is incredible,' South tells his partner. 'Bloggs had to have a singleton heart and Jones had to have the ♠A, otherwise ten tricks are icy.' But they were icy anyway. From the lead of the 9, South can see that any ruff will come from West, so he should win in hand. When East gets in, West can ruff, but only a loser.

Now suppose that the lead is the ♡Q: this time the trick should be taken in dummy, lest East should have a singleton heart and West the ♠A.

In the next deal the defenders have two natural trump tricks and threaten also to gain a ruff. But you can arrange that if the ruff is taken, one of the trump tricks will evaporate:

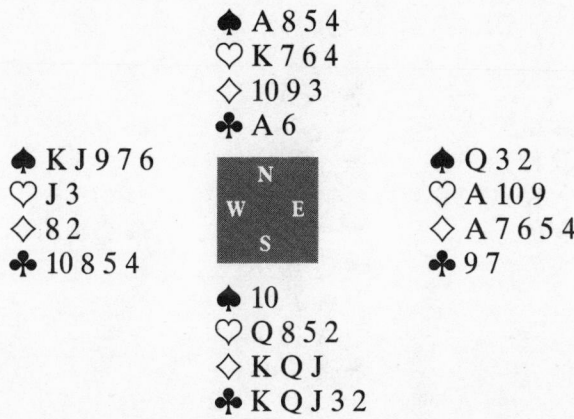

♠ A 8 5 4
♥ K 7 6 4
♦ 10 9 3
♣ A 6

♠ K J 9 7 6
♥ J 3
♦ 8 2
♣ 10 8 5 4

♠ Q 3 2
♥ A 10 9
♦ A 7 6 5 4
♣ 9 7

♠ 10
♥ Q 8 5 2
♦ K Q J
♣ K Q J 3 2

Against 4♥ West leads the ♦8 and East returns the suit. West follows with the 2, so it is clear that he can ruff the next round. And yet, with a 3–2 trump break you can be sure to get home!

Cross to the ♠A and lead a low trump from the table. If East ducks, the queen wins, a second trump is played, and West gets no ruff. If East goes in with the ace to give West a ruff, he forfeits his second trump trick. Finally, if West has the ♥A he wins the first trump lead but cannot put East in.

With this type the idea is to lead the first round of trumps through the partner of the defender who can ruff.

In the next case the declarer again cannot stop the ruff but by controlling when it takes place he gains a vital tempo:

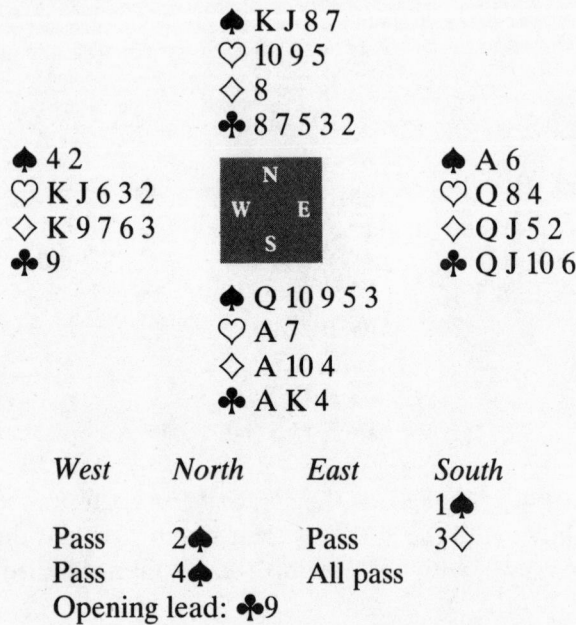

	♠ K J 8 7	
	♡ 10 9 5	
	◇ 8	
	♣ 8 7 5 3 2	

♠ 4 2		♠ A 6
♡ K J 6 3 2		♡ Q 8 4
◇ K 9 7 6 3		◇ Q J 5 2
♣ 9		♣ Q J 10 6

	♠ Q 10 9 5 3	
	♡ A 7	
	◇ A 10 4	
	♣ A K 4	

West	North	East	South
			1♠
Pass	2♠	Pass	3◇
Pass	4♠	All pass	

Opening lead: ♣9

East follows with the 6, so it seems clear that the lead is a singleton. You win and lead a trump, taken by East who returns the ♣Q.

If you cover, West will ruff and return a heart, leaving you with a fatal number of losers. Therefore your thoughts should lightly turn to what will happen if you allow the queen to hold!

In that case West ruffs the next club but, lo, the timing is in your favour: you can win the heart return, cross to a trump, ruff a club, and park a heart on the fifth club.

Chapter 17

THE DEFENCE TO TRUMP CONTRACTS

Counting declarer's winners – Ruffs by defenders –
Preventing ruffs by declarer – Trump promotion –
Forcing plays

A defender seeing the ball clearly will often spot a promising route to the setting tricks. When he cannot, his best bet may be to diagnose the declarer's game plan and try to thwart it. But in some cases he can do neither. There is then a choice: grab tricks quickly or – if it looks as though the contract will be hard to make – exit passively without helping declarer.

How should the choice be resolved? The golden rule is to count declarer's winning tricks, actual and prospective.

COUNTING DECLARER'S WINNERS

Requires mental effort, but rewards are high. You are West:

```
                    ♠ K Q 5
                    ♡ Q 5 2
                    ◇ 10 3 2
                    ♣ K Q 10 9
  ♠ J 10 9 3                      ♠ A 6 4
  ♡ K 10          ┌─────────┐     ♡ J 4
  ◇ Q 6 4         │    N    │     ◇ 9 8 7
  ♣ A J 6 3       │ W     E │     ♣ 8 7 5 4 2
                  │    S    │
                  └─────────┘
                    ♠ 8 7 2
                    ♡ A 9 8 7 6 3
                    ◇ A K J 5
                    ♣ –
```

West	North	East	South
Pass	Pass	Pass	1♡
Pass	2NT	Pass	4♡
Pass	Pass	Pass	

Opening lead: ♠J

East captures the king with the ace and returns the 6. The queen wins, a trump goes to declarer's ace, and another trump puts you in, East following with the jack. You cash a spade and all follow.

You place South with five trump tricks and a spade, and he will surely have the ◇A–K: eight tricks in all. If you exit with a low club he will have nine. Counting the winners was worth the trouble, for any other lead gives him the contract.

At the table you may never get the chance to impress your friends with such a sparkler, but the same kind of reasoning leads directly to accurate defence on everyday deals such as the next, where again you are West:

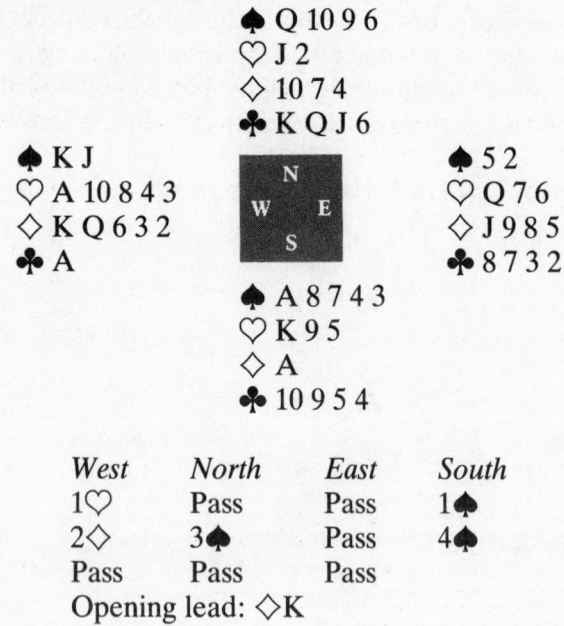

♠ Q 10 9 6
♡ J 2
◇ 10 7 4
♣ K Q J 6

♠ K J
♡ A 10 8 4 3
◇ K Q 6 3 2
♣ A

♠ 5 2
♡ Q 7 6
◇ J 9 8 5
♣ 8 7 3 2

♠ A 8 7 4 3
♡ K 9 5
◇ A
♣ 10 9 5 4

West	North	East	South
1♡	Pass	Pass	1♠
2◇	3♣	Pass	4♠
Pass	Pass	Pass	

Opening lead: ◇K

South wins with the ace and plays the ace and another trump, East following. You lead the ◇Q but South ruffs and returns a club, East playing the 8. Is it time to attack hearts?

East's ♣8 suggests either four clubs or two. If four, South will have only three club winners, four trumps and the ♢A. When you can see that declarer has not enough tricks, you avoid a play that may present him with one, so here you exit with a diamond.

It is not very likely that East has two clubs and South six, but in that case South will have only one heart and the contract will be icy.

RUFFS BY DEFENDERS

Something for nothing is an idea that has such strong appeal that it seems unnecessary to commend the advantage of scoring a ruff with an otherwise useless trump, and better to caution against over-eagerness. In particular:

Do not go for an immediate ruff if you can first establish a high-card trick and still get a ruff afterwards; otherwise you may leave declarer with discards.

Do not play for a ruff in declarer's second suit unless you can see that it will set the contract. When you are short enough to get a ruff, your partner may have a holding that will trouble declarer, and by leading the suit you may damage his holding:

10 4 3

9   Q J 7 5 2

A K 8 6

East will normally make one trick in this side suit if declarer knows his percentages and two tricks if he doesn't, but if West leads the suit East may make no tricks at all.

Even when a ruff is there for the taking, it is usually wrong to ruff declarer's side suit when you will be ruffing only a loser. You are East:

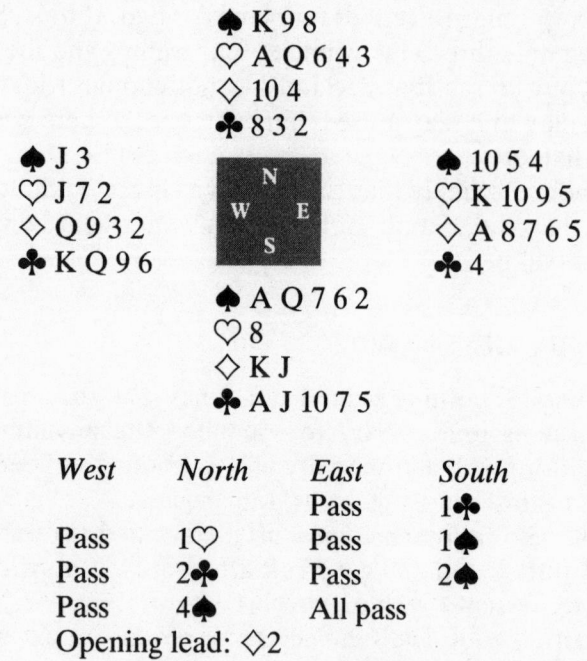

♠ K 9 8
♡ A Q 6 4 3
◇ 10 4
♣ 8 3 2

♠ J 3
♡ J 7 2
◇ Q 9 3 2
♣ K Q 9 6

♠ 10 5 4
♡ K 10 9 5
◇ A 8 7 6 5
♣ 4

♠ A Q 7 6 2
♡ 8
◇ K J
♣ A J 10 7 5

West	North	East	South
		Pass	1♣
Pass	1♡	Pass	1♠
Pass	2♣	Pass	2♠
Pass	4♠	All pass	

Opening lead: ◇2

You win with the ace and return the ♣4; the right shot at this point. West captures South's jack with the queen and plays the ♡2. The ace goes up and a club is led from the table.

From West's switch you should conclude that he has tricks in clubs, so you should not ruff. If you do, you will in effect be ruffing West's trick: South will be able to draw trumps in two rounds and ruff a club to leave his hand high.

You are not necessarily expected to be able to read such positions in detail: you proceed on the basis of general principles. Here, as long as you do not ruff, your trump holding proves fatal to declarer's chances.

Of course, there are many deals where declarer's side suit, once he has dislodged a stopper, will be solid. In such a case defenders should thirst for ruffs as the hart does for cool waters. Accurate signalling is the key:

```
              ♠ 9 7 6
              ♡ K Q 10
              ◇ K Q 10 9
              ♣ 10 5 2
♠ K Q 10 5 2      N           ♠ J 8 3
♡ 6 5 4      W       E        ♡ 7 2
◇ 7 3            S            ◇ A 8 6 2
♣ Q 8 7                       ♣ K 9 4 3
              ♠ A 4
              ♡ A J 9 8 3
              ◇ J 5 4
              ♣ A J 6
```

The contract is 4♡ and West leads the ♠K, which is allowed to hold. On winning the next spade South sees that he needs three diamond tricks for game. He takes two rounds of trumps but leaves dummy's third trump as an entry. However, he cannot succeed against accurate defence. When he leads a diamond, West signals with the 7 and East ducks. If diamonds are continued, West gets a ruff, and if a third trump is drawn, East holds up the ◇A until the third round.

Ruffs for partner

A defender who has length in an enemy side suit should bear in mind that his partner may have failed to try for a ruff in this suit for fear of helping declarer:

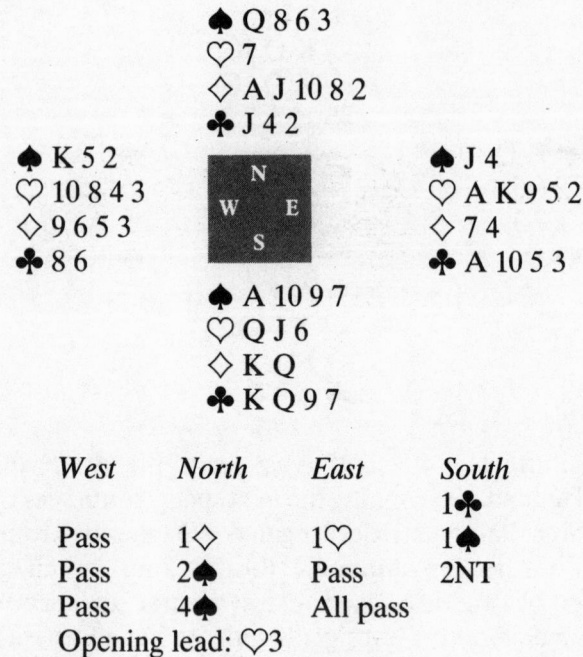

♠ Q 8 6 3
♡ 7
♢ A J 10 8 2
♣ J 4 2

♠ K 5 2
♡ 10 8 4 3
♢ 9 6 5 3
♣ 8 6

♠ J 4
♡ A K 9 5 2
♢ 7 4
♣ A 10 5 3

♠ A 10 9 7
♡ Q J 6
♢ K Q
♣ K Q 9 7

West	North	East	South
			1♣
Pass	1♢	1♡	1♠
Pass	2♠	Pass	2NT
Pass	4♠	All pass	

Opening lead: ♡3

East wins with the ♡K and sees that prospects will be dim unless West has a trick in trumps. In that case a club ruff is on the cards, as South has bid the suit. Which is more likely: that West has doubleton club, or a singleton? He would not have led either.

For his 2NT call South is perhaps more likely to be 4–3–2–4 than 4–3–1–5, so East returns a low club, assuring a happy ending when West comes in with the ♠K.

To ruff one of declarer's losers does him no harm and may strengthen his hold on the trump suit. Sometimes you can work out that a special stroke is needed to ensure that the card ruffed will be a winner. You are West:

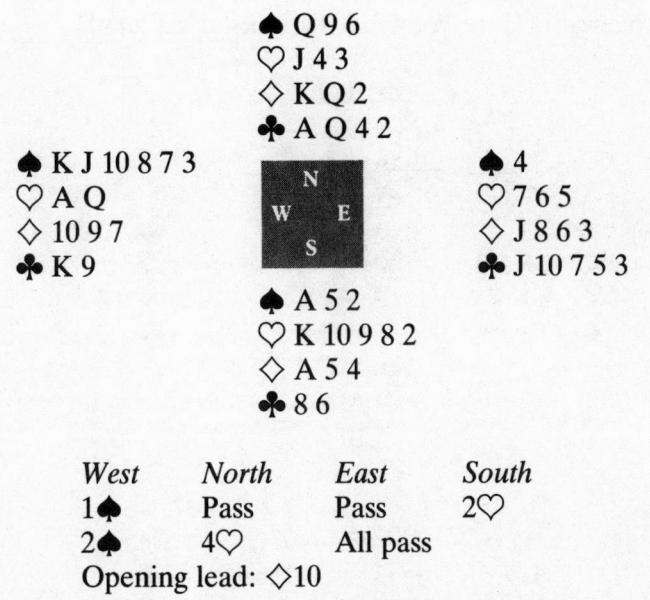

♠ Q 9 6
♡ J 4 3
◇ K Q 2
♣ A Q 4 2

♠ K J 10 8 7 3
♡ A Q
◇ 10 9 7
♣ K 9

♠ 4
♡ 7 6 5
◇ J 8 6 3
♣ J 10 7 5 3

♠ A 5 2
♡ K 10 9 8 2
◇ A 5 4
♣ 8 6

West	North	East	South
1♠	Pass	Pass	2♡
2♠	4♡	All pass	

Opening lead: ◇10

The first trick is won in dummy and a low trump lead brings forth the 7, 10 and queen. The 7 looks like the beginning of an echo, suggesting three trumps and a desire to ruff, but even without this clue you might reckon that with no spade ruff your only tricks will be the ♠K and ♡A–Q.

Now you must consider what will happen if you lead the ♠J and East has the expected singleton. The queen will win and a trump will be led. You can give partner a ruff but he will be ruffing a loser: the natural trick you would have made without going to all this trouble.

To put South in his place you must lead the ♠K on the first round. When in with the ♡A, the lead of the ♠J allows East to ruff away the queen.

Ruffing to kill discards

To ruff a winner that would have provided declarer with a discard is an effective form of defence, even when declarer can overruff. Here West has the reins in his hands:

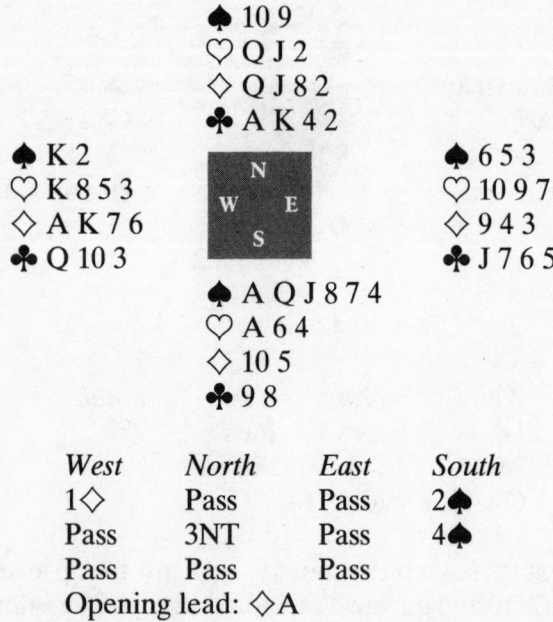

              ♠ 10 9
              ♡ Q J 2
              ♢ Q J 8 2
              ♣ A K 4 2

♠ K 2   ♠ 6 5 3
♡ K 8 5 3   ♡ 10 9 7
♢ A K 7 6   ♢ 9 4 3
♣ Q 10 3   ♣ J 7 6 5

              ♠ A Q J 8 7 4
              ♡ A 6 4
              ♢ 10 5
              ♣ 9 8

West	North	East	South
1♢	Pass	Pass	2♠
Pass	3NT	Pass	4♠
Pass	Pass	Pass	

Opening lead: ♢A

On the first trick East plays the 3 and declarer the 5. West may think he has plenty of defensive tricks but if he counts the winners he sees that five trump tricks, the ♡A, ♣A–K and two diamond tricks will give South game.

One of these winners can be erased. West continues with a second and third diamond, South discarding a heart. When in with the ♠K, a fourth diamond allows East to ruff and leave South wishing he had passed 3NT.

It is sometimes necessary to play a similar defence while holding back a winner in the suit ruffed:

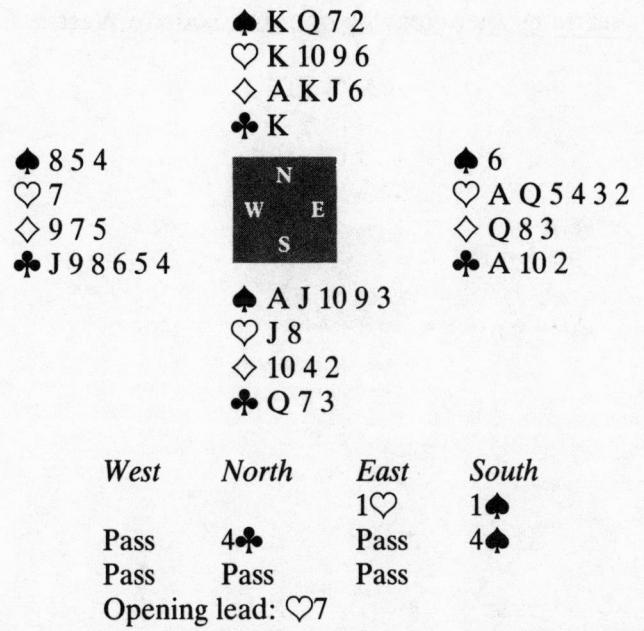

♠ K Q 7 2
♡ K 10 9 6
♢ A K J 6
♣ K

♠ 8 5 4
♡ 7
♢ 9 7 5
♣ J 9 8 6 5 4

♠ 6
♡ A Q 5 4 3 2
♢ Q 8 3
♣ A 10 2

♠ A J 10 9 3
♡ J 8
♢ 10 4 2
♣ Q 7 3

West	North	East	South
		1♡	1♠
Pass	4♣	Pass	4♠
Pass	Pass	Pass	

Opening lead: ♡7

East wins the first trick with the queen and is not misled when South falsecards with the jack. How should he continue?

Suppose that he cashes the ♡A and plays a third heart, hoping to promote a trump trick. South ruffs high, draws trumps, and makes game by discarding a diamond on the fourth heart.

If East leads the ♡2 at the second trick, he prevails whether or not West has a promotable trump holding. East wins the club return and plays a third heart, still retaining the ace. This time South is forced to ruff, eventually losing a diamond trick.

Accessing partner's hand

Often a defender has a ruffing capability but the critical question is how to get partner into the lead. When he has a quick entry in trumps he should not necessarily do the obvious thing: there may be options. You are West:

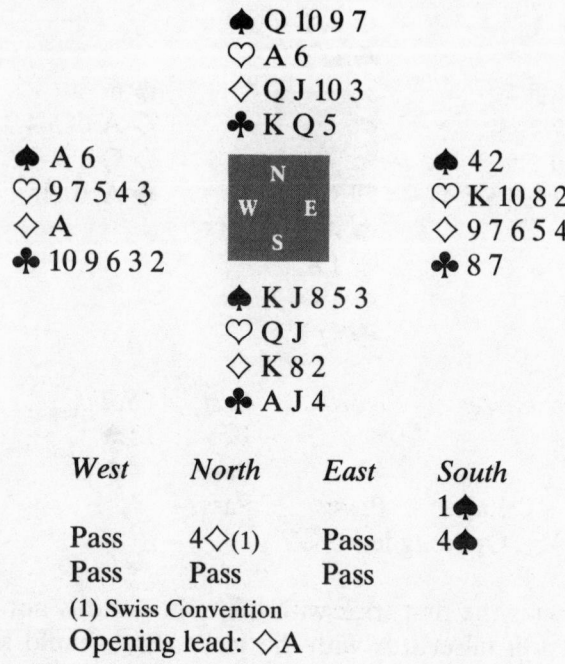

```
                    ♠ Q 10 9 7
                    ♡ A 6
                    ◇ Q J 10 3
                    ♣ K Q 5
♠ A 6                              ♠ 4 2
♡ 9 7 5 4 3          N            ♡ K 10 8 2
◇ A              W       E        ◇ 9 7 6 5 4
♣ 10 9 6 3 2         S            ♣ 8 7
                    ♠ K J 8 5 3
                    ♡ Q J
                    ◇ K 8 2
                    ♣ A J 4
```

West	North	East	South
			1♠
Pass	4◇(1)	Pass	4♠
Pass	Pass	Pass	

(1) Swiss Convention

Opening lead: ◇A

On the first trick East plays the ◇4, which you take as suit-length, not suit-preference. So?

You need to find East with the ♣A or the ♡K, as a defensive trick as well as an entry for a ruff. Had you no trump entry you would have to play him for the ♣A. As it is, a heart lead at this point gives you both chances: either he will signal the king or you will play a club when in with the ♠A.

Looking beyond the ruff

Before giving partner a ruff, a defender should consider whether the situation will be satisfactory after the ruff: perhaps a prior feat of arms is needed.

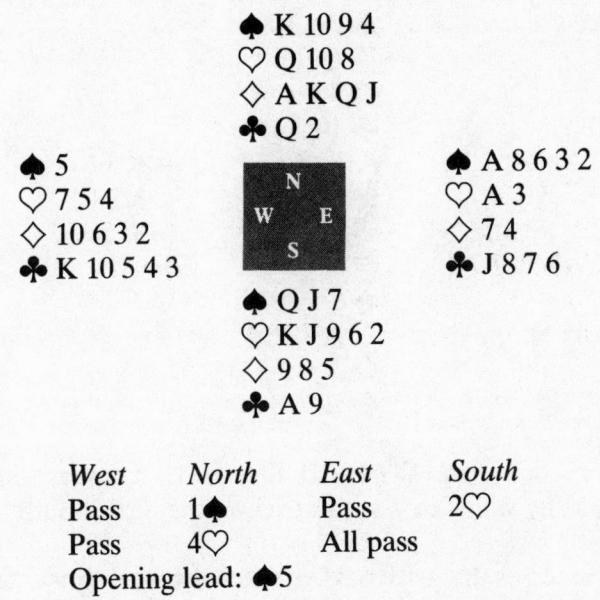

```
                    ♠ K 10 9 4
                    ♡ Q 10 8
                    ◇ A K Q J
                    ♣ Q 2
    ♠ 5                               ♠ A 8 6 3 2
    ♡ 7 5 4                           ♡ A 3
    ◇ 10 6 3 2                        ◇ 7 4
    ♣ K 10 5 4 3                      ♣ J 8 7 6
                    ♠ Q J 7
                    ♡ K J 9 6 2
                    ◇ 9 8 5
                    ♣ A 9
```

West	North	East	South
Pass	1♠	Pass	2♡
Pass	4♡	All pass	

Opening lead: ♠5

The lead is an obvious singleton but if a ruff is given West will have nowhere to go and the defenders will never make a fourth trick. East, however, can see that a club trick is needed, and as he will be coming in with the ♡A he should switch at the second trick. Whether South ducks or not, the defenders gain a club trick as well as a ruff.

PREVENTING RUFFS BY DECLARER

To prevent declarer from ruffing is no less noble a purpose than to gain ruffs oneself. Like all passive forms of defence, it comes more into the reckoning when dummy is below par or when the cards may lie poorly for declarer. Consider this deal from East's angle:

♠ A Q 9 2
♡ Q 9 3 2
♢ 7 4
♣ 10 5 4

♠ 10 5 3
♡ K 6
♢ J 10 8 5
♣ Q J 7 2

♠ K J 6 4
♡ 8 5 4
♢ K Q 9 2
♣ 9 6

♠ 8 7
♡ A J 10 7
♢ A 6 3
♣ A K 8 3

South is in 3♡ and West leads the ♢J. East covers with the queen, as he wants to win this trick or the next. South holds off.

East assesses that with passive defence the contract may be headed for the rocks: he has the spades sewn up, and if South has to take a finesse in trumps or clubs it will fail. There can be no advantage in switching to a club, as South has no discards coming. East therefore returns a trump: further trump leads at each opportunity will beat South with normal play. Without this defence South can ruff a diamond and the fourth club for nine tricks.

When you are fairly sure that a trump lead will prevent a ruff, do not be put off just because the lead may give away a trick in the trump suit itself. The trick may come back:

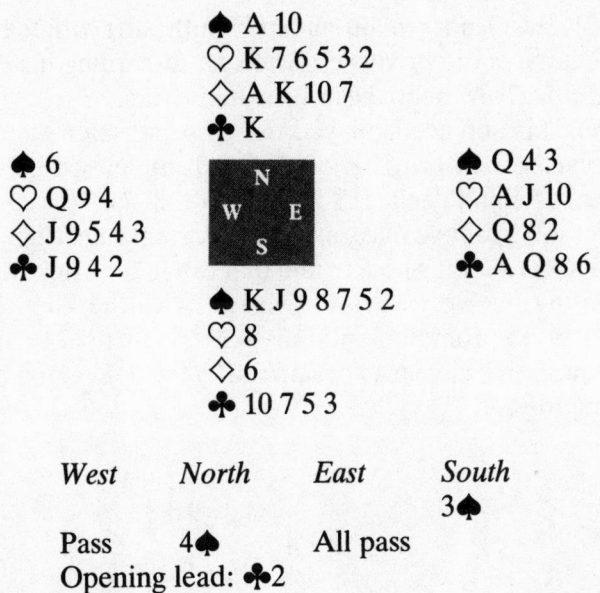

♠ A 10
♡ K 7 6 5 3 2
♢ A K 10 7
♣ K

♠ 6
♡ Q 9 4
♢ J 9 5 4 3
♣ J 9 4 2

♠ Q 4 3
♡ A J 10
♢ Q 8 2
♣ A Q 8 6

♠ K J 9 8 7 5 2
♡ 8
♢ 6
♣ 10 7 5 3

West	North	East	South
			3♠
Pass	4♠	All pass	

Opening lead: ♣2

From the lead, East places South with four clubs as well as seven spades. If he is allowed to ruff clubs twice he will make game despite losing a trump trick, so East returns a trump. Whether South takes a club ruff or not he is held to nine tricks.

TRUMP PROMOTION

This is a powerful form of defence. The threat of an overruff may undermine all but the strongest trump suits in such positions as these:

(1)　　　　　♠1072　　　　(2)　　　　　♠9765

♠J63　　　　　　♠84　　　♠K102　　　　　♠3

　　　♠AKQ95　　　　　　　　♠AQJ84

In (1), if South could get in he would swiftly draw trumps, but if East is on play and can lead a plain suit that West can ruff, South will lose a trump trick whether he ruffs high or low.

In (2), East leads a plain suit and South ruffs with the jack. West exercises the privilege of refusal, discarding instead of overruffing. Now he makes two trump tricks.

When this defence is played twice on the same hand, the effect can be shattering. K–9–2, for example, will be worth two tricks behind declarer's A–Q–J–10–8–7.

Diagram (2) above illustrates an important rule: a defender should not overruff with a trump that can take a trick without overruffing. If West were to overruff with the king the 10 would not be promoted and only one trick would be made.

The same principle may be applied by the defender who sits over dummy:

J 6

8   K 9 5 3

A Q 10 7 4 2

If South ruffs a plain suit with the jack, East makes two trump tricks as long as he does not overruff.

The only exceptions of practical importance are when you wish to gain the lead and when failing to take the trick may expose you to an endplay. Of course, if there is a chance to overruff with a card that will otherwise be useless, you take it.

When the tricks needed to set the contract can come only from the trump suit, the principle of not overruffing is boldly extended:

J 4

10 6 3 2   Q 8

A K 9 7 5

East leads a plain suit and South ruffs with the 9. If West can see that two tricks are needed from the trump suit, he should not overruff, even though he cannot be sure of making a trick at all. As the cards lie, declarer now loses two tricks.

A trump promotion will not work if declarer can discard a loser instead of ruffing. Defenders must first cash all plain winners:

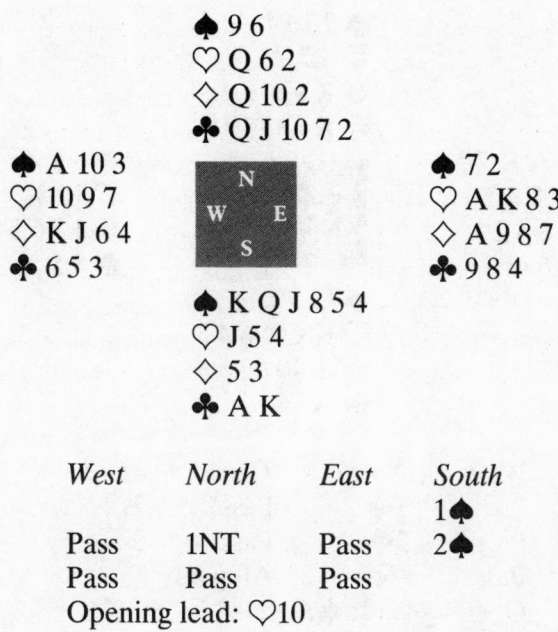

♠ 9 6
♡ Q 6 2
♢ Q 10 2
♣ Q J 10 7 2

♠ A 10 3
♡ 10 9 7
♢ K J 6 4
♣ 6 5 3

♠ 7 2
♡ A K 8 3
♢ A 9 8 7
♣ 9 8 4

♠ K Q J 8 5 4
♡ J 5 4
♢ 5 3
♣ A K

West	North	East	South
			1♠
Pass	1NT	Pass	2♠
Pass	Pass	Pass	

Opening lead: ♡10

East plays off the A–K and, placing West with a trump holding, leads a third round, preparing for a promotion. He returns the 8 rather than the 3, to highlight the higher-ranking side suit.

A trump from dummy goes to the king and ace. East's signal has marked him with the ♢A, so West sees that two diamond tricks and a trump promotion when East leads the last heart will beat the contract.

However, West must not put East in with the ♢A at this point. If he does, when East returns the ♡3 South will discard his remaining diamond. West therefore must make the sparkling play of the ♢K. Now a diamond to the ace and heart return apply the quietus.

Promotion can also be brought about by a play aptly termed the uppercut:

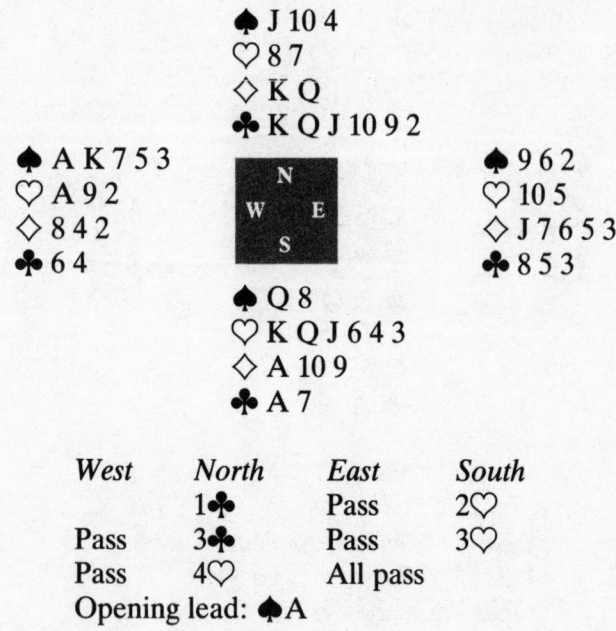

♠ J 10 4
♡ 8 7
♦ K Q
♣ K Q J 10 9 2

♠ A K 7 5 3
♡ A 9 2
♦ 8 4 2
♣ 6 4

♠ 9 6 2
♡ 10 5
♦ J 7 6 5 3
♣ 8 5 3

♠ Q 8
♡ K Q J 6 4 3
♦ A 10 9
♣ A 7

West	North	East	South
	1♣	Pass	2♡
Pass	3♣	Pass	3♡
Pass	4♡	All pass	

Opening lead: ♠A

West cashes two top spades, dropping South's doubleton queen. Only a trump promotion holds hope, so West continues with a third spade. When in with the ♡A, a fourth spade allows East to ruff with the 10.

A trump holding may also be promoted in length. A defender with, say, Q–4–3–2 of trumps should not overruff a declarer who has A–K–J–10: by simply discarding he eventually makes a long trump as well as the queen, provided his trumps cannot be drawn by dummy.

FORCING PLAYS

A powerful defence is to run declarer out of trumps by making him ruff. We saw in the previous chapter that declarer may refuse to ruff, waiting until dummy can take the force, but defenders in turn have a resource: they may hold up a trump winner until dummy has no more trumps. Here East faces a standard situation:

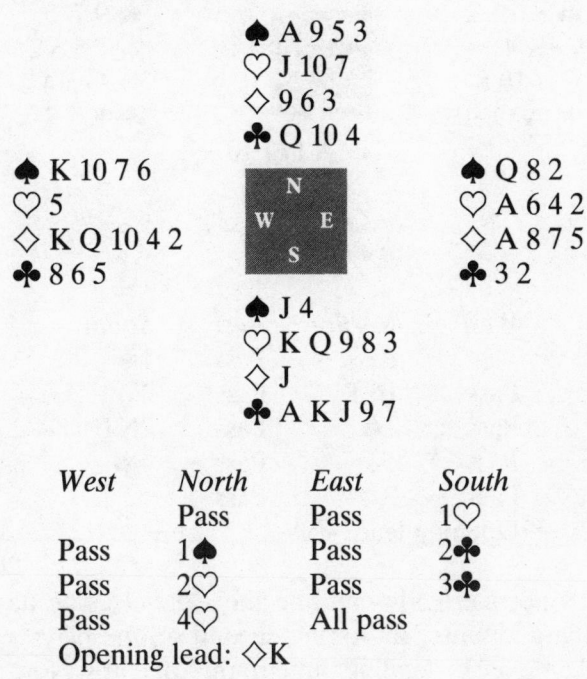

♠ A 9 5 3
♡ J 10 7
♢ 9 6 3
♣ Q 10 4

♠ K 10 7 6
♡ 5
♢ K Q 10 4 2
♣ 8 6 5

♠ Q 8 2
♡ A 6 4 2
♢ A 8 7 5
♣ 3 2

♠ J 4
♡ K Q 9 8 3
♢ J
♣ A K J 9 7

West	North	East	South
	Pass	Pass	1♡
Pass	1♠	Pass	2♣
Pass	2♡	Pass	3♣
Pass	4♡	All pass	

Opening lead: ♢K

West plays a second diamond and South ruffs, returning a heart. If East wins and plays a diamond, South will discard a spade. Any further diamond can be ruffed in dummy and trumps can be drawn.

East must hold up the ♡A, and when South leads a second trump hold up again. Now South is out of business, as a further trump lead will bring a diamond return.

To play such a defence it is not necessary to have a winner in the trump suit. Four small trumps and an entry in declarer's second suit may do nicely.

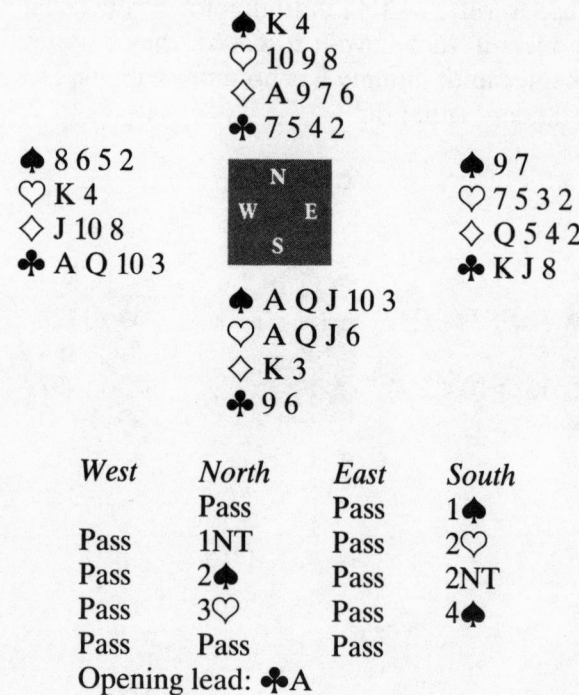

```
                    ♠ K 4
                    ♡ 10 9 8
                    ◇ A 9 7 6
                    ♣ 7 5 4 2
♠ 8 6 5 2                              ♠ 9 7
♡ K 4              N                   ♡ 7 5 3 2
◇ J 10 8       W       E               ◇ Q 5 4 2
♣ A Q 10 3         S                   ♣ K J 8
                    ♠ A Q J 10 3
                    ♡ A Q J 6
                    ◇ K 3
                    ♣ 9 6
```

West	North	East	South
	Pass	Pass	1♠
Pass	1NT	Pass	2♡
Pass	2♠	Pass	2NT
Pass	3♡	Pass	4♠
Pass	Pass	Pass	

Opening lead: ♣A

West's normal lead would be the ◇J but as he has four trumps and an entry in South's second suit he plays a more spirited defence by leading three rounds of clubs. Now South cannot get home, since West will play another club when in with the ♡K.

Shortening declarer with a ruff and discard

It is usually a bad mistake to lead a suit that allows declarer to ruff in one hand while discarding a loser from the other, especially if this allows him to establish a side suit without loss. However, this is not the case when declarer has no useful discard. Here West is the key defender:

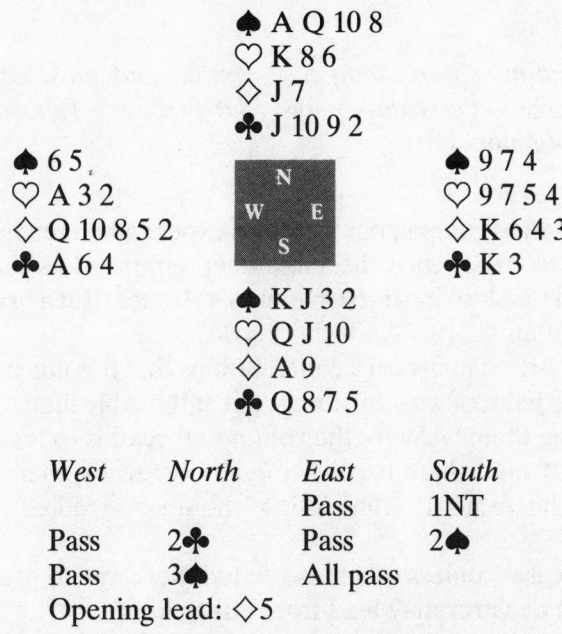

♠ A Q 10 8
♡ K 8 6
◇ J 7
♣ J 10 9 2

♠ 6 5
♡ A 3 2
◇ Q 10 8 5 2
♣ A 6 4

♠ 9 7 4
♡ 9 7 5 4
◇ K 6 4 3
♣ K 3

♠ K J 3 2
♡ Q J 10
◇ A 9
♣ Q 8 7 5

West	North	East	South
		Pass	1NT
Pass	2♣	Pass	2♠
Pass	3♠	All pass	

Opening lead: ◇5

Dummy plays low and South takes the king with the ace. He draws three rounds of trumps, East following each time. A club towards dummy is taken by East's king, the ◇3 comes back and West is in.

If West returns a diamond, conceding a ruff and discard, and plays another when in with one of his aces, he takes out declarer's remaining trumps and is left with the fifth diamond and an entry. Any other return allows South to get home.

Chapter 18

PLAYS IN A SINGLE SUIT

Leading up to strength – Simple and advanced finesses – Percentage plays – Safety plays – Table of probabilities

The seasoned campaigner need not expect when reading this chapter to experience the same deep emotions as the poet Keats on first looking into Chapman's Homer. But a brush-up never did any harm. And who knows . . .?

There are so many card combinations that it is much better to get the habit of working things out at the table than to try to memorize them. Always the common thread is to lessen the chance of one's high cards being clobbered by enemy high cards. The examples that follow should be studied in that context.

In all cases, unless otherwise stated there are no problems of entry: declarer may lead from either hand.

LEADING UP TO STRENGTH

A basic principle of play is to lead a low card from one hand towards a high card or cards in the other hand. You hope to circumvent a high card in between:

(1)	Q 6 4		(2)	K J 10	
K 9 5 3		J 10 7	Q 8 2		A 9 6 4
	A 8 2			7 5 3	

In (1) South leads low towards the queen. When West has the king, the queen makes a trick on this round or later. In (2) South leads twice from hand to the jack and 10.

To find one card well placed is a 50% chance; to find two is 25% (50% of 50%):

(3)   K J 2   (4)   A Q 10

  A Q 9   10 8 7 3   K J 4   9 5 3 2

       6 5 4   8 7 6

In (3) you lead up to dummy, finesse the jack, return to hand in another suit and lead again. You have a 25% chance of two tricks, a 50% chance of one trick, and a 25% chance of no tricks when East has both ace and queen. (4) offers similar odds. Sticklers may object that the figures should be 24% and 76%, but we are not dealing in such trifles.

In the next example there is a new dimension: you have a high card in each hand and the question is, towards which hand should you lead first?

(5)   Q 5   (6)   Q 6 5 2

  A 10 3   J 9 7 4   A 10 8 4   K 9 3

       K 8 6 2   J 7

In general you make more tricks by leading first towards the shorter hand. In (5), South leads low and the queen wins. On the next round a low card is played from both hands. South leads low again on the third round and when West has to play the ace, the king becomes good.

Thus South has avoided having a high card captured by the ace. Were he to lead first from dummy the chances of making two tricks would be poor, as one or other of his high cards would surely be clobbered.

In (6) you have to be lucky to make even one trick. You begin with a low card from dummy towards the shorter hand. West wins with the ace but you play low on the next two rounds and eventually make a trick with the queen.

Always the object is to secure that enemy high cards beat the air. This is distinctly less likely to be achieved if you lead first towards the longer hand.

With two honours in one hand and one in the other, you lead low towards the hand with two honours:

(7)   Q J 3   (8)   J 6 3

  K 9 8 6   10 5   10 9 8 4   A 5

       A 7 4 2   K Q 7 2

In (7) you make three tricks by twice leading low towards dummy. Do not play the ace first. In (8) you lead low twice from the dummy hand, avoiding East's ace when it is doubleton.

SIMPLE AND ADVANCED FINESSES

A finesse is any play that seeks to win or establish a trick with a card that is not the highest available. A simple finesse requires one card to be well placed, as when you lead towards the queen in an A–Q combination. A double finesse requires two cards of different rank to be well placed, as in example (4).

When taking a finesse it does not usually pay to lead a high card unless a strong sequence is held:

```
(9)       A J 7 4                (10)            A Q 10 4
     K 8          10 9 2              K 7 5 3              8 6
          Q 6 5 3                              J 9 2
```

In (9), you would not lead the queen, as West would cover and East's holding would be promoted. Instead, lead low, finesse the jack, and play the ace next.

In (10) it is all right to lead high because there are enough cards in sequence, the Q–J–10–9. In this particular combination there is a fine point. If you start with the 9, four tricks can be run without need for re-entry. If the jack is led, it holds but the next round leaves you in dummy.

Often you have to decide whether you wish to win the maximum or lose the minimum:

```
(11)   A Q 9 6 4      (12)   K 10 8 5

        5 3                   7 3 2
```

To make the maximum you should usually take a deep finesse. In (11) a finesse of the 9 will save a trick when West has J–10–x or J–10–x–x. If the 9 loses to the jack or 10, you finesse the queen next. Of course, if you want to avoid losers you finesse the queen first time.

In (12), to make the maximum you finesse the 8, saving a trick when West holds Q–9–x, or J–9–x, A–Q–9–x or A–J–9–x.

The combination finesse

This is a finesse against two cards of adjoining rank. It is very efficient, with a 75% chance of two tricks:

(13)   *Dummy*
A J 10

Declarer
7 6 4

Declarer leads low and finesses the 10. If it loses he repeats the process.

A combination finesse may also be played when more than two honour cards are missing. Again it is better to begin with a deep finesse:

(14)   A J 9   (15)   K 10 9

7 6 5   4 3 2

In (14) to finesse the jack, playing West for K–Q–x, would offer only a 25% chance of two tricks. Instead, finesse the 9 on the first round: if it fetches the king or queen, finesse the jack next. This requires West to have first the 10, a 50% chance, and then one of the other honours, a net 37½%.

In (15) you finesse the 9. If it loses to the jack or queen, you next finesse the 10, failing only when East started with Q–J–x. Do not change your mind on the second round and put up the king: you would fail when East started with either A–Q–x or A–J–x.

The two-way finesse

This is a finesse that may be taken against either opponent.

However, there is often advantage in finessing one way rather than the other:

(16)   K 5 4   (17)   K 9 7 2

A J 10 6 2   Q 10 4 3

In (16) South may play either defender for the queen but if he wants to make as many tricks as possible he should target East. He cannot make five tricks against Q–9–x–x in West's hand: only in East's.

In (17), again, declarer can guard against four cards in the hand of one defender only. He leads low from dummy and plays the queen. On the next round he leads the 10, exposing West's holding when he started with A–J–8–x. If East has this holding South cannot cope.

When strong intermediate cards are held it does no harm to try to tempt an opponent into an injudicious cover:

(18)   A J 7 3   (19)   Q 10 7 3

K 10 9 8   K 9 8 4

In (18) declarer does not cash a top card but begins by leading the 10 from the closed hand. West may elect to play the queen, which would be the right thing to do in some cases; if he does not, declarer may overtake and finesse the other way. In (19), similarly, he starts with the 9 or 10.

The ruffing finesse

When declarer has a sequence of high cards in one hand and can ruff in the hand opposite, he may take a ruffing finesse:

(20)   Void   (21)   A K J 10

K Q J 5   4 2

In (20), South leads an honour and ruffs West's ace if he covers but lets it run if West plays low.

In (21) South may play either opponent for the queen. If he needs four tricks he takes a normal finesse against West. If he needs only three, he may cash the A–K and lead the jack for a ruffing finesse.

The ruffing finesse is a particularly strong play when a loser can be discarded as the finesse is taken:

(22)

♠ A Q J 10
♡ A 6
♢ A K 2
♣ 9 7 5 4

♣ Q led

♠ 6
♡ K Q J 9 3 2
♢ 8 5 4 3
♣ A 6

Against 6♡ West makes the best lead but South, after drawing trumps, cashes the ♠A and leads the queen, discarding a club if East follows small. If West wins with the king, South loses no other trick, later discarding two diamonds. Were he instead to take a simple finesse against West, he might lose two tricks straight off.

The intra-finesse

This is a clever trick. Defenders seem due for two winners, but one is nullified:

(23)

      Q 9 4 2
J 6   K 10 7
    A 8 5 3

If South starts normally by cashing the ace he loses two tricks, but if he can picture the layout he may start by leading low from hand and inserting the 9. East wins with the 10 but on the next round the queen is led from dummy and the jack is pinned.

The intra-finesse is easier for defenders than for declarer:

```
              J 6
   A 8 5 3            Q 9 4 2
            K 10 7
```

Against a notrump contract, when West leads small and dummy plays low it will be quite normal for East to finesse the 9 and lead the queen when he gets in.

The backward finesse

When the bidding suggests that a normal finesse will fail, a defender's queen may be picked up by leading the unsupported jack if declarer has the 9 behind it:

```
              A 7 2
   Q 8 5              10 6 4 3
            K J 9
```

South leads the jack from hand, takes West's queen with the ace, and finesses the 9 on the way back. The stratagem requires two cards to be well placed.

Like the intra-finesse, the backward finesse is easier for defenders, who may use the same idea here:

```
              9 7 3
   Q 6 5              K 10 8 4
            A J 2
```

If East leads low South will duck and make two tricks. By leading the 10, a backward finesse against the jack, East holds declarer to one trick.

PERCENTAGE PLAYS

This term is often used loosely to describe the better of two close alternatives:

(1)   K J 7 5 2   (2)   6 5

        A 6 4 3   A K J 10 7 3

In (1) declarer could play West for Q–x–x but as he has nine cards the percentage play is to cash the ace and king. The margin is small and if there is anything to suggest that West may have more cards than East, the finesse should be taken.

In (2), with eight cards it is better to finesse against the queen than to play for the drop, but there remains the question of whether to finesse on the first round or play off the ace and enter dummy for a second-round finesse. The percentage play is to take a first-round finesse. It costs if West has the singleton queen but gains against Q–x–x–x in East's hand, which is four times more likely.

Whether to take a combination finesse or play for the drop is a frequent question:

(3)   A K 10 9 4   (4)   A J 10 7 5 3

            7 5   6 4 2

In (3), to make four tricks there are three possible plays: cash the A–K, hoping to drop a doubleton honour; finesse the 10 and if it loses play for the drop; or finesse twice – first the 9, then the 10. The last is best.

In (4) also there are three options: play off the ace, take two finesses, or take one finesse and then play off the ace. Again it is best to take two finesses.

The advantage of the first-round finesse extends to these combinations:

(5)   A 9 2   (6)   A 10 6 2

        K 10 5 4   J 7 4 3

With (5) you finesse the 9, then play the ace and king. With (6) you can play either defender for a doubleton honour: if East is more likely to be short, you may lead either low from dummy or the jack from hand; if West, you lead low to the 10, then cash the ace. The second play is better as it copes with other situations also.

At the table declarer should always be willing to abandon the normal percentage play when there is any clue from the bidding:

(7)   A 4 2
    K J 7   10
        Q 9 8 6 5 3

This is the trump suit. Normally you would lay down the ace, but if West has bid notrumps at any stage, you should lead the queen, hoping to pin the 10 or jack with East.

Finally, there are occasions when only a particular layout of the suit will help:

(8)   A 10 4 2
    J 8 6   K 9 5
        Q 7 3

Playing in notrumps you need three tricks and have no other entry to dummy. Best is to lead the queen and duck whether it is covered or not. On the next round you finesse the 10, playing in effect for West to have J–x–x or K–J–x.

Single-suit plays by defenders

The defenders, seeing the dummy, find it easier than declarer to play accurately: the backward finesse and intra-finesse are examples already noted. In another type the defender holds back a winner so as to allow a lower honour held by his partner to play its part:

(9)   K Q 10 3   (10)   A 10 7 3
    A 9 7 5   J 6 2   J 8 5   K 9 6 2
        8 4   Q 4

In (9), playing in notrumps, South leads twice towards the

dummy hand. Unless West ducks each time South may make three tricks. In (10) also, if East goes in with the king when a low card is led from dummy, declarer makes three tricks.

SAFETY PLAYS

A safety play, properly so called, is one where declarer forgoes the chance of maximum tricks so as to improve his chances of the number he requires:

(1) A J 7 2   (2)   J 6 4

     K 6 3   A K 9 3 2

In (1) there is no sure way to make three tricks but the safety play is to cash the A–K and lead towards the jack. By giving up the finesse you guard against Q–x with East.

In (2), if four tricks will suffice, declarer does not try to drop the doubleton queen but plays the ace and leads low towards the jack, overcoming Q–10–x–x in either hand.

In the next examples if South can afford to lose a trick the safety play is bomb-proof:

(3)   A 9 4   (4)   A 9 8 3

    Q J 7 5 3 2   K 10 7 5 4

With (3) South leads low from the ace. To cash the ace costs when East is void: to lead the queen costs when West is void. With (4) South leads low from either hand and covers if the next hand follows.

In the next two cases declarer can win four tricks against any 4–1 break:

(5)   K J 5   (6)   K 9 4

    A 9 6 4 3   A J 6 5 3

With (5) he cashes the king, enters his hand in another suit and leads up to the J–x. With (6) he plays the ace, then leads low and puts in the 9 if West follows small.

The term 'safety play' is also used of moves that do not deliberately forgo the maximum but are simply the most careful form of play:

<table>
<tr><td>(7)</td><td>K 7 4 2</td><td></td><td>(8)</td><td>A J 9 7 5 2</td><td></td></tr>
<tr><td>Void</td><td></td><td>J 10 6 3</td><td>K 10 8</td><td></td><td>Void</td></tr>
<tr><td></td><td>A Q 9 8 5</td><td></td><td></td><td>Q 6 4 3</td><td></td></tr>
</table>

In (7), you lead the king, guarding against J–10–x–x with East. If West has this holding nothing can be done. A combination such as Q–7–4–2 opposite K–J–8–x–x invokes the same principle: declarer can pick up A–10–9–x on one side only, so must play the queen first.

In (8) South leads the queen. Were he to lead low and finesse the jack, West with K–10–x would score a trick.

There are many situations where a finesse is initiated with an unsupported high card so as to guard against all outstanding high cards being in one hand:

<table>
<tr><td>(9)</td><td>10 5 3 2</td><td></td></tr>
<tr><td>Void</td><td></td><td>K 9 8 6</td></tr>
<tr><td></td><td>A Q J 7 4</td><td></td></tr>
</table>

If a low card is led and the queen finessed, South will have to lose a trick, so he should lead the 10.

In the next combinations South wishes to lose only one trick:

(10)   K 7 3   (11)   J 6 4 2

     A 10 6 4 2   A 10 8 7 5 3

In (10) he plays the king from dummy and continues with the 3, on which East plays low. South puts in the 10, saving a trick when East has Q–J–x–x.

In (11), if the lead is in South's own hand he should play low towards the jack: then he can pick up K–Q–9 with East. Nothing is gained by laying down the ace.

With a 6-card suit opposite a singleton, you have to think of the 4–2 divisions. In the first diagram South needs four tricks, in the second, five:

(12)   5   (13)   7

     A J 10 7 4 2   A Q 10 9 5 3

In (12), to provide for a 4–2 break, South should not finesse the jack but play the ace and continue with a low card. This succeeds when the suit is 3–3 or either defender holds a doubleton honour.

In (13) the best play for five tricks is to finesse the queen, not the 10. This works when West has J–x, whereas a finesse of the 10 does not help when West has K–x. If the suit is 3–3 the plays have equal chances.

This chapter, it will be remembered, began with the suggestion that the diagrams should be seen as examples of how to protect high cards from capture. Figure (12), where South resists the temptation to lead the jack on the second round, is perhaps the clearest demonstration.

The advantage of safety play is often slight and may take second place to other considerations. In particular, before taking a safety play one should be sure that it is really needed:

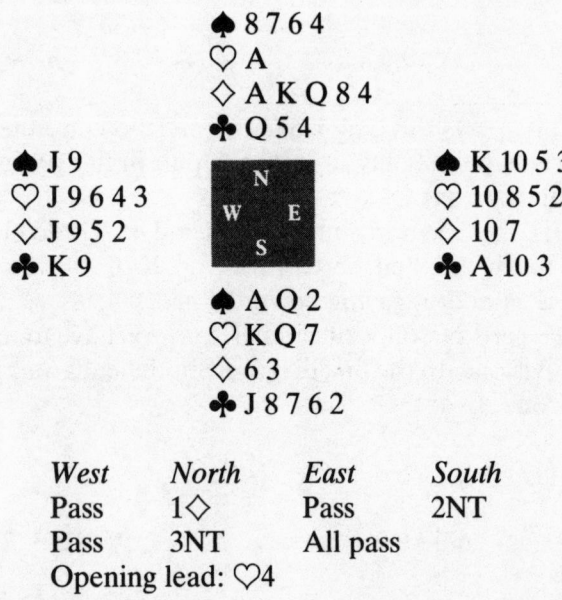

♠ 8 7 6 4
♡ A
♢ A K Q 8 4
♣ Q 5 4

♠ J 9
♡ J 9 6 4 3
♢ J 9 5 2
♣ K 9

♠ K 10 5 3
♡ 10 8 5 2
♢ 10 7
♣ A 10 3

♠ A Q 2
♡ K Q 7
♢ 6 3
♣ J 8 7 6 2

West	North	East	South
Pass	1♢	Pass	2NT
Pass	3NT	All pass	

Opening lead: ♡4

The question is how to play diamonds, as the lead has removed dummy's entry. The safety play is to duck a round; but can you afford it?

To find out, play a spade at trick two, finessing the queen. If it holds, you duck a diamond. If it doesn't, you go after five diamond tricks.

TABLE OF PROBABILITIES

The probabilities at the start of the hand are as follows:

No. of cards held by the defenders:	Likely percentage break	
7 cards	4–3	62.17%
	5–2	30.52%
	6–1	6.78%
	7–0	0.52%
6 cards	4–2	48.45%
	3–3	35.33%
	5–1	14.53%
	6–0	1.68%
5 cards	3–2	67.83%
	4–1	28.26%
	5–0	3.91%
4 cards	3–1	49.74%
	2–2	40.70%
	4–0	9.57%
3 cards	2–1	78.00%
	3–0	22.00%
2 cards	1–1	52.00%
	2–0	48.00%

This table is not something you need paste inside your hat. It is sufficient to know two things. An odd number of cards is likely to divide favourably: 4–3, 3–2, 2–1. The even distributions 3–3 and 2–2, are odds-against.

This often allows two lines of play to be compared. For example, it is better to play for a 3–2 break than for a finesse, but a finesse is better than a 3–3 break.

Chapter 19

ENTRY PLAYS BY DECLARER AND DEFENDERS

Generating entries within a suit – Use of entries in correct order – Entry-killing plays – The entry coups

An entry is a card that will win the trick and allow the player to enter the hand he wants to be in. Entries affect the planning of almost every hand. Some forms of play, such as dummy reversal, make heavy use of them.

When shortage of entries is not fatal it may still constrain declarer's line of play. With K–Q–J–x opposite dummy's x–x–x, for example, he may have to lead the combination from hand instead of leading low towards it.

Declarer can hardly have too many entries, so we look first at ways in which their number may be increased.

GENERATING ENTRIES WITHIN A SUIT

By cashing a suit in a particular way it is often possible to augment the supply of entries:

$$(1) \quad K \ J \ 10 \ 6 \qquad (2) \qquad K \ 6 \ 3$$

$$A \ Q \ 9 \ 7 \ 4 \qquad \qquad A \ Q \ 9 \ 8 \ 7 \ 5$$

In (1), suppose that South needs four entries to dummy. He overtakes the queen with the king, the 9 with the jack, the 7 with the 10 and the 4 with the 6. By a similar process South may instead arrange three entries to his own hand.

In (2), suppose that this suit is trumps and you have to ruff early in the closed hand. You should automatically ruff with the 7 so that dummy will have two entries if trumps are 2–2.

(3) K Q 6 2   (4)   A J 8

10 8 5 4   Q 10 9 7

With (3), the 4 is led towards the table. If the king holds you return to hand and this time lead the 8. Suppose that West goes up with the ace: you are left with Q–6 in dummy and 10–4 in hand, so you have the choice of gaining two entries to dummy by overtaking the 10, or of winning the next round in dummy and the last in your own hand.

In (4) declarer has so many sequential cards that he may think it does not matter how he plays. However, if entries to his own hand are in short supply he should lead the queen. If West follows small, the jack is played. Declarer can then continue with the 10, taking another finesse against the king while keeping the lead in his own hand. If South does not lead the queen on the first round he cannot be sure of winning any subsequent trick in his own hand.

To allow a suit to be run without the use of side entries, it is often necessary to unblock:

(5)   A 10 4   (6)   K 9 4

K Q 9 6 3   A Q 8 3

In (5) South leads the king and unblocks with the 10 in dummy. He continues low to the ace, and if West shows out is poised to finesse the 9 against East's J–x–x–x. Had the 10 not been played, East would refuse to cover it on the third round and declarer would be locked in dummy.

In (6), South leads the ace and unblocks with the 9. Suppose that on the next round, when the 3 is led to the king, West plays the jack or 10. If declarer decides to play West for a doubleton honour, the ground has been prepared for a finesse of the 8.

When defenders lead a suit

Declarer can often improve the entry situation by playing

a high card before he has to:

(7)   J 10 5   (8)   A 8 6

K 7   Q J 4

In (7), against a notrump contract, West leads low to his partner's ace. If you drop the king, defenders cannot clear the suit without letting dummy into the lead.

In (8) West again leads low. Suppose that you expect to need an entry to hand later in the play. If you put up the ace, then either the queen or the jack will be an entry.

In the next examples you are short of entries to dummy:

(9)   K J 4   (10)   A 10 6 3

A 9   Q 5

In (9) West leads low. To take three tricks straight off you should win with the ace, even if East follows small: then the jack can be finessed.

In (10) West leads low and East plays the king. If you want to take two tricks quickly you should unblock with the queen, hoping to take a successful finesse against West's jack.

Entry-creating plays by defenders

Unblocking is not so easy for defenders, as they do not see each other's cards. Often they must go by the way declarer tackles a suit:

10 6 2

Q 9 3   J 8 4

A K 7 5

Suppose that West wants his partner to get in. When declarer plays off the A–K it is safe to drop the queen, for if South held the jack he would have entered dummy and finessed. The next example is only slightly more daring:

$$\begin{array}{c}
\text{Q 10 8 4 2} \\
\text{K 5} \qquad\qquad \text{J 9 3} \\
\text{A 7 6}
\end{array}$$

South, who is not short of entries to either hand, lays down the ace. West should conclude that as he has not finessed he is unlikely to have the jack, so he may drop the king.

Next, an example that not many people think of, simple though it is:

$$\begin{array}{c}
\text{A 10 9 5 4} \\
\text{Q 6} \qquad\qquad \text{J 8 2} \\
\text{K 7 3}
\end{array}$$

When South lays down the king, West should drop the queen. If he does not, South, on the next round, has the option of leaving West on play or putting on the ace and forcing East to win the third round. It does no harm to deny South the choice.

USE OF ENTRIES IN CORRECT ORDER

On any hand that is not open and shut declarer should consider whether there are enough entries for his game plan to succeed. He may find that it will work only if entries are used in an exact order.

```
              ♠ A 10 8 5
              ♡ A Q J
              ◇ A K 6
              ♣ K Q 4
♠ 9 4 2                        ♠ J 7 6 3
♡ 8 7 5 4        N             ♡ 6 3 2
◇ 8 5 2      W       E         ◇ Q 10 4 3
♣ A 9 2          S             ♣ J 5
              ♠ K Q
              ♡ K 10 9
              ◇ J 9 7
              ♣ 10 8 7 6 3
```

West	North	East	South
	2♣	Pass	2NT
Pass	3NT	Pass	4NT
Pass	6NT	All pass	

Opening lead: ♡8

North should have passed 4NT, but the final contract is not terrible. The best chance is to play for four club tricks, leading the suit twice towards dummy. This will require three entries to the closed hand, and it may seem that South has them: ♠K–Q and ♡K. However, he should work out in detail how the play will go.

Suppose that he wins the first trick in hand and leads a club. The king holds and he comes back to hand with a spade, but when the next club is led West nimbly puts in the ace and returns a spade. This takes out South's last entry and he cannot cash the clubs because the suit is blocked in dummy.

This difficulty can be overcome. Win the opening lead not in hand but in dummy. Enter the closed hand twice in spades to lead clubs. The difference is that if West tries the same dodge he cannot remove South's entry, the ♡K.

Next, suppose that there are two developable suits. Only one is needed for the contract, but you want to be able to try both. Entry considerations may dictate which should be tested first:

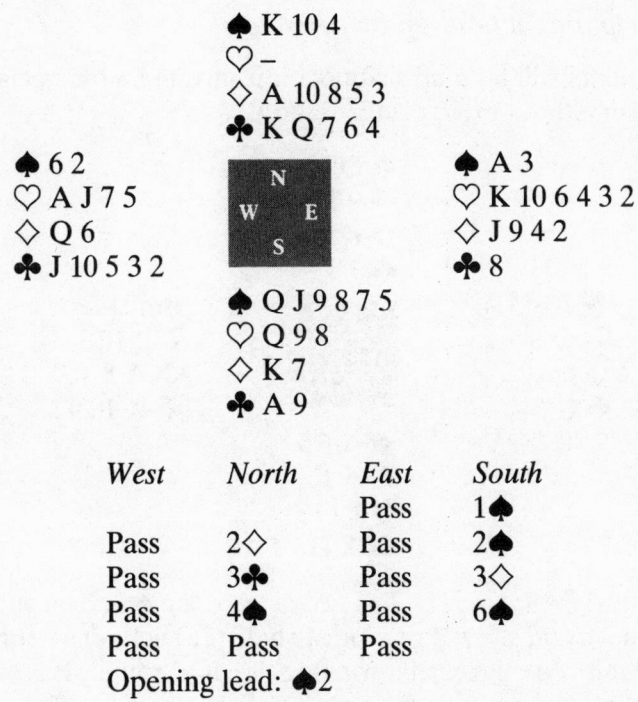

```
                    ♠ K 10 4
                    ♡ –
                    ◇ A 10 8 5 3
                    ♣ K Q 7 6 4
♠ 6 2                                    ♠ A 3
♡ A J 7 5              N                 ♡ K 10 6 4 3 2
◇ Q 6              W       E             ◇ J 9 4 2
♣ J 10 5 3 2          S                 ♣ 8
                    ♠ Q J 9 8 7 5
                    ♡ Q 9 8
                    ◇ K 7
                    ♣ A 9
```

West	North	East	South
		Pass	1♠
Pass	2◇	Pass	2♠
Pass	3♣	Pass	3◇
Pass	4♠	Pass	6♠
Pass	Pass	Pass	

Opening lead: ♠2

North has been at pains to define a heart shortage so South, with two vital cards, has little hesitation in bidding the low point-count slam. East wins with the ace and returns the suit, West following. Plan the play.

You have eleven winners, including a heart ruff. You need to establish only one of dummy's suits, but the question is, which should be tackled first, to cover both chances?

Suppose that you start by playing the ♣A–K. Here, finding the suit 5–1, you switch to diamonds, but cannot overcome the 4–2 break for lack of entries.

Now try playing diamonds first. When opponents follow to the king and ace, you can ruff twice and still reach the long card. The advantage of this sequence is that if diamonds were 5–1 you could switch to clubs and still succeed as long as clubs were no worse than 4–2.

The principle is that, in general, declarer should tackle first the suit that requires more entries for establishment.

Anticipating a hold-up by defenders

Defenders will hold up a stopper if it suits them but declarer may sometimes exact compensation:

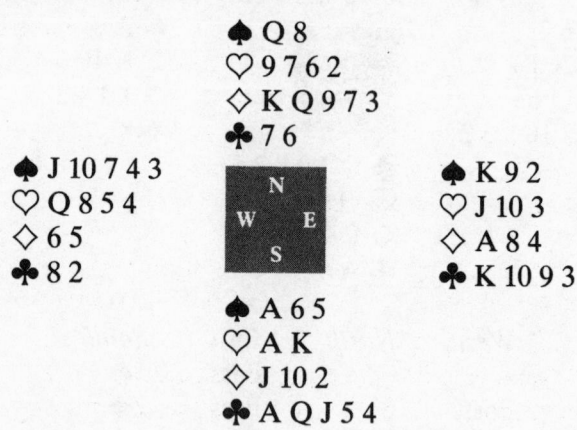

```
              ♠ Q 8
              ♡ 9 7 6 2
              ◇ K Q 9 7 3
              ♣ 7 6
♠ J 10 7 4 3              ♠ K 9 2
♡ Q 8 5 4                 ♡ J 10 3
◇ 6 5                     ◇ A 8 4
♣ 8 2                     ♣ K 10 9 3
              ♠ A 6 5
              ♡ A K
              ◇ J 10 2
              ♣ A Q J 5 4
```

After 1♣–1◇–2NT–3NT, West leads the ♠4. You put up the queen and allow East's king to hold the trick. The 9 comes back and you duck again, winning the third round. It is clear that the contract must fail unless East has both the ◇A and the ♣K. So?

Do not start by leading the ◇J followed by the 10. Anticipating a hold-up, you should overtake the jack with the queen and take the club finesse. Next, overtake the ◇10 and repeat the process. Abandon diamonds, give East his club trick, and make game with two diamonds, four clubs and three top cards.

ENTRY-KILLING PLAYS

Declarer is sometimes able to stop the run of an enemy suit by inserting a winner early and leaving the suit blocked:

```
(1)           A 4          (2)           A 9 4
   K J 8 5 3        Q 7       K 10 7 6 2        Q 5
           10 9 6 2                     J 8 3
```

In (1), when West leads the 5 declarer goes right up with the ace. This is sure to leave East stranded if West has led from a 5-card suit, as West would not have led low from K–Q–J–x–x.

In (2) West leads the 6. If only a 5–2 break will hurt you, and East can be kept out of the lead, you should go up with the ace. This will not be a success if West has led from K–Q–x–x–x, but it stands to gain twice as often when he has K–10–x–x–x or Q–10–x–x–x.

When the enemy layout is known within limits, some effective moves can be improvised at the table. Here the suit has been bid by East:

(3)	7		(4)	5 4	
J 8 6		A K 9 4 3	Q 10 2		A 9 8 6 3
	Q 10 5 2			K J 7	

In (3) the 6 is led to the king, East returning the 4. If you place West with J–x–x, you can block the suit by going in with the queen.

In (4) West leads the 2 and East wins with the ace, returning the 6. This time you have to take a view: the jack will hold if West has led from 10–x–x, but in that case East would have A–Q–x–x–x and would probably have inserted the queen. As the cards lie, if you go in with the king, the suit will be blocked until West's queen has been cashed and East has got the lead in another suit.

Avoidance plays

When declarer is developing a suit and wants to keep a particular defender out of the lead, an avoidance play may be the solution. Here the player to be kept out is West:

(5)   7 4 2   (6)   10 2
  J 8 5   K 10   J 7 4   Q 9 5
     A Q 9 6 3   A K 8 6 3

In each case a trick has to be lost but declarer plans to lose it to East. In (5) he leads low from dummy. If East plays the 10 he finesses the queen and crosses in another suit for the next lead; this time, when the king appears, it is allowed to hold.

In (6) if South cashes the A–K, East will unblock, so he must lead twice from dummy towards the A–K–x–x–x. If East plays the queen on the first or second round it is allowed to hold.

Entry-killing plays by defenders

It is a characteristic of blocking plays – and unblocking plays – that they are available to both sides:

(7)   A Q 2   (8)   K 9 6 3
  9 6 5 3   J 7 4   10 8 7 2   5
     K 10 8   A Q J 4

In (7) the declarer, who is short of entries to his hand, cashes the ace and leads the 2, intending to finesse the 10. East upsets the apple cart by going in with the jack. In (8) South plays off the A–Q and leads the 4. If West plays low South can finesse or not, as he chooses. It should be automatic to put in the 10, denying the choice.

West's plays in the next diagrams are part of the standard repertoire:

(9)   A J 10 6 3   (10)   A J 9 4 2
  Q 4   K 9 5   K 10 3   Q 8 6
     8 7 2   7 5

In (9) declarer has no outside entry to dummy. When he leads low, West goes in with the queen: otherwise South can make four tricks. The best South can do now is to duck this round and the next, allowing the defenders two tricks.

In (10), again with no outside entry, South intends to finesse the 9: as the cards lie, if East wins with the queen South will make four tricks when he regains the lead. East therefore should duck, holding South to two tricks. Better still is for West to put up the king on the first round: now South makes only one trick!

At a trump contract, when dummy has a running suit and no side entry, a strong defence is to keep leading the suit until declarer has no more cards in it. You are West:

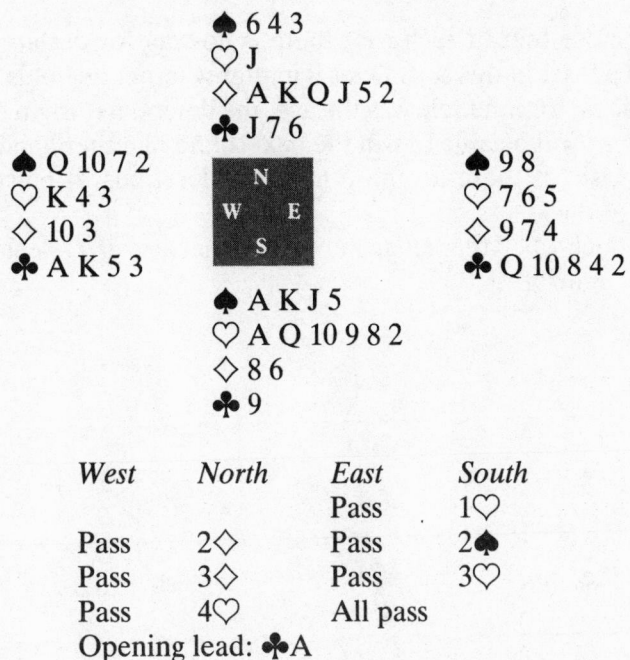

```
                    ♠ 6 4 3
                    ♡ J
                    ◇ A K Q J 5 2
                    ♣ J 7 6
    ♠ Q 10 7 2          N          ♠ 9 8
    ♡ K 4 3        W         E      ♡ 7 6 5
    ◇ 10 3             S          ◇ 9 7 4
    ♣ A K 5 3                      ♣ Q 10 8 4 2
                    ♠ A K J 5
                    ♡ A Q 10 9 8 2
                    ◇ 8 6
                    ♣ 9
```

West	North	East	South
		Pass	1♡
Pass	2◇	Pass	2♠
Pass	3◇	Pass	3♡
Pass	4♡	All pass	

Opening lead: ♣A

East follows with the ♣2, suggesting an odd number of cards, and South with the 9. You should compute that if South is 6–4 in hearts and spades, he can make in his own hand no more than five heart tricks and two spades: the rest must come from diamonds.

By switching to a diamond, you hold declarer to two diamond tricks, as you will be able to lead the suit again when in with the ♡K. Even when South has no diamonds but three losing clubs, he still goes down.

The hold-up at trump contracts

At notrumps, to hold up a stopper in the defenders' suit is a routine measure. At a trump contract its advantage is sometimes less apparent:

(11)   8 7 4   (12)   6 2
  K led   J played   3 led   K played
       A 2   A 8 5

Suppose that in each case there is no way for declarer to avoid a loser in this suit. Does it matter whether he holds up?

It does, for if he releases the ace, the defenders, when they come in, will be able to win the next round in either hand, as they wish. If there are no other considerations, it must be right to duck.

To duck when there is an inevitable loser also gives declarer better control:

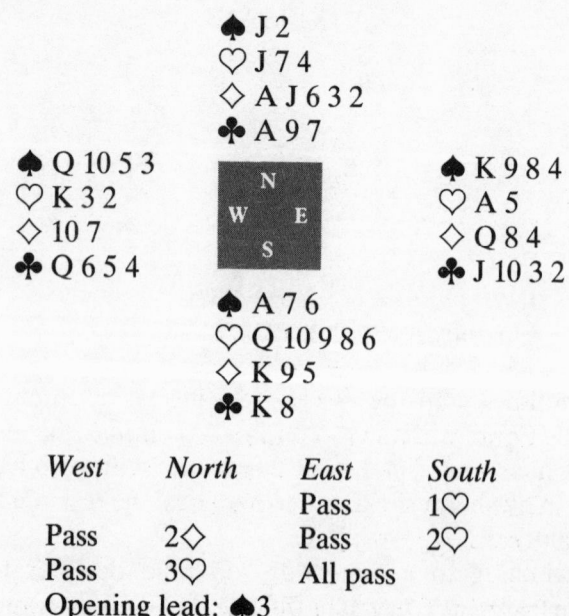

	♠ J 2	
	♡ J 7 4	
	◇ A J 6 3 2	
	♣ A 9 7	

♠ Q 10 5 3   ♠ K 9 8 4
♡ K 3 2   ♡ A 5
◇ 10 7   ◇ Q 8 4
♣ Q 6 5 4   ♣ J 10 3 2

          ♠ A 7 6
          ♡ Q 10 9 8 6
          ◇ K 9 5
          ♣ K 8

West	North	East	South
		Pass	1♡
Pass	2◇	Pass	2♡
Pass	3♡	All pass	

Opening lead: ♠3

Suppose that South wins the first trick. If he returns a spade, the defenders will play three rounds of trumps, leaving him with five losers. If instead he takes a finesse in diamonds, the defenders can play for a diamond ruff. As the cards lie he can get home by playing the ace, king and another diamond, but this is not the most natural line.

By ducking the first trick South gains the upper hand: if trumps are played, he can afford to give up a diamond trick, as he still has the ♠A; otherwise he can take a spade ruff.

THE ENTRY COUPS

There are three celebrated coups that attack entries. The first is the prerogative of the declarer:

The Scissors Coup

Declarer leads a suit solely to cut the defenders' communications, usually with the object of preventing a ruff:

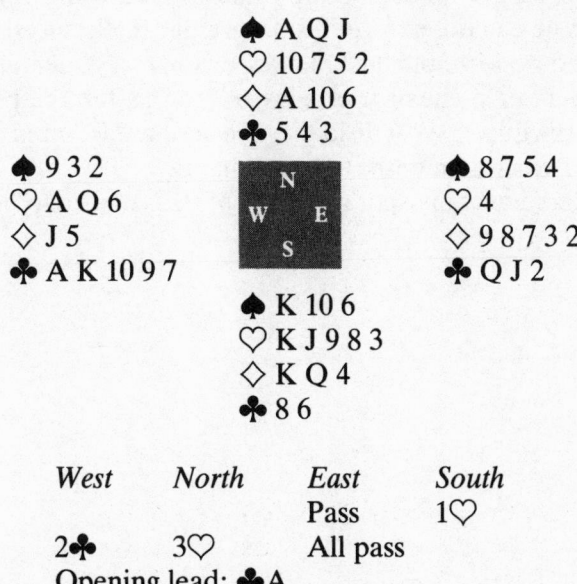

```
              ♠ A Q J
              ♡ 10 7 5 2
              ◇ A 10 6
              ♣ 5 4 3
♠ 9 3 2                        ♠ 8 7 5 4
♡ A Q 6         N              ♡ 4
◇ J 5        W     E           ◇ 9 8 7 3 2
♣ A K 10 9 7     S             ♣ Q J 2
              ♠ K 10 6
              ♡ K J 9 8 3
              ◇ K Q 4
              ♣ 8 6
```

West	North	East	South
		Pass	1♡
2♣	3♡	All pass	
Opening lead: ♣A			

On the first trick East drops the queen. Confident now of an entry to East's hand, West decides to play for a ruff, switching to the ◇J.

If trumps are played now, West will lead a second diamond and later put East in with the ♣J for a diamond ruff. Instead, South should lead a club at the third trick, the Scissors Coup. Now the defenders have no communication.

The next two coups involve the lead of an unsupported high card, but with different objectives:

The Deschapelles Coup

Here the defender aims to force out declarer's winner and create an entry to the other defender's hand. South is in a notrump contract:

```
                 J 9 6 2
     Q 10 4                 K 7 5 3
                 A 8
```

West is on play in the middle game and this is the only suit in which he can hope to get his partner in. If West leads low, East needs to withhold the king to score an entry later and this gives declarer a cheap trick now as well as the tempo. By leading the queen West dislodges the ace on this round or the next and creates an entry to East's hand.

An alert East may spot a variant of the same coup here:

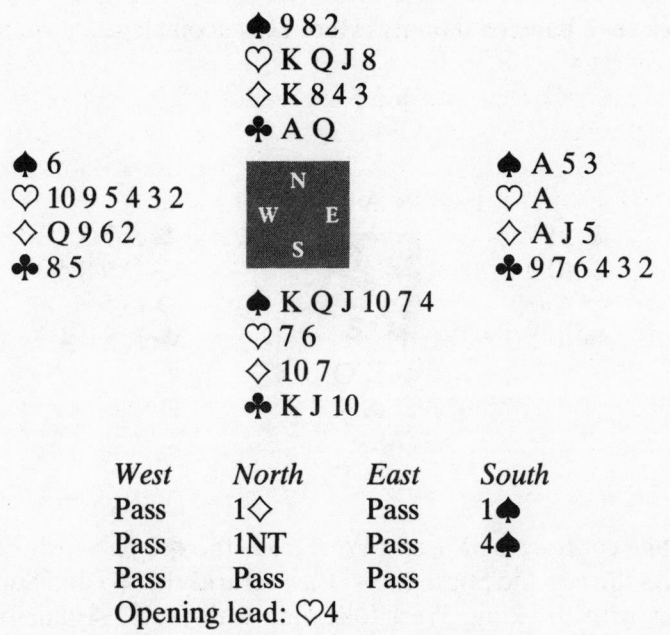

♠ 9 8 2
♡ K Q J 8
◇ K 8 4 3
♣ A Q

♠ 6
♡ 10 9 5 4 3 2
◇ Q 9 6 2
♣ 8 5

♠ A 5 3
♡ A
◇ A J 5
♣ 9 7 6 4 3 2

♠ K Q J 10 7 4
♡ 7 6
◇ 10 7
♣ K J 10

West	North	East	South
Pass	1◇	Pass	1♠
Pass	1NT	Pass	4♠
Pass	Pass	Pass	

Opening lead: ♡4

East takes the king with the ace and computes that South has at least ten winners: two hearts, five trumps and three clubs. The only chance is a spade ruff; but how can he get West in?

At the second trick East returns the ◇J, playing West for the queen. When he comes in with the ♠A, East underleads the ◇A.

The Merrimac Coup

This is similar to the Deschapelles Coup but instead of creating an entry for partner it destroys a vital entry in declarer's hand or dummy. Here East is on stage:

♠ 6 5
♡ J 6 3
◇ K J 10 9 4 3
♣ A 7

♠ J 9 8 2
♡ 10 2
◇ A 6 2
♣ 10 5 3 2

♠ A 7 3
♡ Q 9 8 4
◇ Q 5
♣ K 8 6 4

♠ K Q 10 4
♡ A K 7 5
◇ 8 7
♣ Q J 9

The contract is 3NT and West leads the ♠2 on which East plays the ace and South the 4. East returns the ♠7 and South wins with the king, West following with the 8. A diamond from declarer goes to dummy's jack and East's queen, West following with the 2.

East places his partner with the ◇A and can also read the likely spade layout. A spade continuation will establish no more than one trick, making four in all, so the best chance is to drive out the ♣A, the entry for dummy's diamonds. East therefore returns the ♣K, giving South an extra trick in clubs but killing the diamond suit.

Chapter 20

SIGNALS AND DISCARDS

*Signals when partner leads to the trick – Signals
when declarer plays a suit – Suit-preference signals
when leading to a trick – The trump echo – Making
the right discards – Special signalling conventions*

A signal is a card played with the object of conveying information. Signals are made usually with a high spot card or a low one, and they relate to three subjects:

(i)   Attitude to the suit of the signal; that is, encouragement or discouragement.

(ii)   Length in the suit of the signal; an odd or even number of cards.

(iii)   Liking or dislike for a different suit; that is, suit preference.

In general, signals take precedence in that order. If a signal can plausibly relate to encouragement or discouragement, that is what it means. When it cannot, it is construed as suit-length. When neither message seems necessary or appropriate, it is suit preference.

On partner's lead of the ace (or king) from a suit headed by the A–K, you do not echo with Q–x: the play of the queen, if it is not a singleton, always denotes that the jack is held. Also, you do not signal with a high spot card that may be needed for a successful defence.

Elsewhere in this book there are many hands where signals are touched on. In this chapter, therefore, the emphasis is not on illustrative deals but on protocol, as it were.

SIGNALS WHEN PARTNER LEADS TO THE TRICK

In any situation where your partner will expect you to show attitude, this rule applies: *When partner leads an honour, a high spot card from you will encourage, a low card will discourage.*

(1)	10 6 2		(2)	A 7 5
Q led	K 8 7 3		6 led	Q 4 3 2

In (1), when West leads the queen you play the 8 to invite a continuation.

The same is true when a low card is led and dummy wins the trick. In (2), suppose that dummy's ace is played: the highest card you can afford is the 4, but this will be confirmed as encouraging when you later complete a high-low with the 2.

In the same way, if you wish to discourage a lead and your lowest card is, say, the 7, its meaning will become clear when you later play a higher card.

When playing an encouraging card from 'equals' (two or more cards in sequence), the highest is played. This is logical, and helpful: in (1), why signal with the 7 when you can play the 8 for the same money?

Third hand is not obliged to signal just because he has a high card. The test is whether he wants the suit continued. Here East is the signaller:

```
                  ♠ 10 8
                  ♡ A 6 3
                  ◇ K Q 10 9 3
                  ♣ A Q 10
   ♠ A Q 5          N            ♠ 6 2
   ♡ J 10 9 4    W     E         ♡ K Q 8 2
   ◇ A 6            S            ◇ 8 7 5 2
   ♣ 9 8 7 4                     ♣ K J 5
                  ♠ K J 9 7 4 3
                  ♡ 7 5
                  ◇ J 4
                  ♣ 6 3 2
```

West	North	East	South
	1◇	Pass	1♠
Pass	1NT	Pass	2♠
Pass	Pass	Pass	

Opening lead: ♡J

Whether declarer puts up dummy's ace or not, East plays

the discouraging 2, as he wants West to lead clubs before declarer can get the diamonds going.

In the same way you may encourage a continuation for no other reason than to prevent a costly switch:

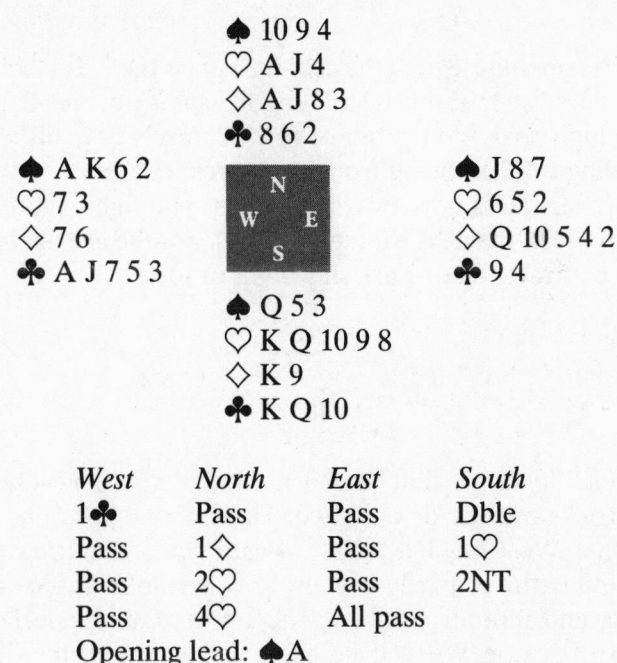

	♠ 10 9 4	
	♡ A J 4	
	◇ A J 8 3	
	♣ 8 6 2	

♠ A K 6 2		♠ J 8 7
♡ 7 3	N	♡ 6 5 2
◇ 7 6	W E	◇ Q 10 5 4 2
♣ A J 7 5 3	S	♣ 9 4

	♠ Q 5 3	
	♡ K Q 10 9 8	
	◇ K 9	
	♣ K Q 10	

West	North	East	South
1♣	Pass	Pass	Dble
Pass	1◇	Pass	1♡
Pass	2♡	Pass	2NT
Pass	4♡	All pass	

Opening lead: ♠A

North might have done better to raise to 3NT, but 4♡ may well be made unless East sends the right signal. He sees that the opening lead has probably blown a trick, but that a switch to diamonds or clubs may do further damage.

East therefore encourages with the 8. West continues the suit and South makes the queen, but he could have done that anyway, once the ace had been led. With normal play South now loses two more tricks.

When to show suit length

It is often more important to show how many cards are held than to show attitude. Bridge players like to have their cake and eat it, so in many situations they expect partner to work out which meaning is intended:

$$Q \; J \; 4$$
$$A \; K \; 10 \; 8 \; 3 \qquad\qquad 9 \; 7 \; 6 \; 2$$
$$5$$

On the opening lead of the ace, East plays the 7. He expects West to realise that this is suit length, as it is obvious that he has no high cards. At the table West will rarely have difficulty in reading the 7 as being from four cards, not two.

However, all is not always sweetness and light: there are grey areas. In the next example, West leads the ace against a trump contract. Does East play high, or low?

$$J \; 9 \; 6 \; 3$$
$$A \; K \; 7 \; 5 \qquad\qquad Q \; 8 \; 2$$
$$10 \; 4$$

East's difficulty is that he may not know whether there are three tricks to take or only two. However, suppose he can infer that West has led from a 4-card suit: in that case he should play the 2, partly because he does not want West to play ace and another, setting up the fourth round for declarer, but also because West, if he has four cards, will be vitally interested in count. The 2 can more comfortably be played if East knows he will get in soon, for then he will be able to cash the queen and lead the 8.

When the over-riding need is to cash quickly, or if he can be sure South has three cards in the suit, East should play the 8 on the first round.

When to show suit preference

Sometimes it is clear that a defender can have nothing useful to say about either attitude or count:

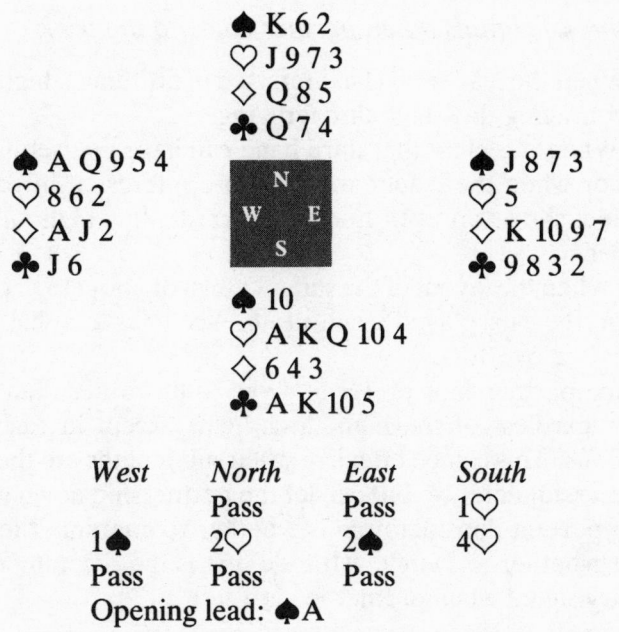

	♠ K 6 2		
	♡ J 9 7 3		
	◇ Q 8 5		
	♣ Q 7 4		

♠ A Q 9 5 4   ♠ J 8 7 3
♡ 8 6 2   ♡ 5
◇ A J 2   ◇ K 10 9 7
♣ J 6   ♣ 9 8 3 2

♠ 10
♡ A K Q 10 4
◇ 6 4 3
♣ A K 10 5

West	North	East	South
	Pass	Pass	1♡
1♠	2♡	2♠	4♡
Pass	Pass	Pass	

Opening lead: ♠A

East sees that a diamond switch will be more promising than a club so he drops the jack on the first trick. This is a suit-preference signal, asking for the higher-ranking side suit. West will not need an Ultra machine to decode the message, as East has no need to show attitude or count. The 3 would have asked for a club, and the 8 would have been neutral.

Suit-preference signals at the first trick are not common, but on later rounds there is more scope:

◇ 10 5 2
◇ A K J 8 4   ◇ 7 6 3
◇ Q 9

South is in a spade contract and West has overcalled in this suit. West leads the ace and East plays the 3, clearly count.

Knowing that it is safe, West continues with the king. Now East, having disclosed his holding, has a choice; the 6 or the 7.

To show preference for the higher side suit, he may play the 7. The lower card will indicate that if he has any preference, it is for the lower suit.

Resumé of signals when partner leads to the trick

i) When the leader will be interested in attitude, a high-low is encouraging, low-high discouraging.

ii) When it is clear that third hand can have no useful high card, or when the leader will be more interested in count, high-low shows an even number of cards, low-high an odd number.

iii) When the layout of the suit is known or about to become known, the card played is suit-preference or at least has suit-preference overtones.

Some partnerships prefer to show count rather than attitude regardless of the high cards held, except in cash-out situations. This can be effective when suit lengths are the key to successful defence, but can let the partnership down when the important consideration is whether to continue the suit led or whether to switch. Attitude first is the recommended primary signal when partner leads a suit.

Discarding on partner's lead

In general, the same principles are followed when discarding as when following suit. When you want a suit led, you discard a high spot card, and when you cannot afford this, you discard low in the suit you don't want led.

SIGNALS WHEN DECLARER PLAYS A SUIT

Whenever a defender will want to know how long to hold up a stopper, his partner should signal count as a matter of course. Here South is in notrumps:

```
(1)     KQ1083              (2)       QJ107
   64          A95             982          A653
       J72                           K4
```

In (1), whichever way South tackles the suit, West must echo to indicate an even number of cards. Now East knows that he must hold up until the third round. In (2) South leads the king and West plays the 2. East ducks but knows that he may safely win the next round.

Defenders should also automatically show count when declarer is cashing an established suit. One benefit is that partner will know how many discards he has to make:

(3)   A K 4
      5   9 7 6 2
            Q J 10 8 3

South begins with the A–K. When East echoes, West has to find four discards: important information.

Aside from those situations, when declarer is developing a suit the defenders either show length or do not signal at all. Thus a defender who plays high-low shows an even number, but a defender who plays low-high may simply have decided not to signal. At the table, each defender will usually have a good idea of whether his partner has elected to signal. A defender with, say, J–x–x–x in front of dummy's K–Q–10–x is obviously not going to.

When suit length has been shown a later signal may denote suit-preference:

(4)   K Q J 10 5 3
      6 2   9 8 4
            A 7

South is cashing and the defenders' only concern is to keep the right suits guarded. Suppose that there are two critical suits: East, by playing first the 4, which is normal suit length, and then the 9, which is suit-preference, can indicate that he intends to keep a guard in the higher-ranking of the two.

A similar signal may be made when partner is about to win a trick:

(5)   K Q 9 4
      A 7 3   8 5 2
            J 10 6

Playing in notrumps, South leads first the jack, then the 10. If East, having defined his length by playing the 2, drops the 8 on the second round, this will be suit-preference.

When partner is about to ruff it is especially important to show suit-preference, to guide his next lead. This is a side suit at a trump contract:

(6)   A Q J 6 2
   8 7   10 9 5 3
      K 4

Declarer plays off three rounds, discarding a loser from hand. On the third round East, knowing that West will ruff, plays high or low to show which suit West should lead. If, in a slightly different layout, East thinks his partner may have a singleton, he should signal earlier by playing the 10, then the 9; or, as the case may be, the 5 then the 3.

Suit-preference when discarding

Sometimes a defender can ill afford an encouraging discard in either of two side suits. It may instead be possible to show suit-preference via the third suit:

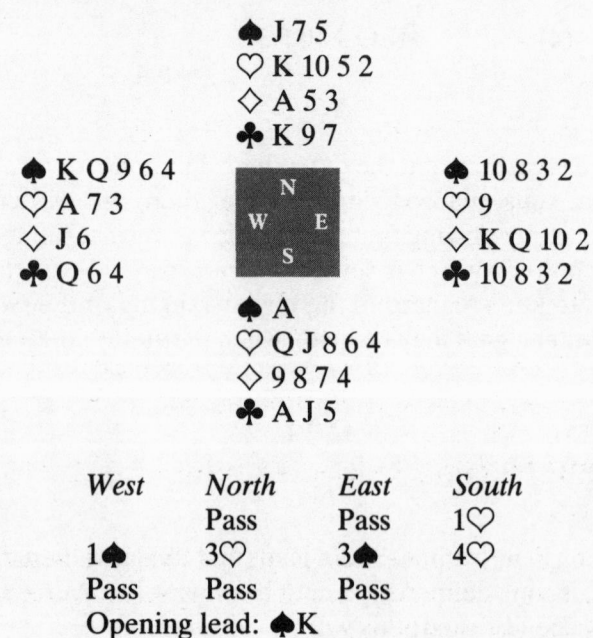

	♠ J 7 5	
	♡ K 10 5 2	
	◇ A 5 3	
	♣ K 9 7	
♠ K Q 9 6 4	N	♠ 10 8 3 2
♡ A 7 3	W E	♡ 9
◇ J 6	S	◇ K Q 10 2
♣ Q 6 4		♣ 10 8 3 2
	♠ A	
	♡ Q J 8 6 4	
	◇ 9 8 7 4	
	♣ A J 5	

West	North	East	South
	Pass	Pass	1♡
1♠	3♡	3♠	4♡
Pass	Pass	Pass	

Opening lead: ♠K

South begins with a trump to the king and a trump back. East would like to show preference for diamonds but does not want to part with either a high diamond or a low club. He therefore discards the ♠10 which, in context, should be taken as suit-preference for diamonds.

Holding up a winner to allow a signal

A winner may sometimes be held up solely to allow partner to issue a signal:

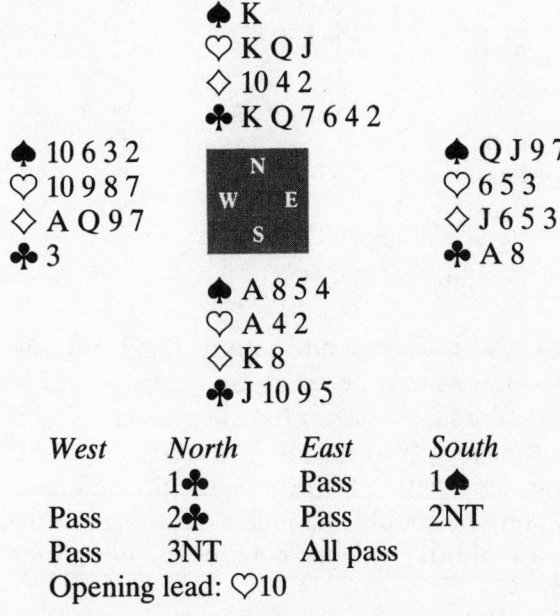

	♠ K	
	♡ K Q J	
	◇ 10 4 2	
	♣ K Q 7 6 4 2	
♠ 10 6 3 2		♠ Q J 9 7
♡ 10 9 8 7		♡ 6 5 3
◇ A Q 9 7		◇ J 6 5 3
♣ 3		♣ A 8
	♠ A 8 5 4	
	♡ A 4 2	
	◇ K 8	
	♣ J 10 9 5	

West	North	East	South
	1♣	Pass	1♠
Pass	2♣	Pass	2NT
Pass	3NT	All pass	

Opening lead: ♡10

The first trick is won in dummy and the ♣K is led. East ducks, as he does not know whether to lead the ◇3, playing West for ◇A–Q–x–x, or the ♠7, playing West for A–10–x. On the second club West discards the ♠2.

SUIT-PREFERENCE SIGNALS WHEN LEADING TO A TRICK

The use of suit-preference signals has over the years been extended to the nth degree, but the original purpose was to cover a specific situation:

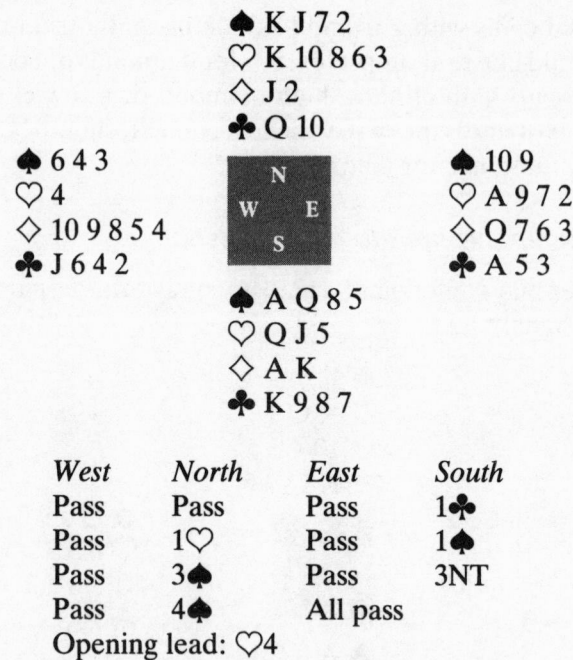

♠ K J 7 2
♡ K 10 8 6 3
♢ J 2
♣ Q 10

♠ 6 4 3
♡ 4
♢ 10 9 8 5 4
♣ J 6 4 2

♠ 10 9
♡ A 9 7 2
♢ Q 7 6 3
♣ A 5 3

♠ A Q 8 5
♡ Q J 5
♢ A K
♣ K 9 8 7

West	North	East	South
Pass	Pass	Pass	1♣
Pass	1♡	Pass	1♠
Pass	3♠	Pass	3NT
Pass	4♠	All pass	

Opening lead: ♡4

East wins with the ace and returns the 2; no other card. Thus he indicates that his entry is in clubs rather than diamonds. So, although declarer has bid the suit, West returns a club and obtains a further ruff. The lead in that situation is always suit-preference, for even when the defender has no quick re-entry he should still indicate the safer return.

There are also many opportunities for suit-preference at notrumps:

7 4
K J 8 6 3   Q 9 5
A 10 2

West leads this suit, the queen wins, and South ducks the return. To the third round, West, if there is one suit that he clearly cannot want led, may lead the king to request the higher-ranking suit or the 3 for the lower-ranking. A middle card indicates no preference unless no suit can be excluded, in which case it will ask for the 'middle' suit.

Suit-preference signals by the opening leader

Exceptionally, a suit-preference signal may be made when leading to the first trick:

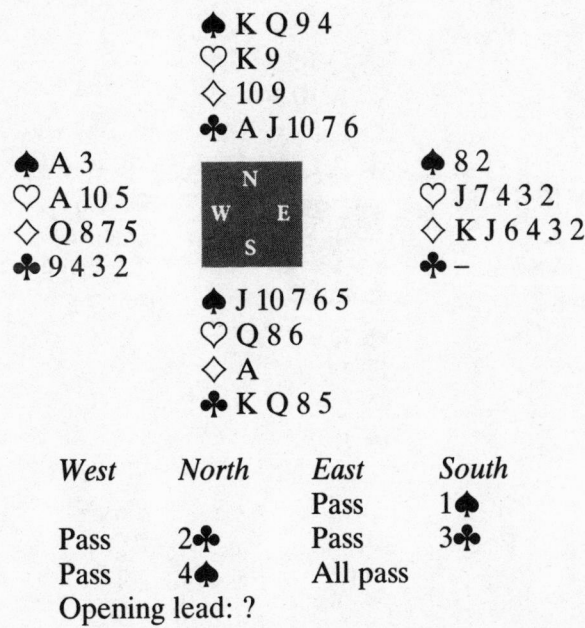

	♠ K Q 9 4	
	♡ K 9	
	◇ 10 9	
	♣ A J 10 7 6	
♠ A 3		♠ 8 2
♡ A 10 5		♡ J 7 4 3 2
◇ Q 8 7 5		◇ K J 6 4 3 2
♣ 9 4 3 2		♣ —
	♠ J 10 7 6 5	
	♡ Q 8 6	
	◇ A	
	♣ K Q 8 5	

West	North	East	South
		Pass	1♠
Pass	2♣	Pass	3♣
Pass	4♠	All pass	

Opening lead: ?

West can be fairly sure that East will have at most one club and that by leading the suit he will be able to give him a ruff when in with the ♠A. Since East may be void and able to ruff twice, West leads the ♣9. East sees that the rank of the card can have no significance except in relation to suit-preference, so he returns a heart and gets a second ruff.

A suit-preference gambit in the next situation may lead to triumph – or disaster:

♠ 10 7 5 3   ♡ –   ◇ 8 7 6 3   ♣ A K 9 8 2

Opponents climb confidently to 6◇ after the defender with this hand has mentioned clubs. It would be extraordinary if there were two club tricks for the taking, so an intrepid defender may come forth with the ♣2, hoping partner can win and return a heart.

THE TRUMP ECHO

When following in the trump suit it is standard for a defender with three or more small trumps to echo to show that he is interested in a ruff:

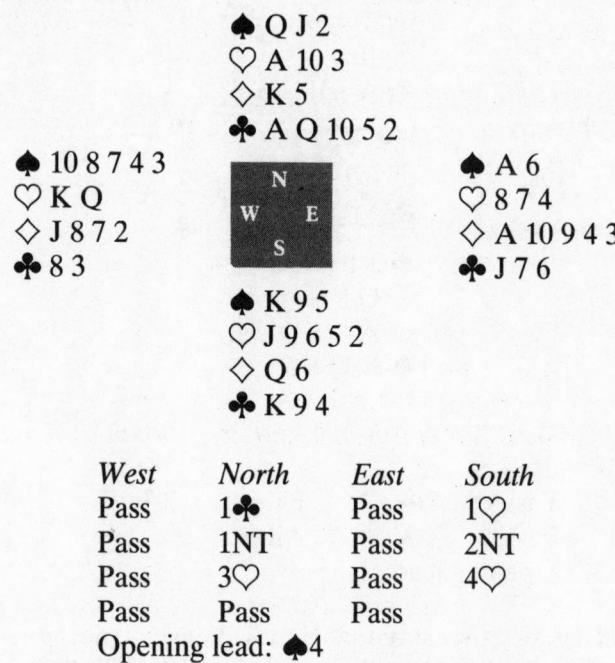

```
                    ♠ Q J 2
                    ♡ A 10 3
                    ◇ K 5
                    ♣ A Q 10 5 2
  ♠ 10 8 7 4 3                        ♠ A 6
  ♡ K Q          N                    ♡ 8 7 4
  ◇ J 8 7 2   W     E                 ◇ A 10 9 4 3
  ♣ 8 3          S                    ♣ J 7 6
                    ♠ K 9 5
                    ♡ J 9 6 5 2
                    ◇ Q 6
                    ♣ K 9 4
```

West	North	East	South
Pass	1♣	Pass	1♡
Pass	1NT	Pass	2NT
Pass	3♡	Pass	4♡
Pass	Pass	Pass	

Opening lead: ♠4

East wins with the ace and returns the 6. South plays first the 9, then the king, so West cannot tell who has the 5. However, when South plays a trump to the ace and a trump back, East echoes with the 8 and 4 confirming not only that he has a third trump but also that he can ruff.

A defender should also echo routinely with three or more trumps when ruffing before trumps have actually been led. With 9–8–6, for example, you ruff with the 9. Suppose that you then exit in a plain suit and declarer plays a trump which your partner wins: when you follow with the 6, he knows that you still have a trump.

The trump echo is useful also in a negative sense: when a player fails to echo, he indicates that no ruff can be had.

MAKING THE RIGHT DISCARDS

It is often difficult to discard well when declarer plays off a long suit. It is important to show suit length by playing high-low or low-high as this will help each defender to work out which suits he must keep. A proviso is that you should not signal length in any suit if this may tip off declarer to a finesse against your partner's holding of, say, J–x–x–x.

A defender should avoid discarding even worthless cards if this means that on a later round he will show out and put his partner's holding at risk:

$$A K Q 10$$
$$J 6 4 3 \qquad\qquad 7 5$$
$$9 8 2$$

If East lets go a card declarer will be able to play off two tricks and expose a proven finesse against West.

It can also be a mistake to discard from worthless cards for another reason:

$$A K Q$$
$$10 7 5 2 \qquad\qquad 9 8 3$$
$$J 6 4$$

You are East and declarer is cashing another suit to which you cannot follow. Even if you have to make an awkward discard, you should not throw away from this suit. If you do, you will still have to make the same discard when declarer plays off the A–K–Q, and meanwhile you will have given him a count of the suit and perhaps the entire hand.

A rule dating from the earliest days is to keep the dummy covered: that is, to keep equal length with any suit, usually a 4-card suit, in dummy, to prevent establishment. When both defenders have length in dummy's suit, the player sitting behind dummy should retain his guard, as this will be more effective against a squeeze. The same applies to any 4-card suit known to be in the closed hand.

One of the most reliable inferences occurs when the declarer makes no attempt to ruff a side suit in dummy. Suppose this is the dummy in a high diamond contract:

♠ J 9 5 2   ♡ K 6   ◇ Q 8 7 6   ♣ A 8 2

Declarer wins the first trick in spades or clubs and plays off several rounds of trumps. It is a certainty that he has no losing heart to ruff: he may hold a doubleton, or A–Q–x, but never A–x–x, so defenders can let go this suit with confidence.

SPECIAL SIGNALLING CONVENTIONS

The scope for innovation is wide and many ingenious schemes have been proposed. Some give too much away, others may raise ethical problems when the correct signal requires consideration. One signal, however, is simple and gives declarer no useful information:

Smith peters

Against notrumps, when third hand wishes his partner to continue the suit led initially, he echoes in the suit first played by declarer:

```
                    ♠ A K J 4
                    ♡ 9 2
                    ◇ 10 9 6
                    ♣ Q 9 8 3
♠ 10 9 5                             ♠ 8 7 6 2
♡ A 10 7 5 3        N                ♡ Q J 4
◇ A 7          W         E           ◇ 8 4 2
♣ 10 6 2            S                ♣ K J 7
                    ♠ Q 3
                    ♡ K 8 6
                    ◇ K Q J 5 3
                    ♣ A 5 4
```

West	North	East	South
		Pass	1◇
Pass	1♠	Pass	1NT
Pass	3NT	All pass	

Opening lead: ♡5

South takes East's jack with the king and returns the ♢Q, continuing with the king when West ducks. From West's angle to continue hearts may be a mistake if South started with K–Q–x. However, if East has initiated a high-low in diamonds, West knows that it is safe.

Smith peters may also be used by the opening leader, but as it is normal to expect a return of one's suit, the message this time is: 'Please find a switch.'

Reverse signals ('Upside down signals')

These are simply the opposite of normal signals: a low card encourages, a high card discourages. They are undoubtedly superior to standard signals:

Q 10 7 3

A 5 4   K J 9 2

8 6

When West leads the ace, East, playing standard, cannot afford the 9. Playing reverse signals, the 2 is encouraging.

A further advantage is that when a high card is played to discourage, the leader is more likely to read its meaning:

9 3

K Q 10 6   8 7 4

A J 5 2

West leads the king against a notrump contract. Playing standard, East drops the 4 to discourage but South contributes the 5 and West cannot tell whether his partner is trying to encourage from, perhaps, J–4–2.

Playing reverse signals, East drops the 8 and the position is clear.

Roman discards ('odd-even discards') and signals

A defender's first discard, whether against notrumps or a suit contract, is encouraging if it is an odd card, discouraging if an even card. When an odd card is discarded, the lower its rank, the more encouraging it is. When an even card is discarded, the choice between high and low indicates suit-preference.

The defender cannot refuse to signal and this may be awkward when he has all odd cards or all even cards, which is not unlikely when there is only one suit from which he can safely discard. Sometimes the problem may be solved by asking for an 'impossible' suit-preference, or by some other device.

Odd-even signals may also be used to encourage or discourage a lead; again with suit-preference overtones when there is a sufficient choice of cards.

Lavinthal discards (Suit-preference)

These are based on the reasonable proposition that it is usually more efficient to discard from a suit you don't want led than to signal with a high card in the suit you do want led.

A discard therefore says: 'Do not lead this suit. If my discard is a low card, lead the lower-ranking of the other two suits. And vice versa.'

Dummy
♠ A Q 8 6
♡ K 7 2
♢ K Q 10 4
♣ 6 2

East
♠ J 10 4 2
♡ A Q J 4
♢ 8 5
♣ J 8 3

South is in 3NT and West leads the ♣5 to the jack and king. South returns the ♢J and continues the suit, West winning the third round with the ace. Clearly is is more convenient for East to discard the ♣3 to ask for a heart lead than to part with either a spade or a heart.

Chapter 21

DISCOVERY AND DEDUCTION

Discovery – Deduction by the declarer – Deduction by defenders – Deduction based on assumption – Tips from the mathematicians

Few things are so satisfying as to work out the cards an opponent holds before he plays them. This is done by deduction, the process by which Sherlock Holmes built his reputation. First you assemble the facts, then you put the tips of your fingers together and consider what logically follows.

But first some legwork may have to be done. If you wish to take Holmes as your role model you should not rest content with facts already to hand but go out on the job and see whether the supply can be augmented.

DISCOVERY

One of the privileges enjoyed by declarer during his term of office is that he has scope for discovery. When short of information about the defenders' hands, he can sometimes force them to cough up:

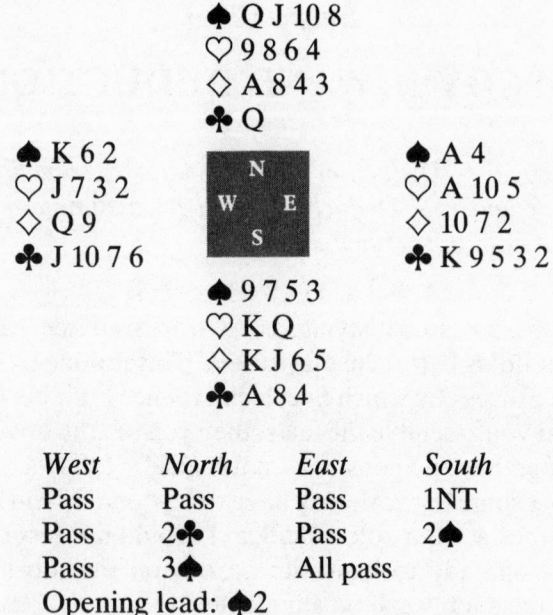

♠ Q J 10 8
♡ 9 8 6 4
◇ A 8 4 3
♣ Q

♠ K 6 2
♡ J 7 3 2
◇ Q 9
♣ J 10 7 6

♠ A 4
♡ A 10 5
◇ 10 7 2
♣ K 9 5 3 2

♠ 9 7 5 3
♡ K Q
◇ K J 6 5
♣ A 8 4

West	North	East	South
Pass	Pass	Pass	1NT
Pass	2♣	Pass	2♠
Pass	3♠	All pass	

Opening lead: ♠2

East wins with the ace and returns the suit. West wins with the king and plays a third round, East discarding the ♣2.

South has two losing clubs and can ruff only one. He is missing the ♡A, so cannot afford to lose a diamond trick. Is there anything better than a normal finesse against East in diamonds?

It would certainly be poor play to take the diamond finesse without trying to learn more about the unseen hands. For starters, South should force out the ♡A. Here, East wins and exits with a heart. South crosses to the ◇A and leads the ♣Q, intending to let it run if not covered. He wants to know who has the king, and since he has to lose a club trick, should give himself the chance that East has the king and may not cover.

Suppose, however, that East does cover. He has shown up with two aces and the ♣K and has failed to open, so South plays for the drop in diamonds.

Such is discovery play: you test the lie of one suit in order to find out more about another suit. Even the most nebulous holdings may lend themselves:

Dummy
10 5 4

Declarer
J 8 2

This is a side suit at a trump contract. If you cannot avoid losing these tricks you should play the suit before touching a more critical suit. You lead low from dummy: if East plays the queen, you place him with K–Q; if the king, you put him with A–K. If he plays low, you may well be able to picture the layout after West has captured the jack.

Discovery of distribution

Suppose that you have a long string of trumps. It is sometimes good play to rattle them off, hoping for a defensive error, but when you are bent on discovery it is often better to use them to ruff dummy's side suits:

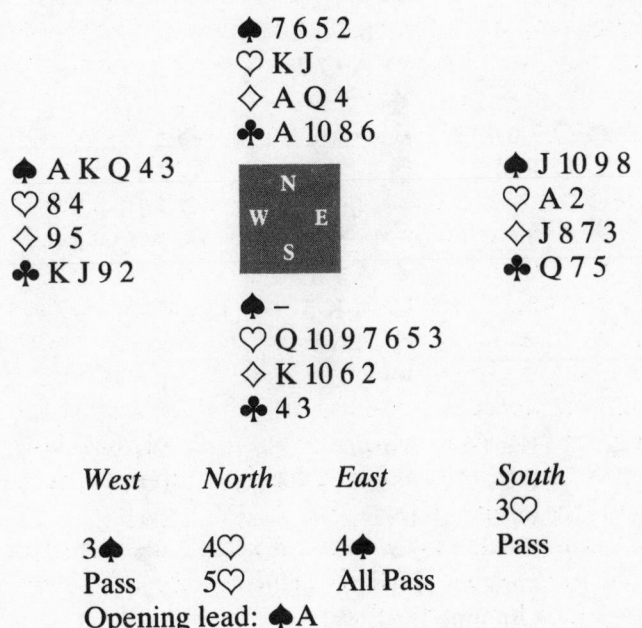

```
                    ♠ 7 6 5 2
                    ♡ K J
                    ♢ A Q 4
                    ♣ A 10 8 6
♠ A K Q 4 3                          ♠ J 10 9 8
♡ 8 4               N                ♡ A 2
♢ 9 5           W       E            ♢ J 8 7 3
♣ K J 9 2           S                ♣ Q 7 5
                    ♠ —
                    ♡ Q 10 9 7 6 5 3
                    ♢ K 10 6 2
                    ♣ 4 3
```

West	North	East	South
			3♡
3♠	4♡	4♠	Pass
Pass	5♡	All Pass	

Opening lead: ♠A

You ruff and lead a trump. East wins and returns a spade which you ruff. All follow to a second round of trumps.

As there is a club loser, you must lose no diamond trick, and of course you will leave this suit until last. To play off the trumps and hope for a defensive error is one possibility. Another is to use your trumps to ruff dummy's clubs, which may tell you something about the distribution.

Duck a club, ruff the spade return, cross to the ♣A and ruff a club. Enter dummy with a diamond and ruff the last club.

Here, West shows up with four clubs, so you may place him with five spades: for with 4–4 he might have opened with 1♣ or 1NT. West is known to have had two hearts, so on the third round of diamonds you can finesse the 10 with confidence.

Were West to show up with three clubs you would play for the drop in diamonds: he could not have fewer than three.

Do not neglect to root out clues that are not conclusive and serve merely to improve the odds slightly. Here you are playing pairs:

```
                    ♠ K 10 9
                    ♡ 8 7 6 3
                    ◇ A Q 7
                    ♣ 7 5 3
     ♠ Q 7 6 4                        ♠ 5
     ♡ Q 10 4 2        N             ♡ J 9
     ◇ 9 8 3       W       E         ◇ J 10 4 2
     ♣ J 10            S             ♣ A Q 9 8 6 4
                    ♠ A J 8 3 2
                    ♡ A K 5
                    ◇ K 6 5
                    ♣ K 2
```

West	North	East	South
Pass	Pass	Pass	1♠
Pass	1NT	Pass	2NT
Pass	3♠	Pass	4♠
Pass	Pass	Pass	

Opening lead: ♣J

East wins with the ace and returns the 8, on which West plays the 10. Game is safe, but an overtrick would be most welcome. If opponents are playing an honest game in clubs and West has no more, you will want to play him for length in trumps, taking a first-round finesse, which is not the normal play. How can you be sure he is not false-carding?

Simple. Cross to dummy with a diamond and lead the remaining club, discarding a heart.

Discovery by defenders

Defenders have fewer opportunities for discovery, and these occur mainly at the first trick. Here East has a chance to shine:

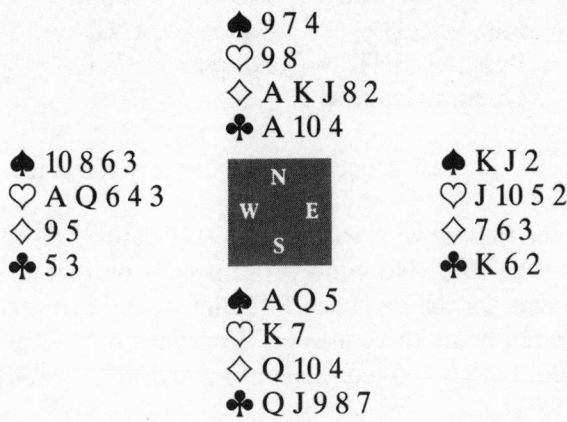

```
              ♠ 9 7 4
              ♡ 9 8
              ◇ A K J 8 2
              ♣ A 10 4
♠ 10 8 6 3                    ♠ K J 2
♡ A Q 6 4 3       N          ♡ J 10 5 2
◇ 9 5          W     E       ◇ 7 6 3
♣ 5 3             S          ♣ K 6 2
              ♠ A Q 5
              ♡ K 7
              ◇ Q 10 4
              ♣ Q J 9 8 7
```

The contract is 5♣ and West leads the ♠3. Suppose that East puts up the king: South wins and runs the ♣Q. In with the king, East cannot be sure whether to return a spade or switch to hearts.

The discovery play is to insert the ♠J at the first trick. If it loses to the queen, East knows that the only chance is to play for two tricks in hearts.

Sometimes the hard part is to spot what it is you need to discover:

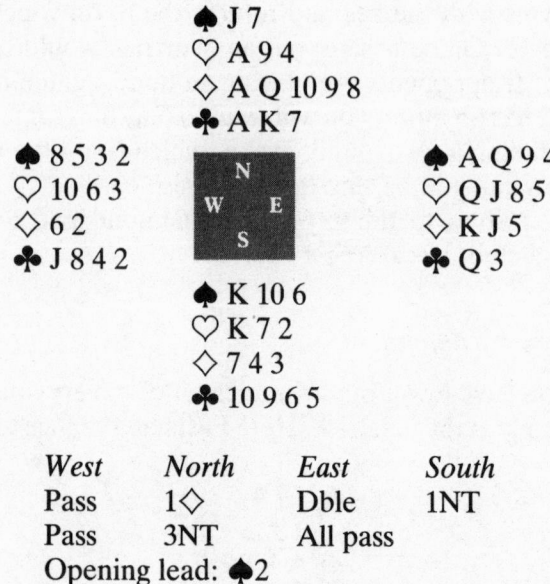

♠ J 7
♡ A 9 4
♢ A Q 10 9 8
♣ A K 7

♠ 8 5 3 2
♡ 10 6 3
♢ 6 2
♣ J 8 4 2

♠ A Q 9 4
♡ Q J 8 5
♢ K J 5
♣ Q 3

♠ K 10 6
♡ K 7 2
♢ 7 4 3
♣ 10 9 6 5

West	North	East	South
Pass	1♢	Dble	1NT
Pass	3NT	All pass	

Opening lead: ♠2

How should East proceed when dummy plays low to the first trick?

Suppose that he wins with the ace and returns either a low spade or the ♠Q. No good: South plays on diamonds and makes game for the loss of two diamonds and two spades. 'A heart switch beats the contract,' East tells his partner, 'But how could I tell? You led the 2 and you didn't even have the 10.'

After this auction there is nothing against leading the 2, to give count. In any case, leading a different card would not change East's problem. But East himself could easily have covered all possibilities. On the opening lead he should play not the ace, nor the queen, but the 9. If this brings forth the king, East continues spades when he comes in. Here, when South wins with the 10, East knows to switch to hearts.

DEDUCTION BY THE DECLARER

So much for clue gathering. We turn now to deduction, the process of figuring what logically follows from facts already known or assumed. Many deductions are automatic – a defender leads the queen, so cannot have the king, and so on and so forth. Here we focus on the less obvious.

Deductions from the opening lead

In earlier chapters there are many examples of inferences from the opening lead. At notrumps, a defender leads the 3 and the declarer, seeing the 2 in dummy, places him with no more than four cards. This is merely scratching the surface. Presumably the leader has no longer suit, and no 4-card suit headed by a sequence. If he leads a short suit against notrumps, then either your side has bid his longest suit or he is playing for his partner's hand, in which case you deduce that the leader has few high cards.

Inferences arise also from third-hand's play. You are South:

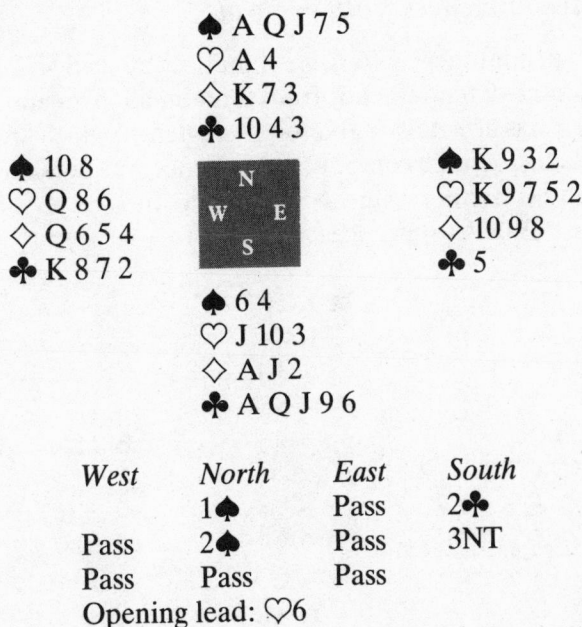

```
              ♠ A Q J 7 5
              ♡ A 4
              ◇ K 7 3
              ♣ 10 4 3

♠ 10 8                        ♠ K 9 3 2
♡ Q 8 6          N            ♡ K 9 7 5 2
◇ Q 6 5 4     W     E         ◇ 10 9 8
♣ K 8 7 2        S            ♣ 5

              ♠ 6 4
              ♡ J 10 3
              ◇ A J 2
              ♣ A Q J 9 6
```

West	North	East	South
	1♠	Pass	2♣
Pass	2♠	Pass	3NT
Pass	Pass	Pass	

Opening lead: ♡6

Over 2♠ it might have been an idea to bid 3◇: then North could have played 3NT from the right side. Still, there you are in 3NT.

East wins the first trick with the king and returns the 5 on which West plays the 8. If East has the ♣K there will be no problem; but what if he has not?

It is seldom a waste of time to work out the precise layout of the suit led, whether or not it seems strictly necessary. It cannot be 4–4, as the 2 has not appeared.

West cannot have five, for then he would have to have the 2. East would then have K–9–5 or K–7–5 and would not have returned the 5.

West, then, has led from three to the queen, a good shot on the bidding. Since he has had to block the suit, the contract can be assured by leading the ♠Q, dislodging East's only possible entry. If East wins the trick, the defenders thereafter take only one heart trick and one club. If the queen is allowed to hold, you shift to clubs.

Negative inferences from the lead

Negative inferences often go unnoticed. Against a trump contract the defender leads from three small in an unbid suit: he surely has no small doubleton or singleton, which are much better leads. After a competitive sequence, the defender does not lead his partner's suit: very likely he has the ace. One of the most reliable inferences is seen here:

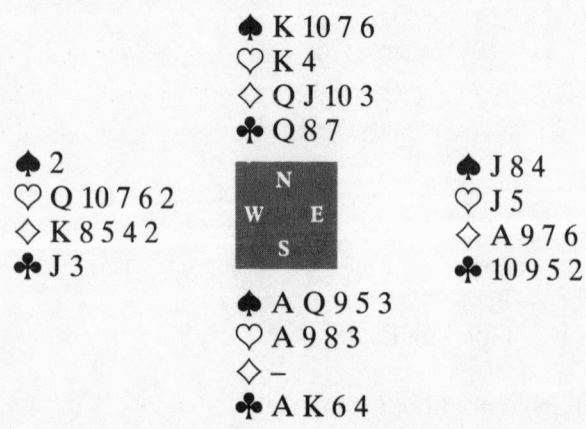

After 1♠–3♠–6♠, West leads the ♡6, taken in dummy. The simple line is to play off the ♠A–K and try to ruff hearts twice in dummy. This would work for most players, but you of course are the original Tough Luck Kid so you are sure to find trumps 3–1 and be overruffed in spades.

There is a blue-chip play. Defenders with A–K of a suit are strongly inclined to lead it, especially against a slam reached with no check on aces. So, draw three rounds of trumps and lead the ◇Q from dummy, discarding a heart if not covered. Later you lead the ◇J for a ruffing finesse. One diamond trick and one ruff in dummy give you the contract.

Deductions from the bidding

Aside from the obvious – a player who has failed to open is unlikely to hold 12 points, a player who passed his partner's opening is unlikely to hold five or six, and so on – the bread-and-butter inferences are these:

(1) When opponents have been bidding their heads off on very little, expect suits to break badly. When there has been an eerie silence despite their having some share of high cards, expect suits to break favourably.

(2) Do not place a defender with any missing jacks or queens just because he has overcalled. These cards are more valuable in defence than in attack and good overcallers take account of this.

(3) Suppose that a particular defender had shown up with a few points: even if these are not enough to entitle him to bid, you should place his partner with any outstanding high cards.

This deal shows why:

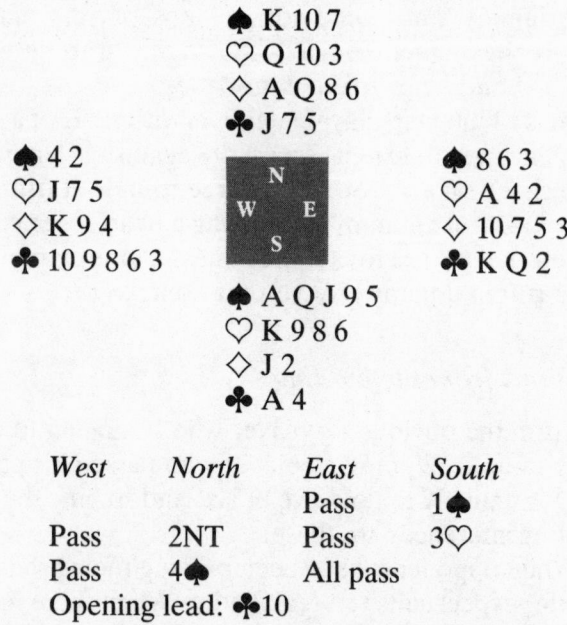

♠ K 10 7
♡ Q 10 3
♢ A Q 8 6
♣ J 7 5

♠ 4 2
♡ J 7 5
♢ K 9 4
♣ 10 9 8 6 3

♠ 8 6 3
♡ A 4 2
♢ 10 7 5 3
♣ K Q 2

♠ A Q J 9 5
♡ K 9 8 6
♢ J 2
♣ A 4

West	North	East	South
		Pass	1♠
Pass	2NT	Pass	3♡
Pass	4♠	All pass	

Opening lead: ♣10

The jack is played and East's queen is allowed to hold. East continues with the king. The contract will be safe if you can pick up the ♡J but first you should try your luck in diamonds. If you can deduce who has the king, you will not need to find the ♡J.

If West has the ♢K, a simple finesse gives you game. If East has it, a low diamond lead from dummy gives you three tricks if East puts up the king, allowing you two heart discards. Which is it to be?

Simply because East, who passed as dealer, has shown up with a few points – the ♣K–Q – and West has not shown anything at all, you should play West for the ♢K. East could hold the ♢K and still have passed – but not if he held the ♡A as well! That is why West is more likely to hold the ♢K.

Deductions from the play

In the middle game the declarer should question at each turn why defenders have done what they have done, or not done what they could have done:

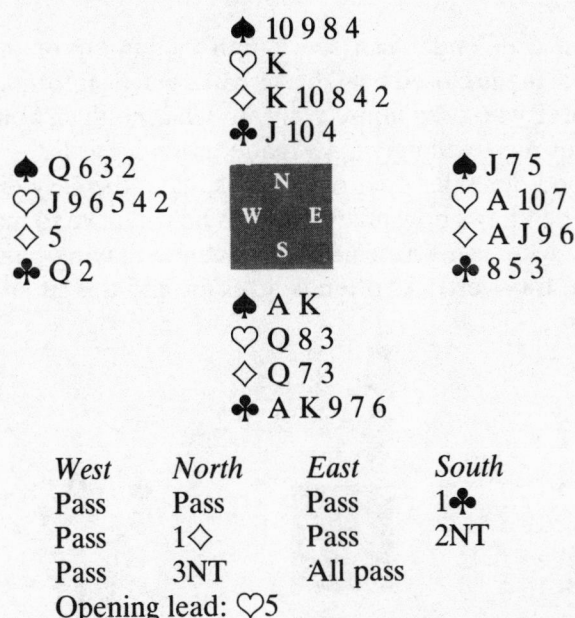

```
            ♠ 10 9 8 4
            ♡ K
            ◇ K 10 8 4 2
            ♣ J 10 4
♠ Q 6 3 2                    ♠ J 7 5
♡ J 9 6 5 4 2      N         ♡ A 10 7
◇ 5            W       E     ◇ A J 9 6
♣ Q 2              S         ♣ 8 5 3
            ♠ A K
            ♡ Q 8 3
            ◇ Q 7 3
            ♣ A K 9 7 6
```

West	North	East	South
Pass	Pass	Pass	1♣
Pass	1◇	Pass	2NT
Pass	3NT	All pass	

Opening lead: ♡5

East wins with the ace and returns the 10 which you duck. He continues with the 7, West following with the 4 and 2.

You play off a top club and nothing happens. You switch to the ◇Q, East winning. A spade comes back and you return a diamond but West shows out, discarding a spade. Now there is nothing for it but to put up the king and try to make five club tricks. When East follows small to dummy's jack, do you finesse?

Suppose you were East and happened to have the ♣Q. Wouldn't you have held up the ◇A, to prevent South from entering dummy? On this reasoning you should decline the finesse and play to drop the queen.

Do not be discouraged when this kind of deduction goes wrong. Bridge is not like noughts and crosses, where you cannot lose if you play correctly.

Deductions from defenders' discards

Defenders often cannot help giving clues when they discard. A player seeing A–K–Q–x in dummy will cling to any 4-card holding, so if he discards you can be sure that he has more or fewer.

When a defender can see length in dummy or infer its presence in the closed hand his discards will be informative to a declarer who asks himself, 'From what holding would the defender most willingly have made those discards?'

A good defender does not always make the easy discards first: if he knows how many discards he will have to make he will try to present a misleading picture. Playing pairs, the struggle for overtricks often centres around this situation:

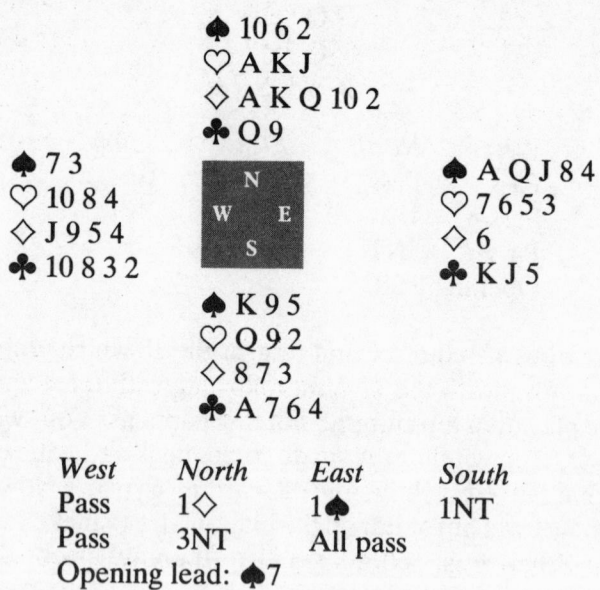

```
              ♠ 10 6 2
              ♡ A K J
              ♢ A K Q 10 2
              ♣ Q 9
♠ 7 3                          ♠ A Q J 8 4
♡ 10 8 4        N             ♡ 7 6 5 3
♢ J 9 5 4     W   E           ♢ 6
♣ 10 8 3 2      S             ♣ K J 5
              ♠ K 9 5
              ♡ Q 9 2
              ♢ 8 7 3
              ♣ A 7 6 4
```

West	North	East	South
Pass	1♢	1♠	1NT
Pass	3NT	All pass	
	Opening lead: ♠7		

East does not insert the jack at the first trick, which would be normal if he thought West might have an entry. He plays the ace, hoping to deprive South of a throw-in card if he has K–x. Here, however, South wins the next trick and tests diamonds, exposing the finesse against West's jack. Then he cashes the red suits, aiming to throw East in with a spade to lead away from the ♣K for +460.

If East discards without guile, he becomes an easy victim. Say he throws a club, a heart and a spade in that order: he winds up having to discard from ♠J–8 and ♣K–J. Declarer knows that he has these cards and he makes eleven tricks.

East must not part with a heart but should bare the ♣K at an early stage. His last four cards are ♠J–8, ♡7 and ♣K. When the last diamond is led he throws a spade. If South attempts a throw-in he is held to ten tricks.

It follows from this illustration that when a defender knows how many discards he is going to have to make, declarer should anticipate that he may organise them in a cunning way.

DEDUCTION BY DEFENDERS

Defenders have at least as much scope for deduction as the declarer. First, because declarer has been obliged to do some bidding. Secondly, because they can draw inferences from his line of play. But most of all because the defenders can empathise, drawing inferences from each other's moves.

7

K Q 10 5 3   A J 6 2

9 8 4

Against a trump contract West leads the king and it holds. West should register that East evidently sees no advantage in overtaking and switching from his side: this in itself may suggest a line of defence. Also, it seems that East does not want to force dummy to ruff: if he did, he would have overtaken and continued.

Inferences from the bidding have been discussed in Chapter 13, but the auction should be revisited when dummy is exposed. Is dummy weaker or stronger than expected? If stronger, a dynamic form of defence may be needed; if weaker, a passive defence may be best. With this in mind, it is good practice to estimate how many points dummy ought to have before the opening lead is made. A separate exercise is that when you see how many points are actually in dummy, you should compute how many points are left for your partner. You are East:

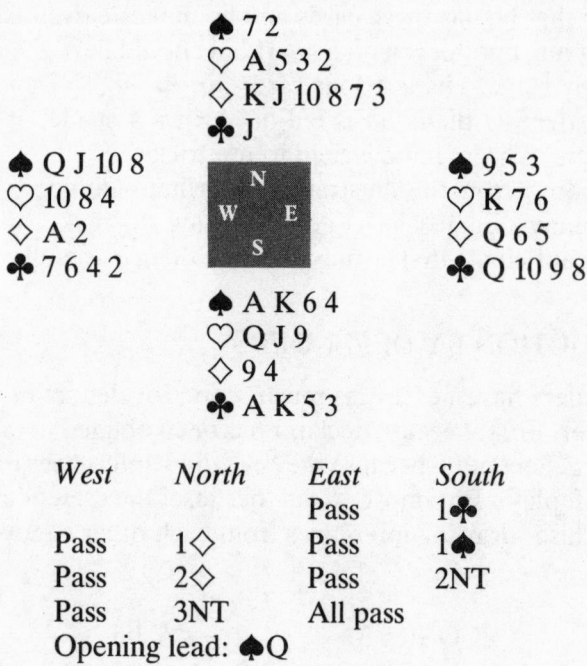

```
                    ♠ 7 2
                    ♡ A 5 3 2
                    ◇ K J 10 8 7 3
                    ♣ J
♠ Q J 10 8                          ♠ 9 5 3
♡ 10 8 4          N                 ♡ K 7 6
◇ A 2          W     E              ◇ Q 6 5
♣ 7 6 4 2         S                 ♣ Q 10 9 8
                    ♠ A K 6 4
                    ♡ Q J 9
                    ◇ 9 4
                    ♣ A K 5 3
```

West	North	East	South
		Pass	1♣
Pass	1◇	Pass	1♠
Pass	2◇	Pass	2NT
Pass	3NT	All pass	

Opening lead: ♠Q

South wins with the ace and returns the ◇9, losing to your queen. You have of course already drawn two inferences about your partner's hand: he has precisely four spades, and six or seven points, as South has 17–18.

Next, a reliable inference from South's play in diamonds: your partner has A–x. His points are therefore entirely accounted for and you can forget about returning the ♣Q, which might otherwise have seemed a bright idea.

Two spade tricks and two diamonds will not beat the contract but, with the information you have assembled, you may hit on the sparkling return of the ♡K, even though South will surely have Q–J–x. To preserve dummy's entry, South has to duck, and now you revert to spades.

It has been previously noted that if declarer draws dummy's trumps, you can assume he has no losers that he could have ruffed. This often indicates which suit may safely be discarded. West's deduction in the next deal is almost as safe:

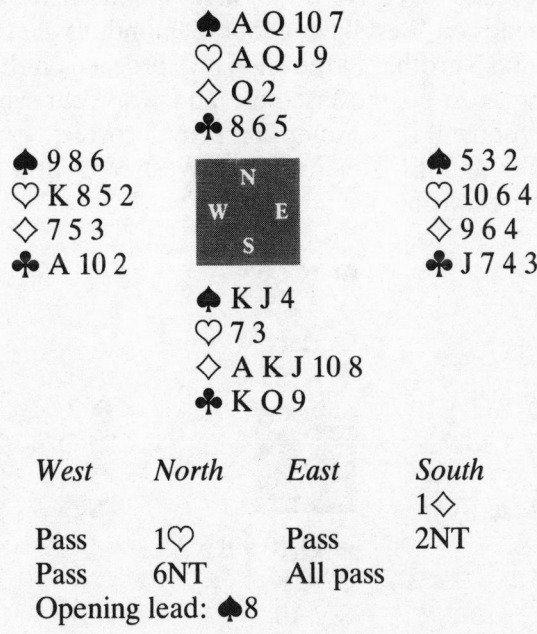

♠ A Q 10 7
♡ A Q J 9
♢ Q 2
♣ 8 6 5

♠ 9 8 6
♡ K 8 5 2
♢ 7 5 3
♣ A 10 2

♠ 5 3 2
♡ 10 6 4
♢ 9 6 4
♣ J 7 4 3

♠ K J 4
♡ 7 3
♢ A K J 10 8
♣ K Q 9

West	North	East	South
			1♢
Pass	1♡	Pass	2NT
Pass	6NT	All pass	

Opening lead: ♠8

The first trick is won with dummy's ace, East playing the 2. A low club goes to declarer's king.

West ducks, of course – and in normal tempo. South cannot conceivably have led up to the unsupported king so early when he has such good holdings elsewhere. He is trying to learn the position of the ace, and if West ducks smoothly South may sooner or later play a second club instead of taking a successful finesse in hearts.

Memo: A competent declarer defers the crunch as long as possible. His early plays are often feelers rather than make-or-break shots.

DEDUCTION BASED ON ASSUMPTION

Deductions may be made not only from what is known but from what is assumed or postulated. This opens up a new field of thought.

We all make extensive use of assumption. When the contract depends on West having four diamonds to the jack, two trumps, and a brother in the Navy, we proceed on that basis. The thing is to go the last mile and work out what must logically follow if the assumption proves correct.

Put your thumbs over the East–West cards and try your hand at three problems:

(1)

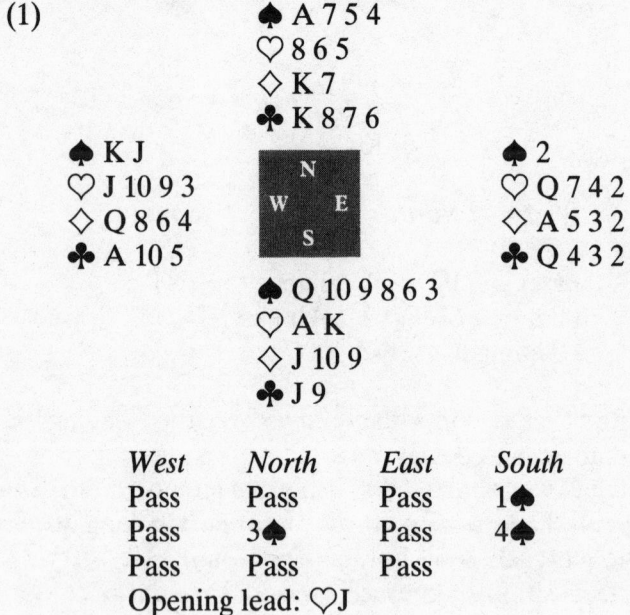

	♠ A 7 5 4	
	♡ 8 6 5	
	◇ K 7	
	♣ K 8 7 6	
♠ K J		♠ 2
♡ J 10 9 3		♡ Q 7 4 2
◇ Q 8 6 4		◇ A 5 3 2
♣ A 10 5		♣ Q 4 3 2
	♠ Q 10 9 8 6 3	
	♡ A K	
	◇ J 10 9	
	♣ J 9	

West	North	East	South
Pass	Pass	Pass	1♠
Pass	3♠	Pass	4♠
Pass	Pass	Pass	

Opening lead: ♡J

You play off the second heart winner and lead a trump to the ace, bringing forth the jack from West and the 2 from East. Next, you ruff dummy's heart and exit with a trump, hoping to put East on play, but West wins and returns the ◇4.

(2)

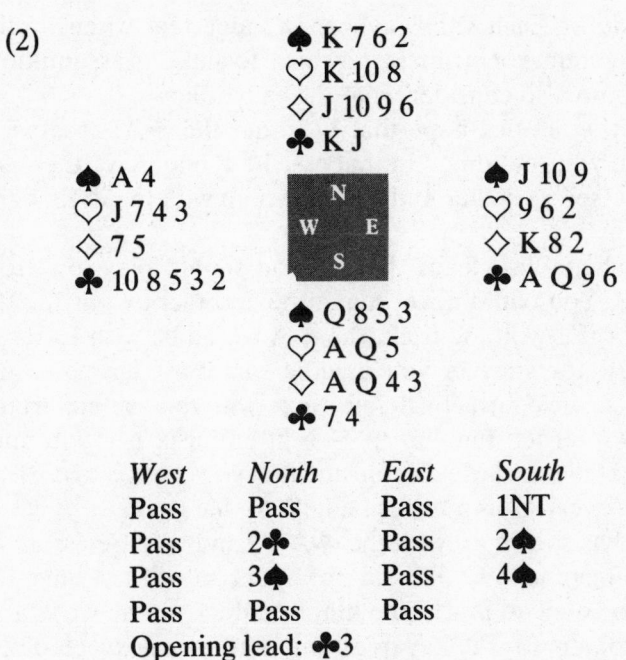

	♠ K 7 6 2	
	♡ K 10 8	
	◇ J 10 9 6	
	♣ K J	
♠ A 4		♠ J 10 9
♡ J 7 4 3		♡ 9 6 2
◇ 7 5		◇ K 8 2
♣ 10 8 5 3 2		♣ A Q 9 6
	♠ Q 8 5 3	
	♡ A Q 5	
	◇ A Q 4 3	
	♣ 7 4	

West	North	East	South
Pass	Pass	Pass	1NT
Pass	2♣	Pass	2♠
Pass	3♠	Pass	4♠
Pass	Pass	Pass	

Opening lead: ♣3

East takes tricks 1–2 with ♣Q, ♣A and exits with a heart.

(3)

	♠ A Q 5 3	
	♡ Q 10	
	◇ 7 6 2	
	♣ A K 8 3	
♠ 9 7 6 2		♠ K 10 8
♡ A K 6 5 2		♡ J 9 8 7 4 3
◇ A 9 4		◇ J 10 8
♣ 5		♣ 6
	♠ J 4	
	♡ –	
	◇ K Q 5 3	
	♣ Q J 10 9 7 4 2	

West	North	East	South
		Pass	3♣
Pass	5♣	All pass	

Opening lead: ♡K

You ruff, and play a club, both defenders following.

Solutions: Each hand invokes the idea that when, in the ordinary course of business, you have to make an assumption, you should also consider what logically follows.

In (1), you must hope that West has the ♣A: otherwise, how can you get home? In that case he cannot have the ◇A, as he passed as dealer and has shown up with the ♠K–J and ♡J.

So, when West leads the ◇4 you should play low from dummy. You could never make the contract by playing the king, for if it won the trick, the ♣A would be with East.

In (2), for starters you assume that East has the ◇K; otherwise the contract will fail. Next, with this skeletal trump holding – all too familiar to 4–4–fit enthusiasts – you must hope that the ace is doubleton and that you can locate it. In no other way can trump losses be held to one trick.

East has shown up with the ♣A–Q and you are assuming that he has the ◇K. He did not open, so will not have the ♠A. So you lead low to the king and duck on the way back.

In problem (3) the key question, perhaps unexpectedly, is who has the ♠K. You have to assume that West has the ◇A, for if East has it you will get home however you play. Next you should realise that you can play either opponent for the ♠K.

The opening lead has marked West with the ♡A–K and we are assuming that he has the ◇A. It is possible that he has the ♠K and was silenced by your 3♣ opening, but it is more likely that East has it. So, after drawing trumps, you lead a low spade from the table. If East puts up the king, you get two diamonds away on the spades.

Assumptions about distribution

It is of course often right to make an assumption about the division of a suit: when the contract will be safe unless trumps are 4–1, you play as though they *are* 4–1; and so on.

In such case you should consider what follows, just as you would in the case of an assumption about high cards:

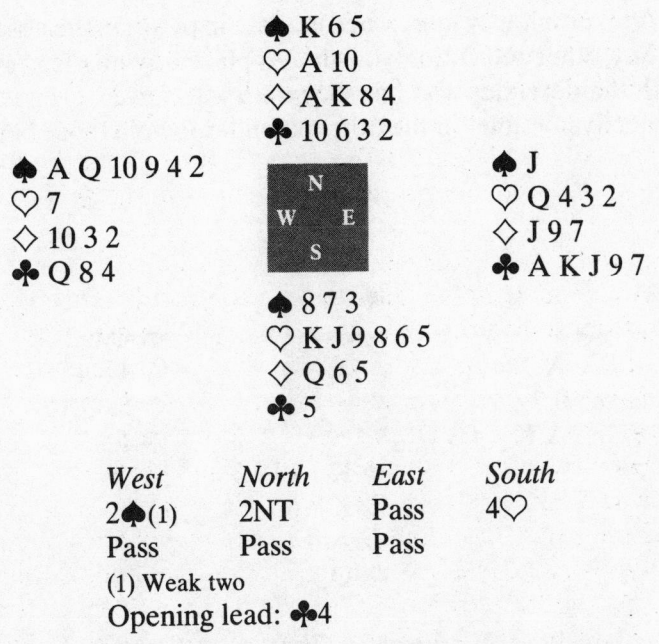

♠ K 6 5
♡ A 10
♢ A K 8 4
♣ 10 6 3 2

♠ A Q 10 9 4 2
♡ 7
♢ 10 3 2
♣ Q 8 4

♠ J
♡ Q 4 3 2
♢ J 9 7
♣ A K J 9 7

♠ 8 7 3
♡ K J 9 8 6 5
♢ Q 6 5
♣ 5

West	North	East	South
2♠(1)	2NT	Pass	4♡
Pass	Pass	Pass	

(1) Weak two

Opening lead: ♣4

East wins with the king and returns the ♠J to West's ace. The ♠Q comes back and East ruffs the king, exiting with the ♣A which you ruff.

You play a trump to the ace and a trump back. East follows, but as he has already ruffed, a question arises: should you put up the king, playing for the suit to have been 3–2?

West has shown up with six spades and appears to have at least three clubs. You have to assume that diamonds are 3–3, for otherwise there will be a spade loser. So you must play West for a singleton trump.

TIPS FROM THE MATHEMATICIANS

Mathematical knowledge is not really needed in bridge, as everything of practical importance that depends on mathematics is already encapsulated in conventional wisdom.

A tip previously mentioned is a case in point: in the absence of any other indication you should place any missing points with the defender who has shown up with fewer, even if it is perfectly possible for the other defender to hold those points:

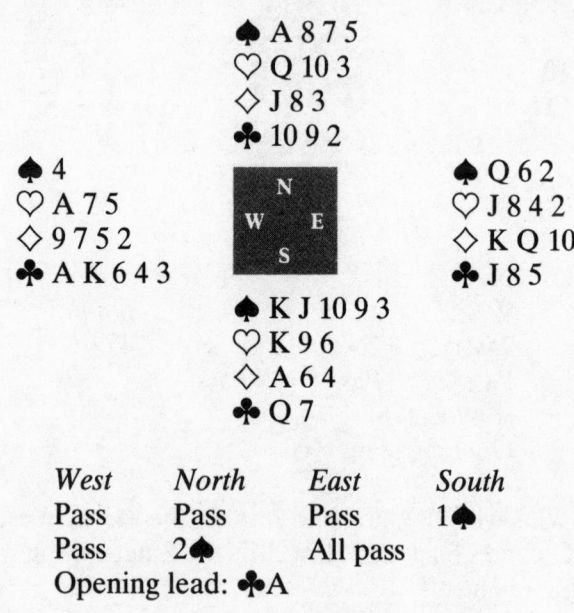

West	North	East	South
Pass	Pass	Pass	1♠
Pass	2♠	All pass	

Opening lead: ♣A

West begins with the ace, king and another club and you ruff East's jack. With this trump holding it is normal to play for the drop, but this has only a narrow edge over the finesse. Here West, who passed as dealer, has already shown up with the ♣A–K, so you should play East for the ♠Q.

The basis for this tip is that, mathematically speaking, East can hold zillions of hands that include the ♠Q whereas West can hold only trillions. This is because if West has the ♡A, which is possible, he cannot have the ♠Q as well.

The chances of a 3–3 break

A second tip from the wranglers is that while a 3–3 break is, at the start, a 36% shot, the chances improve if two rounds of the suit are played off with no one showing out:

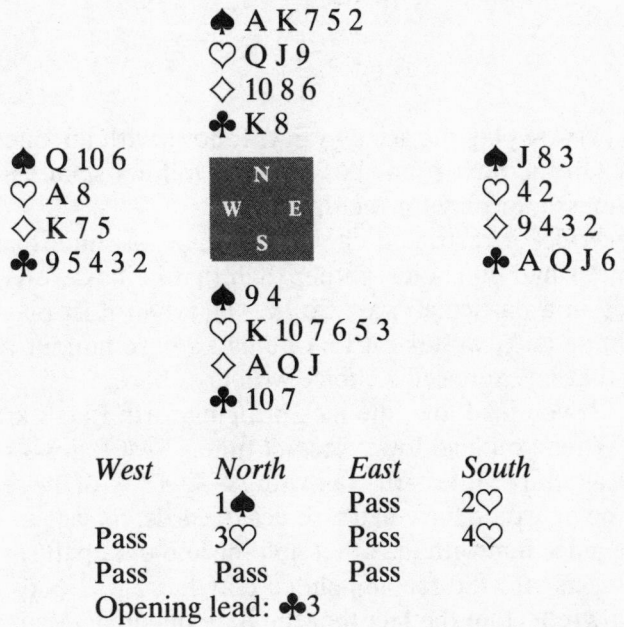

	♠ A K 7 5 2	
	♡ Q J 9	
	◇ 10 8 6	
	♣ K 8	

♠ Q 10 6		♠ J 8 3
♡ A 8	N	♡ 4 2
◇ K 7 5	W E	◇ 9 4 3 2
♣ 9 5 4 3 2	S	♣ A Q J 6

	♠ 9 4	
	♡ K 10 7 6 5 3	
	◇ A Q J	
	♣ 10 7	

West	North	East	South
	1♠	Pass	2♡
Pass	3♡	Pass	4♡
Pass	Pass	Pass	

Opening lead: ♣3

East takes two club tricks and exits with a trump. West wins with the ace and returns a trump to which East follows.

A 3–3 spade break will allow you to get two diamonds away. Alternatively you may play East for the ◇K. There are not enough entries to test spades and still take two finesses.

At this stage the diamond finesse looks better. However, you can afford to play off the ♠A–K, and when you do, both opponents follow. Now the 3–3 break is almost an even chance: this is because the 6–0 and 5–1 divisions have been eliminated. You may therefore be swayed by other indications, however slight. If your reading of the entrails is that West did not lead a diamond because he has the king, you may play for spades to break.

So the tip is: when defenders follow to two rounds, a 3–3 break is almost as good as a finesse, and you may therefore elect to follow any reasonable sort of hunch.

A final tip is the rule of restricted choice:

(1)   K 10 9 4 2   (2)   Q J 9

A 6 5 3   5 4 3

In (1) you play the ace and East follows with the queen or jack. On the next round, when West follows small, should you finesse, or play for the drop?

The rule of restricted choice tells us to assume that the defender had no choice, rather than that he has exercised a choice in a particular way. So, in (1), when East plays the queen or jack, we take it that he had a bare honour rather than that he exercised a choice with Q–J bare.

In (2) you lead low, the jack bringing forth East's king or ace. When you lead low a second time, West follows small. Did East start with K–10–x or with A–K–x? With the second holding he would have had a choice of cards, the ace or king, so we place him with the other holding and put up the queen.

In each case the recommended play has 2 to 1 odds in its favour; reflecting the fact that the bare queen and bare jack are, in aggregate, twice as likely as Q–J doubleton; and similarly in the second example.

Whenever the defender has cards of equal value and is obliged to play one, the rule of restricted choice may apply. But there is a trap:

A Q 9 8 5 3

K 4

South plays the king and East follows with the jack or 10. On the next round South should not finesse but should play high in dummy. East is more likely to have a bare honour than J–10 doubleton, but these are not the only possibilities: he may be falsecarding with J–10–x.

The rule of restricted choice can sometimes be applied to leads made by a defender. South plays in 6NT, no suit having been mentioned, and West leads a club from what turns out to be 7–5–3. Later in the play South has to decide whether, in diamonds, West holds three low cards or three to an honour. It is perfectly logical to say, 'If West had held the same cards in diamonds as in clubs he might have led a diamond. That he led a club makes it likely he has not the same holding in the two suits.'

Chapter 22

DECEPTION AND CONCEALMENT

Deception by declarer at the first trick – Ploys and capers in a single suit – Concealment by declarer – Deceptive opening leads – Concealment by defenders – Offering declarer a losing option – Tromperie

The urge to outwit is ingrained in all of us. Does deception at the bridge table perhaps provide an outlet for tendencies normally suppressed? At all events, schemers whose minds work along these lines have responded to public demand by proposing a great number of cunning moves.

DECEPTION BY DECLARER AT THE FIRST TRICK

When the defending side wins the first trick, declarer may wish to encourage or discourage a continuation. The rule is simple: do as you would if you were the defender's partner. When you want a switch, play your lowest. When you want a continuation, play a card just above RHO's card:

	(1)	8 6 3			(2)	A 5 3	
A K 10 7			J 9 4	K Q 9 8			J 6 4
		Q 5 2				10 7 2	

In (1) the ace is led and East follows with the 4. You would like to make the queen, so you encourage with the 5. Now West has to wonder whether his partner has started an echo with Q–4–2.

In (2) the king is led and East encourages with the 6. To deter a continuation you play the 2. From West's angle East may have played a discouraging card from 10–7–6.

That such plays can work against even the best players is evidenced by an example from a world championship match:

(3)   Q 10 4
         A K J 7 5   6 3
                         9 8 2

At one table West was Lew Mathe, a macho performer who once conceded in a Los Angeles courtroom that he was the world's greatest bridge player. He led the king, on which East played the 6. However, South dropped the 2 and Mathe switched, as he did not want to set up the queen if East held 9–8–6. Thus South averted a killing ruff.

At the other table South was Ira Rubin, equally admissive of his stature. Again East played the 6 but Rubin, instead of the 2, followed with the 8. West now computed that East would not have played the 6 from 9–6–3, 9–6–2 or 6–3–2, so he continued the suit, to South's disadvantage.

The same stratagem may be helpful when the opening lead hits declarer's suit:

(4)   K 6
         J 8 5 4   10 9
                         A Q 7 3 2

After 1NT–3NT, West leads the 4. South should not necessarily go up with the king and clear the suit. If he plays low from dummy and the 7 from hand, East may continue and a tempo will have been gained.

Plays to disguise strength

In the same neck of the woods, it can be sound play to win with a higher card than necessary:

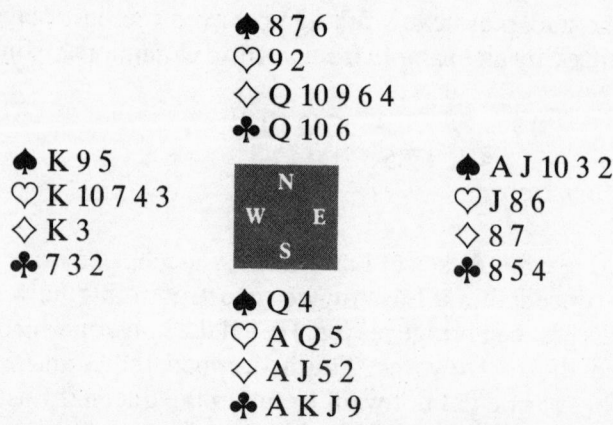

♠ 8 7 6
♡ 9 2
◇ Q 10 9 6 4
♣ Q 10 6

♠ K 9 5
♡ K 10 7 4 3
◇ K 3
♣ 7 3 2

♠ A J 10 3 2
♡ J 8 6
◇ 8 7
♣ 8 5 4

♠ Q 4
♡ A Q 5
◇ A J 5 2
♣ A K J 9

After 2NT–3NT the ♡4 is led and East plays the jack. Since South does not need two heart tricks, and fears a spade switch, he wins with the ace. After declarer crosses with a club and takes a losing finesse in diamonds, West may continue with a low heart.

A similar ploy may be attempted with these holdings:

(5)   6 3   (6)   K 7 4

5 led   9 played   3 led   10 played

A Q 10   A J 6

In (5) it can hardly cost to win with the queen rather than the 10. If East gets in it makes no difference whether South has kept A–Q or A–10, but if West is in first he may play low again from K–J–x–x.

In (6), if a switch to another suit would be unwelcome, declarer may take the 10 with the ace, not the jack. The trick may come back if West again underleads the queen.

To part with a higher card than necessary can be super-effective when it gives defenders the wrong idea of your length:

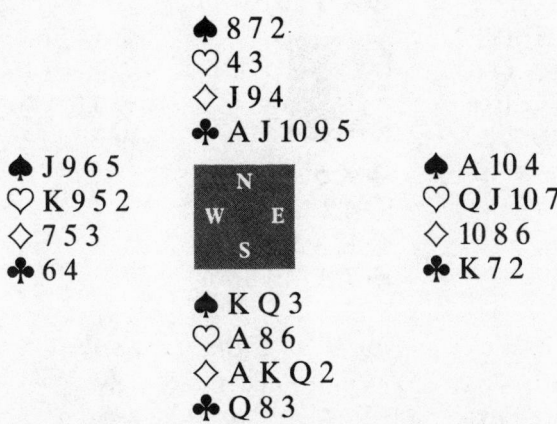

```
              ♠ 8 7 2
              ♡ 4 3
              ◇ J 9 4
              ♣ A J 10 9 5
♠ J 9 6 5                      ♠ A 10 4
♡ K 9 5 2          N          ♡ Q J 10 7
◇ 7 5 3        W     E        ◇ 10 8 6
♣ 6 4             S           ♣ K 7 2
              ♠ K Q 3
              ♡ A 8 6
              ◇ A K Q 2
              ♣ Q 8 3
```

After 2NT–3NT, West leads the ♣5 to his partner's ace. If East switches to a heart, things could turn nasty, so South drops the queen, even though he does not know how spades are breaking. If East continues, South wins and takes the club finesse. If it loses and East has another spade, the defenders make no more than four tricks.

Still at the first trick, here is a deception that could fool most defenders, including the present writer:

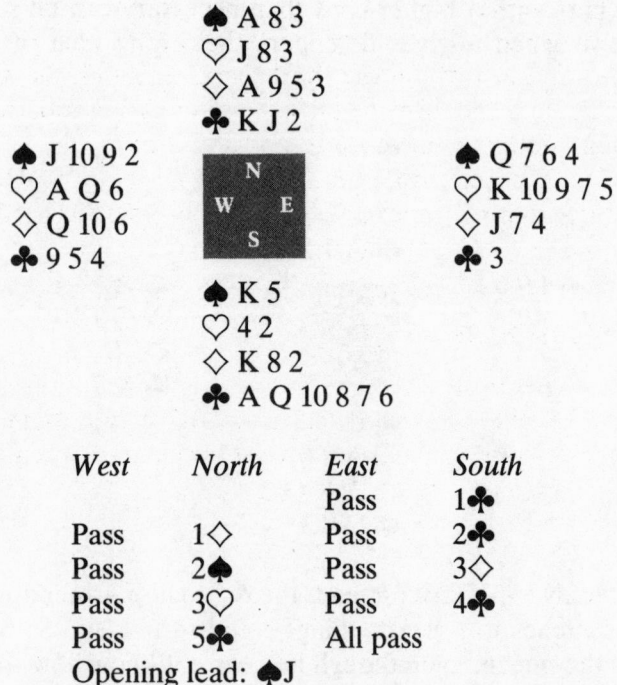

♠ A 8 3
♡ J 8 3
◇ A 9 5 3
♣ K J 2

♠ J 10 9 2   ♠ Q 7 6 4
♡ A Q 6   ♡ K 10 9 7 5
◇ Q 10 6   ◇ J 7 4
♣ 9 5 4   ♣ 3

♠ K 5
♡ 4 2
◇ K 8 2
♣ A Q 10 8 7 6

West	North	East	South
		Pass	1♣
Pass	1◇	Pass	2♣
Pass	2♠	Pass	3◇
Pass	3♡	Pass	4♣
Pass	5♣	All pass	

Opening lead: ♠J

Prospects are dim: you have ten tricks, and nowhere to go except diamonds. If you win, draw trumps, and give up a diamond, hearts will be the only suit for defenders to play.

So, duck at trick one. If West continues you can discard a diamond on a spade, ruff a diamond, and scrape home if the suit is 3–3.

PLOYS AND CAPERS IN A SINGLE SUIT

Suppose that you are developing a suit and logistically it makes no difference which hand you lead from. It must be better to lead from dummy towards the closed hand, as these examples will show. In each case you need two tricks:

(1)   Q 8 6 3   (2)   A Q 5 2
   J 9 2   A 10 7 4   J 9 7 3   K 10
          K 5   8 6 4

In (1) you lead low to the king, which holds. Many players will now return the suit and duck, hoping to find East with A–x–x and to ruff out the third round. Instead, the second lead should come from the table. East may go in with the ace, fearing South may have started with K–J bare.

In (2), if you can afford an immediate loser you should lead low from dummy, putting East under pressure. The finesse can if necessary be taken later.

Deception in the trump suit

This suit has been given special attention by larcenists, who have developed some spectacular ways of crashing defenders' honours. These come especially into their own when a particular defender is thought to be short in the suit:

```
(3)            Q 6 3
      A                    K 10 8
           J 9 7 5 4 2
```

The percentage play is low to the queen, but if you are sure that any singleton or void will be with West, not East, it cannot cost to lead the queen from dummy.

The next two examples are bolder still. Again they depend on East not being short:

```
(4)   Q 5 4 3        (5)   J 6 5 4

      10 8 7 6 2            K 9 8 3 2
```

In (4) you get your name in lights if East with K–J–x or A–J–x covers the lead of the queen. In (5) the normal play is low to the king. Instead, lead the jack. East with Q–10–x or A–Q–x may cover, to his partner's disgust; but you intend to put on the king anyway.

In all these plays the scheme is to lead high through the defender who is more likely to have length.

There is also a group where the lead is risk-free:

(6)   9 6 3

      Q   J 10 8 5

        A K 7 4 2

Lead the 9, intending to run it. East may cover, and moreover you save a trick by force when West has the singleton 8.

There are of course many more combinations where you can afford to lead an unsupported high card, intending to overtake. With 10–x–x–x in dummy and A–K–9–x–x–x in hand, for example, you may persuade RHO to cover with Q–J–8.

CONCEALMENT BY DECLARER

It can hardly be wrong, when it can be done without cost, to play the cards so as to disclose as little as possible:

(1) A Q 10 3   (2)   A Q 3

     J 9 5   K 7 5 4

With (1), if you lead the jack, everyone will know how many tricks you have coming, but if you lead the 5 and finesse the queen, losing to the king, West at any rate may be in doubt. You also make it more difficult for East to hold up the king.

(2) shows a side suit that you wish to test before drawing trumps. If you lay down the A–Q, East, when the queen holds, will know that you have the king and he will ruff the third round if he can. Instead, lead low from hand and play the queen as though finessing against West; then play the ace. Now East may not ruff the third round.

(3)   A J 10 2

    8 7 5 4   9 3

        K Q 6

South hopes to cash three tricks in this side suit before starting a crossruff. It looks as though he is out of luck, but if he plays the king, then the ace, and then leads the jack, he may convince East that he is about to take a ruffing finesse that will lose to West's queen.

When you expect to lose a trick, there is always a better chance of camouflaging your holding if you concede it early rather than late:

(4)   9 7 5 4 2   (5)   9 5 3

A K 6   A Q 7 6 2

In (4), if you lead out three rounds the opponents will see how many tricks have become established and will take suitable action. It may be better to duck the first round.

With (5), if you start with the finesse, opponents will soon know the layout. Instead, lead low from hand, taking the finesse later.

Defenders will always try to suss out declarer's game plan, but sometimes it is possible to keep it under wraps:

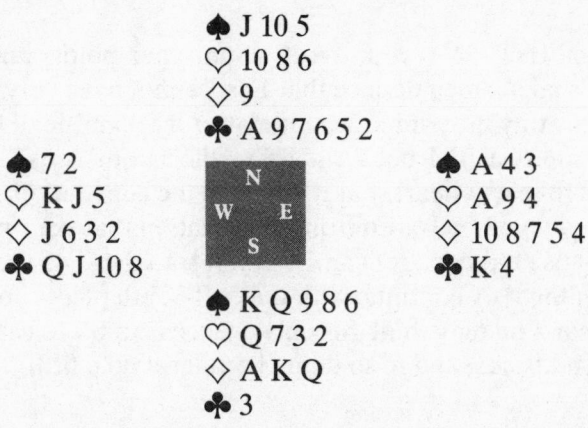

          ♠ J 10 5
          ♡ 10 8 6
          ♢ 9
          ♣ A 9 7 6 5 2

♠ 7 2   ♠ A 4 3
♡ K J 5   ♡ A 9 4
♢ J 6 3 2   ♢ 10 8 7 5 4
♣ Q J 10 8   ♣ K 4

          ♠ K Q 9 8 6
          ♡ Q 7 3 2
          ♢ A K Q
          ♣ 3

After 1♠–2♠–4♠, West leads the ♣Q. There are only eight winners, so you must hope to discard two hearts on the diamonds and gain two heart ruffs. However, if you start by cashing ♢A–K–Q the defenders are sure to play trumps when you now lead a heart. Instead, on winning with the ♣A you should lead a heart from dummy and play the queen. You will be very unlucky if West fires back a heart: if he continues clubs, the rest is easy.

DECEPTIVE OPENING LEADS

The opening leader is expected to play an honest card, but he is not on oath:

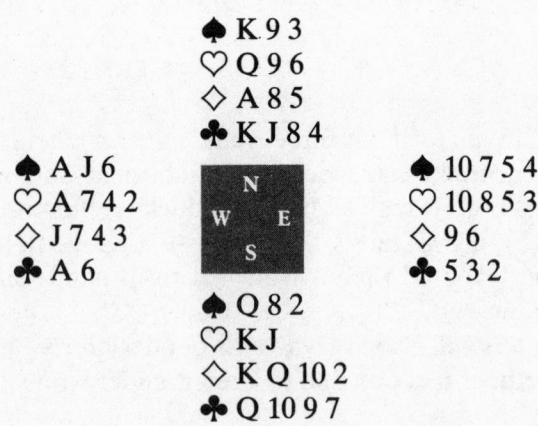

```
              ♠ K 9 3
              ♡ Q 9 6
              ◇ A 8 5
              ♣ K J 8 4
♠ A J 6                      ♠ 10 7 5 4
♡ A 7 4 2       N            ♡ 10 8 5 3
◇ J 7 4 3    W     E         ◇ 9 6
♣ A 6           S            ♣ 5 3 2
              ♠ Q 8 2
              ♡ K J
              ◇ K Q 10 2
              ♣ Q 10 9 7
```

After 1NT–3NT you, West, count your points and with your usual acumen deduce that East cannot have very many. With his tiny little mind, can it matter if you mislead him?

No interest had been shown in the major suits, so you intend to lead a heart, but if you lead the conventional card, the 2, you will be transmitting information that your partner cannot use but declarer can. Why not lead the ♡4, and when in with the ♣A continue with the 2. If South places you with five hearts he may think his only chance is to try to cash four diamond tricks, and in so doing he will set up a fifth trick for you.

If you lead an honest ♡2, South will note that the suit appears to be 4–4. He will dislodge the ♣A, then lead a spade for nine tricks.

When you really do have a 5-card suit, you can keep declarer on his toes by leading the lowest, as if you had only four.

CONCEALMENT BY DEFENDERS

'Never false-card against your partner' is good advice for the beginner, but not for the old hand. There are many holdings where to false-card is not just forgivable but the duty of every conscientious citizen:

(1)   A J 5   (2)   A Q 8 5

Q 10 4   8 6 3   K 9 6 3   J 7 4

        K 9 7 2   10 2

In (1) South leads low, finesses the jack, and cashes the ace. Suppose that West has followed with the 4 and 10. When dummy leads to the next round and East follows, South knows for sure that the queen will fall. Therefore West must drop the queen under the ace: South then has to consider whether to play East for 10–x–x–x.

In (2) South intends to crossruff. He leads low, finesses the queen and plays the ace. Unless West drops the king, South knows he can ruff low with impunity.

From this comes a tip that is always valid: When it can be done without cost, a defender should play the card he is known to hold. Properly speaking, this is not false-carding but concealment:

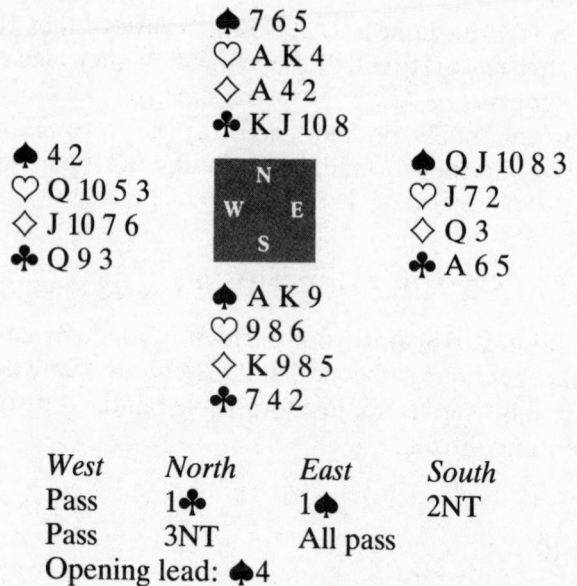

```
                    ♠ 7 6 5
                    ♡ A K 4
                    ◇ A 4 2
                    ♣ K J 10 8
    ♠ 4 2                              ♠ Q J 10 8 3
    ♡ Q 10 5 3         N              ♡ J 7 2
    ◇ J 10 7 6     W       E          ◇ Q 3
    ♣ Q 9 3            S              ♣ A 6 5
                    ♠ A K 9
                    ♡ 9 8 6
                    ◇ K 9 8 5
                    ♣ 7 4 2
```

West	*North*	*East*	*South*
Pass	1♣	1♠	2NT
Pass	3NT	All pass	

Opening lead: ♠4

East plays the 10 and South wins with the ace. He leads a club to the jack, which holds, enters his hand with the ◇K, and leads a second club.

West is known – sticklers would say, 'presumed', – to hold the ♣Q, so he plays it. It is covered by the king and ace, but now South has a problem: East may have started with ♣A–9–x–x, in which case it will pay to play him for a 5–2–2–4 pattern. So South wins the spade return, cashes the top hearts and diamonds, and exits with a spade, hoping that East, after cashing two more spades, will have to lead away from ♣9–x. As it is, East produces a third heart.

When the critical holding is in declarer's hand, not dummy's, the defender may have to do some advance thinking. You are East, defending against a slam contract, and this is the trump suit:

```
(3)                    6 4
        K Q                      10 5 2
                A J 9 8 7 3
```

A low card is led from dummy, you play low, declarer plays

the 9 and West the queen. Straight away it should register that the 10 is now a card you are known to hold. Can you afford to play it when declarer gets into dummy and leads the suit again?

Work on it and you find that it cannot cost. Now, if South follows the rule of restricted choice, he will finesse the jack, playing you for K–10–x or Q–10–x, which is a much more likely holding than K–Q bare in West's hand.

If you do not play the 10 on the second round, South will compute that if you held K–10–5–2 originally the contract cannot be made. He will therefore play the ace and drop your partner's king.

Concealment on opening lead

Sometimes it is immediately clear that the contract depends on whether declarer will guess right in a critical suit. There is nothing against third hand making a concealment play at trick one if partner will not be misled and declarer might be:

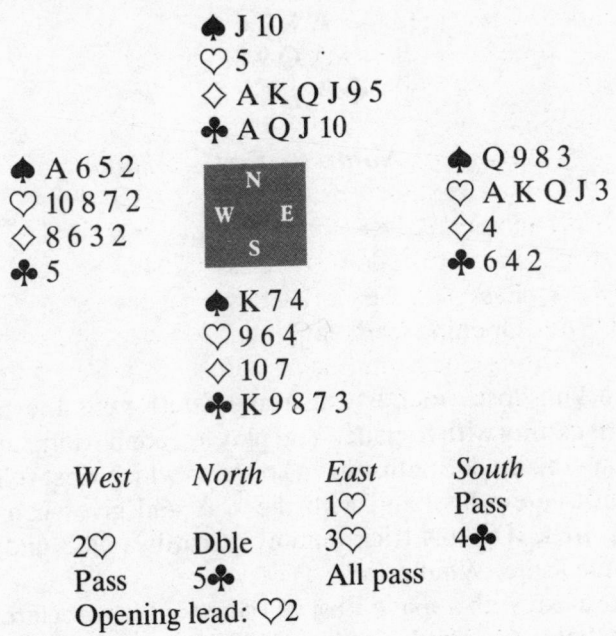

	♠ J 10		
	♡ 5		
	◇ A K Q J 9 5		
	♣ A Q J 10		

♠ A 6 5 2			♠ Q 9 8 3
♡ 10 8 7 2			♡ A K Q J 3
◇ 8 6 3 2			◇ 4
♣ 5			♣ 6 4 2

	♠ K 7 4		
	♡ 9 6 4		
	◇ 10 7		
	♣ K 9 8 7 3		

West	North	East	South
		1♡	Pass
2♡	Dble	3♡	4♣
Pass	5♣	All pass	

Opening lead: ♡2

When dummy goes down East sees at once that he must switch to a spade. If he wins the heart lead with the jack, South will place him with the four top honours and may play West for the ♠A. East gives the defence its best chance if he wins with the ♡A, and plays ♠3.

The concealment of distribution

Concealment can extend to suit lengths as well as high cards. You are West:

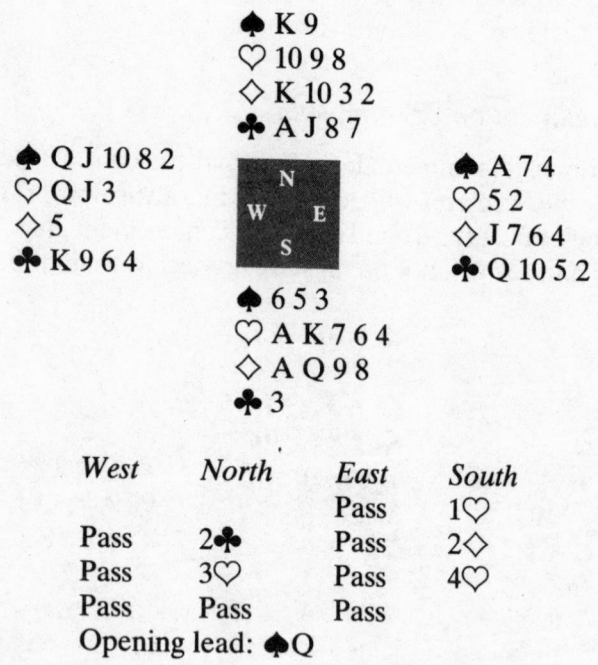

	♠ K 9		
	♡ 10 9 8		
	◇ K 10 3 2		
	♣ A J 8 7		

♠ Q J 10 8 2   ♠ A 7 4
♡ Q J 3   ♡ 5 2
◇ 5   ◇ J 7 6 4
♣ K 9 6 4   ♣ Q 10 5 2

♠ 6 5 3
♡ A K 7 6 4
◇ A Q 9 8
♣ 3

West	North	East	South
		Pass	1♡
Pass	2♣	Pass	2◇
Pass	3♡	Pass	4♡
Pass	Pass	Pass	

Opening lead: ♠Q

The king loses to East's ace and South wins the trump return, exiting with a spade. You play a second trump and on winning this trick South ruffs a spade to which East follows.

South enters his hand with the ◇A and gives you your trump trick. On this trick dummy discards a club and East does the same. What now?

If you exit with a spade East will show out and declarer will know that you started with five. If he now plays the ♣A and ruffs a club, he learns when you follow that you cannot have four diamonds and will play to pick up East's jack.

The best you can do is to exit with a club when in with your trump winner, concealing the spade distribution and leaving South to make his own arrangements.

OFFERING DECLARER A LOSING OPTION

When declarer has only one line of play and this will succeed, defenders should try to offer an alternative that will fail. Sometimes this amounts to an extension of an earlier idea: you release early, not a card you are known to hold, but one that the declarer will surely play you for. South is in notrumps and has no side entry to dummy:

(1)   A Q J 7 3 2
    K 6   10 9 4
              8 5

South leads low, intending to finesse. If West plays low declarer will make six tricks, but if he puts in the king, the card declarer will surely play him for, South may duck, to ensure five tricks.

(2)   A 10 7 5   (3)   A 10 9 3
    K J 6 2   8 3   K J 6   7 4 2
              Q 9 4   Q 8 5

Declarer leads from dummy and plays the 9. If West wins with the jack, declarer will play him for the king, leading the queen from hand and collecting the remaining tricks.

West therefore takes the 9 with the king, the card declarer will later play him for. Expecting East to have the jack, South will play off the queen and ace.

In (3) declarer has not enough entries to play the suit from his own hand so he leads the 10 from dummy and lets it run. If West wins with the king, declarer when next in dummy may finesse against East's expected jack.

Many plays of this kind take place in the trump suit:

(4)   K Q 9 2
          A 10 8 5   3
                           J 7 6 4

South leads low from hand. If West plays the 5, dummy wins with the king and South has only one way to continue: he cannot cope with A–10–8–x in East's hand, so he leads small to the jack, exposing West's holding and allowing him to be held to one trick.

West should therefore play the 8 on the first round, presenting declarer with a losing option. Now, on winning with the king, declarer may continue with the queen, as he can guard against A–10–5–3 with East.

Always a defender who sees that a card has no value because of the way the cards lie should consider playing it early:

(5)   A Q 7 2
           K 6   10 4
                           J 9 8 5 3

South leads low and finesses the queen. If East follows with the 4, South will realise that there is nothing he can do if West is left with the K–10, so he will lay down the ace.

If East drops the 10 on the first round, South may re-enter his hand and lead the jack, in case West has K–x–x. This may waste an entry.

A defender with four trumps can usually picture the precise holding in the closed hand:

(6)   J 8 7 5
          Q 10 9 4   3
                           A K 6 2

South is in dummy and he leads low to the ace. West knows the layout so he drops the 9, his only chance of two tricks. South may now think it safe to cross in another suit and lead the jack, holding East to one trick if he has Q–10–x–x and scooping the pool if West has 10–9 bare.

(7)   A J 8 6 4   (8)   K J 8 7 3
     K 3   10 9 5   10 9 6 5   A Q 4
          Q 7 2   2

In (7) South leads the 2 and puts in the jack. If East drops the 9 or 10, South may return to hand and lead the queen to pin 10–9 bare.

In (8) this is a side suit at a trump contract. South leads the 2 and finesses the jack, losing to the queen. On the next round he leads dummy's 3 and ruffs in hand. West must play the 9 or 10, so that on the third round South may be persuaded to lead the king, which would be winning play if West started with 10–9–x.

(9)   A 8 6 4
     3   J 9 5 2
          K Q 10 7

South leads the king. If East plays the 2 or 5, declarer's next lead will be low to the ace, as he cannot cope with J–9–x–x in West's hand. East therefore must play the 9 on the first round, giving South a losing option.

A fine point: if you ever happen to hold the South cards against Professor Moriarty you should begin by leading low from dummy, still intending to play the king. This time East cannot afford to false-card with the 9, as West could have the bare 10.

Deceptive exit cards

With the right choice of exit card a defender when endplayed may still escape by offering declarer a losing option. In these examples there is no other suit the defenders may safely lead:

(10)   A 10 3   (11)   K 9 5
     Q 6 4   J 8 7 2   10 6 4 2   A J 7
          K 9 5   Q 8 3

In (10), if either defender exits with a low card, declarer will play for split honours and make the balance. By leading his high card, the defender offers South the option of playing him for both honours.

In (11) East leads the jack. It runs to the king but on the next round declarer may decide to play East for J–10–x.

(12)   10 8 5   (13)   K 8 5

A J 3   Q 9 6 2   A Q 3   J 9 6 2

K 7 4   10 7 4

In (12), if East leads low South will duck and West will be endplayed when he wins with the jack. Instead, East should lead the queen (and equally the jack from J–9–x or J–x–x). South may then play low, which would be the right move if East held Q–J–9–x.

In (13), if West is on lead, the queen is the only card that gives South an option. He may play low from dummy and do the same on the next round.

Postponing the setting trick

A defender who knows he is in control may play a cat and mouse game, delaying the kill. In trying to get home, declarer may go down an extra trick. You are East:

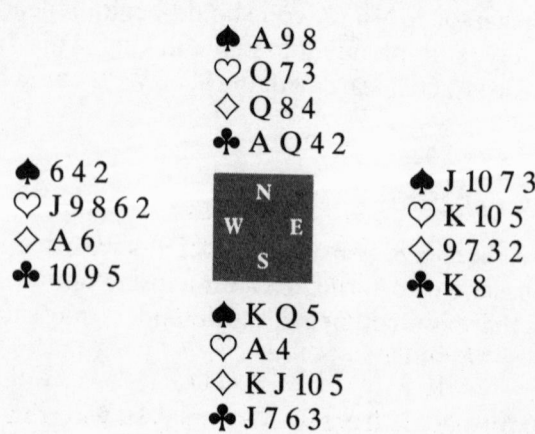

After 1NT–3NT, West leads the ♡6 and the 10 loses to the ace. A diamond from declarer is won by the queen and diamonds are continued, South's king losing to the ace. West returns the ♡J which South elects to cover in dummy. You win with the king and play . . . ?

A heart return puts the contract down one but if you count South's winners you find that he cannot make more than eight tricks before letting you in. Therefore you should exit with a diamond. Thinking you have no more hearts, South may take the club finesse for his contract, going down an extra trick as the cards lie.

At duplicate this type of play can be a prolific bringer-in of tops. When playing for mere lucre, an extra point on the rubber may make no difference to your life-style; but think of the ascendancy it gives you.

Often the best way to conjure up a losing option is by putting yourself in declarer's position. You are East:

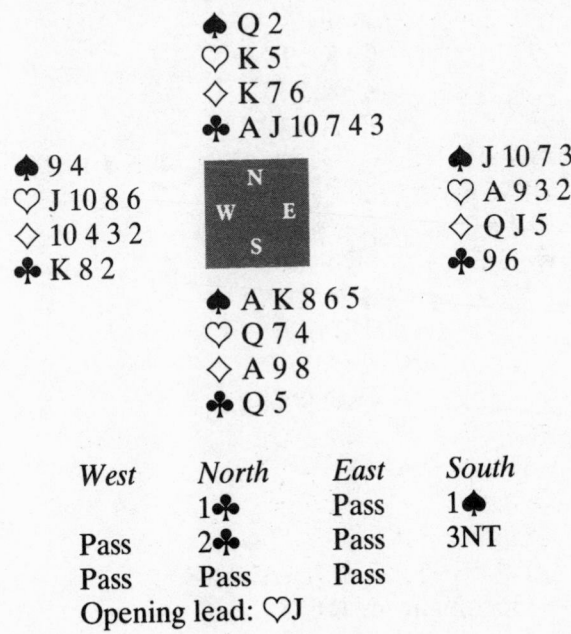

```
                ♠ Q 2
                ♡ K 5
                ◇ K 7 6
                ♣ A J 10 7 4 3
  ♠ 9 4          N          ♠ J 10 7 3
  ♡ J 10 8 6   W   E        ♡ A 9 3 2
  ◇ 10 4 3 2     S          ◇ Q J 5
  ♣ K 8 2                   ♣ 9 6
                ♠ A K 8 6 5
                ♡ Q 7 4
                ◇ A 9 8
                ♣ Q 5
```

West	North	East	South
	1♣	Pass	1♠
Pass	2♣	Pass	3NT
Pass	Pass	Pass	

Opening lead: ♡J

The ♡K is played from dummy and you win with the ace, returning . . . ?

There must be a good chance that South will have to take a finesse in clubs. In that case, he will be concerned to know how hearts are breaking. If you return the 2, South will note that the suit appears to be 4–4 and that there is no point in holding up. He will win with the queen and make twelve tricks as the cards lie.

If you return the ♡9, South may duck, which would be winning play if you held the ♣K and only three hearts.

Winning with an unnecessarily high card

To allow declarer to win a finesse that he is sure to repeat is a standard defensive move. He may be well aware that you could be holding up, but he still has to repeat the finesse, in case you aren't. In so doing he may waste an entry.

This form of play can produce more spectacular results in a deal like this:

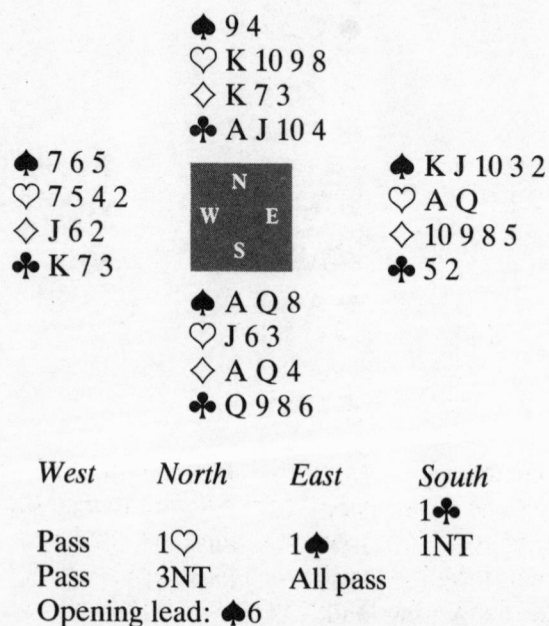

	♠ 9 4	
	♡ K 10 9 8	
	◇ K 7 3	
	♣ A J 10 4	
♠ 7 6 5		♠ K J 10 3 2
♡ 7 5 4 2		♡ A Q
◇ J 6 2		◇ 10 9 8 5
♣ K 7 3		♣ 5 2
	♠ A Q 8	
	♡ J 6 3	
	◇ A Q 4	
	♣ Q 9 8 6	

West	North	East	South
			1♣
Pass	1♡	1♠	1NT
Pass	3NT	All pass	
Opening lead: ♠6			

East plays the 10 and South wins with the queen, returning the ♡J. East wins with the ace, confident of still making the queen. South ducks the spade return, wins the next, and repeats the finesse to go one down.

Had East won the first heart with the queen, South would have abandoned hearts and tried the club finesse.

TROMPERIE

The French word for deception has an extra connotation when applied to trump contracts. One strategy is to play on declarer's nerves by threatening to ruff when you can do no such thing:

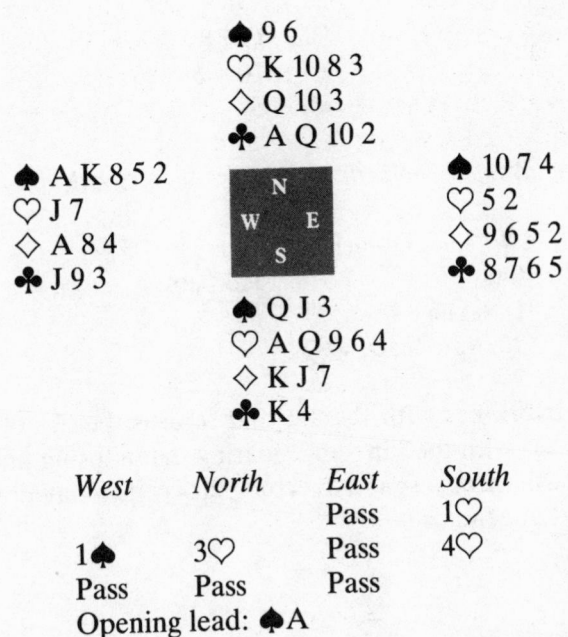

```
              ♠ 9 6
              ♡ K 10 8 3
              ◇ Q 10 3
              ♣ A Q 10 2
♠ A K 8 5 2                      ♠ 10 7 4
♡ J 7              N             ♡ 5 2
◇ A 8 4        W     E           ◇ 9 6 5 2
♣ J 9 3           S             ♣ 8 7 6 5
              ♠ Q J 3
              ♡ A Q 9 6 4
              ◇ K J 7
              ♣ K 4
```

West	North	East	South
		Pass	1♡
1♠	3♡	Pass	4♡
Pass	Pass	Pass	

Opening lead: ♠A

East sees that the contract is surely cold: South can have only two spade losers and perhaps a diamond. But the fat lady isn't singing yet. When West cashes the spades, East puts forth an echo, so South ruffs the next spade with the ♡K. He learns that he has been deceived, but that is no reason why East should not hold ♡J–x–x.

In a related form of play, declarer is bluffed into abandoning a winning finesse in the trump suit:

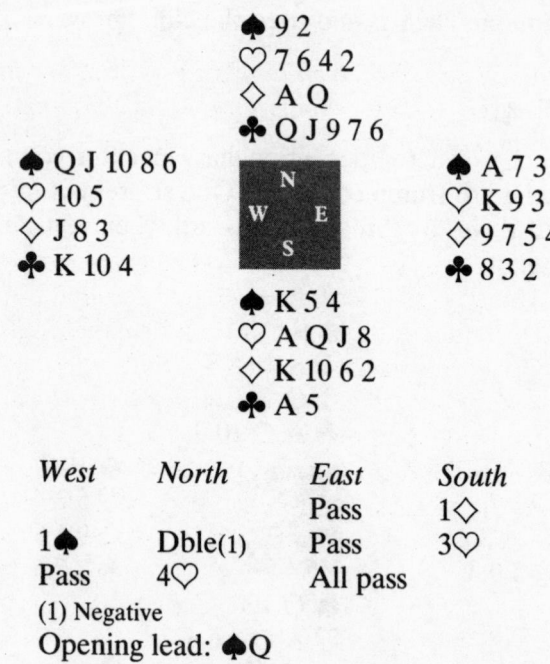

♠ 9 2
♡ 7 6 4 2
◇ A Q
♣ Q J 9 7 6

♠ Q J 10 8 6
♡ 10 5
◇ J 8 3
♣ K 10 4

♠ A 7 3
♡ K 9 3
◇ 9 7 5 4
♣ 8 3 2

♠ K 5 4
♡ A Q J 8
◇ K 10 6 2
♣ A 5

West	North	East	South
		Pass	1◇
1♠	Dble(1)	Pass	3♡
Pass	4♡	All pass	

(1) Negative

Opening lead: ♠Q

East overtakes with the ace and returns the 3, not the 7. South wins with the king and, fearing that a losing finesse in trumps will incur a spade overruff, proceeds to lay down the ♡A and queen.

Chapter 23

ENDPLAYS, COUPS AND SQUEEZES

Eliminations – Partial eliminations – The throw-in –
Defending against eliminations and throw-ins –
Trump coups – The squeeze – Defending against
squeezes

Proficiency in coups and endplays is perhaps not of overwhelming importance in one's early days around the bridge
table, but as one gets on in the world it becomes a necessary
skill. Endplays consist of eliminations, throw-ins, coups and
squeezes, all of which aim to erase losers irremovable by
more straightforward measures.

It is possible to lead a full and happy life without a knowledge of coups such as the smother play, which occurs with
about the same frequency as confirmed sightings of the Loch
Ness monster. But no serious player should lack a thorough
grasp of eliminations.

ELIMINATIONS

These occur only at trump contracts. A defender is on play
and is forced to concede a ruff and discard or lead into a
tenace.

One of the attractive features is that declarer can quite
often bring about this situation without having the slightest
idea of how the cards lie:

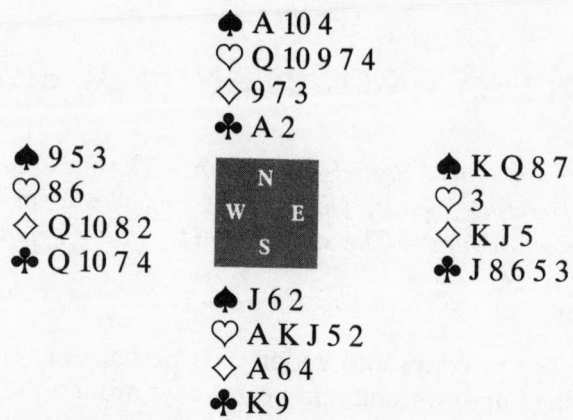

♠ A 10 4
♡ Q 10 9 7 4
♢ 9 7 3
♣ A 2

♠ 9 5 3
♡ 8 6
♢ Q 10 8 2
♣ Q 10 7 4

♠ K Q 8 7
♡ 3
♢ K J 5
♣ J 8 6 5 3

♠ J 6 2
♡ A K J 5 2
♢ A 6 4
♣ K 9

After 1♡–3♡–4♡, West leads the ♢2 and East's king is allowed to hold. East returns the ♢J and declarer wins with the ace.

South can now table his cards, saying: 'Drawing trumps, cashing the A–K of clubs, and exiting with a diamond.' He could not care less who has what or who takes the trick.

Suppose that West wins and returns a spade: dummy plays low and East wins with the queen. This is the defenders' last trick, whether East returns a spade into dummy's tenace or a minor suit for a ruff and discard.

This example was easy and inexorable, but it included a vital ingredient: ducking the first diamond. Had South not done so he would later have had to lead diamonds twice to clear the suit, giving West the opportunity to lead spades and take East off the hook.

Always before exiting declarer must remove any cards the defenders may safely lead. Often this is done by ruffing, a process that may impose a strain on entries:

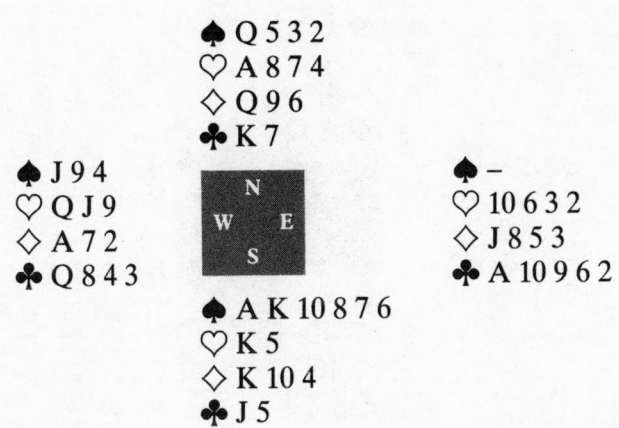

```
            ♠ Q 5 3 2
            ♡ A 8 7 4
            ◇ Q 9 6
            ♣ K 7
♠ J 9 4                      ♠ –
♡ Q J 9         N           ♡ 10 6 3 2
◇ A 7 2      W     E        ◇ J 8 5 3
♣ Q 8 4 3       S           ♣ A 10 9 6 2
            ♠ A K 10 8 7 6
            ♡ K 5
            ◇ K 10 4
            ♣ J 5
```

The contract is 4♠ and West leads the ♡Q. If South can eliminate hearts and throw the lead in clubs, he avoids a guess for the ◇J. He has to ruff hearts twice, and as there are only two sure entries to dummy – the ♠Q and ♡A – he must use them carefully.

He wins the first trick in hand and lays down the ♠A. With East showing out the play goes: ♠K cashed; heart to the ace; heart ruff; spade to the queen; heart ruff.

South still has a trump in each hand, always a necessary condition. He leads a club to the king and does not much care what happens. The defenders may cash a second club but then have to lead a diamond or concede a ruff and discard.

In these examples it did not matter who won the trick when South got off play. Often an elimination will work only when a particular defender can be placed on lead. This may be done very neatly by the device of loser-on-loser.

A loser-on-loser elimination

Diamonds are trumps and the declarer, needing all the tricks but one, has reached this ending with the lead in dummy:

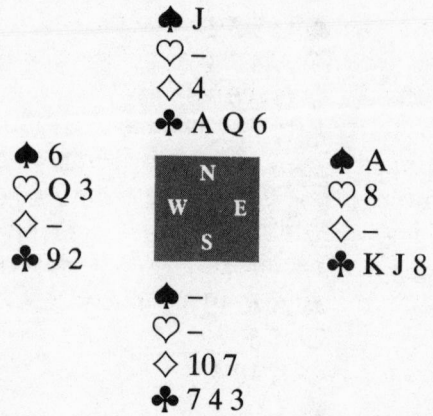

Suppose that he plays the ♠J from dummy, ruffs it and leads a club, hoping to duck into East's hand. This works if West plays the 2, but not if he puts in the 9.

There is a better idea: when the ♠J is led and East covers, South does not ruff but discards a club.

Using the trump suit to place the lead

It is often possible to handle trumps so that if a trick has to be lost, an elimination will follow.

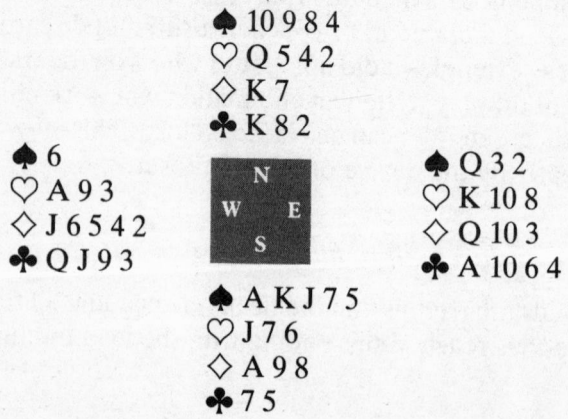

After 1♠–2♠ the ♣Q is led and the suit is continued, South ruffing the third round. His possible losers are three heart tricks and a trump. With this trump holding it is normal to play for the drop, but here the finesse is better because it can be combined with an elimination.

South cashes a top trump and plays off three rounds of diamonds, ruffing. Then he leads a trump and finesses the jack. If West were to win the trick he would be endplayed and South would lose only two hearts.

Always look for an elimination when you have one loser too many, plenty of trumps, and a tenace in a side suit.

PARTIAL ELIMINATIONS

In any elimination, declarer must have trumps in dummy and his own hand. Life is easier if the defenders have no trumps, but in a partial elimination one defender is left with a trump and the lead is placed with the other:

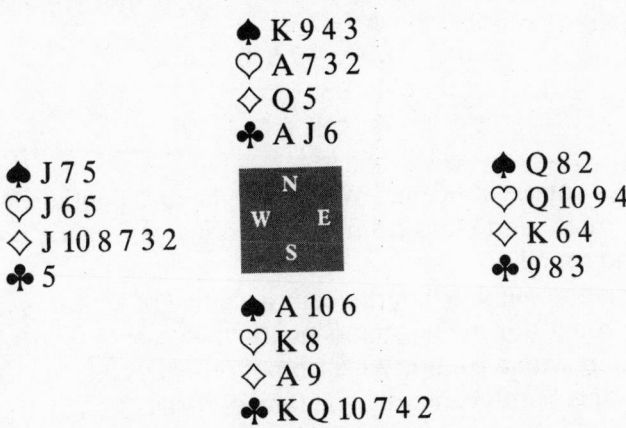

```
                    ♠ K 9 4 3
                    ♡ A 7 3 2
                    ◇ Q 5
                    ♣ A J 6
  ♠ J 7 5            N            ♠ Q 8 2
  ♡ J 6 5        W       E        ♡ Q 10 9 4
  ◇ J 10 8 7 3 2     S            ◇ K 6 4
  ♣ 5                             ♣ 9 8 3
                    ♠ A 10 6
                    ♡ K 8
                    ◇ A 9
                    ♣ K Q 10 7 4 2
```

Against 6♣ West leads the ◇J and the queen is covered by the king and ace. There are squeeze possibilities but an elimination, forcing defenders to open up spades, is a more promising route to twelve tricks.

South plays off the ♣K and takes three rounds of hearts, ruffing. Then he crosses to the ♣A. If both defenders followed he would complete a normal elimination by ruffing the last heart and exiting with a diamond, not caring who won. On a spade return he would play for split honours.

Here, West shows out on the ♣A. South cannot afford to draw East's last trump as he has to keep a trump in dummy. However, the elimination still works because when he ruffs the last heart and exits with a diamond the trick is won by West, who has no more trumps.

In the same way, declarer may be able to draw trumps but unable to eliminate a side suit from the hand of a particular defender. Again, he places the lead with the other:

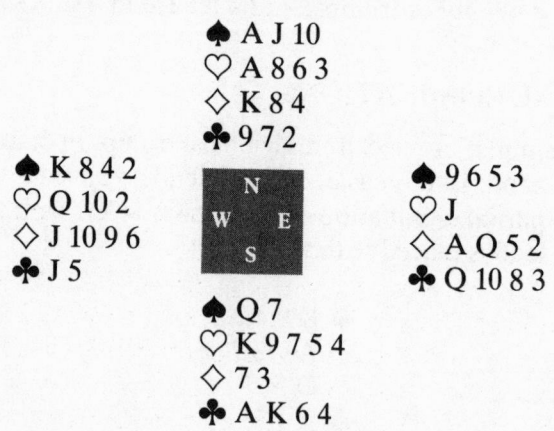

```
                ♠ A J 10
                ♡ A 8 6 3
                ◇ K 8 4
                ♣ 9 7 2
  ♠ K 8 4 2                      ♠ 9 6 5 3
  ♡ Q 10 2        N             ♡ J
  ◇ J 10 9 6   W     E          ◇ A Q 5 2
  ♣ J 5           S             ♣ Q 10 8 3
                ♠ Q 7
                ♡ K 9 7 5 4
                ◇ 7 3
                ♣ A K 6 4
```

The contract is 4♡ and West leads the ◇J. South ruffs the third round and plays trumps. East discards a spade on the second round.

To get home now South needs a change of luck. He takes three rounds of spades, finessing; then he cashes the ♣A–K and exits with a trump. West cannot return a club, so after a poor start South comes up smelling of roses.

THE THROW-IN

The throw-in differs from eliminations in that the defender is forced to concede a trick in the suit he exits with: a ruff and discard is not an option, since declarer is either playing in notrumps or does not have a trump in each hand.

Like eliminations, a throw-in can sometimes be foreseen early in the play:

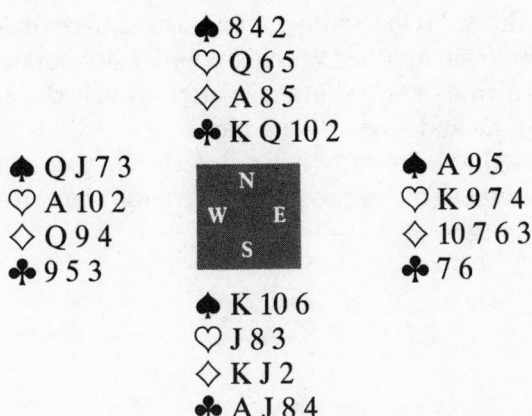

After 1NT–2NT, West leads the ♠3 and East wins with the ace, returning the 9. South does not duck as he intends to use the 10 as a throw-in card.

South has seven winners and will have eight if West can be made to lead a red suit. West appears to have only four spades, so this seems manageable: South removes West's exit cards in clubs and puts him in with the ♠10.

In a throw-in, declarer must be able to discard comfortably on any winners the defender may cash, and he must also have enough entries to benefit from the enforced return. In the last deal, had South taken a fourth round of clubs he could not have met these conditions. As it is, he still has to play carefully. When West leads the last spade, this is the position:

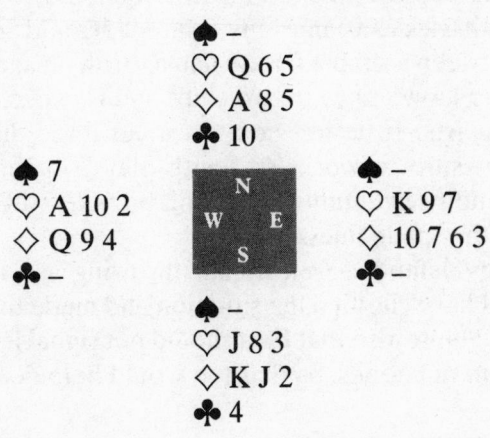

When the ♠7 is led South discards a heart from dummy and a diamond from hand. If West exits with a diamond, the ♣10 provides a vital entry. South may alternatively discard a club from dummy and a heart from hand.

Not all throw-ins are so tidy: declarer may not have a reliable count of the opposing hands, or may have to rely on a favourable lie:

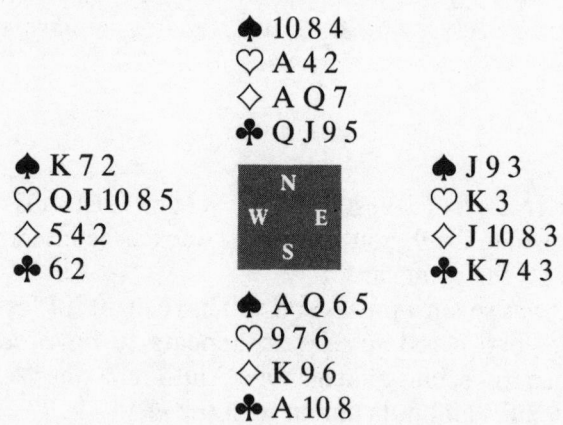

	♠ 10 8 4	
	♡ A 4 2	
	◇ A Q 7	
	♣ Q J 9 5	

♠ K 7 2		♠ J 9 3
♡ Q J 10 8 5		♡ K 3
◇ 5 4 2		◇ J 10 8 3
♣ 6 2		♣ K 7 4 3

	♠ A Q 6 5	
	♡ 9 7 6	
	◇ K 9 6	
	♣ A 10 8	

After 1NT–3NT, West leads the ♡Q and East overtakes with the king. When he returns the 3, South does not duck, as the suit seems to be 5–2.

The ♣Q is led and holds the trick, then a low club is won by declarer's 10. The ♣A is cashed but West discards a spade; the 2, as he does not wish to help South.

The ninth trick can come only from spades and South has to choose between a simple finesse and a throw-in against West.

West has shown up with two clubs and is expected to have had five hearts. If he has no more than three diamonds, a throw-in is sure to work, so South plays off the diamond winners, ending in dummy. Up to this point he still retains the option of the spade finesse.

West has defended well by not throwing a diamond, for that would have clarified the situation and made the throw-in a certainty. Note also that East should not signal length when following in diamonds, as that too would help declarer.

Nevertheless, the throw-in still offers better odds, so South exits with a heart. West cashes his hearts but then has to lead into the ♠A–Q. Had West begun with two spades and four diamonds the throw-in would have failed.

Throw-in with a trump

Trumps are not essential in throw-in play but declarer may use trumps to clear suits that the defenders could safely play. Trumps may also be used as the throw-in suit:

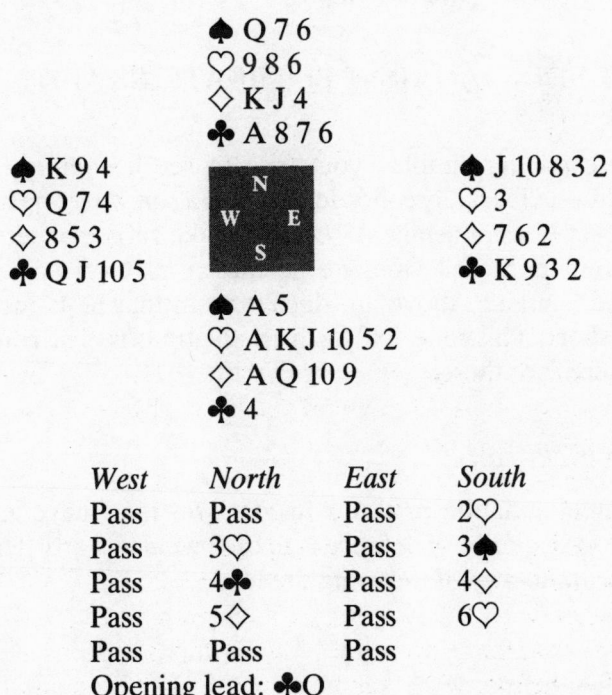

```
                    ♠ Q 7 6
                    ♡ 9 8 6
                    ◇ K J 4
                    ♣ A 8 7 6
    ♠ K 9 4                          ♠ J 10 8 3 2
    ♡ Q 7 4            N             ♡ 3
    ◇ 8 5 3        W       E         ◇ 7 6 2
    ♣ Q J 10 5         S             ♣ K 9 3 2
                    ♠ A 5
                    ♡ A K J 10 5 2
                    ◇ A Q 10 9
                    ♣ 4
```

West	North	East	South
Pass	Pass	Pass	2♡
Pass	3♡	Pass	3♠
Pass	4♣	Pass	4◇
Pass	5◇	Pass	6♡
Pass	Pass	Pass	

Opening lead: ♣Q

As South you win the first trick and see that the slam will be icy unless there is a trump loser. In that case a throw-in will be almost the only chance of avoiding a spade loser.

You are in dummy and must make use of the entry by ruffing a club. Then you lay down the ♡A–K. East discards a spade on the second round, so you cross to dummy twice in diamonds and ruff the remaining clubs. Then you take out the diamonds and exit with a trump. If West happened to have another club you would be out of luck, but here he is forced to lead away from the ♠K.

The throw-in would also have failed if West had been able to ruff a diamond and exit in clubs, or to overruff in clubs and exit in diamonds. Those are points to watch when planning a throw-in or an elimination.

DEFENDING AGAINST ELIMINATIONS AND THROW-INS

To prevent an endplay you have to see it coming. Does declarer deliberately concede a trick in a suit where he has no prospect of establishment? Does he take ruffs that serve no apparent purpose? Does he needlessly play off an unsupported winner? Above all, does it seem that he is just one trick short of his contract? Such are the tip-offs. The counter-measures are these:

Cash tricks early

In any elimination or throw-in, declarer must have an exit card, so one form of defence is to cash winners early, leaving him with no way of throwing the lead:

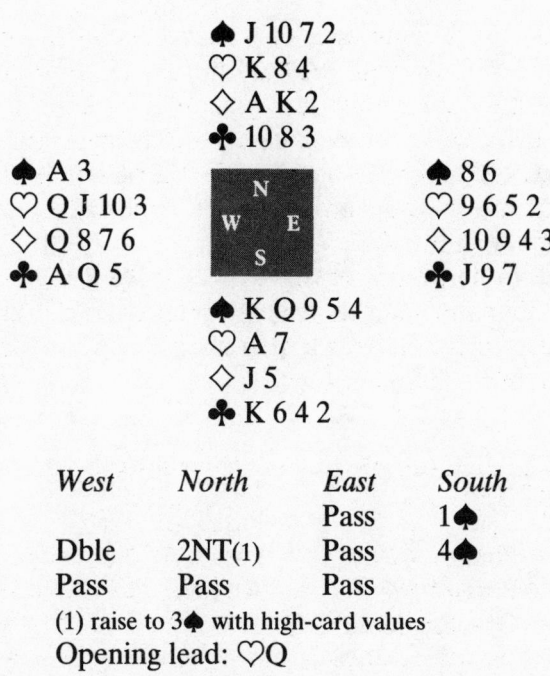

♠ J 10 7 2
♡ K 8 4
◇ A K 2
♣ 10 8 3

♠ A 3
♡ Q J 10 3
◇ Q 8 7 6
♣ A Q 5

♠ 8 6
♡ 9 6 5 2
◇ 10 9 4 3
♣ J 9 7

♠ K Q 9 5 4
♡ A 7
◇ J 5
♣ K 6 4 2

West	North	East	South
		Pass	1♠
Dble	2NT(1)	Pass	4♠
Pass	Pass	Pass	

(1) raise to 3♠ with high-card values

Opening lead: ♡Q

Dummy plays low and East, knowing that South will win the trick, gives count by playing the 6.

South's best shot is to return a low spade but West, seeing that there is no trick to be had in hearts, hastens to play the ace while he can still exit safely. It is most unlikely that East has the ♠K, but in any case it is a risk that must be taken. Eventually, South loses three club tricks.

If West does not play the ♠A he will be put in with it after South has eliminated the red suits. A defender who is the likely target of an endplay should always be on watch for that situation.

A defender should also consider whether his partner may be targeted by declarer. Here East has to rise to the occasion:

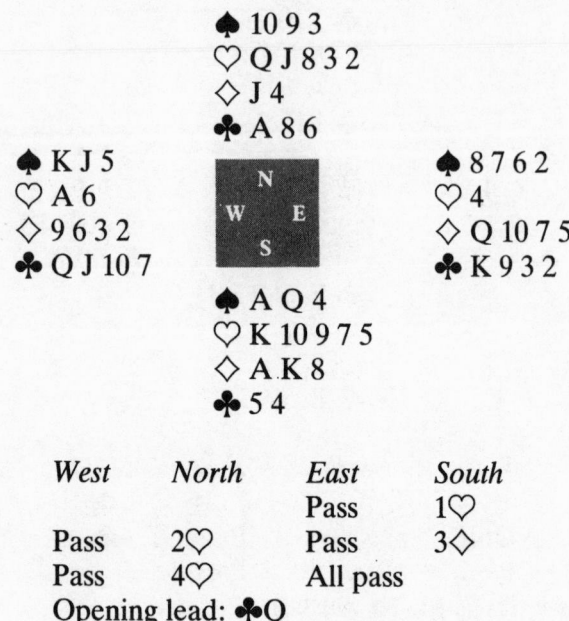

♠ 10 9 3
♡ Q J 8 3 2
◇ J 4
♣ A 8 6

♠ K J 5
♡ A 6
◇ 9 6 3 2
♣ Q J 10 7

♠ 8 7 6 2
♡ 4
◇ Q 10 7 5
♣ K 9 3 2

♠ A Q 4
♡ K 10 9 7 5
◇ A K 8
♣ 5 4

West	North	East	South
		Pass	1♡
Pass	2♡	Pass	3◇
Pass	4♡	All pass	

Opening lead: ♣Q

When dummy plays low to the first trick East should already suspect that South may be planning an elimination. If he allows the ♣Q to hold, South will draw trumps, eliminate clubs and diamonds, and run the ♠10 to endplay West. East therefore should overtake and lead a spade. Now West cannot be endplayed as long as he does not let himself be left with the bare ♡A.

Do not lead suits for declarer to ruff: instead, attack entries

Many eliminations succeed only because a defender at some point exits lazily in a suit declarer can ruff, when he could instead have attacked an entry:

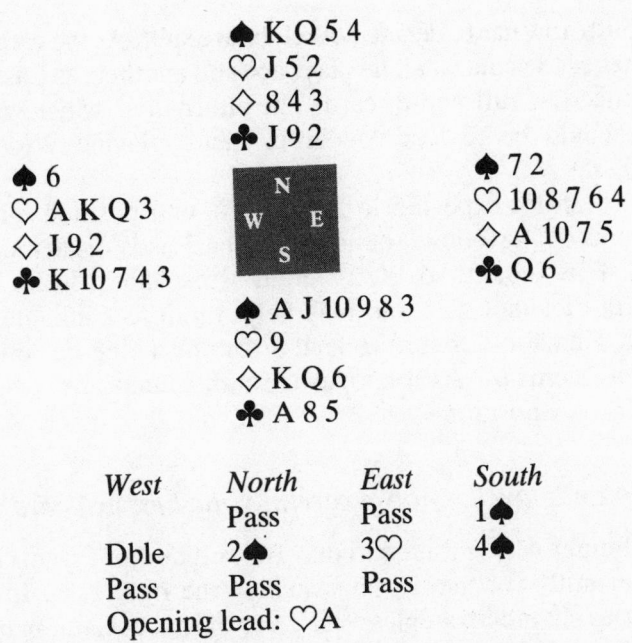

West	North	East	South
	Pass	Pass	1♠
Dble	2♠	3♡	4♠
Pass	Pass	Pass	

Opening lead: ♡A

East follows with the 4 and South with the 9. Suppose that West leads a second heart. South ruffs, crosses to a trump, and leads a diamond. The king wins and he repeats the process. This time East puts up the ace and exits with a diamond. South again crosses with a trump and ruffs the last heart, leaving this:

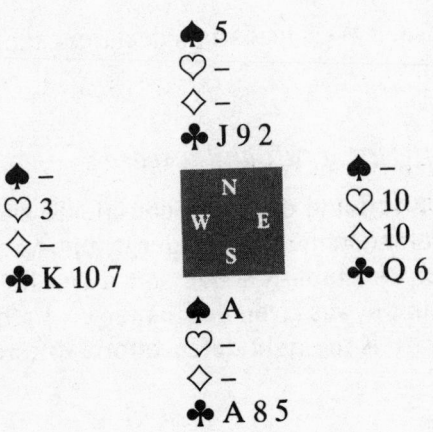

South now has to decide how clubs are split. As the cards lie he makes the contract if he plays ace and another, as East has to concede a ruff-and-discard. The alternative, which would fail, would be to lead low from hand, playing West for K–Q–x.

West is not expected to foresee the end position but he prevents it if he follows sound principles. East's ♡4 at the first trick shows count, so West should assess that a heart continuation cannot gain and may help South to eliminate the hand. He should therefore lead a trump, taking out one of dummy's entries. As it happens, South cannot now reach a satisfactory position.

When endplayed, choose carefully the best exit card

A defender who is forced to play the suit declarer wants him to may still save the day by selecting the right card. In the previous chapter examples were given of how declarer may be presented with a losing option. There are also many plays that have no element of deception but are logistically correct. Here South has no side entries to dummy:

(1)	A Q 4 3		(2)	A K 2	
K 9 6		10 8 5 2	Q 8 6 5		10 9 7 3
	J 7			J 4	

In each case, if West leads high declarer cannot profit from the endplay.

Consider offering a ruff and discard

To concede a ruff and discard is considered such a solecism that many defenders never consider it, but when it does not help declarer to establish a side suit it can be the lesser of evils. An example was given in Chapter 17. In the next deal a ruff and discard is the right defence for a different reason:

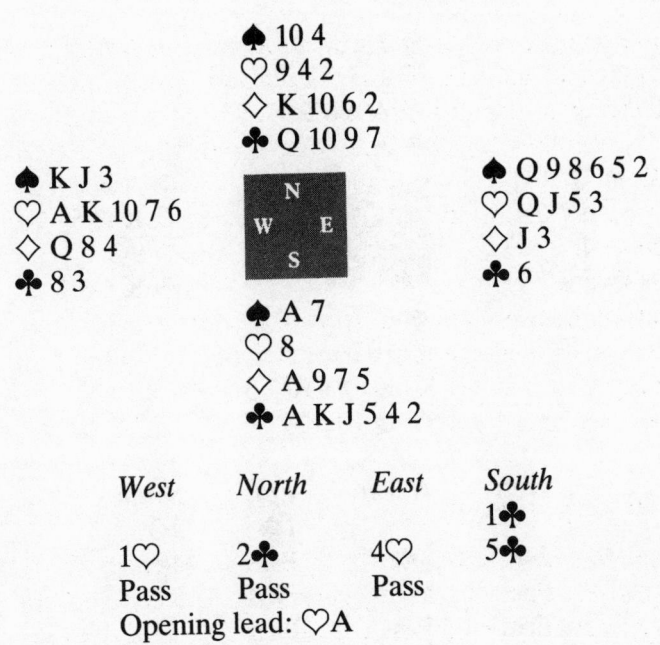

	♠ 10 4		
	♡ 9 4 2		
	◇ K 10 6 2		
	♣ Q 10 9 7		

♠ K J 3		♠ Q 9 8 6 5 2
♡ A K 10 7 6		♡ Q J 5 3
◇ Q 8 4		◇ J 3
♣ 8 3		♣ 6

	♠ A 7	
	♡ 8	
	◇ A 9 7 5	
	♣ A K J 5 4 2	

West	North	East	South
			1♣
1♡	2♣	4♡	5♣
Pass	Pass	Pass	

Opening lead: ♡A

On the first trick East plays the queen, so West underleads the king, but South ruffs, draws trumps, ruffs dummy's last heart and exits with ace and another spade, hoping for a diamond return.

Whoever wins this trick may safely return a spade. South has shown up with one heart and no more than six clubs. If he is out of spades he will have four diamonds and cannot profit from a ruff and discard.

When genuinely endplayed, concede a trick that will not be decisive

A count of declarer's winners may show that a trick given away in one suit may be less helpful to him than a trick conceded in another:

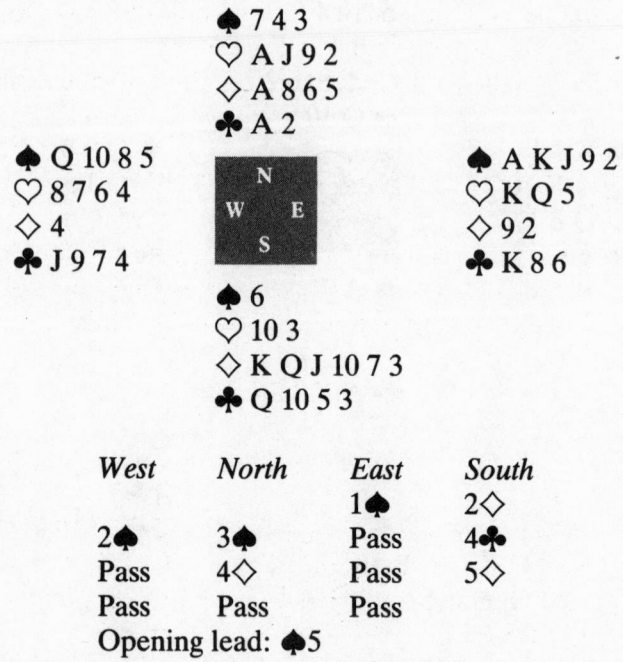

                    ♠ 7 4 3
                    ♡ A J 9 2
                    ◇ A 8 6 5
                    ♣ A 2

♠ Q 10 8 5   ♠ A K J 9 2
♡ 8 7 6 4   ♡ K Q 5
◇ 4   ◇ 9 2
♣ J 9 7 4   ♣ K 8 6

                    ♠ 6
                    ♡ 10 3
                    ◇ K Q J 10 7 3
                    ♣ Q 10 5 3

West	North	East	South
		1♠	2◇
2♠	3♠	Pass	4♣
Pass	4◇	Pass	5◇
Pass	Pass	Pass	

Opening lead: ♠5

East wins the first trick and South ruffs the continuation. He draws two rounds of trumps, West following once, and ruffs dummy's last spade. Then he leads the ♡10 and runs it to East's queen, West playing the 8. In which suit should East exit?

East can be sure that South's pattern is 1–2–6–4, so a club must be fatal if South has the queen. A spade return allows South to throw a club from dummy, ruff two clubs, and make the eleventh trick by means of a ruffing finesse against the ♡K.

A heart return concedes three heart tricks but six trumps, three hearts and the ♣A add up to only ten tricks, so East will still make the ♣K.

TRUMP COUPS

The peculiar properties of the trump suit can lead to endings that appear to defy the normal rules of card play. For example, the defenders may be denied a trick with a seemingly impregnable holding such as Q–x–x opposite J–x; or with K–x of trumps when declarer's ace is bare.

We look at the coups in the order of their practical importance.

Coup en passant

The name is apt, yet a player unfamiliar with the coup might study this deal at some length without seeing how declarer avoids losing two trump tricks and two diamonds:

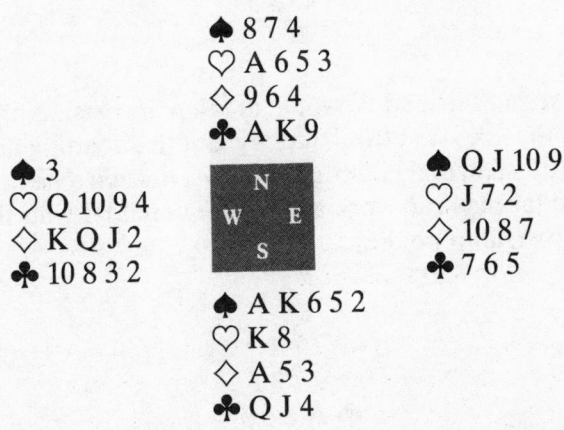

```
                    ♠ 8 7 4
                    ♡ A 6 5 3
                    ◇ 9 6 4
                    ♣ A K 9
    ♠ 3                              ♠ Q J 10 9
    ♡ Q 10 9 4        N             ♡ J 7 2
    ◇ K Q J 2      W     E          ◇ 10 8 7
    ♣ 10 8 3 2        S             ♣ 7 6 5
                    ♠ A K 6 5 2
                    ♡ K 8
                    ◇ A 5 3
                    ♣ Q J 4
```

The contract is 4♠ and the ◇K is led. South wins and cashes the ♠A–K. West shows out on the second round, but as long as East has to follow when the side winners are cashed, the defenders can do nothing to beat the contract.

Declarer plays three rounds of hearts, ruffing, and plays off the clubs, ending in dummy and needing just one more trick:

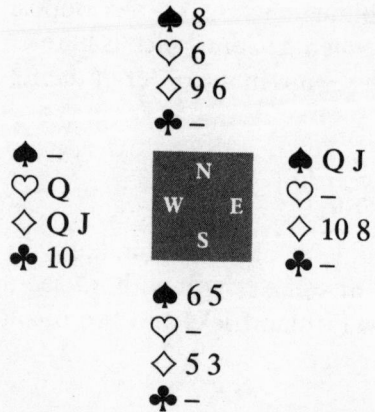

If East had the lead he would mop up the remaining tricks. As it is, the ♡6 is led from dummy. South discards a diamond if East ruffs and makes a trump trick *en passant* if he does not.

A similar play can work against the defender who sits over declarer's trump holding:

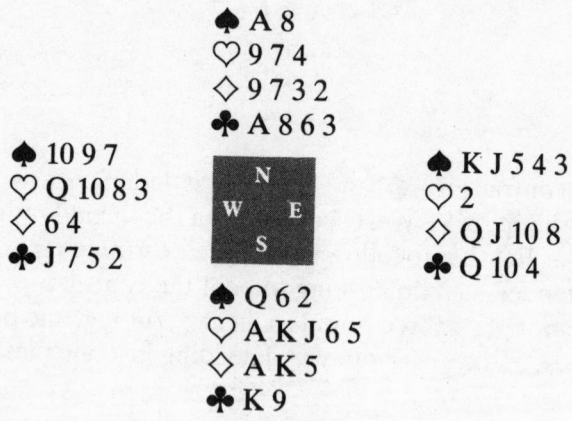

Against 4♡ West leads the ♠10 to East's king. South wins the diamond return, cashes the ♡A, and crosses to the ♠A to lead a low heart, on which East shows out.

It looks as though South must lose two hearts and a diamond, but if he plays the ♡K, ◇K and three rounds of clubs, ruffing, he reaches this position with the lead in hand:

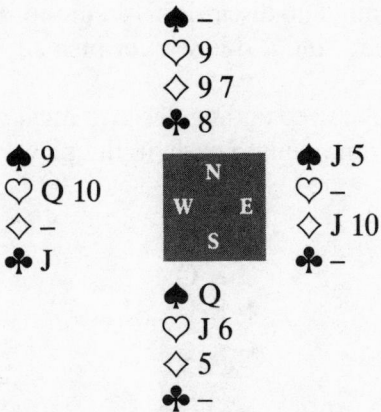

South enters dummy by ruffing his own winning spade. Then he ruffs the fourth club for ten tricks. This is the typical end position, with opponents' side winners and trump winners falling together.

Trump reduction plays

To complain of having too many trumps might be thought ungrateful, but in this common ending South wishes he had one trump fewer:

```
              ♠ –
              ♡ Q J
              ◇ 6
              ♣ –
♠ —                        ♠ 9 4
♡ 9 2          N           ♡ –
◇ –          W   E         ◇ 10
♣ 8            S           ♣ –
              ♠ J 8 3
              ♡ –
              ◇ –
              ♣ –
```

Spades are trumps, the lead is in dummy and South needs the balance. He leads a heart winner, hoping East will ruff, but East can count and discards his diamond. Had South held one trump fewer, and a side winner instead, he would have been all right.

To reach the desired ending declarer must often take steps to reduce his trump length early in the play:

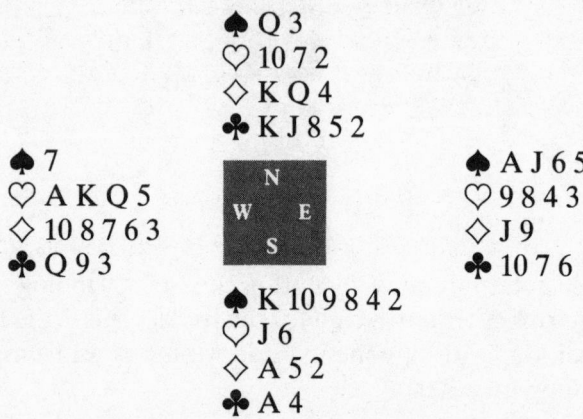

The contract is 4♠ and West begins with three top hearts. South ruffs and leads a trump to the queen and ace. East exits with a diamond, taken in dummy, and South finesses the ♠10 but West shows out.

Three tricks have been lost, East still has the ♠J–6, and dummy has no more trumps. South must now try to reduce his trumps to the same length as East's. He cashes the ♣A–K and ruffs a club, leaving this:

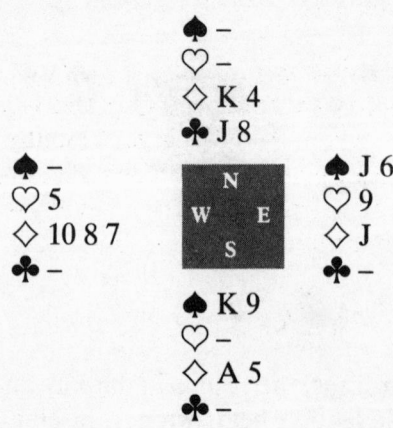

South crosses to the ♢K and leads a club. He has achieved his object, for if East declines to ruff, South discards the ♢A.

Here South was able to form his plan after the trump distribution had shown up, but sometimes it has to be done earlier. In fact it is a good practice to reduce one's trumps as a matter of routine whenever there is a surplus.

It follows that a defender with long trumps, or who can judge that his partner has long trumps, should not help the declarer shorten his trumps.

Devil's Coup and Smother Play

These coups are so rare as to be of little practical usefulness, but they do have curiosity value:

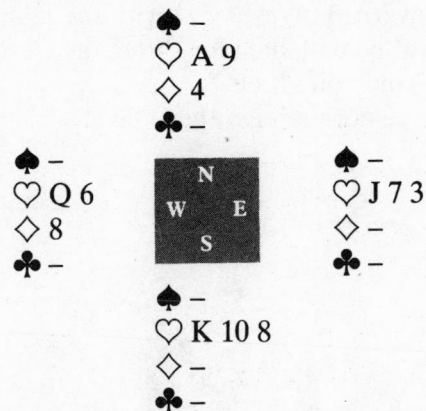

This is the Devil's Coup. Hearts are trumps and the lead is in dummy. A defensive holding of Q–x and J–x–x is normally invincible, but when the ♢4 is led, South can take the balance, no matter whether East ruffs high or low. Declarer may play for this ending when he has A–9–x opposite K–10–8–x–x and cannot afford a trump loser.

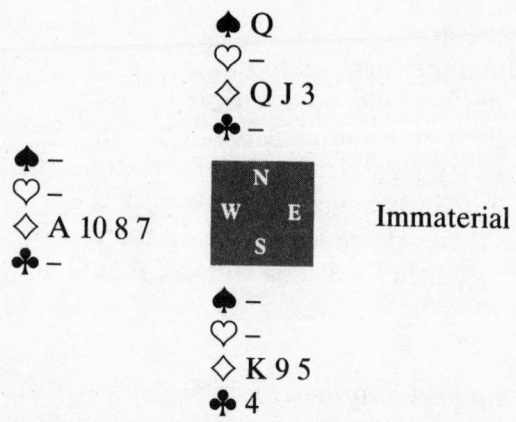

Immaterial

This is another diabolical ending. Diamonds are trumps and West may think he has two tricks coming, but South leads his club and overruffs West's ◇7 with the jack. The ♠Q is then led and ruffed with the king. Whether West overruffs or not, he makes only one trick.

Finally, the celebrated Smother Play:

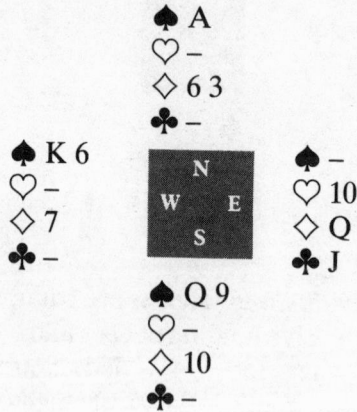

Spades are trumps and South needs two more tricks. He must lose a diamond but does not have to lose a trump, for when he puts East on play with a diamond, West is out of business.

THE SQUEEZE

A defender is squeezed when forced to discard a winner or an essential guard. Squeezes present a mental hazard to many players, as it is often necessary to visualise the end position several tricks in advance.

Before studying the endings it will be convenient to define the terms used.

Terms used in squeeze play

The squeeze card. The declarer must be able to lead a card to which the victim cannot follow and on which he can discard only at the cost of a trick. This is called the squeeze card.

Threat cards (or menace cards). These are cards held by declarer or dummy that will become winners if a defender can be made to discard a winner or essential guard. Here West is squeezed:

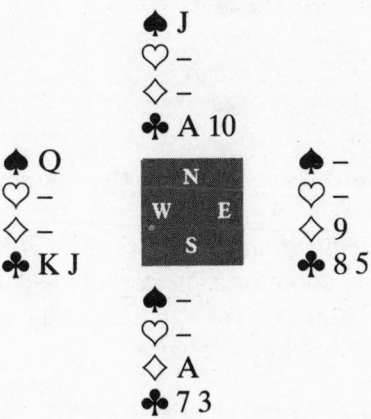

At notrumps South leads the squeeze card, the ◇A. North's holdings are menaces against West, who has to unguard one suit or the other.

A two-card menace consists of a winner and a loser, such as the ♣A–10 in the above diagram. In the common squeezes there must always be a two-card menace in the hand opposite the squeeze card. A further essential is that declarer must be able to enter the hand opposite the squeeze card, usually in the suit of the two-card menace.

A single menace is a single losing card. In the above diagram the single menace is the ♠J. When it is in the same hand as the two-card menace, the squeeze works only against the defender in front. This is called a simple squeeze.

When the single menace is in the same hand as the squeeze card, as in the next diagram, the squeeze works against either opponent:

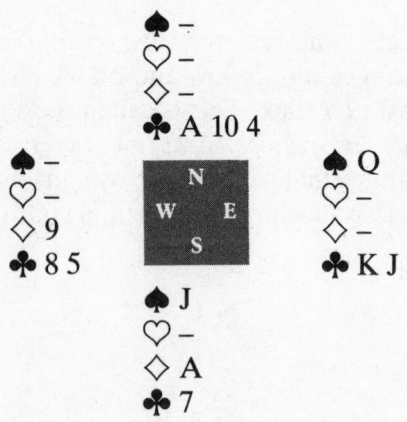

This is an automatic squeeze, the commonest and most useful squeeze.

The simultaneous double squeeze sounds forbidding but is simple and fairly common. There is the usual two-card menace in the hand opposite the squeeze card, and there are two single menaces, one in each hand:

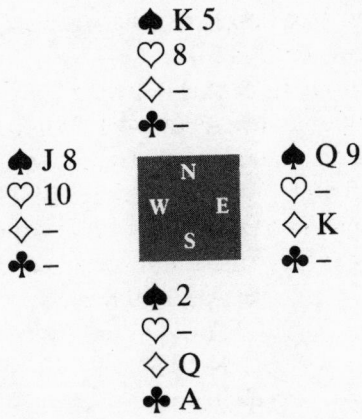

Spades are the two-card menace: the ♣A is the squeeze card: the ♡8 and ◇Q are single menaces.

On the lead of the ♣A West has to keep the ♡10 so he throws a spade. Dummy's heart is discarded and East is squeezed in spades and diamonds.

Timing

When the squeeze card is led the victim must hold no card that can be thrown without cost. This usually means that declarer must be able to win all the tricks but one. To meet this condition declarer may have deliberately to concede one or more tricks, so that he can win by force all but one of the balance:

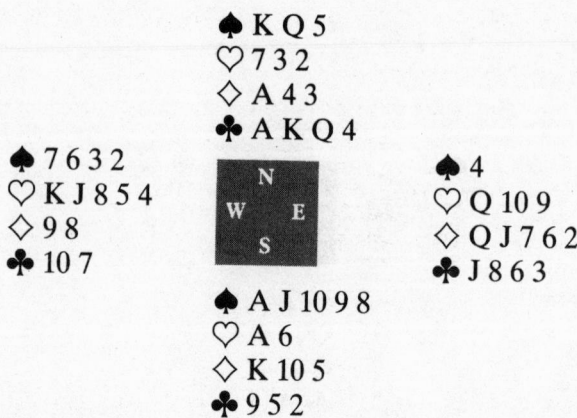

Against 6NT West leads the ◇9 and South takes East's jack with the king. From the lead it is clear that the ◇10 will be a menace against East. If East also has four or more clubs he can be squeezed.

However, South cannot win all the tricks but one, and if he were to play out the winners East would be able to discard comfortably. South must therefore concede a trick. The only suit in which this can be done is hearts, so he plays a low heart from each hand. This is called rectifying the count. He then plays to reach this position:

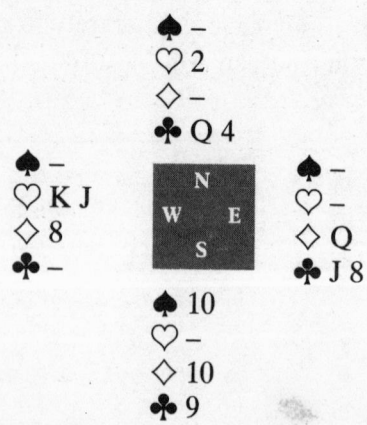

West's cards are of no account. When South leads the ♠10, throwing the heart from dummy, East is squeezed.

Isolating the menace

When there is no single menace because both defenders can guard the suit, it may be possible to put one defender out of court by a procedure known as isolating the menace:

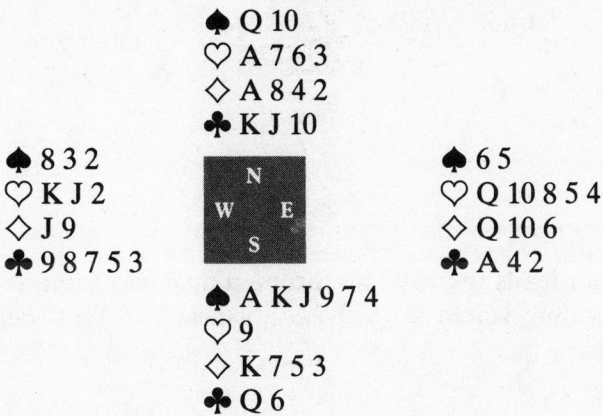

```
                   ♠ Q 10
                   ♡ A 7 6 3
                   ◇ A 8 4 2
                   ♣ K J 10
   ♠ 8 3 2                          ♠ 6 5
   ♡ K J 2          N               ♡ Q 10 8 5 4
   ◇ J 9         W     E            ◇ Q 10 6
   ♣ 9 8 7 5 3      S               ♣ A 4 2
                   ♠ A K J 9 7 4
                   ♡ 9
                   ◇ K 7 5 3
                   ♣ Q 6
```

Against 6♠ West leads the ♣9 and East plays the ace, returning the suit.

A squeeze is almost the only hope, the potential menaces being in hearts and diamonds. Diamonds can be controlled by only one opponent, but at present both can control hearts. If hearts are 4–4, nothing can be done, but if they are 5–3 South, by ruffing twice, can leave only one opponent with a guard. If this is the opponent who controls diamonds, there will be a squeeze. South therefore plays a heart to the ace and ruffs a heart. After two rounds of trumps ending in dummy, the ♣K is cashed and a third heart ruffed. After the last trump is drawn, South has reached this ending:

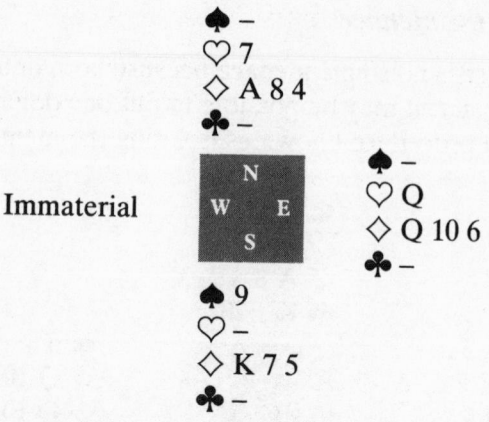

Immaterial

```
        ♠ —
        ♡ 7
        ◇ A 8 4
        ♣ —

              ♠ —
              ♡ Q
              ◇ Q 10 6
              ♣ —
        ♠ 9
        ♡ —
        ◇ K 7 5
        ♣ —
```

South leads the ♠9 and throws a diamond from dummy. The ending would be just as satisfactory if West held the guards.

Transferring the menace

Sometimes only one defender can control a critical suit, but he is the wrong one:

```
            K 5 4
   J 7 6 3             Q 9 2
            A 10 8
```

West leads this suit initially and South takes East's queen with the ace. Later in the play he needs to have in his own hand a single menace against East. Since West is marked with the jack, South leads the 10, forcing a cover. His luck is in as East has the 9, and after winning with dummy's king the 8 is a menace against East.

Squeeze without the count

At notrumps a defender may be squeezed and forced to discard from his own long suit even when declarer still has several tricks to lose:

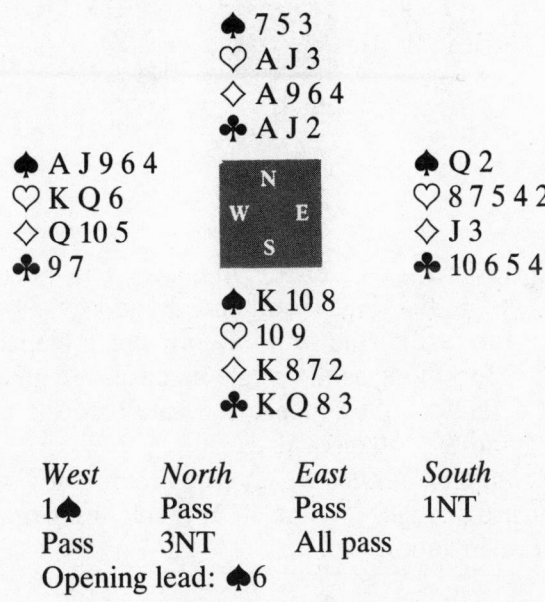

♠ 7 5 3
♡ A J 3
◇ A 9 6 4
♣ A J 2

♠ A J 9 6 4
♡ K Q 6
◇ Q 10 5
♣ 9 7

♠ Q 2
♡ 8 7 5 4 2
◇ J 3
♣ 10 6 5 4

♠ K 10 8
♡ 10 9
◇ K 8 7 2
♣ K Q 8 3

West	North	East	South
1♠	Pass	Pass	1NT
Pass	3NT	All pass	

Opening lead: ♣6

South takes East's queen with the king and plays off the clubs. On the third round West can spare a heart, but on the next has to let go a winning spade, allowing South to develop a trick in diamonds or hearts.

Automatic double squeeze

The distinctive feature is that the suit controlled by both opponents is a three-card menace headed by two winners. Now the hand opposite has room for two single menaces as well as the squeeze card:

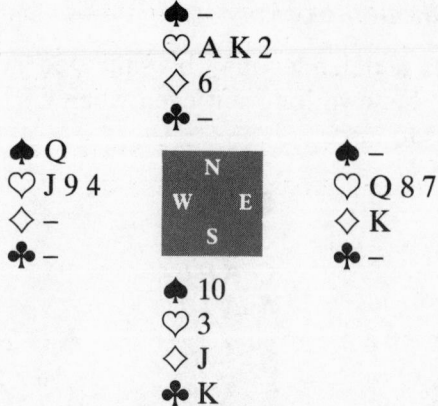

The three-card, or extended, menace is in hearts. The squeeze card is the ♣K. South needs only one heart for communication so is able to hold both single menaces, the ♠10 and ◇J. So long as the single menaces are guarded by different defenders, the squeeze is bound to work when the ♣K is led and the ◇6 discarded.

A non-simultaneous double squeeze occurs when there are two two-card menaces – one in the suit both opponents control, one in another suit:

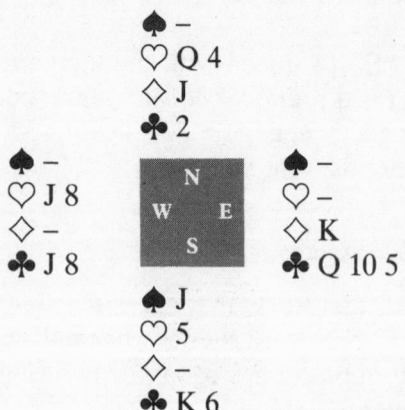

The two-card menace controlled by both opponents is clubs. It is in the same hand as the squeeze card, which is not unusual, and moreover the ◇J is under the opponent whom it threatens. The compensating feature is an extra entry in hearts. The ♠J is led and West has to throw a club: he is now out of the picture. The ♡4 is discarded and East is able to let go a club, but when South continues with a heart to the queen, East is *kaput*.

The criss-cross squeeze lacks the usual two-card menace headed by a winner but has extra entries:

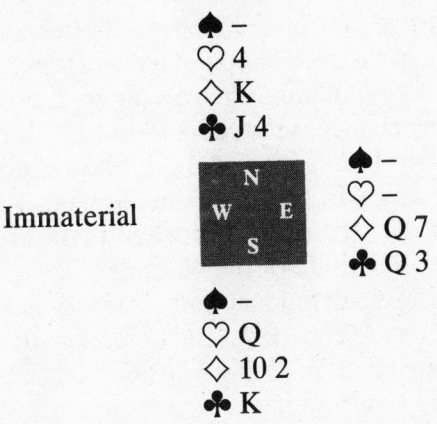

```
              ♠ —
              ♡ 4
              ◇ K
              ♣ J 4
                            ♠ —
                            ♡ —
Immaterial                  ◇ Q 7
                            ♣ Q 3
              ♠ —
              ♡ Q
              ◇ 10 2
              ♣ K
```

South leads the ♡Q and takes the balance no matter which suit East unguards. The typical feature is the presence of a singleton winner in each hand.

The trump squeeze is possible only because of the ruffing factor. Clubs are trumps:

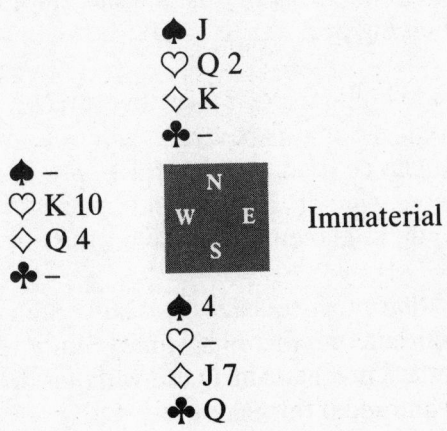

```
              ♠ J
              ♡ Q 2
              ◇ K
              ♣ —
♠ —
♡ K 10
◇ Q 4                       Immaterial
♣ —
              ♠ 4
              ♡ —
              ◇ J 7
              ♣ Q
```

A spade to the jack squeezes West. There must be two entries in the hand opposite the trump, but one may lie in a suit where there is no menace card, as in the diagram above, or in a menace suit.

DEFENDING AGAINST SQUEEZES

At rubber bridge a declarer who has made his contract seldom plays out the cards in the hope of an overtrick. At duplicate, players will do so not only when a squeeze is possible but also when the only chance is that defenders may throw the wrong cards. In general, defenders should follow these rules:

(i) Keep a guard in a suit held on the right in preference to one held on the left; especially when there are two double menaces, one each side of the defender.

(ii) When both defenders can guard against a two-card menace and a single menace, the defender sitting under the two-card menace should give up his guard in it and keep control of the single menace.

(iii) Do not inadvertently help declarer to isolate a menace:

$$7\,6\,4\,3$$
$$A\,K\,Q\,10\,8 \qquad\qquad J\,5\,2$$
$$9$$

West wins the first trick in this side suit but if he continues he may be helping declarer to establish the fourth card as a menace.

(iv) When exiting, prefer a suit that attacks a removable entry card to a lead that is neutral.

(v) With a choice of entries to attack, prefer a suit where declarer has one winner in each hand.

(vi) Kill a potential menace by playing the suit until none is left.

It is a fact that most squeezes can be beaten if defenders lead the right suits at the right time. Study the next few squeezes that are made against you, whether deliberately or by accident, and see if this is not so.

Chapter 24

THE PLAY AT PAIRS

*How to play 'room' contracts – Unusual contracts –
Sacrifice contracts – Match-point defence – Playing
for tops*

The play of the cards at duplicate is a sufficient pleasure all by
itself, but players who have a competitive nature and want to
win as well must develop two particular attitudes. To be
willing to fight tooth and nail for every trick, whether it is an
overtrick in a part-score or the fulfilling trick in a grand slam.
And to have in mind at all times what is likely to happen at
other tables.

The second consideration governs the game plan on most
deals.

HOW TO PLAY 'ROOM' CONTRACTS

The Stoic principle that a man should look not to what his
neighbour has said, thought or done, but only to his own
affairs, does not apply to duplicate. Quite the contrary: as
soon as you see the dummy you should start to worry about
the bidding and the contract at other tables.

Your game plan is clearest when you think you are in the
room contract – the one most other tables will reach. You
then focus on making more tricks than other tables. However, that is not the same as going flat out to make as many
tricks as possible. The distinction is important:

     (1) A K Q 5 2   (2) A Q 6 4 3

          7 3   K 7 2

Suppose that you are in notrumps and have no side entry to
dummy. With (1) you should duck a round: a 4–2 break is

more likely than 3–3. In the long run you make more tricks by ducking than by not ducking. Even if you needed five tricks for your contract, you might still duck, a play that would have your rubber-bridge partners jumping up and down.

With (2), suppose that you need only four tricks for your contract, so can afford to duck a round. You should not do so. A 3–2 break is odds-on and you should go for all the tricks even though a 4–1 break may wreck the contract.

Be clear in your mind that these examples do not conflict. In each case you make the play that collects most tricks in the long haul.

Taking risks for an overtrick

In the next deal South would have no problem at rubber bridge:

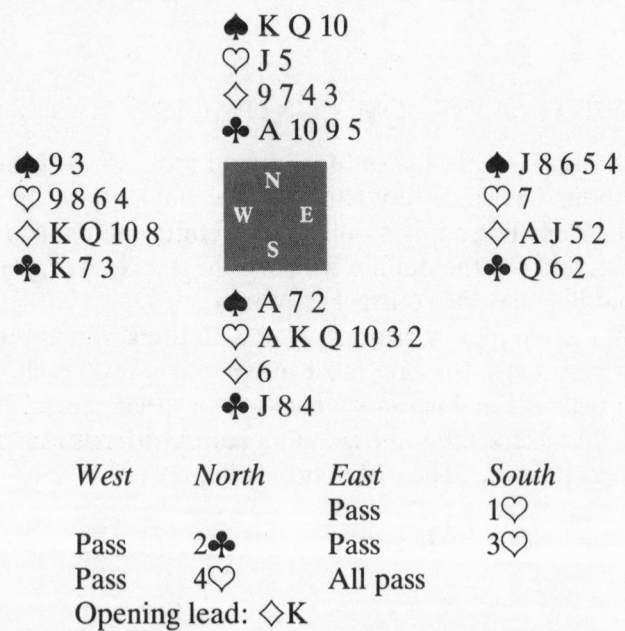

```
              ♠ K Q 10
              ♡ J 5
              ◇ 9 7 4 3
              ♣ A 10 9 5
♠ 9 3                          ♠ J 8 6 5 4
♡ 9 8 6 4        N             ♡ 7
◇ K Q 10 8    W     E          ◇ A J 5 2
♣ K 7 3          S             ♣ Q 6 2
              ♠ A 7 2
              ♡ A K Q 10 3 2
              ◇ 6
              ♣ J 8 4
```

West	North	East	South
		Pass	1♡
Pass	2♣	Pass	3♡
Pass	4♡	All pass	

Opening lead: ◇K

West continues with the ◇8 and South ruffs East's ace. He draws trumps, finding West with four, and runs the ♣J, losing to East's queen. He ruffs the diamond return with his last trump and after cashing the spades has to decide whether to risk the contract by taking a second finesse in clubs or settle for ten tricks.

The contract and sequence of play are likely to be the same at all or most tables, so South should play for the maximum expectation of tricks. The rule of restricted choice suggests that the second finesse will succeed twice as often as it will fail, so if South takes it he will get a good score twice as often as a bad one.

Suppose that you are in game or slam in a suit and can see that half the field may be in notrumps. It is easy to fall into a logical trap. The genial Charles Goren had just displaced Ely Culbertson as 'Mr Bridge' when he played this deal:

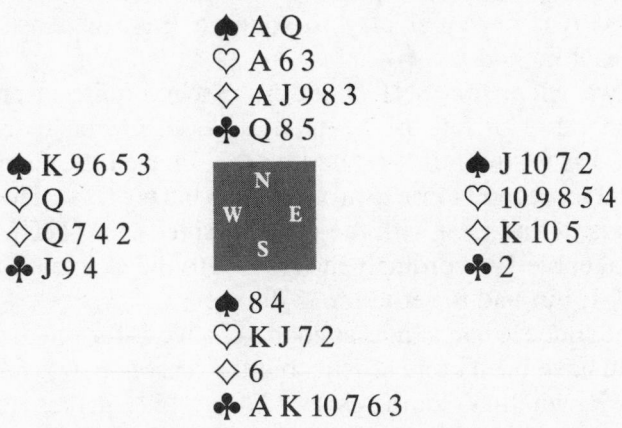

Goren was in 6♣ and West led the ♡Q. He set about ruffing diamonds, reaching this position with the lead in his hand:

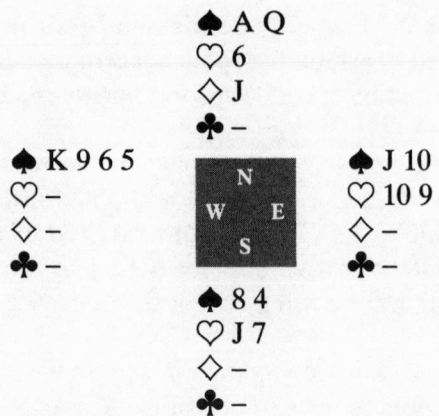

The ◇J was good so Goren was sure of 1370 and could take a risk-free finesse in spades for 1390. But there was an alternative: he could play to squeeze East in hearts and spades if he had the ♠K.

It was clear that 6NT would be reached quite often and would stand or fall by the spade finesse. Goren therefore argued as follows: 'If West has the ♠K I have little chance of a good score, and I lose to all those who bid 6NT . . . The only hope is to find East with the ♠K, in which case 6NT will be unmakeable.' Accordingly, he crossed to the ♠A and cashed the ◇J, but had to settle for 1370.

The squeeze had almost as good a chance as the finesse, and would have been more artistic, but the reasoning was flawed. At 6♣, whether South scores 1370 or 1390 makes no difference vis-à-vis players who are in 6NT, so he should concern himself only with beating those in 6♣.

The unquantifiable risk

In pursuit of overtricks, declarer sometimes has to address a risk that cannot be precisely assessed, such as whether defenders will find a killing switch. The more certain you are of being in the room contract, the more willing you should be to accept this risk:

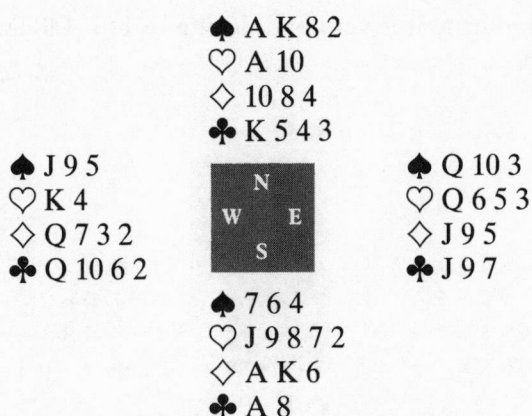

```
              ♠ A K 8 2
              ♡ A 10
              ◇ 10 8 4
              ♣ K 5 4 3
♠ J 9 5                        ♠ Q 10 3
♡ K 4          N              ♡ Q 6 5 3
◇ Q 7 3 2   W     E           ◇ J 9 5
♣ Q 10 6 2     S              ♣ J 9 7
              ♠ 7 6 4
              ♡ J 9 8 7 2
              ◇ A K 6
              ♣ A 8
```

The contract is 3NT and West leads the ♣2. Nine tricks can be made by winning in either hand and playing ace and another heart, aiming to force out the K–Q: you lose at most two clubs and two hearts. But can you afford to pass up a possible overtrick? If West has ♡K–Q–x or a doubleton honour, ten tricks can be made by winning in hand and finessing the ♡10.

The snag is that if the finesse loses to East and he is clever enough to return a diamond, you will be short of an entry to hand and will not be able to establish hearts if the remaining honour is still guarded. And even when the ♡10 holds the trick, if either defender has K–Q–x–x, entries will again be a problem.

If you thought some tables might not reach game, you would play for nine tricks, but here it is hard to see anyone not being in 3NT. In general, one should not play as though defenders have x-ray eyes. Here, South should go boldly for the heart finesse.

How to be down but not out

There are many opportunities to score well by playing to go one down instead of trying to make the contract when this could result in two down, especially when vulnerable. At rubber bridge, minus 200 is merely twice as much as minus

100: at duplicate it is very bad, losing to 110, 140 and 170 at other tables.

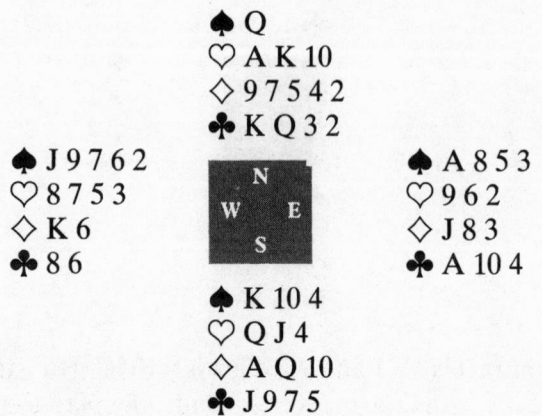

♠ Q
♡ A K 10
◇ 9 7 5 4 2
♣ K Q 3 2

♠ J 9 7 6 2   ♠ A 8 5 3
♡ 8 7 5 3   ♡ 9 6 2
◇ K 6   ◇ J 8 3
♣ 8 6   ♣ A 10 4

♠ K 10 4
♡ Q J 4
◇ A Q 10
♣ J 9 7 5

After 1NT–3NT, West leads the ♠6 and East wins with the ace, returning the 3. The 10 loses to the jack and the ♠2 comes back, East playing with the 8.

The rubber-bridge player, blithe spirit, crosses with a heart and tries his luck in diamonds, finessing the 10. He gets home 14% of the time, making five diamond tricks, three hearts and a spade. Mostly, he goes down two or more tricks, but his partner willingly agrees that he had to try it.

At duplicate, in a normal contract one cannot afford to back outsiders. With 27 points and no major suit, 3NT will be the room contract and a spade will be led from either defender's hand. South's aim is to make most tricks most of the time, so he forces out the ♣A and accepts down one.

UNUSUAL CONTRACTS

The challenge of trying to extract points from an unpromising contract can stimulate the imagination, as Mike Lawrence, one of the Dallas Aces, demonstrated with these cards. The East–West cards have not come down to us.

♠ A 3 2
♡ K Q 3
◇ K J 8
♣ K J 5 3

♠ K Q 4
♡ 9 7 5
◇ A Q 10
♣ A Q 9 6

Lawrence opened 1NT and was raised to 5NT. Taking this as a grand slam invitation, he bid 7NT. West led the ♠J and Lawrence saw that with an ace missing his contract qualified as unusual: at other tables the contract would be 6NT. But he had one advantage.

Lawrence knew that East held the ♡A and that the popular contract would fail. If West had it he would have doubled and led it.

In a bold attempt for parity with pairs in 6NT, Lawrence won the opening lead in dummy and led a low heart! East hesitated but went up with the ace, Lawrence gaining a near average.

Lest the newcomer to duplicate should have his imagination fired by examples such as this, a word of caution: Do not look for an off-beat line of play or go flat out for overtricks just because you are playing duplicate. Do keep always in mind that your true opponents are not the pair at your table but the players with your cards at other tables.

The next deal is more ordinary but exemplifies the same principle: when the contract is bad, one must think up a scenario that allows points to be salvaged.

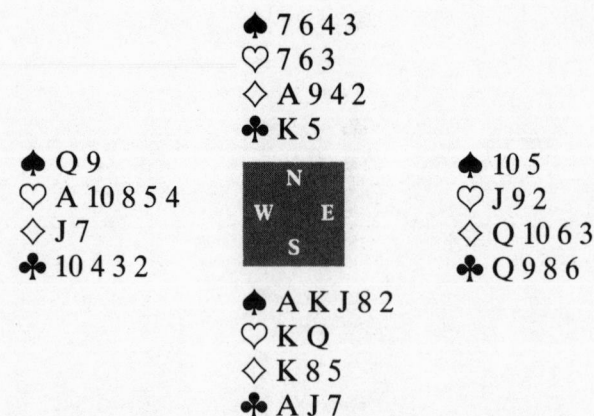

♠ 7 6 4 3
♥ 7 6 3
♦ A 9 4 2
♣ K 5

♠ Q 9
♥ A 10 8 5 4
♦ J 7
♣ 10 4 3 2

♠ 10 5
♥ J 9 2
♦ Q 10 6 3
♣ Q 9 8 6

♠ A K J 8 2
♥ K Q
♦ K 8 5
♣ A J 7

After 2NT–3NT West leads the ♥5 to East's jack and your king. You play off the ♠A–K, dropping Q–x from West.

The contract counts as unusual; not because you opened 2NT with this pattern but because North elected not to use Stayman. Most pairs will reach 4♠ and make eleven easy tricks by ruffing a club in dummy.

You can't join them, so you must beat them. Cross to the ♣K and finesse the jack on the way back. If it loses, West may not realise that the ♥Q is bare, but in any case this is your best chance to score points.

Desperate measures may also be needed when the opening lead is unusually damaging:

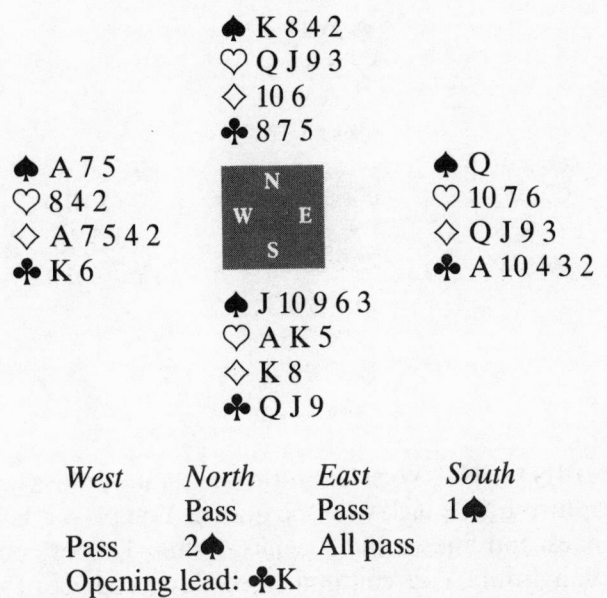

♠ K 8 4 2
♡ Q J 9 3
◇ 10 6
♣ 8 7 5

♠ A 7 5
♡ 8 4 2
◇ A 7 5 4 2
♣ K 6

♠ Q
♡ 10 7 6
◇ Q J 9 3
♣ A 10 4 3 2

♠ J 10 9 6 3
♡ A K 5
◇ K 8
♣ Q J 9

West	North	East	South
	Pass	Pass	1♠
Pass	2♠	All pass	

Opening lead: ♣K

West continues with the ♣6 to East's ace and ruffs the next round, exiting with the ♡4. After this venomous defence, how can you recover?

With a neutral lead, declarer will take a normal finesse in trumps, playing West for the queen. If he has it, your chances are dim. So, lead a trump from hand and climb boldly up with the king, continuing trumps if it holds. You may prevent East from ever getting in to lead diamonds, and may score very well by getting a diamond away on the hearts.

Sometimes even you will get a lucky lead and when that happens the slogan should be not, 'Who dares, wins,' but, 'What we have, we hold':

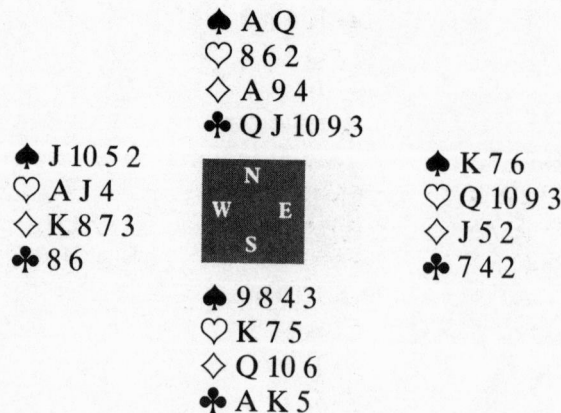

```
              ♠ A Q
              ♡ 8 6 2
              ♢ A 9 4
              ♣ Q J 10 9 3
♠ J 10 5 2                      ♠ K 7 6
♡ A J 4          N             ♡ Q 10 9 3
♢ K 8 7 3     W     E          ♢ J 5 2
♣ 8 6            S             ♣ 7 4 2
              ♠ 9 8 4 3
              ♡ K 7 5
              ♢ Q 10 6
              ♣ A K 5
```

After 1NT–3NT, West leads the ♢3, dummy plays low and you capture East's jack with the queen. You play a diamond right back and finesse the 9, which holds. This of course is most delightful. You continue with three rounds of clubs, finishing in the closed hand so that you can still take the spade finesse. On the third club West discards a spade.

Now you must decide whether to play for an overtrick by finessing in spades. If the finesse loses and the ♡A is offside you might go down, but the risk of finding two cards badly placed would normally be worth taking.

However, the play to the first trick gave you three tricks where normally you would make no more than two. After such a lucky start you should be content with nine tricks – sure to be a good score. Note that the diamond lead cannot have been automatic, since West, having a doubleton club, must have another 4-card suit.

When there will be various contracts

When there is scope for different bidding sequences – and especially when there is likely to be competitive bidding – there are two general rules, which sometimes point in different directions. One is to strive for a plus score. The other is to avoid the kiss of death; minus 200.

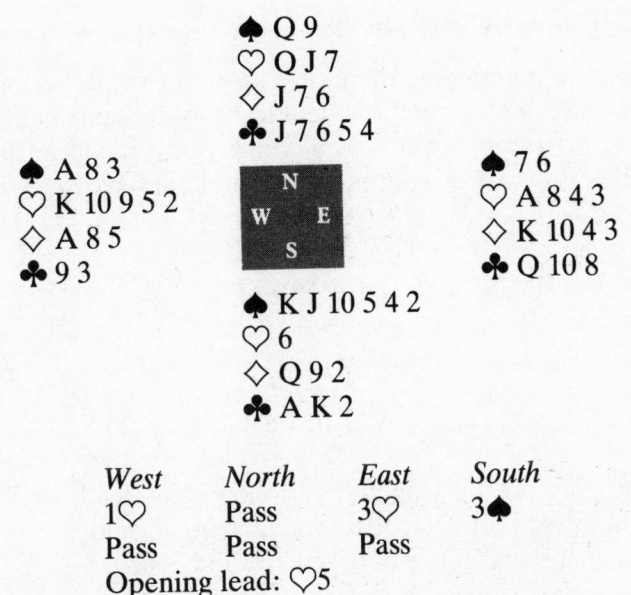

♠ Q 9
♡ Q J 7
◇ J 7 6
♣ J 7 6 5 4

♠ A 8 3
♡ K 10 9 5 2
◇ A 8 5
♣ 9 3

♠ 7 6
♡ A 8 4 3
◇ K 10 4 3
♣ Q 10 8

♠ K J 10 5 4 2
♡ 6
◇ Q 9 2
♣ A K 2

West	North	East	South
1♡	Pass	3♡	3♠
Pass	Pass	Pass	

Opening lead: ♡5

East takes the ♡J with the ace and returns the 3. Should South accept down one by discarding a diamond, or should he ruff and try to get home? Nine tricks may be there if you can drop the ♣Q, but if you cannot you may be down two, as you have a number of key cards to force out and will run short of trumps.

If you play for down one, how many match points will this be worth? It looks as though opponents can make at least 2♡, but you cannot tell how many pairs will get as high as 3♠ on your hand.

Vulnerability is the deciding factor. Not vulnerable, you should probably try to make the contract, as the difference between minus 50 and minus 100 may not matter, compared with part-scores made by East–West at other tables. Vulnerable, you should settle for eight tricks. Minus 200 can hardly be worth much, but minus 100 will pick up points against pairs who have let East–West play in a makeable part-score.

SACRIFICE CONTRACTS

You are in a non-vulnerable save against a vulnerable game and expect perhaps half the field to be in the same contract. This is the trump layout, and we will suppose it is clear to you that if trumps are 3–2, opponents could not have made their contract:

Dummy
K 3

Declarer
A Q 10 7 5 4

You play off the king and all follow. You lead the 3 and East follows again. Do you finesse, playing East for J–x–x–x? It makes the difference between 300 and 500.

Some players will say: 'I shall play East for J–x–x–x, for if trumps are 3–2 I have made a phantom save.' But this is itself phantasmal. However you play, if you could have set the opponents you will lose to all the pairs who don't sacrifice. If you could not have set the opponents, you will beat all the pairs who don't sacrifice. Therefore, you should consider only those who have sacrificed, and in the absence of any contrary indication should play for the drop.

Nevertheless, there are occasions when you should play for a special lie of the cards. To identify them, follow this rule: *When only one division of the cards will allow you to score match points, assume that this division exists.* Here, opponents only are vulnerable:

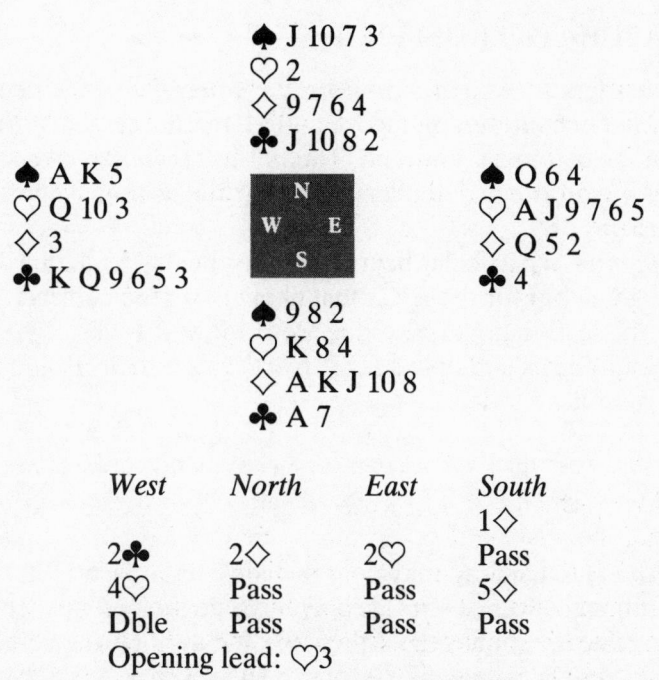

```
              ♠ J 10 7 3
              ♡ 2
              ◇ 9 7 6 4
              ♣ J 10 8 2
♠ A K 5                        ♠ Q 6 4
♡ Q 10 3         N            ♡ A J 9 7 6 5
◇ 3          W       E        ◇ Q 5 2
♣ K Q 9 6 5 3    S            ♣ 4
              ♠ 9 8 2
              ♡ K 8 4
              ◇ A K J 10 8
              ♣ A 7
```

West	North	East	South
			1◇
2♣	2◇	2♡	Pass
4♡	Pass	Pass	5◇
Dble	Pass	Pass	Pass

Opening lead: ♡3

South's final bid is questionable, but there he is in 5◇ doubled. East wins with the ace and switches to the ♣4. South wins, takes a round of trumps, crosses with a heart ruff and leads a trump on which East plays low. A wrong view will cost 800 instead of 500.

This time South may rightly say, 'If diamonds are 2–2 I have made a phantom, so I will play East for Q–x–x.' The difference between this and the previous example is that this time South can out-score North–South pairs who have not saved – but only if diamonds are 3–1.

MATCH-POINT DEFENCE

Defenders face their simplest task when there has been a normal uncontested sequence and there is no reason to think that the contract is unsound. Their object then is to take more tricks than other defenders, whether this will beat the contract or not.

This has a particular bearing on the opening lead: one does not go all out for the lead most likely to set the contract, but for the lead that will hold declarer to fewest tricks.

South deals and opens 1NT, North raises to 3NT, and you as West have to lead:

(1)   ♠ 10 5   ♡ 10 9 8 6   ◇ K J 8 5 3   ♣ A 7

(2)   ♠ 7 6 4   ♡ J 8 5 3   ◇ J 6   ♣ K Q 7 2

With (1) a diamond may beat the contract if partner has the queen, and a rubber-bridge player would look no further. At duplicate the sound lead is the ♡10: it may not bring South to his knees, but is less likely to give away a trick.

With (2), the lead should be a spade, which is likely to hold declarer to fewer tricks than a club or heart. Short-suit leads against notrumps are much more common at duplicate.

Defending against the room contract

At rubber bridge, defenders assume that by hook or by crook the contract can be beaten. At duplicate against a normal contract, this credo has no place: plays that have a good chance of killing an overtrick are preferred to those that have a limited chance of beating the contract:

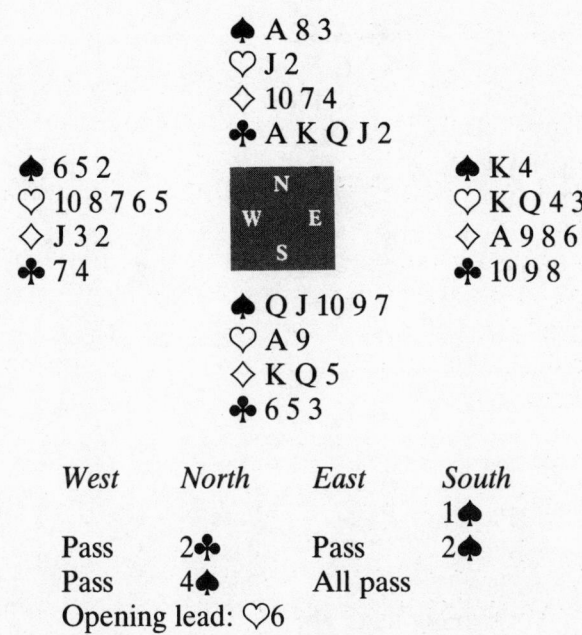

```
              ♠ A 8 3
              ♡ J 2
              ◇ 10 7 4
              ♣ A K Q J 2
♠ 6 5 2                          ♠ K 4
♡ 10 8 7 6 5                     ♡ K Q 4 3
◇ J 3 2                          ◇ A 9 8 6
♣ 7 4                            ♣ 10 9 8
              ♠ Q J 10 9 7
              ♡ A 9
              ◇ K Q 5
              ♣ 6 5 3
```

West	North	East	South
			1♣
Pass	2♣	Pass	2♠
Pass	4♠	All pass	

Opening lead: ♡6

Dummy plays low and East's queen loses to the ace. The ♠Q comes back and East is in with the king. He cashes the ♡K, but what next?

At rubber bridge East would underlead the ◇A: at duplicate such romantic ideas are put aside: South might have the K–J and mis-guess, but he is more likely either to guess right or to have ◇K–x or ◇K–Q and not to have to guess at all. So, cash the ◇A and hold South to his contract.

Defenders at duplicate have an advantage in that they are often the first to realise that the contract cannot be beaten. They can therefore focus on stamping out overtricks while declarer is still worrying about his contract:

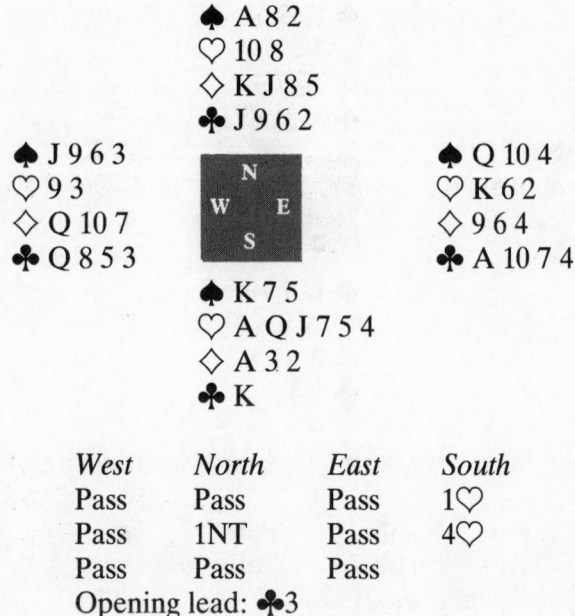

```
                    ♠ A 8 2
                    ♡ 10 8
                    ◇ K J 8 5
                    ♣ J 9 6 2
♠ J 9 6 3                              ♠ Q 10 4
♡ 9 3            N                     ♡ K 6 2
◇ Q 10 7    W       E                  ◇ 9 6 4
♣ Q 8 5 3       S                      ♣ A 10 7 4
                    ♠ K 7 5
                    ♡ A Q J 7 5 4
                    ◇ A 3 2
                    ♣ K
```

West	North	East	South
Pass	Pass	Pass	1♡
Pass	1NT	Pass	4♡
Pass	Pass	Pass	

Opening lead: ♣3

As East you win with the ace and South follows with the king: surely a singleton. At rubber bridge you would switch to a spade, as a club return would give up all hope of beating the contract: declarer would discard a loser and later throw another on the established ♣J.

At duplicate you should compute that the only question is how many overtricks South will make, as the red suits lie favourably for him. He, however, does not know this. If you return a club, he will very likely play safe by discarding. As the cards lie he will make one overtrick. If you make any other return and he has to play the hand out, he will make twelve tricks.

Defenders have many opportunities for semi-deceptive plays in which they hold up key cards or postpone the cashing of winners. This was a fine example by the Italian player, Benito Garozzo, against two of the Dallas Aces:

```
              ♠ K Q 10 8
              ♡ Q J 7
              ♢ 10 8 2
              ♣ K 8 5
♠ 9 6 4 3 2        N          ♠ 5
♡ 8 3          W       E      ♡ A K 9 2
♢ J 9 6            S          ♢ K 5 4 3
♣ Q 9 2                       ♣ A J 10 4
              ♠ A J 7
              ♡ 10 6 5 4
              ♢ A Q 7
              ♣ 7 6 3
```

West	North	East	South
Belladonna	Lawrence	Garozzo	Goldman
	Pass	1♢	Pass
Pass	Dble	Pass	1NT
Pass	Pass	Pass	

Opening lead: ♢6

East put up the king, which South would have done well to duck, but he won and led a heart. East returned a diamond and this time South played low, the jack winning.

West switched accurately to the ♣Q, which held, and continued with the 9, East winning with the 10. Most defenders would automatically cash the ♣A–J, but Garozzo took only the card he was known to hold, the ace, exiting with a diamond.

In with the ♢Q, South could have settled for down one. However, placing West with the outstanding club, and no entry, he saw no harm in playing a second heart. If East had opened a short diamond, which was possible in his system, the contract might still have been made. As it was, South went two down.

PLAYING FOR TOPS

Most players estimate their match-point score as they go along, a process that stretches the mind and can give satisfaction in its own right. Some become very proficient and can usually get within 2% or less. To have an idea of how you are doing is helpful, as this may dictate how some hands should be played.

In a club duplicate the winners' final score is likely to be between 60 and 63%. If, towards the end, you think you are in the running, you should play down the middle, but if your estimate is, say, 57%, then perhaps you should play for tops. A good way to do this is to make a play that is only slightly inferior to a standard play that everyone else will make:

♠ K 7 5
♡ Q 4
♢ A 7 2
♣ A 8 6 4 3

♠ A J 10 6 3
♡ A K J 7
♢ 8
♣ J 5 2

West	North	East	South
		Pass	1♠
Pass	2♣	Pass	2♡
Pass	3♢	Pass	4♣
Pass	4♠	All pass	

Opening lead: ♢Q

A few pairs may be in 3NT but the majority will reach 4♠ and your job is to beat their score. The only point to the hand is that the right guess in trumps will bring you an overtrick.

Normally, every declarer will make the standard play: cash the king and finesse the jack against East, the only way to pick up Q–x–x–x in one hand.

If you are sure you need a good board you should lay down the ace, then run the jack. This is only slightly against the odds, and it will separate you from the field.

To play duplicate is to take part in a mental assault course but, in an age dominated by non-participant forms of entertainment, the appeal of the game has never been greater.

SCORING

CHICAGO (FOUR-DEAL) BRIDGE

This form of scoring is popular with players who wish to avoid prolonged rubbers. Four deals, sometimes called a chukker, are played.

Each player deals in turn. If a deal is passed out it does not count and the same player deals again. Vulnerability is as follows:

First deal: neither side vulnerable.

Second and third deals: dealer's side vulnerable.

Fourth deal: both sides vulnerable.

The game bonus is 300, not vulnerable, 500 when vulnerable. Bonuses are earned for each separate game but there is no additional premium for winning two or more games.

A part-score made in the current deal may be combined with one or more made previously to make a game. The game bonus is determined by vulnerability when the game is completed. When a game is made, part-scores made previously by either pair no longer count towards the next game. A part-score in the fourth deal, if it does not complete a game, earns a bonus of 100 points. No other part-score earns a bonus.

RUBBER BRIDGE SCORING TABLE

A rubber is best of 3 games. A game ends when one side scores 100 or more points *below the line*. Only the declarer's side can score points under the line. They are awarded for contracts actually bid and made. Overtricks are scored above the line. The 100 points for game can be made over more than one deal. 'Vulnerable' = having won one game. A side that has not won a game yet is 'not vulnerable'.

POINTS TOWARDS GAME BELOW THE LINE:

No-trumps – First trick 40
Subsequent tricks 30
Spades or Hearts (major suits) 30
Diamonds or Clubs (minor suits) 20
Final contract doubled and made : Double above values
Final contract redoubled, made : Above values × 4

POINTS ABOVE THE LINE:
OVERTRICK:

		Not vulnerable	*Vulnerable*
For each	Not doubled	Trick value	Trick value
overtrick	Doubled	100	200
	Redoubled	200	400

SLAMS BID AND MADE:

	Not vulnerable	*Vulnerable*
Small slam	500	750
Grand slam	1000	1500

FOR DEFEATING A CONTRACT:

Not doubled, each undertrick is 50 not vulnerable, 100 vulnerable
Doubled but not vulnerable, 1st undertrick 100, 2nd and 3rd 200, 4th and subsequent undertricks 300
Doubled and vulnerable, 1st undertrick 200, others 300
Redoubled: all undertricks score at twice the doubled rate

FOR MAKING A DOUBLED CONTRACT: 50 ('for the insult')

FOR MAKING A REDOUBLED CONTRACT: 100

FOR HONOURS:

Four trump honours in one hand 100
Five trump honours in one hand 150
Four aces in one hand if contract is NT 150
(Either side can score honours, which are claimed at the conclusion of play.)

WINNING THE RUBBER:

For winning by two games to nil 700
For winning by two games to one 500
For one game if rubber is unfinished 300
For part-score if rubber is unfinished 50

INDEX